This book comes with access to more content online.

Quiz yourself, track your progress,
and score high on test day!

Register your book or ebook at
www.dummies.com/go/getaccess.

Select your product, and then follow the prompts
to validate your purchase.

You'll receive an email with your PIN and instructions.

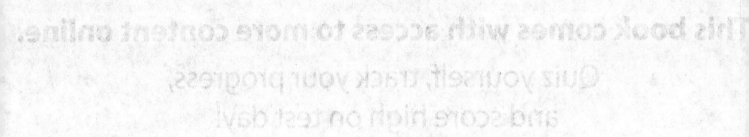

Praxis® Core Study Guide

with Online Practice
5th Edition

by Carla C. Kirkland and Chan Cleveland

A Wiley Brand

Praxis® Core Study Guide For Dummies® with Online Practice, 5th Edition

Published by: **John Wiley & Sons, Inc.,** 111 River Street, Hoboken, NJ 07030-5774, www.wiley.com

For general information on our other products and services, please contact our Customer Care Department within the U.S. at 877-762-2974, outside the U.S. at 317-572-3993, or fax 317-572-4002. For technical support, please visit https://hub.wiley.com/community/support/dummies.

Wiley publishes in a variety of print and electronic formats and by print-on-demand. Some material included with standard print versions of this book may not be included in e-books or in print-on-demand. If this book refers to media such as a CD or DVD that is not included in the version you purchased, you may download this material at http://booksupport.wiley.com. For more information about Wiley products, visit www.wiley.com.

Library of Congress Control Number: 2024943876

ISBN 978-1-394-28185-5 (pbk); ISBN 978-1-394-28187-9 (ebk); ISBN 978-1-394-28186-2 (ebk)

SKY10081753_081224

Contents at a Glance

Table of Contents

Introduction

I f you want to be a teacher, you generally have to take the Praxis Core Academic Skills for Educators exam at least once. "What?! What do you mean by 'at least once'?" Yes, it's true that you may have to take the Praxis twice in your quest to shape the minds of future generations. Many colleges and universities require that students who want to enroll in an education major take the exam. And if that isn't bad enough, most states and some U.S. territories require that you pass the Praxis in order to be licensed to teach. But don't panic. You've come to the right place for help in acing the exam.

The goal of this book is to help you brush up on what you need to know to pass the Praxis with flying colors. We don't cover every topic that will be tested in detail; instead, we offer an overview of those topics. The overview allows you to review a topic and say to yourself either, "Yep, got it! I can move on to the next topic" or "I don't get it. I'd better focus on my statistics knowledge." (If you decide you need more review on a topic, check out a *For Dummies* book that relates specifically to that topic.)

You can also use the two practice tests in this book and the additional four practice tests online to test yourself in an almost-real testing situation. You may want to take one test before you read any chapters to see where your strengths and weaknesses are; then, you'll know where to focus your attention. After you've studied your weak areas and reviewed the topics you're better at, you can take another practice test to see how much you've improved and where you still may need more work.

So, we have you covered when it comes to studying for and passing the Praxis. Take a couple of tests, review the chapters, and get the confidence you need to score well on the test when it really counts.

About This Book

Praxis Core Study Guide For Dummies, 5th Edition, breaks down the exam's main objectives into understandable sections. This book is organized into parts that align with the test's subsections so that you can find the answers to your most challenging areas quickly. If you're struggling with math, you can find all those topics grouped together in Part 2. If writing makes you want to pull your hair out, you can get a comprehensive overview in Part 4.

In addition to reviewing Praxis topics, we offer strategies that you can practice and keep in mind so that you don't fall for the booby traps that the test creators put in your way. We outline the different types of questions so that you know where to expect the hurdles you'll see on the Praxis Core Academic Skills for Educators exam. (Okay, this is the last time we'll spell out the official title of the test. From now on, we'll refer to it as the Praxis or the Praxis Core.)

A test-prep book wouldn't be a test-prep book without a couple of practice tests. This book offers two tests in the book itself, those same two tests online, and then another four tests online to help you become familiar with the content and question types you'll encounter when you take the exam. They say practice makes perfect. With these practice tests, you can put that theory to the test.

This new edition has information in Chapter 2 on how to budget your study time in preparation for the Praxis Core. Understanding how to divide your study time is important for making sure you have time to cover the topics you need to study the most and how to break up your time.

Foolish Assumptions

In writing this book, we've made some assumptions about you. The biggest assumption we've made is that you've decided to teach, which is one of the most rewarding professions known to man. Beyond that, you fall into one of the following categories:

» You're a first-time exam-taker who wants to pass the test on your first try.

» You're an exam re-tester who has taken the exam and failed based on your state cut score requirement. You can still successfully reach the passing score goal. You're actually in a better situation than the first-time exam-taker because you possess a detailed report that outlines your strengths and weaknesses. With that information, you can truly attack the sections that challenge you the most.

» You're a traditional teacher candidate in college who's currently enrolled or trying to enroll as an education major in an undergraduate program, and you need to pass this exam to start taking your specialized courses.

» You're an alternative-route teacher candidate who possesses a four-year degree, and you need to pass this exam as one of your first steps toward certification.

Regardless of your category, we've written this book to fit your specific needs.

Icons Used in This Book

Icons are the drawings in the margins of this book, and we use several icons to call out special kinds of information.

EXAMPLE

Examples are sample test questions that appear in sections and that highlight particular ideas that you should be familiar with. We provide an answer and explanation immediately after the question. (And there's more — at the end of a chapter, you usually find a handful of numbered sample questions, which we don't mark with the icon because they're in their own practice-questions section.)

REMEMBER

The Remember icon points out something you should keep in mind while you're taking the exam.

TIP

A Tip is a suggestion that usually points out a trick for remembering information for the test.

WARNING

The Warning icon flags traps and tricks that the creators of the Praxis often employ to trip you up when it comes to choosing the correct answer. Pay special heed to these paragraphs.

Beyond the Book

This product also comes with some access-anywhere goodies on the web. For some quick and helpful advice to help you prepare for and succeed on the Praxis Core exam, check out the online Cheat Sheet. Just go to www.dummies.com and type in "Praxis Core For Dummies Cheat Sheet" in the search box.

In addition to the two complete practice exams contained in this book, your book purchase also comes with a free one-year subscription to additional practice questions that appear online — enough to fill four more exams. You can access the content whenever you want. Create your own question sets and view personalized reports that show what you need to study most.

So you can take six full-length online practice tests and review hundreds of flashcards. To gain access to all of this online practice, all you have to do is register. Just follow these simple steps:

1. Register your book or ebook at Dummies.com to get your PIN. Go to www.dummies.com/go/getaccess.

2. Select your product from the dropdown list on that page.

3. Follow the prompts to validate your product, and then check your email for a confirmation message that includes your PIN and instructions for logging in.

If you do not receive this email within two hours, please check your spam folder before contacting us through our Technical Support website at https://support.wiley.com or by phone at 877-762-2974.

Now you're ready to go!

You can come back to the practice material as often as you want — simply use the username and password you created during your initial login. No need to enter the access code a second time.

Your registration is good for one year from the day you activate your PIN.

Where to Go from Here

Use this book as a reference. You don't need to read this book from front to back. Feel free to skip around to the sections that you find most useful. If you can't decide, begin with Chapter 1 — it includes an overview of the Praxis, and you'll probably need to read it at some point. If you know that geometry (Chapter 6) is your Achilles heel or that reading comprehension questions (Chapter 9) make your eyes cross, go straight to the corresponding chapter. We give you an index, too, at the back of the book to help you find specific information. Or, if you like, you can take one of the tests to see how well you do and determine what you need to brush up on.

1

Getting Started with the Praxis Core

IN THIS PART . . .

Get the details about who takes the Praxis, what's on the test, and how your score is calculated.

Figure out how to schedule your study time in advance of test day, find out what to expect on test day, and get some pointers if you're retaking the test.

Try out some practice Praxis questions to discover the areas in which you're strong and the areas where you need more review. Then develop a plan to strengthen the areas where you could improve.

Chapter **1**

Previewing the Praxis

For decades, teacher candidates have been taking assessments to meet certification requirements. Praxis Core Academic Skills for Educators is the latest version of these tests that measures core skills in the areas of reading, writing, and mathematics for potential teacher candidates. This chapter gives you an overview of what you need to know about the exam.

Why Take the Praxis?

If you want to become a teacher, you may face the Praxis at some point on the road to certification. You may need to take it to get into a teaching program at college, or you may take it to get your teaching license before starting a second career. If you're lucky, you may take it only once, but you might need to take it two or more times before you're fully qualified to work in a classroom.

Colleges and universities use the Praxis Core testing series to determine whether teaching program candidates meet the minimum requirements to enter into the field of teaching. Most colleges and universities won't allow admission into their teacher preparation programs until candidates complete this basic skills exam. Undergraduate students generally take the Praxis early in their college careers. Educational Testing Service (ETS), the company that creates and administers the Praxis tests, may allow some students to skip taking certain parts of the Praxis if they have high scores on college entrance exams, such as the ACT.

Most states also use the Praxis as a certification test to show that you've mastered the skills that you need to be a highly competent teacher. In many cases, teaching licenses are directly tied to this test. Age doesn't get you out of this standardized test.

TIP

Almost every state in the country uses some form of the Praxis. Contact your state department of education for specific licensure details.

Breaking Down the Praxis

The updated Praxis Core evaluates the core academic abilities of prospective educators in the areas of reading, writing, and math. Previously, this test was called the Praxis I Pre-Professional Skills Test, but ETS decided to make a change to reflect the requirement to get potential teachers up to the level needed to meet ever-changing standards, mainly because of the application of Common Core. ETS breaks down the exam into the following three parts:

>> **The reading test:** Poses multiple-choice questions based on reading passages and statements.

>> **The writing test:** Divided into two sections. The multiple-choice section tests grammar usage, sentence correction, revision in context, and research skills. The test also requires you to write two essays based on information presented; one is an argumentative essay, and the other is an explanation of a topic.

>> **The mathematics test:** Measures multiple mathematics topics up to the advanced high-school level. The format of the test has numeric entry questions and multiple-choice questions that may require you to select one or more choices. (You have access to an on-screen calculator, so you don't have to sweat the simple stuff.)

The following sections give you more details about the subtests and the question types so that you don't encounter any (or too many) surprises when you sit down to take the test.

Knowing what topics the Praxis covers

Just like most other standardized tests, the Praxis includes long reading passages, complicated math problems, and detailed essay topics. You get a set number of questions about certain topics to answer in a given amount of time. Check out Table 1-1 for the breakdown.

TABLE 1-1 Breakdown of the Praxis

Test Subject	Number of Questions	Time
Reading	56 questions	85 minutes
Writing	40 questions and 2 essays	100 minutes
Mathematics	56 questions	90 minutes

Each subject is broken down further into specific concepts.

The Reading test requires you to display proficiency in certain areas:

>> **Key ideas and details:** Closely read text, make logical inferences, connect specific details, address author differences, and determine uncertain matters. (Includes 17 to 22 questions.)

>> **Craft, structure, and language skills:** Interpret words and phrases, recognize the tone of word choices, analyze text structure, assess points of view, apply language knowledge to determine fact or opinion, determine word meanings, and understand a range of words and word nuances. (Includes 14 to 19 questions.)

>> **Integration of knowledge and ideas:** Analyze diverse media content, evaluate arguments in texts, and analyze how two or more texts address similar themes. (Includes 17 to 22 questions.)

The Writing test requires you to understand these concepts:

>> **Text types, purposes, and production:** Produce one argumentative and one informative/explanatory essay. This section also requires you to edit and revise text passages. (Includes 6 to 12 multiple-choice questions and two essays.)

>> **Language and research skills:** Demonstrate command of English grammar, usage, capitalization, and punctuation. This section also requires you to apply and recognize research skills. (Includes 28 to 34 multiple-choice questions.)

The Mathematics test evaluates your understanding and ability in a number of areas:

>> **Number and quantity:** Order among integers, representations of numbers in more than one way, place value, whole-number properties, equivalent computational procedures, ratios, proportions, and percentages. (Includes approximately 20 questions.)

>> **Algebra:** Handling equations and inequalities, recognizing various ways to solve a problem, determining the relationship between verbal and symbolic expressions, and interpreting graphs. (Includes about 11 questions.)

>> **Geometry:** The characteristics and properties of geometric shapes, the Pythagorean theorem, transformation, and use of symmetry to analyze mathematical situations. The test assumes that you have a knowledge of basic U.S. and metric systems of measurement. (Includes approximately 7 questions.)

>> **Data interpretation, statistics, and probability:** Read and interpret visual displays of quantitative information; understand the correspondence between data and graph; make inferences from a given data display; determine mean, median, and mode; and assign a probability to an outcome. (Includes around 18 questions.)

The good news about the math test is that you have access to an on-screen, four-function calculator, which reduces the chance that you'll select a wrong answer choice based on a simple arithmetic error.

Seeing what types of questions you can expect

The Praxis Core gives you multiple types of questions. Taking all of the practice tests offered in this book can give you a consistent idea of what you'll see on the actual test. Before you get to the practice tests, this section gives you a list of question types you'll encounter in the different subtests.

The reading test has four categories of text analysis:

>> **Reading Category 1:** Questions deal with paired passages of about 150 to 200 words combined with four to seven questions, such as "Unlike the author of Passage 2, the author of Passage 1 mentions . . ." or "Which of the following statements best describes the relationship between the two passages?"

>> **Reading Category 2:** Questions deal with lengthy paragraphs of about 175 to 200 words combined with four to seven questions that may ask, "Which of the following best describes the organization of the passage?" or "The author would be *most* likely to agree with which of the following statements?"

>> **Reading Category 3:** Questions deal with abbreviated passages of 75 to 100 words, asking two or three questions, such as "The passage is primarily concerned with . . ." or "Which of the following is an unstated assumption made by the author of the passage?"

>> **Reading Category 4:** Short statements followed by a single question.

The writing test has four categories of multiple-choice questions and two essays:

» **Multiple-choice writing questions:** Straightforward questions covering sentence correction, revision in context, usage, and research skills.

» **Essays:** The argumentative and informative/explanatory essay sections test your skills to write a detailed essay in a very short period of time. See Chapter 11 for more on the essay questions.

The mathematics test has several question categories:

» **Numeric entry:** These types of questions require you to input an integer or decimal into a single box or a fraction into two separate boxes.

» **Multiple-choice questions:** Each question has five possible answers, with one or more correct choices. Be aware that a test question may tell you to select all answer choices that apply without telling you how many of the choices are correct.

Understanding How the Test Is Scored

The Praxis Core exam is divided into three tests: reading, writing, and mathematics. Take careful note of the fact that the *exam* is made up of the three *tests*. Each test is scored separately, and most states that require passing scores for the exam require that the exam-takers pass each of the three tests that compose the exam. Some states consider an exam to have a passing score when the exam's composite (overall) score is high enough. Professional educators, who apply ETS standards, score a given test by taking the raw score and adjusting it to a scale that ranges from 100 to 200 points.

Your *raw score* is the number of questions you answer correctly. You don't lose any points for answering a question incorrectly. If you answer every single question incorrectly, you end up with a raw score of 0 (which translates to an adjusted score of 100), the exact same score you get if you don't answer any questions at all. So you have nothing to lose by guessing if you don't know the answer to a question.

Your score for each test involves taking your raw score and comparing it to the number of questions on the test. This comparison, along with the level of rigor involved in the particular test you take, determines your *final score*, the number that exists in the range from 100 to 200. Your final score determines whether you pass the test. *Note:* When you take the practice tests in the book or online, you can't convert your raw score to a final score. You pass the test in most states by answering at least 60 percent of the questions correctly, which gives you a benchmark to measure yourself against while you go through the practice tests.

TIP

If you fail the Praxis the first time you take it (or if you've already failed it), you can look at your scores for each content category to see where you did well and where you struggled. Use those scores to direct your studies in anticipation of taking the test again.

Each state that requires passing the exam has its own minimum scores for each of the tests that make up the exam, except for states in which a high enough composite score qualifies as passing. What constitutes a passing score in one state may not be a passing score in another state. Contact your state department of education for the actual cut scores.

IN THIS CHAPTER

» Signing up to take the test

» Making the most of your time

» Knowing what to expect on test day

» Making a study plan

» Preparing to take the test again

Chapter **2**

Getting Ready for Test Day

You've known for months, if not years, that you need to take the Praxis exam to be certified to teach in your state. And just like any other major undertaking in life, you need to prepare for the test. You wouldn't run a marathon without doing some training, would you? You shouldn't just show up to take the Praxis either.

Before you take the Praxis, you should put a strategy in place. Ideally, give yourself a couple of months to get ready for the test. In that time, you'll study and review concepts that the test covers, take practice tests to familiarize yourself with the format and timing of the test, and brush up in areas where you're weak so that you can ace the test.

In this chapter, we offer suggestions about how to prepare for the test, whether you're taking it for the first time or taking it again.

Registering for the Test

TIP

Before you register to take the Praxis, check with the local department of education to make sure you're taking the right test. Don't ask ETS, or your mom, or anyone else who isn't in a position to admit you to a teaching program; they may give you wrong information, which can lead to wasted time and money.

You can find out how to register to take the Praxis Core by going to www.ets.org. The Praxis Core is offered during testing windows at more than 300 Prometric testing sites across the country. Contact your local testing site for specific questions regarding its testing windows. Test-takers must register at least three days prior to their intended test date, and you must pay the testing fee online. At the time of this writing, individual tests (reading, writing, or mathematics) cost $90; the price to take all three tests at the same time (on the same day) is discounted to $150.

After you register, read all the admission ticket info to make sure all the content, including your test center and reporting time, is correct. Contact ETS if you have any disabilities that require accommodations.

Consider taking one test per day rather than multiple tests per day. You know your limits and abilities. Some people take all three tests on the same day, and they bomb all three. If you aren't super confident that you can pass multiple tests in one sitting, you may want to schedule them for different days. This approach can also help you map out your study plan more strategically (see the following section). You can study for one test at a time, rather than all three.

A test session includes time for taking a test or tests, and it also includes time for tutorials and collection of background information. If you take one test on a given day, the session lasts two hours. If you take all of the tests in one day, the session takes five hours.

Using Your Time Wisely

When preparing for the Praxis, you need to think of time in two different ways. First, you need to plan your study time. Expect to spend many hours over the next several weeks reviewing the material that could be on the test. Then, you need to know how much time is allotted for the test itself. Knowing these details can help you pace yourself while you answer questions during the test when it really counts. We cover both aspects of using your time wisely in the following sections.

Budgeting your study time leading up to test day

When you budget your study time ahead of your test date, you increase your chances of passing the first time. Do you really want to face the Praxis more than once to enroll in a teacher education program? We didn't think so.

If you can't put in adequate study time before taking the test, seriously consider rescheduling. The Praxis Core is given several times each year at your local testing center. Rather than taking the test with no preparation, contact the testing center or go online to reschedule to take the test at a later date. You must do this at least three days before your scheduled testing time, and doing so requires a $40 fee.

Creating a schedule and penciling in the practice tests

The best way to prepare to take the Praxis is to set up a study schedule and then stick to it. Block off an amount of time each day to prepare for the test and note what topics you plan to study or review. You may need to ask your sister to baby-sit the kids, or you may need to turn down drinks with friends for a few weeks — but it will be worth it. Preparing for this test will affect your life for a short amount of time. After you receive a passing score, you can commit to the bowling league. Use all of your extra time before the test to focus on the Praxis.

Create an adjustable timetable that you can revise to best meet your needs while test time gets closer. The latest that you should begin studying is four to six weeks before the test.

During your study sessions, familiarize yourself with the question types for each section. Not all the questions are straightforward, multiple-choice questions. Some of them ask you to choose *all* the right answers. Other questions require you to calculate an answer and write it in a box. Knowing the variations in question types gives you a better chance of answering them correctly. While you get familiar with the question types, also pay attention to the test's directions. Understanding the directions ahead of time can save you valuable time on test day and can reduce test anxiety.

This book includes two full-length tests in Part 5, plus four additional tests online. You may want to take a test now and save the others to take in the days leading up to the exam.

When you take the practice tests, take them under timed conditions in a quiet setting where you won't be disturbed. This creates a test-like environment and gives you a better sense of how you'll perform on the Praxis when it counts. After you take a practice test, be sure to review the answer explanations. These explanations help you see what you did right or where you went wrong; they're another learning opportunity beyond the review material.

Joining forces with others

Sometimes, people gain more knowledge when they study with others. Other people may have a different way to solve an algebra problem or a better way to get to the heart of a reading passage, and their explanations may help you learn what you need for the test. So, consider creating or joining a study group.

If you can't find a group to study with, look for a Praxis prep course. The instructors of these courses know the ins and outs of what's on the test, and during the class, they review material that you're likely to encounter. Yes, you'll have to pay for the course, but the advantage is that the instructor should know the material in depth and be able to answer your questions or explain the material in a way that suits your learning style. The Kirkland Group has been conducting Praxis workshops for several years. For more details, go to www.kirklandgroup.org.

Take the test within a week after the prep class ends. Jumping right into the test can increase your chances of remembering the information you learn in the prep class. Don't wait six months after completing the course before you take the test, or you may end up back in the same boat you were in before you took the prep class.

Employing other study techniques

Even when you're not officially studying, try to sneak in some learning or review. Pull out your old textbooks for grammar, reading, and math, and skim through them during lunch or while you're on the treadmill. The info in your old textbooks may jog your memory about something you learned a while back. The only way to study math is to practice math problems. You need to know certain grammar rules that may only be explained in a traditional grammar book.

Gather up crossword puzzle books, Sudoku challenges, and other mind games, and work them while you're relaxing in front of the TV. If you're a whiz at English, work numbers games. If numbers are your thing, try your hand at crossword puzzles. Your goal is to strengthen the areas where you're weak, and puzzles or games are a fun way to accomplish that.

You are what you eat. You can't run a marathon by eating candy bars and drinking soft drinks every day for breakfast. Some foods assist you during the learning process. They naturally improve your memory and release chemicals that are helpful to the brain. These foods include eggs, fish, whole grains, leafy greens, fruits, and — thank goodness — coffee.

Budgeting your time while taking the test

On test day, it's all about pacing yourself. We like to look at the test from the perspective of how many questions you have to answer per minute:

>> **The reading test:** Gives you 85 minutes to answer 56 questions. This gives you a little over a minute and a half to answer each question.

>> **The math test:** Gives you 90 minutes to answer 56 questions. This allows you about a minute and 36 seconds to answer each question.

>> **The writing test:** Gives you 40 minutes to answer 40 multiple-choice questions. That comes out to one question per minute. This test also has an essay section, which gives you 60 minutes to write two essays. So you get 30 minutes per essay.

>> **The essay section:** Gives you 60 minutes to write two essays. So you get 30 minutes per essay.

You may look at those numbers and think, "There's no way I can answer questions that quickly!" But fear not. Here are some tips that will help you shave seconds off the amount of time it takes you to answer many of the questions:

>> **Watch the clock on the computer screen.** Monitor the time on the computer screen like it's your million-dollar countdown. Remember that you'll have at least one minute per question, and you need to use every minute wisely.

WARNING

>> **Don't make time your sole focus.** Don't get so caught up on timing that you aren't paying attention to what the questions are asking. Strike a balance between monitoring the time and concentrating on the task at hand.

>> **Watch for the traps.** The people who write the assessment questions always add "trap" answers into the mix. These incorrect answers look like they're correct, but they're not. For example, you may see an answer to a word problem that's achieved by multiplying when you should be dividing. It's a trap. Watch out for it.

>> **Use the process of elimination.** If you don't know the answer immediately after reading the answer choices, try to eliminate as many answers as possible. Then guess at the answer. Your chances of guessing correctly increase while you eliminate more answer choices.

>> **Read all possible answers.** Sift through each answer choice and ensure that you aren't overlooking a better answer. Don't select Choice (A) before looking at the alternative answer choices.

>> **Save unusually time-consuming questions for last.** If you come across a question that you know will require much more time to answer than most of the other questions, skip the question and go back to it, and perhaps others like it, at the end. You do not want to spend so much time on one question that you could have answered several others in that time instead.

Following an Effective Study Schedule

Putting together a study schedule ahead of time is wise when you're preparing to take the Praxis Core to make sure you're ready as you can be on exam day. As you get closer to that day, you'll gain a better understanding of what information you need to cover the most in the time remaining. Your perspective on where you are and what you need to know will evolve, and you can adjust your schedule as needed.

The exam covers large volumes of concepts of three major subjects, and cramming near exam day isn't something we recommend. We might even venture to say that anybody who does recommend cramming should write a book about how not to pass the exam. We want you to be prepared for the Praxis Core when exam day comes, so we recommend creating and following a study schedule. The following sections provide three study guides and when you should follow which depends on how much time you have before taking the exam. Feel free to customize these plans to meet your needs.

Studying six months before the exam

Perhaps you're a top-notch planner and have more than six months before the exam. In fact, starting with a good amount of time to studying and preparing is ideal. Six months is a standard recommendation for when to begin studying. Even if you have a few months before taking the exam, this advice here applies.

The exam covers three subject areas — math, reading comprehension, and writing. Depending on your background, established abilities in each subject area and specific topic, study pace, and other related factors, you may need to adjust the time frame. This study plan is a general model that you can modify according to your needs.

We recommend following this advice:

>> **Answer practice questions.** The first step we recommend is to work the practice questions in Chapter 3 of this book. Try to answer them all in order to give you a strong understanding of where you are in each subject area and how you can get where you need to be by exam time. The questions in each subject area provide an overview of the various topics involved. Together, they can help you have a much improved idea of your order of study priorities.

>> **Read the initial subject-related chapters.** After you answer the practice questions in Chapter 3 of this book, you can figure out what subject area you need to read about first. For math, reading comprehension, and writing, we include multiple chapters to help you form a foundation of knowledge. Read those chapters and work the practice test questions in them.

   You can find the initial math-related chapters in Part 2, covering number and quantity, algebra, geometry, and statistics and probability. Part 3 deals with reading comprehension. Part 4 provides information about grammar and writing the essay.

>> **Read Part 6, The Part of Tens.** The two chapters in this part can help you fine-tune your understanding of the subject areas by giving you advanced explanations of possible mistakes and how to avoid them.

>> **Take the practice tests.** Part 5 has two full practice exams, correct answers, and explanations of the correct answers. We highly recommend that you read explanations for any answers you may get wrong. After you've established a comfortable level of knowledge of a subject area, you can try taking a practice test for it and reviewing the answers and explanations to garner more understanding of what you need to do. You can take four additional exams at www. dummies.com with answer explanations. (Refer to the book's Introduction for complete details.)

>> **Read the initial subject-matter chapters again.** After you have taken a test for a subject area, or a full exam, go back and read the subject-related chapters again. Which chapters you need to read, or the parts of them you need to review, and when to read them, is something you can determine based on your time schedule. More than likely the subject-related material will make more sense to you, and the repetition can help you strengthen the knowledge you've gained.

>> **Take the practice tests more than once.** You can take the same practice tests or full exams multiple times if necessary a couple of weeks later. In fact, we recommend taking the practice tests more than once. Becoming extra familiar with specific questions and the reasons behind their correct answers can help you remember the principles involved. Remembering principles is key, unlike remembering principals.

>> **Rinse and repeat.** Following the pattern discussed up to this point, you can eventually be ready for the Praxis Core exam. Stay on the path we describe here until you have about a month of studying left to do.

Studying one month before the exam

If you have only a month to study before the exam, focus on establishing a solid foundation for the math, reading comprehension, and writing. You can then identify what areas you need to concentrate on the most, what you need to focus on the least, and everything in between. You'll also have a better perspective on what specific topics are within each subject area you need to study. For instance, if you've mastered reading comprehension and writing but still aren't solid with some math concepts, spend the majority of your remaining study time on math concepts and practice tests. If you're ready to teach math and grammar and you can write a stellar essay, but you need much more practice with reading comprehension, then your top area of study needs to be reading comprehension.

You can read the subject-related chapters and take subject-area tests accordingly. (Part 2 focuses on math, Part 3 on reading comprehension, and Part 4 on writing.) You'll also have a clearer idea of which specific subjects and topics you need to work on. The amount of time you spend on each topic should be based on where each topic ranks in the importance hierarchy.

Near the end of this stage of studying, take at least one full practice exam, even if you've done so already. Doing so helps with your knowledge and understanding and also your mental endurance. You don't want to experience taking your first full practice exam on exam day.

Studying one week before the exam

If you've been regularly studying and preparing, about a week before test day, take at least one more full exam and read the explanations for the answers to any questions you missed. Make sure you know all the definitions and rules you need for reinforcement. You can do that quickly by hitting the key concepts of each subject area.

REMEMBER

This recommendation is for people who have been preparing for the exam since long before the point one week ahead of the exam. If you're rusty on the material and begin studying a week before the exam, we recommend rescheduling the exam.

The following is a study plan for the last week before exam day (at this point, your attention should be on reinforcing your understanding of concepts):

» **Quickly skim through the subject-related chapters.** Part 2 focuses on math, Part 3 on reading comprehension, and Part 4 on writing. Focus on the headings, boldfaced words, and diagrams and look for anything that stands out that you don't fully grasp. After doing so, review those specific concepts until you understand them clearly.

» **Make sure you know how to convert among number forms.** Chapter 4 is about number and quantity, the basic concepts and rules of math. Much of that chapter focuses on the types of numbers and operations with numbers. It builds to number conversions among fractions, decimals, mixed numbers, percents, and integers. When you can freely convert to and from all of these number forms in all possible directions, you'll have mastered the major concepts of number and quantity.

» **Review the major principles of algebra.** Ensure you know how to solve algebraic equations because doing so requires knowing the basics of variables, variable expressions, and operations with variable expressions. You can then work algebraic inequalities and systems of equations. Chapter 5 can help if you have any questions.

» **Memorize the rules of geometry:** Geometry sits on a foundation of rules, so knowing the rules is what matters most in geometry. Although geometry may bring up some painful memories, it doesn't have to if you know the rules when solving word problems.

For example, the sum of the interior angles of every triangle is 180 degrees. You can find the measure of an interior angle of a triangle if you know the measures of the other two interior angles. Such a problem is a nightmare if you don't know the rule, but not so bad if you do.

In the down-to-the-wire stage of your geometry studying, read every boldfaced word in Chapter 6, and define it. Then go through the rules and recite them without reading them. You can then apply these rules when answering geometry questions on the exam.

>> **Condense statistics and probability to a few ideas.** The subject of statistics and probability is mostly about data, a few ways data can be represented, and how data can be interpreted. When you're trying to cover a lot in a little bit of time in the last days before the exam, list the main ways data can be presented. The presentation forms in Chapter 7 are bar graphs, line graphs, pie charts, stem-and-leaf plots, box-and-whisker plots, Venn diagrams, scatter plots, and line plots. Each form entails a few principles you need to know.

In addition, focus on the measures of central tendency (mean, median, mode, and range) and explain to yourself what they are and how to determine them. If you can't remember something, review the section in the book and try to recite it without looking.

>> **Know the parts of speech.** In the few days before the exam, make sure that you can name and define the eight parts of speech (nouns, pronouns, verbs, adverbs, adjectives, prepositions, conjunctions, and interjections). Understanding the parts of speech is important to conceptualize the rest of grammar.

>> **Study punctuation rules.** The writing section tests your knowledge of the rules of grammar, which includes punctuation. Review the rules around comma and semicolon usage. In addition, brush up on the principles of independent and dependent clauses because they cover a large portion of what will be on the writing test. You'll see many questions that test your understanding of those rules.

>> **Do a lot of reading.** Reading anything is practice for the reading section, even this book. While you're studying directly for the Praxis Core, reading a novel or two can help prepare you for the reading comprehension test. Follow the reading comprehension advice in Chapter 9. Most importantly, you should never assume anything a passage doesn't say directly or indirectly. *Remember:* The reading comprehension test is more about practice than memorization.

When Test Day Has Arrived

If you've followed the advice in the section "Using Your Time Wisely," earlier in this chapter, you'll begin test day well prepared for the task at hand. By this time, you should be in shape and ready to concentrate on the test.

Print testing-center map directions to make sure you know where you're going. Drive to the testing center the day before to find out exactly where the testing center is located. Try to make the drive at the same time that you'll make the drive on test day; that way, you'll know what traffic may be like and can plan accordingly for leaving home earlier than you had planned or taking an alternate route. You should consider using an app for real-time traffic information on the day of the test.

Arrive at the testing center at least 30 minutes early. Arriving late could cause you to forfeit registration. And make sure you bring a picture ID. Without your ID, you won't be admitted to the test center, and you'll lose your registration fee.

WARNING

Don't take the test while you're fatigued. Sleep deprivation can lead to failing test scores. Make sure you get a good night's sleep the night before you're scheduled to take the test.

After you arrive at the testing center, you'll need to follow a few rules and sit through a bit of training. We cover those details in the sections that follow.

Knowing what to bring and what to leave at home

You must bring two items to the testing center:

>> **Your admission ticket:** You receive your printed admission ticket when you register online.

>> **Picture identification:** The picture ID must include your name, signature, and photo. Acceptable IDs include a valid government-issued driver's license, a passport, a state-issued ID, a national ID, or a military ID. See www.ets.org for more details.

WARNING

If you don't have the items in the preceding list, you won't be allowed to take the exam.

Thousands of people take the Praxis every year. To make sure everyone has a fair chance at passing, ETS has set up guidelines for what isn't allowed in the test center. Here's a list of items to leave at home:

>> **Cellphones, smartwatches, laptops, tablets, MP3 players, or any other electronic devices:** You can't even bring these into the building, so lock them in your car or leave them at home. ETS takes the confidentiality of the test *seriously*.

>> **Dictionaries, books, or other reading materials:** Yes, that includes this book. Study *Praxis Core For Dummies* either in the car or at home.

>> **Scratch paper:** The testing center will provide scratch paper that you can use for math computations, notes, and outlines.

>> **Writing utensils:** The testing center will also provide you with pens or pencils.

>> **Personal items:** You may be asked to empty your pockets before entering the test room. You'll be given a place to store your belongings while you take the test, but don't plan on leaving anything valuable in there.

TIP

Be sure you wear the right clothing. Sometimes, buildings are colder or warmer than expected. Dress in layers so that you can make adjustments for the temperature.

Getting familiar with computer testing

You'll take the Praxis Core on a computer. This allows you to take the test any day of the week and almost on demand at the local Prometric testing center. It also allows for faster scoring of your test, meaning you'll get your results faster than you would if the test were administered on paper. According to ETS, score reports for selected response-only tests that are given continuously (pretty much every day) are available 10–11 business days after the day of the test. On the other hand, score reports for constructed-response tests (such as the writing test that contains the essays) given continuously are available 15–16 business days after the day of the test.

Before you take the test, ETS gives you 30 minutes of practice time during which you can figure out how the computer test works. Pay attention during this online computerized testing tutorial session. Tips such as how to use the computer, answer questions, and review previous pages can be helpful. Take advantage of this time because you're on your own after the test starts.

TIP

Make sure to figure out how to mark questions. Occasionally, you'll come to an item that you aren't sure about. If you have extra time left at the end of the test, you can go back and check your answers.

If You're Retaking the Test

The reality is that sometimes you study for, prepare for, and focus on the Praxis Core only to receive the bad news that you didn't achieve a passing score. Don't panic. According to ETS, you can take the test once per calendar month (but no more than six times within a 12-month period).

If you do need to retake the test, spend some time analyzing the areas where you fell short and then create a plan to improve your score the next time. Examine your previous test scores. The numbers can tell you how close you were to passing and how much work you have to do to bring up your score.

A wise saying defines insanity as doing the same thing over and over again and expecting different results. Don't repeat your previous mistakes on subsequent tests. If you didn't pass because you just don't understand decimals or grammatical rules, spend extra time studying those areas.

Some people miss passing the test by 15 points or more. If that's the case, don't rush to retake the test. Enroll in a review course in order to increase your chances of passing the test on your next try. You may spend a little money on the class, but you'll save money in the long run because you won't have to take the test repeatedly. Sometimes, individuals who work together, take the same college course, or go to the same church can form a study group. Or you can look for a personal tutor.

When test day rolls around again, try to minimize negative circumstances and know that uncontrollable ones aren't likely to reoccur. You may have argued with your spouse on the morning you took the first test. Maybe the baby contracted diarrhea the night before, or perhaps the chicken salad you ate didn't agree with your stomach. These factors may have contributed to your failure to pass the test the last time you took it. Take it again, and the conditions will probably be better.

Chapter **3**

Practicing the Praxis: Sampling Some Practice Questions

I f you're just beginning to prepare to take the Praxis, this chapter is a good place to start. It gives you a sense of the types of math, reading, and writing questions you'll encounter when you face the real exam.

In this chapter, we give you an opportunity to see where your strengths and weaknesses lie. You can determine whether you need to spend the next few weeks studying statistics and probability questions, grammar rules, or reading comprehension strategies. Or maybe you'll decide that you just need to fine-tune one or two specific areas of knowledge, and that's fine, too.

REMEMBER

Focus first on the areas you need to study most. Later, you can review the areas you're more familiar with.

Going through the Pre-Assessment Questions

In the following sections, we toss some practice questions at you. Actually, because there are complete practice tests in Part 5 of this book, maybe you should think of the questions in the following sections as "practice for the practice." The questions in this chapter can help you determine your strengths and weaknesses, and then align your study appropriately.

When you answer the questions in the following sections, we don't recommend setting a timer or anything like that yet. You should learn how to do something right before you start to worry about doing it fast, and there'll be plenty of time to time yourself later.

Because time won't be an issue, you also don't need to worry about skipping hard questions and coming back to them later. Try your best to answer each one, even if it's just a guess (there's no penalty for guessing on the Praxis, so on the actual test, there's no reason to leave a question blank).

Finally, we recommend that you resist the urge to flip to the answers after each question to see whether you got it right. That can wait until you complete all the practice questions. Seeing that you got a few questions wrong early on can dishearten you, and seeing that you got a bunch right in a row can make you paranoid about jinxing yourself. Either way, there's no advantage to checking your answers on a question-by-question basis: Take your time and complete all the questions to the best of your ability. You can worry about how many you got right when you finish, and you can worry about your speed in the practice tests in Part 5 of this book.

Note: We don't provide essay questions in this chapter for you to practice because we want you to get an overview of your skills. If you want to spend some time on essay writing, flip to Part 4.

When you're ready to try your hand at a full-length practice test, head to Part 5, where you can find two full-length Praxis exams (with essay questions included).

Reading practice questions

DIRECTIONS: Each passage in this test is followed by a question based on its content. After reading each passage, choose the best answer to each question from among the five choices given. Answer all questions following a passage on the basis of what is stated or implied in that passage. You are not expected to have any previous knowledge of the topics treated in the passages.

Although "an elephant is an elephant" to the untrained eye, African elephants and Asian elephants are actually two distinct species, and it's not so hard to tell the difference. In African elephants, the head is higher than the back, whereas the Asian elephant's back is higher than its head. Among African elephants, both males and females are almost always born with tusks, while female Asian elephants are usually tuskless. If you can get close enough to examine the trunk, you'll notice that African elephants have two finger-like protrusions at the tip of the trunk, as opposed to an Asian elephant's one.

1. According to the passage, an elephant with no tusks is

    (A) definitely a female elephant.

    (B) definitely an Asian elephant.

    (C) probably a male Asian elephant.

    (D) probably a female Asian elephant.

    (E) more likely to be a male Asian elephant than a female African elephant.

Nowadays, most people are aware that Christopher Columbus was not only a pretty terrible guy, but that he also didn't really discover America. Even leaving out the obvious objection that vast populations of indigenous peoples were already living here, there's also indisputable evidence that the Vikings reached North America and established settlements centuries before Columbus (it was a quicker and an easier trip for them, however, as all they had to do was sail along the ice of the Arctic Circle as though it were a coastline). What far fewer people know is that it seems likely that seafaring Pacific Islanders reached the west coast of South America in the early second millennium, possibly even before the Vikings touched down in the Northeast. Archaeological evidence indicates the sudden appearance of yams (originally native to South America) in Polynesia and of chickens (originally native to Asia) in Chile at about the same time.

2. The primary purpose of the passage is to

   (A) explain how chickens appeared in South America.

   (B) discern whether the Vikings or Pacific Islanders reached the Americas first.

   (C) argue that Columbus Day should no longer be celebrated as a holiday.

   (D) examine the question of whose journey to the Americas was most difficult.

   (E) provide information about journeys to the Americas before that of Columbus.

Though many might understandably assume that it was a long and complex process, the transformation of the Republican Party from a single-issue organization dedicated to ending slavery into the "party of big business" was both predictable and, more or less, instantaneous. Knowing that freed slaves would have no choice but to travel north and take factory jobs, which would result in more competition for employment and therefore lower wages, northern industrialists joined forces with idealistic abolitionists. When slavery ended, the abolitionists considered their duty done and got out of politics, and the captains of industry were left in charge of the party.

3. The passage characterizes the shift in priorities of the 19th-century Republican Party as

   (A) very nearly inevitable.

   (B) the surprising result of a long struggle.

   (C) the fault of naïve abolitionists.

   (D) a logical reaction to unforeseen circumstances.

   (E) an attempt to reduce competition for employment.

It is arguably Shakespeare's finest comedy, but modern productions of *As You Like It* find themselves awkwardly having to negotiate a plot point that doesn't sit right with contemporary audiences: In this day and age, we roll our eyes at the idea that the intelligent, resourceful, and independent heroine Rosalind would fall madly in love with Orlando simply because she sees him win a wrestling match.

4. The author of the passage uses the word *negotiate* most nearly to mean

   (A) imperceptibly alter.

   (B) make the best of.

   (C) draw attention away from.

   (D) apologize for.

   (E) rush through safely.

Perhaps no issue in popular music divides both critics and fans more bitterly than the seemingly endless debate over what music, and which bands, do or do not count as "punk rock." People can't even seem to agree on whether punk is a genre of rock or was a historical movement within rock, specific to a particular place and time. Were 1990s rock groups like Nirvana and Blink-182 punk bands, or were they only bands that were influenced by punk as it was "authentically" played in the 1970s by bands like the Ramones and the Clash? Did punk "end" at a certain point in music history, and if so, then when, and what case is to be made for saying it ended then, as opposed to at an earlier or later date? After all, if a word refers only to a style of music, then music of that style can be played by anyone at any time — but if the word refers to a contextualized historical movement, then calling contemporary bands "punk" would be as absurd as calling contemporary feminists "bluestockings" or calling contemporary Midwesterners "settlers."

5. The organization of the passage can best be described by which of the following?

   (A) A compromise between two sides in a controversy is suggested.

   (B) A popular misconception is corrected.

   (C) A tricky question is analyzed for a general audience.

   (D) A comparison is made between seemingly dissimilar things.

   (E) A problematic term is suggested to be meaningless.

I don't feel old, but when I examine all the data, it seems to point to the fact that I just might be. Perhaps the most crucial piece of evidence is that I haven't dressed up for Halloween in nearly four years. This wasn't a decision I made; it was just a string of bad luck. One year, I happened to be moving on Halloween. The next year, I was helping a friend move. Last year, there was a hurricane — surely that's not my fault, right? I can make all the excuses I want, but deep down inside I know that if I were ten years younger, I would have found a way to dress up on Halloween no matter what. Maybe that's what getting old is: a loss of energy disguised as a series of coincidences.

6. In the passage, the author's tone can best be described as one of
   (A) nostalgic self-justification.
   (B) annoyed defensiveness.
   (C) paranoid hypothesizing.
   (D) blissful ignorance.
   (E) melancholy philosophizing.

Writing practice questions

1. Don't <u>be offended</u> when the cat head-butts <u>you, you</u> should <u>be flattered because it's</u> a sign <u>of affection</u>. <u>No error</u>.

2. When I <u>saw you</u> covered in <u>feathers, I just</u> naturally assumed <u>that you were</u> the person <u>to which</u> I mailed all those ducks. <u>No error</u>.

3. <u>You're computer</u> seems to have a <u>virus, but,</u> as far as I can <u>tell, it should be possible</u> for us to remove it without any <u>of the data being</u> lost. <u>No error</u>.

4. <u>It's</u> remarkable <u>that, even though</u> you are not <u>any taller than he,</u> you are still <u>heavily favored to win the scheduled</u> one-on-one basketball game. <u>No error</u>.

5. Coulrophobia is the fear of clowns, and a phenomenon more widespread than many realize.

   (A) Coulrophobia is the fear of clowns, and a phenomenon more widespread than many realize.

   (B) Coulrophobia, it is the fear of clowns, a phenomenon more widespread then many realize.

   (C) Coulrophobia, the fear of clowns, is a phenomenon more widespread than many realize.

   (D) Coulrophobia, which is the fear of clowns, being a phenomenon more widespread then many realize.

   (E) Coulrophobia is the fear of clowns, it is a phenomenon more widespread than many realize.

6. The octopus is a surprisingly smart animal, they can solve mazes amazing skillfully.

   (A) The octopus is a surprisingly smart animal, they can solve mazes amazing skillfully.

   (B) The octopus is a surprisingly smart animal, that can solve mazes amazing and skillful.

   (C) The octopus is a surprisingly smart animal, it can solve mazes amazingly skillful.

   (D) The octopus is a surprisingly smart animal; which can solve mazes amazingly skillfully.

   (E) The octopus is a surprisingly smart animal: It can solve mazes amazingly skillfully.

7. Whomever parked the car, that is in the driveway, could of done a better job.

   (A) Whomever parked the car, that is in the driveway, could of done a better job.

   (B) Whoever parked the car that is in the driveway could have done a better job.

   (C) Whoever parked the car that is in the driveway, could of done a better job.

   (D) Whomever parked the car which is in the driveway could have done a better job.

   (E) Whomever parked the car, which is in the driveway, could have done a better job.

Mathematics practice questions

DIRECTIONS: Questions 1–20 are followed by five suggested answers. Select the one that best answers the question.

The following graph shows the number of bicycles sold by Brad's Bicycle Company for the years 2006–2011. Use the graph to answer Questions 1–4.

Brad's Bicycle Company Annual Sales

© John Wiley & Sons, Inc.

1. Which year showed the greatest number of bicycles sold by Brad's Bicycle Company?

   (A) 2006

   (B) 2007

   (C) 2008

   (D) 2009

   (E) 2010

2. What is the average number of bicycles sold for the six-year period?

   (A) 1,125,000

   (B) 11,250

   (C) 19,000

   (D) 187,500

   (E) 18,750

3. What is the median number of bicycles sold for the six-year period?

   (A) 210,000

   (B) 220,000

   (C) 215,000

   (D) 430,000

   (E) 225,000

Following are the results from Mrs. Lowe's science test. Use the stem-and-leaf plot to answer Questions 5–7.

Science Test Results	
Stem	Leaf
5	0 0 5 5 5 9
6	0 9
7	0
8	5 5 5 5
9	0 0 0 9

Key: 8|5 = 85

© John Wiley & Sons, Inc.

4. In which interval did most students score?

   (A) 50–59

   (B) 60–69

   (C) 70–79

   (D) 80–89

   (E) 90–99

5. What is the mode of the data set?

   (A) 85

   (B) 55

   (C) 90

   (D) 95

   (E) 50

Use the Venn diagram that follows to answer Question 6.

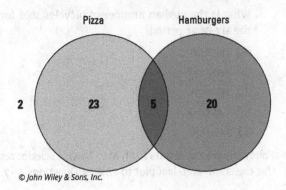

**Favorite Food
of 50 Students**

Pizza   Hamburgers

2   23   5   20

© John Wiley & Sons, Inc.

6. Pizza is the only favorite food of what percentage of students in the Venn diagram?

(A) 46 percent

(B) 40 percent

(C) 10 percent

(D) 23 percent

(E) 4 percent

7. The Hornet football team won eight football games and lost four games. Find the ratio of wins to total games in simplest form.

(A) 8:4

(B) 2:1

(C) 1:4

(D) 2:3

(E) 4:12

8. A grocery store sells 5 pounds of apples for $50. How much would you pay for 2 pounds of apples?

(A) $0.70

(B) $0.75

(C) $1.40

(D) $1.50

(E) $1.43

9. Which problem situation could be solved with the following equation?

$$15d + 50 = m$$

(A) Cassie earns $15 each day she works plus a flat rate of $50 per month. What is m, the total amount she earns in a month when she works d number of days?

(B) Cassie earns $15 for every purchase she sells at her job. What is m, the total amount she earns in 100 months?

(C) Cassie earns $50 each day she works plus a flat rate of $15 per month. What is m, the total amount she earns in a month when she works d number of days?

(D) Cassie earns d amount of dollars for every 15 items she sells. She makes $50 per day at her job. What is m, the total dollar amount Cassie earns in a year?

(E) Cassie earns d amount of dollars for every 50 items she sells. She makes $15 per day at her job. What is m, the total dollar amount Cassie earns in a year?

10. There are 10 yellow counters and 15 red counters in a bag. What is the probability of picking a yellow counter from the bag?

(A) 5/8

(B) 1/2

(C) 2/5

(D) 2/3

(E) 3/8

11. A spinner with the numbers 1 through 15 is spun. In simplest form, what is the probability of the spinner landing on a prime number?

(A) 2/5

(B) 5/15

(C) 6/15

(D) 3/5

(E) 7/15

12. In the following rectangle ABCD, $\overline{AC}$ is 6 inches long. If the rectangle's perimeter is 34 inches, how many inches long is $\overline{AB}$?

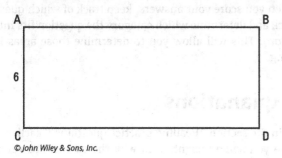

© John Wiley & Sons, Inc.

- (A) 28
- (B) 13
- (C) 22
- (D) 11
- (E) 17

13. What is the length in centimeters of the hypotenuse of a right triangle with legs of 5 centimeters and 12 centimeters?

- (A) 13
- (B) 17
- (C) 7
- (D) 4.12
- (E) 5

14. The length of each leg of an isosceles triangle is 17 centimeters, and the perimeter is 62 centimeters. What is the length of the base?

- (A) 45
- (B) 17
- (C) 28
- (D) 14
- (E) 20

15. Simplify $\left(-3a^5\right)^2$.

- (A) $-9a^{10}$
- (B) $-9a^7$
- (C) $9a^{-7}$
- (D) $9a^{10}$
- (E) $-3a^7$

Looking at the Pre-Assessment Answers

After you answer the practice questions in the preceding sections, see how you did by checking your answers in the following sections. When you score your answers, keep track of which questions you answered incorrectly. Then go back and determine which category the question fits into (algebra, subject-verb agreement, and so on). This will allow you to determine those areas in which you need to spend more time studying.

Reading answers and explanations

Use this answer key to score the questions in the section "Reading practice questions," earlier in this chapter. The answer explanations give you some insight as to why the correct answer is better than the other choices.

1. **D. probably a female Asian elephant.** The passage explicitly states that "female Asian elephants are usually tuskless." While the passage implies that it's possible for a male or female of either elephant species to be born without tusks, it remains the case that only female Asian elephants are tuskless *most of the time.*

    Choice (A) is wrong because there's no reason to think that a tuskless elephant is *definitely* female. The passage states that female Asian elephants are usually tuskless, but it also mentions that female African elephants usually have tusks, and that it's possible, though rare, for a male of either species to be tuskless. (As a general rule, on reading-comprehension tests like the Praxis, you should never go for a "definitely" when a "probably" will do.)

    Choice (B) is wrong because the passage states that "among African elephants, both males and females are *almost* always born with tusks." The "almost" implies that it's possible, though rare, for an African elephant of either gender to be tuskless.

    Choice (C) is wrong because, although the text doesn't explicitly state whether male Asian elephants are usually tusked or tuskless, the construction of the sentence "Among African elephants, both males and females are almost always born with tusks, while female Asian elephants are usually tuskless" clearly implies that male Asian elephants usually have tusks.

    Choice (E) is wrong because the structure of the sentence "Among African elephants, both males and females are almost always born with tusks, while female Asian elephants are usually tuskless" implies that both male Asian and female African elephants have tusks most of the time. Although the passage doesn't say that a male Asian elephant *isn't* more likely to be tuskless than a female African elephant, it *also* doesn't say that it *is* more likely. The passage implies that most male Asian elephants have tusks, and it directly says that the vast majority of female African elephants have tusks, but the passage does not say, directly or by implication, anything about whether male Asian elephants are more likely to have tusks than female African elephants. This answer choice tries to trick you into going for an unsupported complex answer, even though another, simpler answer choice is much more soundly supported by the passage. Don't be fooled!

2. **E. provide information about journeys to the Americas before that of Columbus.** Look at it this way: *Does* the passage "provide information about journeys to the Americas before that of Columbus?" Yes, indisputably. And is it doing this pretty much *the whole time?* It sure is. So there's no real way that Choice (E) can be wrong. There's no reason to go for an overly specific answer choice when another answer choice contains a broad statement that isn't wrong.

    Choice (A) is wrong because, although the passage *does* provide an explanation of how chickens ended up in South America, this isn't the *primary purpose* of the passage — it's a detail brought up in the course of exploring a larger idea. If something isn't brought up until the end, it's probably not the primary purpose of the passage. (Did you notice how the passage *closed* with the chicken detail, and then that detail was mentioned in the *first* of the wrong choices so it would be fresh in your mind? Watch out for that trick!)

Choice (B) is wrong because, although the passage does seem to be unsure about whether Vikings or Pacific Islanders reached the Americas first ("*possibly* even before . . ."), it doesn't seem to be primarily concerned with which of them "won." The passage only seeks to establish that both the Vikings and the Pacific Islanders got here before Columbus.

Choice (C) is wrong because, although it may be logical to assume that the author isn't a big fan of Columbus Day, based on the fact that he calls Columbus a "terrible guy" and point out that he didn't really discover America, the passage never gets into the issue of whether Columbus Day should still be celebrated. If arguing this were really the *primary purpose* of the passage, then the author would have made his opinion clear.

Choice (D) is wrong because although the passage mentions that the Vikings' journey was easier than Columbus's, it does so in a parenthetical, and this is the only comparison in the entire passage involving the difficulty of the respective journeys. A concern brought up only once isn't likely to be the *primary purpose* of a passage.

3. **A. very nearly inevitable.** The first sentence of the passage ends by calling the transformation of the Republican Party from an abolitionist organization to a pro-business party "predictable and, more or less, instantaneous." The rest of the passage offers an explanation for this appraisal, framing the course of events as the only thing that could realistically have happened — in other words, *very nearly inevitable.*

Choice (B) is wrong because the opening sentence establishes that the transformation of the Republican Party was *not* "a long and complex process" (a near-paraphrase of "the surprising result of a long struggle"), despite the fact that "many might understandably assume" it was. As an argumentative passage will often do, this passage opens by explaining what is *not* the case before going on to explain what *is* the case.

Choice (C) is wrong because, while the passage explains that the abolitionists who founded the Republican Party "considered their duty done and got out of politics" after the end of slavery, it doesn't call them naïve and blame them for the party's subsequent course. This answer choice is too strongly worded — something that should make you suspicious on the actual exam.

Choice (D) is wrong because while the passage does characterize the shift in priorities of the Republican Party as "logical" in the sense that it happened due to a series of identifiable and predictable steps, it does *not* bring up any "unforeseen circumstances." On the contrary, the passage explains that northern businessmen *did* foresee the desirable financial effect that the abolition of slavery would have on their businesses and that they joined the party specifically for that reason.

Choice (E) is wrong because the passage clearly states that the businessmen who joined the Republican Party *wanted* there to be "more competition for employment," so they were hardly trying to *reduce* such competition.

4. **B. make the best of.** The close-in-context adverb *awkwardly* is a clue to the fact that a troupe playing *As You Like It* would expect the wrestling-inspired love scene to seem cheesy or even sexist to a modern audience and would therefore have to try and find a way to present the plot device as inoffensively as possible — in other words, to "make the best of" it.

Choice (A) is wrong because there is no indication in the passage that modern troupes are in the habit of actually *changing* the scene in question. They have to "play it down," but the passage doesn't say that they *rewrite* Shakespeare.

Choice (C) is wrong because, while "draw attention away from" is possibly the best of the wrong answers, it's not as good as "make the best of." Why not? Drawing attention away from the plot point in question *would be a form of* making the best of it — so if Choice (C) is right, then *so is* Choice B, but only *one* answer choice can be right. Conversely, Choice (B) can be right on its own because Choice (C) goes too far. There's no real way to "draw attention away from" a scene in a play. You can, however, make decisions about different ways of staging it — so "make the best of" works, but "draw attention away from" goes too far.

Choice (D) is wrong because the passage never implies that modern troupes "apologize for" the wrestling plot point in *As You Like It*. It's implied that they have to stage it cautiously and creatively, but "apologize for" is too extreme.

Choice (E) is wrong because, while "rush through safely" can be a good synonymous phrase for *negotiate* in other contexts — one might speak of *negotiating* hurdles or river rapids, for example — it doesn't fit here.

5. **C. A tricky question is analyzed for a general audience.** At the very least, the passage definitely implies that the question of which bands count as "punk" bands is *tricky* — it does hardly anything aside from explain why the question is difficult to answer. And the passage does definitely appear to have been written for a general audience. Because these things are all that Choice C asserts to be true of the passage, there's really no way it can be wrong.

Choice (A) is wrong because the passage never implies that there are precisely *two sides* to the debate about punk rock. On the contrary, the passage gives the impression that there are as many opinions as there are people involved in the discussion! Additionally, the passage never really "suggests a compromise." It summarizes what others have said, but the author never offers an argument of their own.

Choice (B) is wrong because the passage never says anything along the lines of "many people think that such-and-such is true, but it's not, and here is what's true instead." It summarizes points that many music critics and fans have made, but it never says anything about who's wrong or who's right.

Choice (D) is wrong because the passage never makes any comparisons.

Choice (E) is wrong because, while the passage certainly characterizes "punk" as "a problematic term," it never goes so far as to suggest that it is *meaningless*. The idea of the passage seems to be that the term does mean *something*, but that people can't agree on what.

6. **E. melancholy philosophizing.** The author is certainly *philosophizing* — in other words, they are tossing out analyses and characterizations of a particular concept (aging). And it seems inarguable that they are *melancholy* — that is, mournful and blue. Because those two things are all that Choice (E) asserts and they're both true, there's no way that Choice (E) can be wrong.

Choice (A) is wrong because the passage is not really *nostalgic* — the author is talking more about a present that they aren't enjoying than about a past that they did enjoy. And they certainly aren't being *self-justifying*. If anything, they're beating up on themselves, which is exactly the opposite.

Choice (B) is wrong because the author seems more sad than *annoyed*. They don't like what they're talking about, but it's making them depressed, not angry. And they aren't being *defensive* about anything. They're admitting their faults, rather than making excuses for them.

Choice (C) is wrong because, while the author is *hypothesizing* — in other words, coming up with possible explanations for a phenomenon — nothing in the passage suggests that they're *paranoid*. The author is feeling blue about getting older, not freaking out because they think people are out to get them.

Choice (D) is wrong because the author seems much more sad than they do *blissful*. And as for *ignorance*, it seems as though they're only too aware of their problems, not oblivious to them.

Writing answers and explanations

Use this answer key to score the questions in the section "Writing practice questions," earlier in this chapter. The answer explanations give you some insight as to why the correct answer is better than the other choices.

1. **B. you, you.** This section of the sentence contains a comma splice.

   Choice (A) is wrong because this imperative clause is properly constructed. Choice (C) is wrong because no comma before the *because* clause is necessary, and the correct spelling of *it's* is used.

   Choice (D) is wrong because the correct preposition is used, and *affection* is spelled correctly. Choice (E) is wrong because there is in fact an error in the sentence.

2. **D. to which.** The speaker is talking about a human being, and the pronoun is the object of a preposition, so it should be *whom* instead of *which*.

   Choice (A) is wrong because the normal past tense is correct here. Choice (B) is wrong because the comma correctly joins an initial subordinate *when* clause and a subsequent independent clause.

   Choice (C) is wrong because *that* is the appropriate relative pronoun for an essential clause. Choice (E) is wrong because there is in fact an error in the sentence.

3. **A. You're computer.** The possessive pronoun is spelled *your*, and that's the one you need here (*you're* means "you are").

   Choice (B) is wrong because a comma after a coordinating conjunction is correct in the rare instances where a subordinate clause follows the coordinating conjunction. Choice (C) is wrong because the comma here correctly marks the end of the subordinate clause and the beginning of the final independent clause.

   Choice (D) is wrong because *data* is plural. Choice (E) is wrong because there is in fact an error in this sentence.

4. **E. No error.** There is no error in this sentence.

   Choice (A) is wrong because this is the correct spelling of *it's* in this context (the one that means "it is"). Choice (B) is wrong because a comma is necessary here, as the subordinate *even though* clause interrupts the subordinate *that* clause.

   Choice (C) is wrong because, although many people would say "taller than *him*," it is actually correct to say "taller than *he*" because *than* is not necessarily a preposition in this case. Choice (D) is wrong because the infinitive ("to win") is correct in this context.

5. **C. Coulrophobia, the fear of clowns, is a phenomenon more widespread than many realize.** This sentence correctly presents a single independent clause that is interrupted by an appositive phrase set off with a pair of commas.

Choice (A) is wrong because a comma before the conjunction is not necessary here, as an independent clause does not follow it. Choice (B) is wrong because the comma and *it* after the subject of the sentence are unnecessary, and the spelling should be *than* instead of *then*.

Choice (D) is wrong because the sentence has no main verb, and the spelling should be *than* instead of *then*. Choice (E) is wrong because this sentence contains a comma splice.

6. **E. The octopus is a surprisingly smart animal: It can solve mazes amazingly skillfully.** Both independent clauses are correctly constructed, and a colon is an acceptable way (though not the only way) of joining them.

Choice (A) is wrong because the sentence contains a comma splice, the subject and pronoun do not agree in terms of number, and you need the adverb *amazingly* rather than the adjective *amazing*. Choice (B) is wrong because a comma is not needed before the *that* clause and because the adjectives *amazing* and *skillful* appear to modify the noun *mazes*, when you want them to be adverbs (*amazingly* and *skillfully*) modifying the verb *solve*.

Choice (C) is wrong because the sentence contains a comma splice and because you want the adverb *skillfully* rather than the adjective *skillful*. Choice (D) is wrong because the semicolon does not join two independent clauses (a *which* clause is not an independent clause).

7. **B. Whoever parked the car that is in the driveway could have done a better job.** The subjective case *whoever* is correctly used for the subject of the sentence, the essential *that* clause is not set off with any commas, and the correct *could have* is used in place of the incorrect *could of*.

Choice (A) is wrong because *whoever*, rather than *whomever*, should be used for the subject of the sentence, a *that* clause should not be set off with commas, and *could have* is correct, not *could of*. Choice (C) is wrong because no comma is needed and because *could have* is correct, not *could of*.

Choice (D) is wrong because *whoever*, rather than *whomever*, should be used for the subject of the sentence, and because a *which* clause would need to be set off with commas. Choice (E) is wrong because *whoever*, rather than *whomever*, should be used for the subject of the sentence.

Math answers and explanations

Use this answer key to score the questions in the section "Mathematics practice questions," earlier in this chapter.

1. **E. 2010.** The year 2010 yielded the highest bicycle sales of 230,000.

2. **D. 187,500.** The average sales are found by adding the total sales for all years and dividing the total by the number of years:

$$100,000 + 140,000 + 210,000 + 225,000 + 230,000 + 220,000 = 1,125,000 \div 6 = 187,500$$

3. **C. 215,000.** Put the sales in order from least to greatest:

~~100,000~~, ~~140,000~~, 210,000, 220,000, ~~225,000~~, ~~230,000~~

Cross out the numbers, starting with the highest and then crossing out the lowest, then the second highest and second lowest, and so on, until you reach the numbers in the middle of the data set. There are two numbers in the center; if you take the average of them, you will have the median:

$$(210,000 + 220,000) \div 2 = 215,000$$

You could also write the numbers in numerical order and identify the two in the middle. Their average (mean) is the median of the data set.

4. **A. 50–59.** The stem of 5 indicates that six people scored in the interval of 50–59 with the scores of 50, 50, 55, 55, 55, 59.

5. **A. 85.** The score that occurs the most often is 85, so 85 is the mode.

6. **A. 46 percent.** Fifty people were surveyed regarding their favorite foods. $\frac{23}{50}$, or 46 percent, chose pizza. The people in the overlap do not count since they picked both pizza and hamburgers. The number of people who chose just pizza is 23. That number is out of 50 people, so 46 percent of the people chose pizza.

$$\frac{23}{50} = 0.46$$
$$= 46\%$$

7. **D. 2:3.** The ratio of wins to total games played is 8:12. Set up the ratio of wins to total games played and reduce your answer by dividing both numbers by 4.

$$\frac{\text{wins}}{\text{total games}} = \frac{8}{12} \div \frac{4}{4} = \frac{2}{3}$$

8. **C. $1.40.** Set up a proportion to compare the cost for 5 pounds of apples to the cost for 2 pounds of apples. Cross multiply to find that 2 pounds of apples cost $1.40.

$$\frac{3.50}{5} = \frac{x}{2}$$
$$3.50(2) = 5x$$
$$7.00 = 5x$$
$$\frac{7.00}{5} = \frac{5x}{5}$$
$$1.40 = x$$

9. **A. Cassie earns $15 each day she works plus a flat rate of $50 per month. What is m, the total amount she earns in a month when she works d number of days?** The amount for m is the total Cassie earns each month she works at a rate of $15 per day, plus a flat rate of $50.

10. **C. 2/5.** There are 25 counters in the bag; 10 out of 25 are yellow, or 2/5 when simplified.

11. **A. 2/5.** There are six prime numbers from 1 to 15: 2, 3, 5, 7, 11, and 13. This is 6/15, which is 2/5 when simplified

12. **D. 11.** The perimeter, in this case 34, is the sum of all the sides. You were given the width of 6 in the problem. Using $P = 2l + 2w$, you can find the missing side.

$$P = 2l + 2w$$
$$34 = 2l + 2(6)$$
$$34 = 2l + 12$$
$$22 = 2l$$
$$l = 11$$

13. **A. 13.** Using the Pythagorean theorem formula $a^2 + b^2 = c^2$, substitute the value of the legs for a and b and solve for c.

$$a^2 + b^2 = c^2$$
$$5^2 + 12^2 = c^2$$
$$25 + 144 = c^2$$
$$169 = c^2$$
$$\sqrt{169} = c$$
$$13 = c$$

14. **C. 28.** An isosceles triangle has two sides of equal length. Given that the perimeter or distance around the triangle is 62, you can solve for the base.

$$\text{length of side } 1 + \text{length of side } 2 + \text{base} = 62$$
$$17 + 17 + \text{base} = 62$$
$$34 + \text{base} = 62$$
$$\text{base} = 62 - 34$$
$$\text{base} = 28$$

15. **D. $9a^{10}$.** The exponent of 2 on the outside of the parentheses indicates that you are to raise everything inside the parentheses to the second power.

$$(-3)^2 = 9$$
and
$$\left(a^5\right)^2 = a^{10}$$
so
$$9a^{10}$$

Assessing Your Results

After you answer and review a representative sample of Praxis questions in the preceding sections, you can evaluate how you did and figure out which subjects you need to spend more time reviewing. Even if you missed a couple of questions, don't worry. That was the point of answering the assessment questions. You're still at an early stage in your process of preparation for the Praxis, and there's a lot of book left to go.

REMEMBER

Every time you take a practice test, you can benefit by assessing your results and focusing your studying and skills improvement accordingly.

Identifying categories where you struggled

The areas where you struggled the most are the areas you need to focus on the most. To figure out where you struggled, focus on each section of the practice test and outline the areas in which you need the most improvement. Briefly describe everything you missed and look for patterns. Under each test subject (math, reading, writing), write the names of more specific categories, and then write even more specific categories under those. (Use the table of contents for help identifying specific categories within each test.) You may need to have a subcategory titled "Other."

For example, the first level of subheadings for math consists of the four major categories of Praxis Core math questions — number and quantity (basic math), algebra and functions, geometry, and statistics and probability. Each of those categories has its own subcategories (look at the chapters for each of the broad categories to break them down further). Continue to drill down into the topics until you identify the specific area you need to review. What matters is that you organize your weakest areas in a way that you can keep up with them and work on them.

After you identify the categories that gave you trouble, look at the answer choices you picked incorrectly. Compare them to the correct answer choices. Review your mistakes and be sure you understand why any incorrect answers were incorrect.

Taking notes on the areas where you succeeded can also help you. Improving your knowledge and skills concerning those areas can give you an edge for getting difficult questions correct.

Understanding where you went wrong specifically

Along with making an outline of the types of questions you missed, look for reasons for not getting the ones you missed. Did you lack knowledge that you need to review? Did you simply make an error? Did you confuse one idea with another? Did you not use a strategy you could have used that would have made the difference? Make a list of these reasons and keep them in mind as you work on gaining the necessary knowledge and practice, as well as the test-taking skills, that will help you.

The Praxis Core exam requires critical thinking beyond mere knowledge. But knowledge is extremely important, and so is strategy. The chapters in Parts 2, 3, and 4 review the knowledge you need to know for each topic on the Praxis, and the Parts conclude with a strategy chapter to help you increase your chances of answering a question right when you're not 100 percent sure of the answer.

However, don't focus only on how many questions you missed and what types of questions they were. You can improve your future scores by asking yourself right now: *What did the wrong answers you picked have in common?* After all, if you failed to pick the right answer to a given question, that means you were fooled by one of the wrong answers. Go back over the explanations to the questions you missed, examine the differences between the right answers and the wrong answers that fooled you, and try to develop a sense of *what type of wrong answers you tend to be fooled by.* Then you'll know what to watch out for!

When it comes to math questions, you'll likely have to go back and look at how you worked the problem to identify where you went wrong.

When it comes to the reading and writing questions, think about these questions: Do you tend to jump after the wrong answer with the biggest words in it? Or are you fooled by something that's probably true in real life, but that the passage never actually mentions? Did they get you with the wrong answer that mentions a detail from the end of the passage because they know it's fresh in your mind? Do you have a weakness for the wrong answer that uses the greatest number of exact words from the passage?

There's an old saying among test-prep tutors: "I can tell you how to get a question right, but only you can tell yourself why you got one wrong." Okay, fine, it's not an old saying — we made it up. But it *should* be an old saying, because it makes a good point.

2

Mastering Math Concepts

Review the major categories of numbers, the different ways to represent values, and basic operations.

Brush up on how to use variables to represent quantities, perform operations with variable expressions, and solve equations and inequalities.

Strengthen your understanding of geometric concepts, principles, and formulas.

Gain mastery of the major forms of data representation and analysis.

Understand the best test-taking strategies for math.

IN THIS CHAPTER

» Brushing up on integers, fractions, and mixed numbers

» Determining decimal and percent forms of numbers

» Looking at number lines and the order of operations

» Converting quantities in math problems

» Practicing some math questions and reviewing the answers

Chapter **4**

Count on It: Number and Quantity

A good review of math begins with the basics of numbers and the major operations you do with them. The Praxis Core exam involves the basic operations, as well as more complicated ones, using different types of numbers. About 36 percent of the 56 math questions on the exam fall into the "number and quantity" category (that's about 20 questions if you haven't warmed up your math muscles yet). Plus, you have to understand these basics in order to perform more complicated math problems.

If you were reviewing how to ride a bike, you might want to start with a discussion of pedals and tires, and how to make them move. Doing math is like riding a bike, and this chapter starts at the beginning of your ride down the road to complete preparation for Praxis Core math.

REMEMBER

You'll have an on-screen calculator to use when you take the Praxis Core exam.

Working with Integers: Whole Numbers and Their Opposites

Think about the first numbers you ever learned. The first numbers you named belong to the most basic category of numbers — *whole numbers.* They begin with 0 and go on forever: 1, 2, 3, and so on. Each whole number is separated from the next by a quantity of 1. Partial numbers — that is, fractions such as $\frac{2}{5}$ and decimals such as 0.4 — are *not* whole numbers. (We go into fractions and decimals in the sections "Computing with Fractions and Mixed Numbers" and "Working with Decimals and Percents," later in this chapter.)

All whole numbers other than 0 are *positive*, which means that they're greater than 0. A number other than 0 that has no sign before it is understood to be positive. All numbers less than 0 are *negative* and are represented with a minus sign (–). Every negative number is the opposite of a positive number, and vice versa. For example, the opposite of 8 is –8, and the opposite of –12 is 12.

The *integers* are all the whole numbers and their opposites. In other words, all the whole numbers and all the negatives of whole numbers make up the entire set of integers. The only integer that doesn't have an opposite is 0. (Poor thing.)

Every integer is either *even* or *odd*. Also, integers are the only numbers that can be even or odd. The even integers include 2, 4, 6, 8, and so on, and the opposites of those numbers. Zero is an even number, also. If any even integer is divided by 2, the result is an integer. Every even integer is 2 more than the previous even integer and 2 less than the next. All of the other integers are odd. The odd integers are 1, 3, 5, 7, and so on, and also –1, –3, –5, –7, and so on. Half of an odd integer is never an integer. Like even integers, each odd integer is 2 greater than the previous and 2 less than the next odd integer.

Doing basic operations with integers

The basic operations you can perform with integers are addition, subtraction, multiplication, and division. You perform the same operations with all real numbers, but this part of the review focuses on integers because they're the best numbers to use in the early part of your math review. After all, they're basic numbers, and this discussion is about basic operations. They make a good fit, basically.

To add or subtract integers, it may help to understand *absolute value*, which is an integer's distance from 0 on a number line. The absolute value of any integer is its value without a negative sign. So, the absolute value of any positive integer is the number, and the absolute value of any negative integer is its opposite, or the integer that remains when you drop the negative sign. The | | symbols represent absolute value. Here are a couple examples:

>> The absolute value of a positive number: $|7| = 7$

>> The absolute value of a negative number: $|-7| = 7$

Remember a few facts about working with integers:

>> Subtracting an integer is the same as adding its opposite, and adding an integer is the same as subtracting its opposite.

>> If an even number of negative integers are multiplied or divided, the product or quotient is positive. If an odd number of negative integers are multiplied or divided, the product or quotient is negative.

>> To add two integers that have the same sign, add their absolute values and give the sum the sign that both numbers have.

>> To add two integers that have opposite signs, subtract the smaller absolute value from the greater absolute value and give the difference the sign of the number with the greater absolute value.

EXAMPLE

Find the product of the following numbers: $-2 \cdot 4 \cdot -1 \cdot -3 \cdot -2$

(A) -48

(B) 24

(C) 48

(D) 25

(E) -24

The correct answer is Choice (C). The product of the absolute values of the integers is 48. Because the number of negative integers in the problem is four ($-2, -1, -3$, and -2), an even number, the product is positive.

$$(-2)(4)(-1)(-3)(-2) =$$
$$(-8)(-1)(-3)(-2) =$$
$$(8)(-3)(-2) =$$
$$(-24)(-2) = 48$$

Therefore, the answer is 48.

If addition or multiplication is the only operation used with a group of integers, the order of the integers doesn't matter (an idea with the fancy name *commutative properties*), and the placement of parentheses doesn't matter (called *associative properties*). The sum or product will be the same, regardless of the order in which you perform the operations.

Commutative Property of Addition
$$1 + 2 + 3 + 4 = 3 + 1 + 4 + 2$$

Commutative Property of Multiplication
$$1 \times 2 \times 3 \times 4 = 3 \times 2 \times 4 \times 1$$

Associative Property of Addition
$$(1 + 2 + 3) + 4 = 1 + (2 + 3 + 4)$$

Associative Property of Multiplication
$$(1 \times 2) \times 3 \times 4 = 1 \times (2 \times 3) \times 4$$

REMEMBER

These rules apply to all real numbers. We just used integers in the preceding examples to show you the basics.

WARNING

No matter how well you understand a mathematical concept or process, the threat of careless errors exists. To help avoid them on the Praxis Core exam, make sure you work every step, talk the problem out in your head while you work it, and, if you have time, go back over all the problems you worked after you reach the end of the math section. Danger lurks in the shadows, so be careful out there!

Finding factors of whole numbers

A *factor* of a whole number is a whole number that can be divided into the original whole number a whole number of times. (That's a lot of whole numbers!) For example, 4 is a factor of 20 because 4 can be multiplied by the whole number 5 (which is also a factor of 20) to get 20. The number 4 isn't a factor of 21, 19, or any other number that's not evenly divisible by 4. And if you can break down a number's factor even further into its own factors, those smaller factors are also factors of the original number you started with. For example, because 2 is a factor of 4, 2 is also a factor of 20. The number that 4 must be multiplied by to get 20 is 5, so 5 is also a factor of 20. That makes 4 and 5 a *factor pair* of 20.

The factors of a whole number are also known as the whole number's *divisors*. You're perhaps familiar with the term *divisor* as a number that a dividend is divided by in a division problem. In long division, the divisor is the number that appears to the left of the long-division symbol. Because the factors of a whole number are what that number can be divided by, under the specific requirement of having to be whole numbers, the factors can also be referred to as divisors. The math test of the Praxis Core exam may use that terminology.

REMEMBER

Every whole number has itself and 1 for factors. If those are the only two factors of a number, it's a *prime number*. For example, 3, 17, 31, and 79 are prime numbers.

To determine the factors of a number, first determine one factor and what it has to be multiplied by to get the number. Then find factors of those numbers the same way. Continue the process until no numbers can be broken down further. At this point, you've found the *prime factorization* of the number — a representation of the number as a product of all its prime factors. From there, all the number's other factors, except for 1, can be found by multiplying every possible combination of the prime factors.

A common method for determining the prime factorization of a number is use of the *repeated division* method, but a historically more common method is use of a *factor tree*, in which factors of a number are broken down into their own factors until the only factors at the bottom of the tree are prime numbers. Usually, factor pairs are broken down into other factor pairs. Here's a factor tree for 60:

EXAMPLE

Find all the factors of 30.

(A) 30 and 1

(B) 2, 3, and 5

(C) 1, 2, 3, 5, 6, 10, 15, and 30

(D) 2, 3, 5, 6, 10, and 15

(E) 2 and 15

The correct answer is Choice (C). All the numbers listed are either prime factors of 30, products of combinations of those prime factors, or 1. However, Choice (C) is the only choice that includes all of them.

Employing some helpful divisibility rules

Knowing the divisibility rules concerning single-digit numbers and 10 can be helpful for finding factors of numbers. Check out Table 4-1.

TABLE 4-1 **Divisibility Rules**

A whole number is divisible by . . .	. . . if . . .	Examples
0	No number is divisible by 0.	Sorry; nothing to see here.
1	All whole numbers are divisible by 1.	Every whole number is an example of this rule.
2	The last digit is an even number (0, 2, 4, 6, 8).	12; 728; 4; 962
3	The sum of the digits of the number is divisible by 3.	27 (2 + 7 = 9); 138 (1 + 3 + 8 = 12); 10,011 (1 + 0 + 0 + 1 + 1 = 3)
4	The last two digits form a number that's divisible by 4.	124 (24); 736 (36); 13,112 (12)
5	The last digit is 0 or 5.	25; 360; 40; 195
6	The number is divisible by both 2 and 3.	12; 54; 270; 906
7	You can remove the last digit, double it, and subtract the result from the rest of the original number to get either 0 or a number with an absolute value that's divisible by 7.	14; 63; 175; 707
8	The last three digits form a number that's divisible by 8. (This rule, of course, is useful only with numbers that have more than three digits.)	2,800; 16,384; 596,656
9	The sum of the digits is divisible by 9.	18; 72; 108; 918
10	The last digit of the number is 0.	100; 810; 21,370

Finding multiples of integers

A *multiple* of a number can be obtained by multiplying the number by an integer. For example, multiples of 5 include 5, 10, 15, 20, 25, and so forth. The phrases *a multiple of* and *divisible by* have basically the same meaning, but *divisible by* generally refers specifically to whole numbers, while *multiple* is used to label whole numbers, as well as other types of numbers. If an integer is evenly divisible by another integer, that original integer is automatically a multiple of the other integer. In other words, if a number is a factor of another number, the second number is a multiple of the first number. For example, because 8 is a factor of 40, 40 is a multiple of 8.

EXAMPLE

Each of the following is a multiple of 3 EXCEPT

(A) 96

(B) 123

(C) 3,000

(D) 761

(E) 903

The correct answer is Choice (D). By using the divisibility rule for 3 (see Table 4-1), you can determine that 96, 123, 3,000, and 903 are divisible by 3. The digits of each number add up to a number that's divisible by 3. That means each one is a multiple of 3 because you can multiply 3 by another integer to obtain each number. However, the digits of 761 add up to 14, which isn't divisible by 3. You can also use long division to determine whether each number is a multiple of 3 by seeing whether 3 goes into it a whole number of times, but that takes longer. Fortunately, you can use a calculator to save time.

Determining the greatest common factor and least common multiple

Two whole numbers can have factors in common. Such factors are called *common factors*. The greatest of those factors is the *greatest common factor* of the two numbers. To find the greatest common factor of two numbers, find all the factors of both numbers, determine which factors the numbers have in common, and then determine which of those common factors is the greatest (largest).

For example, to determine the greatest common factor of 20 and 45, you must first determine the factors of both numbers. You can use a prime factorization technique to find them. (We talk about prime factorization techniques in the section "Finding factors of whole numbers," earlier in this chapter.)

20: 1, 2, 4, 5, 10, 20

45: 1, 3, 5, 9, 15, 45

What factors do 20 and 45 have in common? The common factors are 1 and 5. Because 5 is the greatest of the common factors, 5 is the greatest common factor.

An alternative method for finding the greatest common factor of two or more numbers is to write the prime factorization of each number, match up the prime factors they have in common in every instance, and multiply all instances of prime factors they all have in common. For example, if you are looking for the greatest common factor of 50 and 75, you can first write out the prime factorization of each.

$50 = 2 \cdot 5 \cdot 5$
$75 = 3 \cdot 5 \cdot 5$

The two prime factorizations have $5 \cdot 5$ in common. The number 5 appears twice in both of the prime factorizations. There are no other matches. The greatest common factor of 50 and 75 is therefore $5 \cdot 5$, which is 25.

The *least common multiple* of two numbers is like the greatest common factor, except that it's the lowest number instead of the highest one, and it's a multiple instead of a factor. Although multiples of numbers can be negative, the term *least common multiple* refers only to positive numbers. To find the least common multiple of two numbers, write out several positive multiples of each, and then determine the lowest positive multiple that they have in common.

For example, to find the least common multiple of 3 and 5, first write positive multiples of both numbers until you see one that they have in common.

3: 3, 6, 9, 12, 15, 18, 21

5: 5, 10, 15

For 5, you can stop at 15 because 15 is also a multiple of 3. Because 15 is the lowest of the positive multiples that 3 and 5 have in common, 15 is the least common multiple of 3 and 5.

Another way to find the least common multiple of two or more numbers involves writing the prime factorization of each number and looking for matches. You can multiply all of the instances of prime factors, multiplying only once for each instance of a factor that matches between the two numbers.

For example, consider finding the least common multiple of 60 and 75. First, write the prime factorizations of 60 and 75. Then, take note of every instance of a prime factor that they have in common.

$60 = 2 \cdot 2 \cdot 3 \cdot 5$
$75 = 3 \cdot 5 \cdot 5$

The prime factorizations have one matching 3 and one matching 5, so multiply by 3 once and by 5 once. (If the factorizations had another matching 3, you would multiply by 3 one more time.) From there, multiply by every instance of all of the remaining prime factors. The remaining non-matching prime-factor instances are 2, 2, and 5. If you multiply all of the factors in matching instances once and the remaining instances, you get 300. That's the least common multiple of 60 and 75.

$$2 \cdot 2 \cdot 3 \cdot 5 \cdot 5 = 300$$

WARNING

You can't just multiply the factors together to get the least common multiple. Multiplying the factors will give you a common multiple, but it may not be the smallest one. For example, if you want the least common multiple of 4 and 6, you can't multiply them because that gives you 24, when the least common multiple is actually 12.

Exponents and square roots

Have you ever taken a shortcut? If so, you're not alone, and you can relate to the idea of using exponents to represent multiplication. The people who invented the language we use to represent numbers decided to use shortcuts in representing multiplication that involves the same factor more than once. Imagine reading and writing stuff like this all the time:

$$7 \times 7 =$$

Fortunately, an easier way was created. In the preceding example, 7 is multiplied 21 times. That 21 can be used as an exponent.

$$7 \times 7 = 7^{21}$$

An *exponent* represents how many times a number is a factor. A number that has an exponent is said to be set to that *power*. 7^{21} is "7 to the 21st power," for example. On the Praxis Core exam, you're almost guaranteed to see exponents. You may also see two very common exponents: 2 and 3. When a number has 2 for an exponent, the number is *squared*, which means the number is multiplied by itself. When a number has an exponent of 3, the number is *cubed*, or multiplied three times. An example of a squared number is 10^2. That is 10 to the second power, and it is also called 10 squared. An example of a cubed number is 8^3, or 8 cubed.

5^2 is "5 squared" $(5 \cdot 5)$, or 25.

10^3 is "10 cubed" $(10 \cdot 10 \cdot 10)$, which equals 1,000.

Math questions on the Praxis Core exam can involve numbers that have exponents as parts of larger operations, but they can also ask you flat out what the value of a number with an exponent is.

EXAMPLE

Which of the following numbers is 4 cubed?

(A) 16

(B) $\frac{1}{4}$

(C) 43

(D) 64

(E) 256

The correct answer is Choice (D). 4 cubed is 4^3, which represents $4 \cdot 4 \cdot 4$. The value of $4 \cdot 4 \cdot 4$ is 64.

Often, in math, if you can ride one way down a road, you can turn around and ride the other way. As you can find the value of the square of a number, you can find what has to be squared to get a number. The non-negative number you have to square to get a number is the number's *square root*. For example, the square root of 81 is 9 because 9 squared $(9 \cdot 9)$ is 81. The symbol for square root is $\sqrt{}$. The number that you're taking the square root of goes inside the symbol.

EXAMPLE

$\sqrt{9}$ represents "the square root of 9." The positive number that's squared to get 9 is 3, so the square root of 9 is 3. Thus, $\sqrt{9} = 3$ because $3^2 = 9$.

What is the value of $\sqrt{36}$?

(A) 36

(B) 6

(C) 1,296

(D) 72

(E) 18

The correct answer is Choice (B). The positive number that's squared to get 36 is 6; $6^2 = 36$. Choice (A) is incorrect because 36 is simply the number in the square root symbol. Choice (C) is false because 1,296 is 36 squared ($36 \cdot 36$). Choice (D) is the product of 36 and 2. Choice (E) is the value of $6 \cdot 3$ and also the value of $\frac{1}{2} \cdot 36$, but it's not the square root of 36.

Computing with Fractions and Mixed Numbers

Not all numbers are integers. Fractions can represent partial numbers and are represented through the use of integers. The integer on top is the *numerator*, and the integer on the bottom is the *denominator*. In the fraction $\frac{3}{4}$, 3 is the numerator, and 4 is the denominator. What the fraction represents is "3 out of 4." If 3 of the people in a rock group have music degrees, and the band has 4 members, $\frac{3}{4}$ of the members of the band have music degrees. A fraction also represents a *ratio*, which is a comparison of two quantities. The fraction $\frac{3}{4}$, for example, represents the ratio "3 to 4."

If you eat a whole pie and $\frac{2}{3}$ of another one, the number of pies you eat can be represented by a mixed number, $1\frac{2}{3}$. A *mixed number* is an integer followed by a fraction. Every mixed number has an absolute value that is greater than 1.

TIP

A fraction also represents division. The numerator is divided by the denominator. Every integer is understood to be that number over 1. For example, $8 = \frac{8}{1}$.

Simplifying fractions

Different fractions can have equal values. The fractions $\frac{1}{2}$ and $\frac{100}{200}$ represent the same amount, for example. They both represent half. If 20 out of 50 people vote for a political candidate, 2 out of every 5 people vote for the candidate. The difference is that a group of 50 people involves multiple sets of 5 people, while a group of 5 people does not. It only involves one set. The fraction $\frac{2}{5}$ is *simplified*, which means it can't be written with two integers that have smaller absolute values. It's written in the simplest form possible.

To simplify a fraction, find the greatest common factor of the numerator and the denominator, and then write the number of times the greatest common factor goes into each. The greatest common factor of 20 and 50 is 10. To simplify $\frac{20}{50}$, write the number of times 10 goes into 20 and write it over the number of times 10 goes into 50.

$$\frac{20}{50} = \frac{2}{5}$$

Using any common factor will lead you in the right direction. If you don't use the greatest common factor, however, you'll have to repeat the process of finding common factors and simplifying the fractions until they can't be simplified anymore.

EXAMPLE

Which of the following represents $\frac{18}{24}$ in simplest form?

(A) $\frac{3}{4}$

(B) $\frac{9}{12}$

(C) $\frac{36}{48}$

(D) -6

(E) $\frac{3}{24}$

The correct answer is Choice (A). The greatest common factor of 18 and 24 is 6, which goes into 18 three times and 24 four times. The simplest form of the fraction is therefore $\frac{3}{4}$. Choice (B) is another form of the fraction, but not the simplest form. If you arrive at such an answer, you must continue to look for common factors. Choice (C) results from multiplying the numerator and denominator by 2, and Choice (D) is the result of subtracting 24 from 18. Choice (E) is the result of dividing only the numerator by the greatest common factor.

REMEMBER

Knowing how to simplify fractions is important because answers that are the results of operations that involve fractions must always be in simplest form unless otherwise indicated.

Converting between fractions and mixed numbers

Mixed numbers can be written as fractions. Knowing how to write mixed numbers as fractions is important when you perform operations with mixed numbers, and writing fractions as mixed numbers is necessary if your answer choices on the Praxis Core exam are mixed numbers.

To write a mixed number as a fraction, multiply the denominator of the fraction by the absolute value of the integer. Then add the numerator to that product. Write the result over the denominator of the fraction.

$$4\frac{3}{7} = \frac{(7 \cdot 4) + 3}{7}$$
$$= \frac{28 + 3}{7}$$
$$= \frac{31}{7}$$

Put a negative sign before the fraction if the mixed number is negative.

To go the opposite way down that road and convert a fraction to a mixed number, write the highest integral (the adjectival form of *integer*) number of times the denominator fits completely into the numerator. Then write what remains as the numerator of a fraction beside the integer. The denominator of the fraction part will be the denominator of the improper fraction you're converting. The number 7 goes into 31 completely 4 times because $7 \cdot 4 = 28$, which is 3 short of 31.

You can also write the multiples of the denominator up to the last multiple that is less than the numerator. The number of multiples you write will be the integer (followed by a negative sign if the improper fraction is negative) in the mixed number. The value of the numerator of the improper fraction minus the last multiple you wrote will be the numerator of the fraction in the mixed number.

Multiples of 7: 7, 14, 21, 28...

That's a set of 4 multiples, so the integer in the mixed number is 4.

The numerator of the improper fraction minus the highest multiple of the denominator that is less than the numerator equals 3.

$$31 - 28 = 3$$

Therefore, the numerator of the fraction in the mixed number is 3. The denominator is the same for an improper fraction and an equal mixed number, except in cases in which simplification is necessary. The denominator in this case is 7.

$$\frac{31}{7} = 4\frac{3}{7}$$

Performing basic operations on fractions and mixed numbers

Knowing how to convert between fractions and mixed numbers is useful in performing basic operations with them. We highly recommend converting mixed numbers to fractions when performing addition, subtraction, multiplication, or division. Working with fractions is much easier than working with mixed numbers.

Adding and subtracting fractions

To add fractions that have the same denominator, add the numerators and write the sum over the denominator that both fractions have, which is called the *common denominator*. If you add two apples and three apples, you get five apples. Similarly, if you add two sevenths and three sevenths, you get five sevenths.

$$\frac{2}{7} + \frac{3}{7} = \frac{5}{7}$$

Now, what do you do if you want to add two fractions that don't have the same denominator? You turn them into two fractions that do have the same denominator, by force. The way to do that is to write at least one of the fractions in a different but equal form. Usually, you need to convert both fractions into new forms. To convert fractions into new forms, you can multiply the numerator and the denominator by the same number, which should be the number you have to multiply by to get the denominator you want. Multiplying a fraction's numerator and denominator by the same number is a way of multiplying by 1 because a number over itself is equal to 1. Multiplying a number by 1 does not change the original number's value, but it can change the way the original number is written. For example, if you multiply both the numerator and denominator of $\frac{3}{5}$ by 2, the product is equal to $\frac{3}{5}$ but presented in another form.

$$\frac{3}{5} = \frac{3(2)}{5(2)} = \frac{6}{10}$$

$$\frac{1}{5} + \frac{3}{7} = \frac{1(7)}{5(7)} + \frac{3(5)}{7(5)}$$

$$= \frac{7}{35} + \frac{15}{35}$$

$$= \frac{22}{35}$$

TIP

Any common multiple of the denominators of fractions will work as a common denominator, but the best common denominator to use is the least common multiple. If you use another common denominator, you'll have to simplify the sum of the fractions. A guaranteed way to find a common multiple of two numbers is to multiply them by each other. However, this doesn't always result in the least common multiple. It only guarantees a common multiple, not necessarily the smallest one.

You follow the same procedure to subtract fractions, except you, well, subtract. That's the only difference.

$$\frac{5}{8} - \frac{1}{6} = \frac{5(3)}{8(3)} - \frac{1(4)}{6(4)}$$
$$= \frac{15}{24} - \frac{4}{24}$$
$$= \frac{11}{24}$$

A whole can be divided into fractions that add up to the whole, or 1. For example, suppose three people ate a whole pie together. If you know the fraction of the pie the first person ate and the fraction the second person ate, you can determine the fraction the third person ate by subtracting the sum of the first two fractions from 1.

EXAMPLE

Ginger, Mary, and Skip are the only owners of an island. Ginger owns $\frac{1}{4}$ of the island, and Mary owns $\frac{2}{5}$ of it. What fraction of the island does Skip own?

(A) $\frac{1}{5}$

(B) $\frac{1}{4}$

(C) $\frac{2}{7}$

(D) $\frac{7}{20}$

(E) $\frac{9}{13}$

The correct answer is Choice (D). Together, Ginger and Mary own $\frac{13}{20}$ of the island.

$$\frac{1}{4} + \frac{2}{5} = \frac{1(5)}{4(5)} + \frac{2(4)}{5(4)}$$
$$= \frac{5}{20} + \frac{8}{20}$$
$$= \frac{13}{20}$$

Ginger and Mary are, together, the owners of $\frac{13}{20}$ of the 1 island. Skip owns the rest of the 1 island, so the fraction he owns is $\frac{13}{20}$ less than 1. Any integer can be written as itself over 1, so 1 is equal to $\frac{1}{1}$.

$$1 - \frac{13}{20} = \frac{1}{1} - \frac{13}{20}$$
$$= \frac{1(20)}{1(20)} - \frac{13}{20}$$
$$= \frac{20}{20} - \frac{13}{20}$$
$$= \frac{7}{20}$$

Skip owns $\frac{7}{20}$ of the island.

Multiplying fractions

To multiply fractions, multiply the numerators, and then multiply the denominators. Write the product of the numerators over the product of the denominators.

$$\left(\frac{3}{10}\right)\left(-\frac{5}{8}\right) = -\frac{15}{80}$$
$$= -\frac{3}{16}$$

REMEMBER

Unless otherwise suggested by the Praxis Core exam instructions for a question, all fractions that are final answers must be in simplest form.

Dividing fractions

Dividing by a fraction is the same as multiplying by its *reciprocal*, which is what you get when you switch the numerator and denominator of a fraction.

$$\frac{6}{7} \div \frac{2}{3} = \frac{6}{7} \cdot \frac{3}{2}$$
$$= \frac{18}{14}$$
$$= \frac{9}{7}$$

The fraction $\frac{9}{7}$ is an example of an *improper fraction*, which is a fraction in which the numerator has a greater absolute value than the denominator. Improper fractions make acceptable answers as long as they're simplified and the correct one is among the choices you're given. However, answer choices on the Praxis Core exam are not always in improper fraction form. Knowing how to convert among number forms is important.

Working with mixed numbers

To perform the basic operations on mixed numbers, convert those mixed numbers to improper fractions, and then perform the operations like you would with any fractions.

$$5\frac{4}{7} + 3\frac{6}{7} = \frac{39}{7} + \frac{27}{7}$$
$$= \frac{66}{7}$$
$$\left(-3\frac{4}{5}\right)\left(-2\frac{1}{6}\right) = \left(-\frac{19}{5}\right)\left(-\frac{13}{6}\right)$$
$$= \frac{247}{30}$$

EXAMPLE

If every section of each box is the same size, what is the sum of the fractions of the boxes that are shaded?

(A) $\frac{12}{17}$

(B) $\frac{17}{12}$

(C) $\frac{7}{12}$

(D) $\frac{9}{24}$

(E) $\frac{3}{8}$

The correct answer is Choice (B). The fraction of the first box that's shaded is $\frac{8}{12}$, and the fraction of the second box that's shaded is $\frac{9}{12}$. The sum of those two fractions is $\frac{17}{12}$. Choice (A) is the reciprocal of the answer, Choice (C) is the result of adding the unshaded fractions of the boxes, and Choice (D) is the numerator of one fraction over the sum of the fractions' denominators. Choice (E) is the simplified form of Choice (D).

Working with Decimals and Percents

This section deals with one of the most famous types of portions — the percent. A *percent* is a representation of a number of hundredths, and it's represented by the symbol %. The word "percent," the % sign, and the word "hundredths" all have the same meaning. (Their meanings are 100% the same.) A percent greater than 100% represents a quantity greater than 1.

Percents are related to decimals. Decimals represent whole and partial numbers. Both 0.17 and 64 are decimals. The number 64 is equal to 64.0, but the ".0" in "64" is implied. The first place after a decimal point represents tenths, the second place represents hundredths, the third place indicates thousandths, and so on. For a number that's in decimal form, every digit is in a place and has a *place value*. The ones place comes immediately before the decimal point, and the tens place is the next to the left. Every place represents a type of value that is $\frac{1}{10}$ that of the place (not necessarily the number in the place) on its immediate left and 10 times that of the place immediately to its right. This is why moving a decimal point one place to the right makes the new number 10 times the previous number and moving a decimal point one place to the left makes the new number $\frac{1}{10}$ the previous number. Moving a decimal point two places to the right results in a new number that is 100 times the original number, and moving a decimal point two places to the left brings about another number that is $\frac{1}{100}$ the first number. That pattern continues infinitely in both directions.

Decimals can be written as percents, and percents can be written as decimals. Both decimals and percents can be written as fractions. Techniques can be used to convert numbers from any one of those forms to either of the other two. (Note that the word *decimal* refers to both the punctuation mark and numbers that use the punctuation mark but not a %. In other words, *decimal* can be used to mean both *decimal point* and *decimal number*.)

Converting among decimals, percents, fractions, and mixed numbers

Percent means "per centum" or per 100 (divided by 100).

REMEMBER

A fraction represents division. The numerator is divided by the denominator.

Dividing the numerator by the denominator will change the fraction to decimal form.

When you divide by 100, you move the decimal two places to the left. So, when working with percents, you want to be skillful at moving between whole numbers, fractions, and decimals.

$$5\% = \frac{5}{100\%} = \frac{1}{20} = .05$$

Changing a decimal to its equivalent percentage requires multiplying by 100 (because 100% is equal to 1). Multiplying by 1 doesn't result in a different value. Decimals can be written as percentages by moving the decimal point two places to the right and including the percent sign.

$$0.589 \times 100\% = 58.9\%$$

So multiplying by 100 and dividing by 100 undo each other. It's like taking a step forward and taking a step back.

EXAMPLE

Which of the following percents is equal to the fraction $\frac{3}{5}$?

(A) 60%

(B) 30%

(C) 35%

(D) 65%

(E) $\frac{3}{5}$%

The correct answer is Choice (A). When dividing 3 by 5, you get 0.6. If you move the decimal two places to the right and add a percent sign, you get 60%. Choices (B), (C), and (D) involve miscalculations, and Choice (E) results from the false method of simply adding a percent symbol.

To convert a decimal to a fraction or a mixed number, ask yourself what the digits after the decimal point represent, based on their place values. The last digit's place will tell you what number should be on the bottom of the fraction that you need to write at first, before simplification (if simplification is necessary). If the decimal point is preceded by a non-zero digit, you may need to convert the decimal number to a mixed number. The fraction part of the mixed number will follow the rules on how to convert a decimal number to a fraction.

The number 0.43 represents "0 and 43 hundredths." Those words spell out what the number is in fraction form. It is $\frac{43}{100}$. The 0 could precede the fraction to form a mixed number, but what would be the point? The number 8.256 is "8 and 256 thousandths." The "thousandths" part means you need to write, or at least think of, the initial fraction of the mixed number with 1,000 in the denominator. That fraction will follow the 8, forming a mixed number. In this case, it's necessary to simplify the result.

$$8.256 = 8\frac{256}{1,000}$$
$$= 8\frac{32}{125}$$

Of course, you can convert the mixed number to an improper fraction by using the method we discuss in the section "Converting between fractions and mixed numbers," earlier in this chapter.

$$8\frac{32}{125} = \frac{1,032}{125}$$

Because dividing by a fraction is the same as multiplying by its reciprocal, multiplying by a decimal is the same as dividing by the reciprocal of its equivalent fraction. For example, multiplying by 0.1 is equivalent to multiplying by $\frac{1}{10}$ and therefore equivalent to dividing by 10. By the same principle, dividing by 0.1 is the same as multiplying by 10.

Determining percent change

An adjustment from one value to another involves a *percent change*, which is the percent of the original number that the new number is greater than or less than the first. A percent change can be a *percent increase* or a *percent decrease*. For example, a shirt that costs $10 may increase in price to $12. That change consists of a $2 increase.

$$12 - 10 = 2$$
$$\frac{2}{10} = 0.2$$
$$= 20\%$$

Since 2 is 20% of 10, the change in price is 20%. The adjustment is an increase, so it's a 20% increase. If the price of the shirt were lowered instead, there would be a percent decrease. A percent increase or decrease is always a percent of the original number.

Performing basic operations on decimals

Doing the basic operations on decimals isn't very different from doing the same operations on integers. The only major difference is that decimal placement has to be taken into account. Beyond that, everything is pretty much the same.

Adding and subtracting decimals

To add or subtract decimal numbers, line up the decimal points (even the one in the answer) and then add the numbers as if they were integers. Digits that have nothing under them can be dropped, although some may have digits carried over that need to be added. Also, after the last non-zero digit following a decimal point, you can add as many 0s as you want (although it's not a requirement). Doing so doesn't change the value of the number.

$$\begin{array}{r} 3,542.1478 \\ +85.4120 \\ \hline 3,627.5598 \end{array}$$

Multiplying decimals

You multiply decimals exactly the same way you multiply integers, except the total number of digits after the decimal point in the answer equals the number of places after the decimal points in the numbers you're multiplying. So, if you have a total of three places after the decimal points in the numbers you're multiplying, you need to have three digits after the decimal point in your answer.

Don't line up the decimal points if they don't happen to already be lined up when you align the numbers to the right, unless you want to confuse yourself.

$$
\begin{array}{r}
89.7 \\
\times 3.48 \\
\hline
7176 \\
35880 \\
269100 \\
\hline
312.156
\end{array}
$$

A number *of* a number is the same as the first number *times* the second number. In other words, "number of" means "number times." That applies to integers, fractions, mixed numbers, decimals, and percents. Be careful not to confuse a number of a number with a number out of a number. The "out of" terminology implies division. A number of a number indicates multiplication.

$$3 \text{ of } 14 = 3 \times 14$$
$$\tfrac{1}{4} \text{ of } 20 = \tfrac{1}{4} \times 20$$
$$7\tfrac{1}{2} \text{ of } 41 = 7\tfrac{1}{2} \times 41$$
$$0.02 \text{ of } (-100) = 0.02 \ (-100)$$
$$34\% \text{ of } 73 = 34\% \times 73$$

Dividing decimals

To divide decimals, you can use long division the way you would with integers. However, you move the decimal in the number you're dividing by as many places to the right as you need to in order to get an integer. To make up for the change, you move the decimal in the number it's divided into the same number of places to the right. Then, you place the decimal in the answer (above the division symbol) in the same place that it appears in the number being divided into (below the division symbol).

$82.64\overline{)305.768}$ is the same as $8264\overline{)30576.8}$. If you put the decimal in the answer directly above the decimal in 30576.8, you can divide like you would without the decimal. Just remember where the decimal belongs in the answer, which is 3.7.

Keep in mind that a calculator is available for you to use when you take the Praxis exam.

Understanding the Number Line

The *number line* is a tool that's used to illustrate orders of numbers. The numbers represented on it can vary. On all versions of the number line, numbers decrease to the left and increase to the right. Although only a few numbers are shown in any given instance, the line suggests that the numbers represented are all the real numbers. The arrows at both ends of the line indicate that the numbers go on infinitely in both directions.

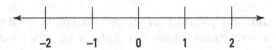

Interpreting numeration and place values

The numbers represented by points on the number line are *coordinates.* The points are named not only by their coordinates, but also sometimes by letters that appear above the points. The coordinate of Point C could be 4, for example. The point can also be called 4.

Questions on the Praxis Core exam may go beyond identifying points by the numbers under them. Questions can involve distances, and those questions are rooted in placements of coordinates.

Point C is not labeled, but it is halfway between Points A and D. What is the distance from Point C to Point D?

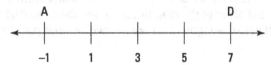

(A) 4

(B) 3

(C) 5

(D) 2

(E) 7

The correct answer is Choice (A). Because the coordinate of Point A is −1 and the coordinate of Point D is 7, the distance between them is 8. Half of that distance is 4, and 3 is 4 units from both −1 and 7. Choice (B) is the coordinate of Point C. Choice (C) is the coordinate of the point that is halfway between Points C and D. Choice (D) is the distance from one labeled coordinate to the next, and Choice (E) is merely the coordinate of Point D.

TIP

The number that's halfway between two numbers is the average of the two numbers. Recall that the *average* of a group of numbers is the sum of the numbers divided by the number of numbers in the group.

Knowing the basics of order

The number line can be helpful for putting numbers in order. A question about order on the Praxis Core exam can involve differing types of numbers. For example, an order question can involve a mixture of integers, fractions, mixed numbers, and decimal numbers. The best way to put such an assortment of numbers in order is to rewrite all of them as one type of number, such as all fractions or all decimals. Then you can use the number line as a mental and visual aid to put the numbers in order.

Suppose you need to put the numbers 2.78, $\frac{5}{2}$, 2, and $\frac{8}{3}$ in order from least to greatest. You can put all these numbers in improper fraction form and get a common denominator, but it may be easier to convert all the numbers to decimal form.

$$2.78 = 2.78$$
$$\frac{5}{2} = 2.5$$
$$2 = 2.0$$
$$\frac{8}{3} = 2.666\ldots$$

Because the order of the decimal forms is 2.0, 2.5, 2.666 . . ., 2.78, the order of the numbers as given is $2, \frac{5}{2}, \frac{8}{3}, 2.78$. Placing the decimal form numbers on the number line, or at least thinking about where they are on the number line, can help put the task into focus.

TIP The number line can also be useful for addition and subtraction problems that involve negative numbers. Left is the negative direction, and right is the positive direction.

Finding orders of magnitude

The *magnitude* of a number is its *absolute value*, meaning its positive distance from 0. A question on the Praxis Core exam can involve the order of the magnitudes of numbers. To find the answer to this type of question, just drop all negative signs that may be involved and put the remaining numbers in order.

EXAMPLE Determine which answer choice has the following numbers in order of magnitude from least to greatest: $9, -2, 5.7, -\frac{15}{2}$.

(A) $-\frac{15}{2}, -2, 5.7, 9$

(B) $9, 5.7, -2, -\frac{15}{2}$

(C) $9, -\frac{15}{2}, 5.7, -2$

(D) $-2, 5.7, -\frac{15}{2}, 9$

(E) $-\frac{15}{2}, 9, 5.7, -2$

The correct answer is Choice (D). Without the negative signs taken into account, the order of the numbers from least to greatest is $-2, 5.7, -\frac{15}{2}, 9$, so that's the order of magnitude from least to greatest. Choice (A) is the order of the numbers from least to greatest without magnitude taken into account, Choice (B) is the actual order of the numbers from greatest to least, and Choice (C) is the order of magnitude of the numbers from greatest to least. Choice (E) has no excuses for itself.

Finding numbers in sequences

A *sequence* is a list of numbers in a certain type of order. Have you ever heard a person talk about doing something in sequence? It means doing the parts of the task in order. Sequences are important because many types of orders of numbers exist. For example, a sequence can be a list of prime numbers in which order increases. One of the most common classifications is the *arithmetic sequence*, in which the same quantity is added to each number to get the next. In the following arithmetic sequence, 4 is added to each number to determine the next number.

3, 7, 11, 15, 19, 23, 27 . . .

Another is the *geometric sequence*, for which each number is multiplied by the same quantity to get the next.

2, 6, 18, 54, 162, 486 . . .

On the Praxis Core exam, you may be asked to determine a number that should appear in a certain position in a sequence. To make the determination, first decide what's done to each number in order to create the value of the one that follows. Then, make the calculation for each number up to the position in question.

EXAMPLE

What is the ninth term of the following sequence? 3, 6, 12, 24, 48 . . .

(A) 96

(B) 2,304

(C) 768

(D) 72

(E) 1536

The correct answer is Choice (C). The sequence is geometric, so each term must be multiplied by 2 to result in the next. The fifth term is 48, so it must be multiplied by 2·2·2·2 for the multiplication to result in the ninth term of the sequence, which is 768. Choice (A) is the sixth term, Choice (B) is the square of 48, and Choice (D) is the sum of 48 and 24. Choice (E) is the tenth term of the sequence.

Following Orders: The Order of Operations

After you have the basic mathematical principles down (which you can review in the sections "Working with Integers: Whole Numbers and Their Opposites" and "Computing with Fractions and Mixed Numbers," earlier in this chapter), you're ready to tackle the order of operations.

When multiple computations are involved in finding a value represented by multiple numbers and operations signs, the rules concerning the order in which the operations are to be worked must be applied. Doing them in the wrong order can cause answers to be false, which isn't the ideal situation. To avoid such examination misfortune, you must follow the *order of operations*, or the correct procedure for working multiple computations.

Think about how you would determine the value of the following expression:

$$3 + 2^3 + 5(4 - 7)$$

What would you do? Hold that thought. We have an idea.

Remembering GEMDAS

The acronym GEMDAS is formed by the initials of the order of operations, in order:

>> **G:** *Grouping* symbols (such as parentheses, brackets, and fraction bars)

>> **E:** *Exponents*

>> **MD:** *Multiplication* and *Division* in order from left to right

>> **AS:** *Addition* and *Subtraction* in order from left to right

Notice that multiplication and division are represented together, as are addition and subtraction. That indicates that you must do those operations in the order in which they appear. For example, you don't want to add all the way from left to right, and then go back and do all the subtraction from left to right.

Okay, we believe an unresolved issue is still waiting for an answer. How do you find the value of $3+2^3+5(4-7)$? Well, the first step is to find the value within the grouping symbols, the parentheses. Then the exponent needs to be used. Next comes the indicated multiplication, and then the addition.

$$\begin{aligned} 3+2^3+5(4-7) &= 3+2^3+5(-3) \\ &= 3+8+5(-3) \\ &= 3+8-15 \\ &= 11-15 \\ &= -4 \end{aligned}$$

Using the order of operations within itself

What should you do if the issue of operations order arises within a step of the order of operations? Don't worry. The order of operations is a principle of its word. It applies even within steps of itself. If multiple operations are needed within parentheses, for example, apply the order of operations inside the parentheses.

EXAMPLE

$$\left[(8-3)^2+2\cdot 5\right]-7+4\cdot 6 =$$

(A) −52

(B) 22

(C) 52

(D) 152

(E) 192

The correct answer is Choice (C). The value within the parentheses must be determined first, and then it must be squared because exponents come next in the order of operations. The product of 2 and 5 should be added to the value. At this point, the value within the brackets can be determined. Then, you need to find the product of 4 and 6 and add it to the result of subtracting 7 from the value within the brackets. Here's how the math looks when you work it out:

$$\begin{aligned} \left[(8-3)^2+2\cdot 5\right]-7+4\cdot 6 &= \left[5^2+2\cdot 5\right]-7+4\cdot 6 \\ &= [25+2\cdot 5]-7+4\cdot 6 \\ &= [25+10]-7+4\cdot 6 \\ &= 35-7+4\cdot 6 \\ &= 35-7+24 \\ &= 28+24 \\ &= 52 \end{aligned}$$

Reasoning with Quantities

The Praxis Core exam tends to involve questions about quantities and how they're related. Various categories of quantities exist, and two major systems are used for measuring them.

Using the two major systems of measurement

The two mainstream systems of measurement in the United States are the English system and the metric system. Table 4-2 shows the basic units of measurement for each system.

TABLE 4-2 Systems of Measurement

Form of Measurement	English System	Metric System
Distance	Inch, foot, yard, mile	Meter
Volume	Cup, pint, quart, gallon	Liter
Weight	Ounce, pound, ton	Gram

The metric system has fewer units because each category of measurement uses the same base unit. However, you can add prefixes to the units that give you more specific information about the sizes of the measurements. For example, 1,000 grams is the same as 1 kilogram. All the prefix meanings in the metric system are multiples of 10 or multiples of $\frac{1}{10}$. Check them out in Table 4-3.

TABLE 4-3 Metric System Prefixes

Metric Prefix	Meaning
Milli–	$\frac{1}{1,000}$
Centi–	$\frac{1}{100}$
Deci–	$\frac{1}{10}$
Main unit (meter, liter, gram)	1
Deca–	10
Hecto–	100
Kilo–	1,000

The English system doesn't have consistent base units for categories of measurement. The English units for each type of measurement are based on each other, but not in ways that mere prefixes can reflect the changes that you need to make between varying levels. Here's how the different units of measurement relate within each form:

>> **Distance:** 12 inches = 1 foot, 3 feet = 1 yard, and 5,280 feet = 1 mile

>> **Volume:** 2 cups = 1 pint, 2 pints = 1 quart, and 4 quarts = 1 gallon

>> **Weight:** 16 ounces = 1 pound, and 1 ton = 2,000 pounds

There's also the issue of how English measurements relate to metric units. These are some key comparisons:

>> 1 meter ≈ 1.0936 yards

>> 1 kilogram ≈ 2.20462 pounds (on Earth)

>> 1 liter ≈ 0.264172 gallon

>> 1 inch = 2.54 cm

Converting units of measurement

Problems on the Praxis Core exam may involve converting one unit of measurement to another. For example, you may need to determine that 5 feet is the same as 60 inches or figure out how many deciliters are in 3 hectoliters.

To make such conversions, use the more basic unit to divide if the answer involves the bigger unit and multiply if the answer involves the smaller unit. For example, say you want to know how many inches of twine are in 4 yards. You have to convert yards to feet to inches:

1. **Convert yards to feet.**

4 yards = 4(3 feet) = 12 feet

2. **Convert feet to inches.**

(12)(12 inches) = 144 inches

Therefore, 4 yards is equal to 144 inches.

To convert from greater to lesser units, multiply instead of divide. The same applies to metric units, but the conversions are easier because you can simply multiply by multiples of 10 or $\frac{1}{10}$.

The more involved conversions require what's called *dimensional analysis*, which is a strategy that involves multiplying by fractions that are equal to 1 but have different units in the numerator and denominator of each. Doing so allows units to be cancelled so that the two desired units will be the only ones remaining. It's important then to know the units and make sure they align first before performing any calculations.

For example, say that Jan is preparing punch for the party. She expects that each guest will drink 3 cups. How many gallons does she need to prepare for the expected 15 guests?

First, figure the number of cups; 15 guests would need 15×3 cups of drink.

$$15 \times 3 = 45 \text{ cups}$$

Next, use the conversions for cups to gallons. You have to go from cups to pints to quarts to gallons — unless you already know the relationship between cups and gallons.

$$45 \text{ cups} \times \frac{1 \text{ pint}}{2 \text{ cups}} \times \frac{1 \text{ quart}}{2 \text{ pints}} \times \frac{1 \text{ gallon}}{4 \text{ quarts}} = \frac{45 \times 1 \times 1 \times 1}{2 \times 2 \times 4} \text{ gallons} = \frac{45}{16} \text{ gallons} = 2.8125 \text{ gallons}$$

So 2.8125 gallons would be needed.

In order to ensure the appropriate numbers are calculated, the conversions have to be set so that units cancel themselves out and you end up with the one unit that you want in the numerator. In this instance, cups, pints, and quarts all canceled out. Gallons stood alone.

EXAMPLE

How many kilograms are in 7 centigrams?

(A) 0.00007

(B) 7,000

(C) 700

(D) 70

(E) 7

The answer is Choice (A). Moving from centigrams to kilograms, the number gets smaller, so multiply 7 by $\frac{1}{10}$ for every space the prefixes are apart on Table 4-3. Choice (B) falsely involves the result of multiplying 7 by 10^3 instead of by $\frac{1}{10}$ as a factor five times. Choices (C) and (D) involve too few factors and multiplying in the wrong direction. Choice (E) falsely implies that a kilogram is the same as a centigram.

Basic word problems

Conversions with units can be involved in answering word problems, but often they also require performing other operations. You need to memorize the meanings of the units and prefixes for the Praxis Core exam because they won't be provided. You also need to understand how words used in each system for each type of measurement are connected to each other.

If a cook pours 5 quarts of water out of a full 3-gallon container, and then another cook takes his place and adds 2 pints of water, how many cups of water are in the container?

(A) 8

(B) 16

(C) 72

(D) 32

(E) 64

The correct answer is Choice (D). The best way to determine the answer is to convert all the measurements to numbers of cups, and then calculate the number of cups remaining. You could also convert the measures to numbers of pints and convert to cups on the last step. Five quarts is equal to 5(4) cups; 3 gallons is the same as 3(16) cups; and 2 pints is a measure equal to 2(2) cups. $48 - 20 + 4 = 32$, so the answer is 32. Choice (A) is the number of quarts that result, and Choice (B) is the equivalent measure in pints. Choice (C) is the number of cups that would result if all of the mentioned quantities were added, and Choice (E) could be the correct answer if there were 4 cups in a pint instead of 2.

Working with unit rates

Some measurements involve more than one unit of measure. A measurement can entail a number of one unit per another unit. Examples of that include numbers of miles per hour, gallons per mile, and calories per gram. Such ratios are known as *unit rates*. Numbers of units of measurement can be converted to other numbers of other units of measurement, and through the same processes, numbers of units per other units can be converted.

Michael ran a 40-yard race during football practice. The time Michael took to run the full distance was 4.2 seconds. Which of the following is closest to Michael's average speed in miles per hour?

(A) 10.57 miles per hour

(B) 15.01 miles per hour

(C) 17.33 miles per hour

(D) 19.48 miles per hour

(E) 28.81 miles per hour

The correct answer is Choice (D). To answer the question, you can convert yards to miles and seconds to hours, and then divide. Because there are 5,280 feet in a mile and 3 feet in a yard, the number of yards in a mile is $\frac{1}{3}$ of 5,280, which is 1,760. That means a yard is $\frac{1}{1,760}$ mile. The number of seconds in a minute is 60, and the number of minutes in an hour is 60, so the number of seconds in an hour is $60 \cdot 60$, or 3,600.

$$40 \text{ yards} = 40\left(\frac{1}{1,760} \text{ mile}\right)$$

$$= \frac{40}{1,760} \text{ mile}$$

$$= 0.0227\ldots \text{ mile}$$

$$4.2 \text{ seconds} = 4.2\left(\frac{1}{3,600} \text{ hour}\right)$$

$$= \frac{4.2}{3,600} \text{ hour}$$

$$= 0.00116 \text{ hour}$$

With those conversions, you can write Michael's time in miles per hour.

$$\frac{0.0227 \text{ miles}}{0.00116 \text{ hours}} = 19.48051948\ldots \text{ miles/hour}$$

$$\approx 19.48 \text{ miles/hour}$$

Rounded to the nearest hundredth, Michael's average speed for the 40-yard race was 19.48 miles per hour.

There's another method you can use to answer the problem, and many people find the method easier than the preceding one. Like with basic unit conversions, you can multiply unit rates by unit rates that are equal to 1 in order to cancel units and end up with the desired ratio units. Each ratio that's equal to 1 has a numerator measure that's equal to the denominator measure, but the numerator and denominator have different units.

$$\frac{40 \text{ yards}}{4.2 \text{ seconds}} \times \frac{3 \text{ feet}}{1 \text{ yard}} \times \frac{1 \text{ mile}}{5,280 \text{ feet}} \times \frac{60 \text{ seconds}}{1 \text{ minute}} \times \frac{60 \text{ minutes}}{1 \text{ hour}}$$

$$= \frac{432,000 \text{ miles}}{22,176 \text{ hours}}$$

$$= 19.48051948\ldots \text{ miles/hour}$$

$$\approx 19.48 \text{ miles per hour}$$

Practice Questions about Number and Quantity

These practice questions are similar to the questions about number and quantity that you'll encounter on the Praxis.

1. In the most recent basketball season, Marty scored 168% of the number of points his coach predicted he would score. Which of the following is that percentage expressed as a mixed number in simplest form?

   (A) $1\frac{17}{25}$

   (B) $1\frac{68}{100}$

   (C) $\frac{168}{100}$

   (D) $100\frac{68}{100}$

   (E) $168\frac{1}{100}$

2. $\left[(9-4)^3 - 25 \cdot 2\right] - \left[7 + 4(2-3)\right] =$

   (A) -3
   (B) 64
   (C) 72
   (D) 103
   (E) 172

3. Which of the following numbers is the lowest?

   (A) $3\frac{1}{3}$
   (B) 3.25
   (C) $3\frac{1}{2}$
   (D) $\frac{23}{7}$
   (E) 3.271

4. The following table represents the percentages regarding the favorite movie categories of students at a college attended by 1,000 students. How many students have a favorite movie category that is either drama, comedy, or horror?

Movie Category	Percent of Students
Comedy	26%
Musical	11%
Drama	22%
Documentary	6%
Horror	19%
Science Fiction	12%
Other	4%

   (A) 26
   (B) 67
   (C) 220
   (D) 670
   (E) 6,700

5. Each of the following numbers is a common factor of 150 and 300 EXCEPT

   (A) 5
   (B) 25
   (C) 50
   (D) 75
   (E) 300

Answers and Explanations

Use this answer key to score the practice number and quantity questions in the preceding section.

1. **A.** $1\frac{17}{25}$. To convert 168% to a mixed number, you can first write it as an improper fraction. Because *percent* means "hundredths," you can write 168% as $\frac{168}{100}$. Simplify the fraction now to make it easier to work with and also because simplification will be necessary at some point in the process of working the problem.

$$\frac{168}{100} \div \frac{2}{2} = \frac{84}{50}$$

$$\frac{84}{50} \div \frac{2}{2} = \frac{42}{25}$$

Next, convert $\frac{42}{25}$ to a mixed number by dividing the numerator by the denominator.

$$42 \div 25 = 1 \text{ with a remainder of } 17$$

$$= 1\frac{17}{25}$$

2. **C. 72.** Follow the order of operations to solve this correctly (remember GEMDAS).

$$\left[(9-4)^3 - 25 \cdot 2\right] - \left[7 + 4(2-3)\right] = \left[5^3 - 25 \cdot 2\right] - \left[7 + 4(2-3)\right]$$
$$= \left[125 - 50\right] - \left[7 + 4(2-3)\right]$$
$$= 75 - \left[7 + 4(-1)\right]$$
$$= 75 - \left[7 + (-4)\right]$$
$$= 75 - 3$$
$$= 72$$

All other answer choices can be reached through following an incorrect order of operations.

3. **B. 3.25.** The best way to determine the answer is to write all the numbers in the same type of form. For example, you can write all the numbers as decimal numbers: $3.3\overline{3}$, 3.25, 3.50, 3.2857..., and 3.271, respectively. The orders of such numbers can be clearer if you give each number the same number of digits after the decimal point. Remember that after the last non-zero digit after a decimal point, you can put as many zeros as you want to. It doesn't change the value of the number. Then, you can put them in order and see that 3.25 is the lowest number, making Choice (B) correct.

4. **D. 670.** The sum of the drama, comedy, and horror percentages is 67 percent, and 67 percent of 1,000 is 670. To get 67 percent of 1,000, you can write 67 percent in decimal form by dropping the percent sign and moving the decimal two places to the left. That gives you 0.67, which you can multiply by 1,000 to get 670. Choice (A) is merely the numerical part of the term 26 percent, the percent of students whose favorite genre is comedy. Choice (B) is 6.7 percent of 1,000, Choice (C) is the number of students whose favorite type of movie is drama, and Choice (E) is 670 percent of 1,000.

5. **E. 300.** If you find the prime factorizations of 150 and 300 and use those prime factors to find all the other factors, you can see that Choices (A), (B), (C), and (D) are common factors of 150 and 300. However, 300 is a factor of 300 but not 150, though it is a multiple of 150. A factor of a whole number can't be greater than that whole number. Any positive number divided by a number greater than itself equals a fraction less than 1, and those don't qualify as factors of whole numbers.

$$\frac{150}{300} = \frac{1}{2}$$

Therefore, 300 isn't a factor of 150.

IN THIS CHAPTER

» **Coming to terms with variables**

» **Solving equations and inequalities**

» **Facing the facts of factoring**

» **Making quick work of word problems**

» **Looking at patterns and conditional statements**

Chapter **5**

Introducing Letters: Algebra

Now's the time to revisit your days as an algebra student. When you start treating letters like numbers, you're entering algebra territory. This chapter can help you safely navigate that territory. The Praxis Core exam tests basic algebra knowledge — generally, the material that's covered in pre-algebra and perhaps some Algebra I courses, depending on where you went to school and when. Algebra questions make up 20 percent of the math section of the Praxis Core. Also, many of the geometry questions on the test involve algebra, so this chapter goes a long way toward preparing you for the entire math test of the Praxis exam.

Variables: When Letters Represent Numbers

You're very familiar with letters, and algebra just involves using letters in some different ways. Algebra is the area of math that focuses on the basics of working with *variables*, which are letters that represent numbers. That's all it is. A large portion of algebra involves determining the numbers represented by variables, which requires knowledge of some basic rules.

The most common letter used to represent numbers is x. Other letters that are commonly used are y, n, a, and b. Most of the letters in our alphabet, and many of the letters in the Greek alphabet, are used as variables at times. (But thankfully, you don't have to know Greek to take the Praxis Core exam.)

Here's an example of an equation that uses a variable:

$x + 3 = 7$

This equation means that when 3 is added to some number (x), the result is 7. In this case, the number that the variable x represents is 4. When 3 is added to 4, the result is 7, so x equals 4. In the section "Solving for x and other variables," later in this chapter, you can review how to determine what a given variable represents. In the following sections, we cover the basics of variables.

Laying out the terms: Variable terms and expressions

What makes algebra interesting is when variables and numbers meet. When a number comes right before a variable, it means that the number is multiplied by the variable. For example, $3y$ means "3 times y." A number can also be multiplied by more than one variable at a time. $10xyz$ means "10 times x times y times z." A number that precedes a variable or variables to indicate that it's multiplied by them is a *coefficient*. In $10xyz$, 10 is the coefficient. If no coefficient is given, the coefficient is understood to be 1. In other words, x is the same as $1x$, and xyz is the same as $1xyz$.

A variable or group of variables next to a coefficient, or with an understood coefficient of 1, is called a *term*. A number followed by no variables is also a term. In a term, variables can have exponents, which indicate how many times a variable is multiplied by itself in the term (see Chapter 4 for a review of exponents). All of the following are examples of terms:

x

$-17n^2$

5

$156abc$

xy

A single term or a group of terms separated by + or − forms an *expression*. There's no maximum number of terms an expression can have, but the minimum number is one. Yes, a term is an expression, but not all expressions are terms. $48x^3y^5$ is a term, so it's an expression. $48x^3y^5 + 15x^2y^2 - xy + 87x - 9$ has five terms, but it's one expression.

Let's get together: Combining like terms

After you come to terms with terms (see the preceding section), it's time to see how to make them join forces and become one term (when they can). *Like terms* are terms that have either exactly the same variable, variables that have only one exponent for each variable, or no variables at all. In other words, the variable parts of like terms are exactly the same. They're identical in appearance.

If two terms are like terms and both have x, y, and z, every x has the same exponent, every y has the same exponent, and every z has the same exponent. Numbers without variables, such as 3 and 5, are also like terms. $17x$ and $12x$ are like terms, and so are $15a^3b^{15}c^8$ and $4a^3b^{15}c^8$.

Like terms can be combined. In other words, one can be added to or subtracted from the other to form one term. To combine like terms, combine their coefficients to get a new coefficient and follow that with the common variables and their exponents.

$$17x + 12x = (17 + 12)x = 29x$$
$$15a^3b^{15}c^8 - 4a^3b^{15}c^8 = (15 - 4)a^3b^{15}c^8 = 11a^3b^{15}c^8$$
$$5 + 7 = 12$$

If you have 2 apples and you add 3 apples, you have 5 apples. The same principle works with variables. If you have 2 of x and add 3 of x, you have 5 of x.

$$2 \text{ apples} + 3 \text{ apples} = 5 \text{ apples}$$
$$2x + 3x = 5x$$

Multiplying and dividing terms and expressions

Just like you can add and subtract terms and expressions (see the preceding section), you can multiply and divide them. Remember that variables represent numbers, which means operations that include variables involve the same principles that apply to operations that don't include variables. So, when in doubt, just think about how numbers work.

Multiplying expressions

In multiplying algebraic expressions, the number of times a number or variable is a factor is part of what determines the product. To multiply different variables, simply put them next to each other.

$$x \cdot y = xy$$
$$a \cdot b = ab$$

To multiply a number times a variable or variables, put them all next to each other.

$$3 \cdot a \cdot b = 3ab$$

The next question is what you should do when the same variable is a factor more than once. Do you write the variable next to itself? Nope. The product is written with an exponent next to the variable. The exponent says how many times the variable is multiplied by itself. The letters have to remain the same after multiplication, but their exponents don't. The final answer should have exponents representing how many times a variable is a factor.

$$(x)(x)(x) = x^3$$
$$j \cdot j = j^2$$
$$p \cdot p \cdot p \cdot p = p^4$$

REMEMBER

Showing 1 as an exponent isn't necessary. A variable without an exponent shown is understood to have an exponent of 1.

Now, put these principles together in your mind, and you're ready to multiply algebraic terms that have coefficients.

$$(4ab)(2ab) = 4 \cdot 2 \cdot a \cdot a \cdot b \cdot b$$
$$= 8a^2b^2$$

What do you do when the terms you're multiplying have variables with exponents other than 1? For each variable, you just add its exponents.

$$(5p^2q^4r^3)(3p^3q^2r^2) = (5 \cdot 3)p^2p^3q^4q^2r^3r^2$$
$$= 15p^{2+3}q^{4+2}r^{3+2}$$
$$= 15p^5q^6r^5$$

To multiply a term by an expression that involves addition or subtraction, you can use the *distributive property*, which entails multiplying a term by each term that's added or subtracted in the expression, and then combining the resulting products. The multiplication is distributed to each term of the expression that has addition or subtraction.

$$5(x+3) = 5(x) + 5(3)$$
$$= 5x + 15$$

With these skills, you can multiply any algebraic terms. On the Praxis Core, you may be asked to multiply two-term expressions. For example, you may need to multiply $(x+2)(x+3)$. You can use the distributive property to multiply the expressions.

$$(x+2)(x+3) = (x+2)(x) + (x+2)(3)$$
$$= (x)(x+2) + (3)(x+2)$$
$$= x(x+2) + 3(x+2)$$
$$= (x^2 + 2x) + (3x + 6)$$
$$= x^2 + 2x + 3x + 6$$
$$= x^2 + 5x + 6$$

To find the product of two two-term expressions, the best method to use is FOIL, which is the best-known algebra acronym. FOIL is a specifically ordered application of the distributive property. It stands for "first, outer, inner, last." The words apply to the terms in the problem. In this case, the first terms in each expression are x and x, the outer terms are x and 3, the inner terms are 2 and x, and the last terms in each expression are 2 and 3. To use FOIL, multiply the first, outer, inner, and last terms, and then add their products together (according to the rules for combining terms) in the same order.

$$(x+2)(x+3) = (x \cdot x) + (x \cdot 3) + (2 \cdot x) + (2 \cdot 3)$$
$$= x^2 + 3x + 2x + 6$$
$$= x^2 + 5x + 6$$

REMEMBER

Subtracting a number is the same as adding its opposite. A minus sign in a FOIL problem must be treated as a negative sign.

EXAMPLE

Find the following product: $(3j+4)(2j-5)$

(A) $5j^2 - 7j - 20$

(B) $6j^2 - 7j - 20$

(C) $6j^2 + 7j + 20$

(D) $13j^3 - 1$

(E) $5j^2 - 1$

The correct answer is Choice (B). By using FOIL, you can determine that the product of the two expressions is $(3j)(2j) + (3j)(-5) + (4)(2j) + (4)(-5)$, which is $6j^2 - 15j + 8j - 20$. By combining those terms, you get $6j^2 - 7j - 20$.

You can also find values when entire terms are given exponents. In such cases, the exponent for the term applies to every factor presented in the term.

$$(xyz)^3 = xyz \cdot xyz \cdot xyz$$
$$= x \cdot y \cdot z \cdot x \cdot y \cdot z \cdot x \cdot y \cdot z$$
$$= x \cdot x \cdot x \cdot y \cdot y \cdot y \cdot z \cdot z \cdot z$$
$$= x^3 y^3 z^3$$

If a fraction has an exponent, the exponent applies to the numerator and the denominator. That's because you're multiplying the fraction by itself the exponent number of times, and multiplying fractions involves putting the product of the numerators over the product of the denominators.

$$\left(\frac{g}{h}\right)^5 = \frac{g}{h} \times \frac{g}{h} \times \frac{g}{h} \times \frac{g}{h} \times \frac{g}{h}$$

$$= \frac{g \times g \times g \times g \times g}{h \times h \times h \times h \times h}$$

$$= \frac{g^5}{h^5}$$

To raise a power to a power, just multiply the exponents. An exponent shows how many times a factor is a factor. When a factor with an exponent is raised to a power, simply multiply those numbers to get the correct exponent.

$$(m^2)^4 = m^{2\cdot4}$$

$$= m^8$$

Here's the reason:

$$\left(m^2\right)^4 = m^2 \cdot m^2 \cdot m^2 \cdot m^2$$

$$= m^{2+2+2+2}$$

$$= m^{2\cdot4}$$

$$= m^8$$

Dividing expressions

Dividing algebraic terms isn't as common as multiplying them, but it does happen, so you should know how to perform this operation.

REMEMBER

In a fraction, the numerator is divided by the denominator.

$$\frac{8x^3y^4z^2}{2x^2y^2z^2} = \frac{8 \cdot x \cdot x \cdot x \cdot y \cdot y \cdot y \cdot y \cdot z \cdot z}{2 \cdot x \cdot x \cdot y \cdot y \cdot z \cdot z}$$

Recall that factors that appear in a term that's a numerator and also appear in a term that's the denominator of the same fraction can be cancelled once in both the numerator and the denominator for every appearance in both. In other words, anything that's a factor of a fraction's numerator and denominator can be cancelled from both, but it can be cancelled only one time for each instance.

$$\frac{8x^3y^4z^2}{2x^2y^2z^2} = \frac{8 \cdot \cancel{x} \cdot \cancel{x} \cdot x \cdot \cancel{y} \cdot \cancel{y} \cdot y \cdot y \cdot \cancel{z} \cdot \cancel{z}}{2 \cdot \cancel{x} \cdot \cancel{x} \cdot \cancel{y} \cdot \cancel{y} \cdot \cancel{z} \cdot \cancel{z}}$$

What's left in the preceding ratio? $\frac{8}{2} = 4$, so 4 is left in the numerator. With three x's on top and two on the bottom, one is left on top because $3 - 2 = 1$. By the same reasoning, two y's are left in the numerator. The z's cancel each other out. Therefore, you're left with $4xy^2$.

Because of this principle, you can easily find the difference of a variable's numerator and denominator exponents. Just subtract the smaller exponent from the bigger exponent and make the difference the variable's resulting exponent. Put the variable with that exponent in the place where the bigger exponent was before you subtracted. If a variable in a problem has the same exponent in the numerator and denominator, you can cancel the variable completely. The result of exponent subtraction would be the variable with an exponent of 0, and any value (other than 0) with an exponent of 0 equals 1.

$$\frac{12a^3b^4c^7d^5}{9a^5b^2c^2d^5} = \frac{4b^{4-2}c^{7-2}}{3a^{5-3}}$$

$$= \frac{4b^2c^5}{3a^2}$$

Similarly, when you divide one product of multi-term expressions by another, you can cancel expressions that are factors of both the dividend and the divisor.

$$\frac{(y+2)(y-3)}{(y-1)(y+2)} = \frac{\cancel{(y+2)}(y-3)}{(y-1)\cancel{(y+2)}}$$

Now you're left with one expression on top and one on the bottom. The quotient is $\frac{y-3}{y-1}$.

On the Praxis Core exam, you may be asked to divide with expressions that have three or more terms. The section "Factoring in Algebra," later in this chapter, shows you how to work such problems.

Combining fractions that have variables

Like with addition and subtraction of fractions that don't contain variables, combining fractions that have variables is easiest when the fractions have common denominators. If an original problem doesn't present common denominators, you need to create them. The method for doing so is the same with variables as it is without them. (We cover this rule without variables in Chapter 4.) Multiply a fraction's denominator by whatever's necessary to get a common denominator, and then multiply the numerator by the same thing. When all fractions have the same denominator, combine the numerators and put the result over the common denominator.

$$\frac{3}{m} + \frac{7}{m^2} - \frac{11}{2m} = \frac{3\,(2m)}{m\,(2m)} + \frac{7\,(2)}{m^2\,(2)} - \frac{11\,(m)}{2m\,(m)}$$

$$= \frac{6m}{2m^2} + \frac{14}{2m^2} - \frac{11m}{2m^2}$$

$$= \frac{-5m+14}{2m^2}$$

Multiplying a fraction's numerator and denominator by the same value doesn't change the value of the fraction because doing so is the same as multiplying by 1.

You can always get a common denominator by multiplying all of the original denominators, but if you don't use the least common multiple of the denominators when combining fractions, you'll need to simplify the first fraction that results from combining the fractions in the problem. Try to make the common denominator as simple as possible to save yourself some work (and possible errors).

When variable values are given

The values of expressions can be determined when the values of the variables in them are known. To find the value of an expression is to *evaluate* the expression. When you evaluate an expression, you replace each variable with its given value. Then, you can solve for the value of the expression. Follow these steps:

1. **Replace each variable with its given value.**

2. **Follow the order of operations.**

   Recall GEMDAS from Chapter 4.

3. **Simplify the resulting expression.**

   You simplify by following the order of operations as many times as necessary.

4. **Mark the final number as your answer.**

EXAMPLE

Evaluate the following expression for $p = 2$, $q = 5$, and $r = 1$.

$5p - q + 2r$

(A) -1

(B) 2

(C) 7

(D) -16

(E) 17

The correct answer is Choice (C). To evaluate the expression, simply replace each variable with its value.

$$5p - q + 2r = 5(2) - 5 + 2(1)$$
$$= 10 - 5 + 2$$
$$= 5 + 2$$
$$= 7$$

REMEMBER

A number immediately next to a variable indicates that the number is multiplied by the variable.

Working with Equations

An *equation* is a mathematical statement in which one expression is set equal to another. For example, $8n + 1 = 17$ is an equation. Very commonly in algebra, the value of a variable in an equation can be determined when the value is not given. To determine the value of a variable in an equation is to *solve* the equation.

The two sides of an equation have the same value. If $8n + 1 = 17$, then $8n + 1$ has the same value as 17. The value of n can be determined from the equation.

Solving for *x* and other variables

Solving equations is an enormous part of algebra. Understanding how to do it puts you in an excellent position for conquering Praxis Core algebra completely.

To solve an equation, you need to get the variable by itself on one side of the equal sign ($=$). If you're solving for x, the goal is to work with the equation until you have $x =$ something, such as $x = 4$ or $x = -12$. Notice that in both cases, x is by itself on one side of the equal sign and a value is on the other side. After you reach that point correctly, you have solved the equation. The point of solving an equation is to determine what the variable equals.

To get a variable by itself on one side of the equal sign, you need to perform whatever operations are necessary. Then, if necessary, combine like terms so that the variable is in only one term in the equation. The next step is to undo everything that's being done to the variable by doing the opposite. Addition and subtraction are opposite operations, and multiplication and division are opposite operations. You can use opposite operations to undo each other.

Because the two sides of an equation are equal, anything done to one side of the equation must be done to the other side so that the two sides will remain equal. If you have a set of weights with 50 pounds on one side and 50 pounds on the other side, and you want to add a certain amount of weight to one side, you must add the same amount of weight to the other side to keep the weights of the two sides equal. The values on either side of an equation work the same way. If you add 10 to one side of an equation but not the other, the two sides will no longer be equal. An equation is wrong if its sides aren't equal.

Follow these steps to get a variable by itself so that you can determine its value (also known as solving for x):

1. **Isolate the variable.**

   Get all the x's on one side of the equal sign and the numbers without variables on the other side.

2. **Combine like terms.**

   Add or subtract all the x's on one side; add or subtract whatever is on the other side of the equal sign.

3. **Divide both sides of the equation by whatever number (coefficient) is in front of the x (or other variable).**

You can see how these steps work by solving for y in this equation: $3y - 12 = y + 6$.

1. **Isolate the variable.**

   Move the y to the left side of the equation by subtracting y from both sides. Move the 12 to the right side by adding it to both sides of the equation. This gives you $3y - y = 6 + 12$.

2. **Combine like terms.**

   Do the operations to get $2y = 18$.

3. **Divide both sides of the equation by whatever number (coefficient) is in front of the y.**

   When you divide 18 by 2, you get 9. Therefore, $y = 9$. Problem solved!

Undoing addition and subtraction

Consider the equation $y + 4 = 9$. The variable y is not by itself on one side of the equal sign because 4 is being added to y. Getting rid of the addition of 4 will cause y to be by itself on one side of the equation. By subtracting 4, the addition of 4 will be undone. If you add 4 to a number and then subtract 4 from the result, you're back at the original number. If you have 5 sandwiches and someone gives you 4 sandwiches, and then you give away those 4 sandwiches, you'll be back to having 5 sandwiches. Algebra works the same way.

$y + 4 = 9$	Original equation
$y + 4 - 4 = 9 - 4$	Subtract 4 from both sides to get y by itself on one side.
$y = 5$	Determine the value of each side.

The equation has been solved. The value of y is 5 because $y = 5$. If you replace y with 5 in the original equation, you'll see that the value of y is 5 because $5 + 4 = 9$. All solutions to equations can be checked that way.

REMEMBER

Keep in mind that anything done to one side of an equation must also be done to the other side.

Just like subtraction can be used to undo addition, addition can be used to undo subtraction.

$$j - 8 = 12$$
$$j - 8 + 8 = 12 + 8$$
$$j = 20$$

In the solution, j is by itself on one side of the equal sign, so the value of j is on the other side of the equal sign. The value of j is 20, so 20 is the solution to the equation. It's true that $20 - 8 = 12$, so j is 20.

Undoing multiplication and division

Like addition and subtraction (see the preceding section), multiplication and division are opposite operations. When a variable is multiplied by a number, the multiplication can be undone if the term is divided by the same number. (Recall that a fraction represents a numerator divided by a denominator.) The easiest way to divide a term by a number is to create a denominator with that number. However, you must create that denominator on both sides.

$$5m = 30$$
$$\frac{5m}{5} = \frac{30}{5}$$
$$m = 6$$

Now m is by itself on one side of the equation. The solution is 6 because that's what m equals.

Because multiplication and division are opposite operations, multiplication can undo division. Think about how to solve the following equation:

$$\frac{p}{4} = 10$$

The variable, p, is not by itself on one side of the equal sign because it's being divided by 4. Because you don't have any addition or subtraction to worry about, you can go ahead and multiply by 4 to undo the division by 4. Multiplying by 4 gets p by itself on one side of the equal sign. The equation is then solved because you're left with the statement of what p equals.

$$\frac{p}{4}(4) = 10(4)$$
$$p = 40$$

The solution is 40 because $p = 40$.

WARNING

Whatever you do to a side must be done to the entire side, not just some small part of it. A common mistake is to do something like multiply a term on one side by a number and then multiply just one term among several on the other side by the same number. So not only do you have to do the same thing to each side, but you must do that operation to the complete value of each side to make both sides equal.

Multistep equations

In many algebraic equations, you have to undo more than one operation. The best way to solve such equations is to use whatever addition or subtraction is necessary first, and then use multiplication or division.

The following equation requires undoing both multiplication and subtraction. Undo the subtraction first so that you can then divide both entire sides by the same number.

$$5x - 3 = 12$$
$$5x - 3 + 3 = 12 + 3$$
$$5x = 15$$
$$\frac{5x}{5} = \frac{15}{5}$$
$$x = 3$$

The solution is 3 because 3 is what x equals.

Proportions

A *ratio* is a comparison of two or more quantities. If there are 2 boys for every 3 girls in a classroom, the ratio of boys to girls is 2 to 3, which can also be written as 2:3 or $\frac{2}{3}$. Fractions are ratios, and in math, ratios are usually written as fractions.

A *proportion* is an equation in which one ratio (usually in the form of a fraction) is set equal to another. This is an example of a proportion:

$$\frac{9}{3} = \frac{12}{4}$$

On the Praxis Core exam, you may need to solve one or more proportions in which one number in a numerator or denominator is unknown (represented by a variable). You can save a lot of time in finding the unknown if you cross multiply. To cross multiply, you multiply the numerator of the left fraction by the denominator of the right fraction, and then you do the same with the right numerator and left denominator. These products are set equal to each other. Finally, divide both sides by the coefficient to get the variable by itself and solve the equation.

$$\frac{20}{x} = \frac{15}{3}$$
$$20(3) = 15(x)$$
$$60 = 15x$$
$$\frac{60}{15} = \frac{15x}{15}$$
$$4 = x$$
$$x = 4$$

EXAMPLE

$$\frac{10}{5} = \frac{6a}{21}$$

For the value of *a* in the preceding proportion, what is the value of $a^2 - 2a$?

(A) 35

(B) 42

(C) 63

(D) 49

(E) 7

The correct answer is Choice (A). To answer this question, you need to first determine the value of *a*. By cross multiplying, you get the equation $210 = 30a$, the solution to which is 7. Next, substitute 7 in for *a* in $a^2 - 2a$.

$$a^2 - 2a = 7^2 - 2(7)$$
$$= 49 - 14$$
$$= 35$$

The other choices are misleading because all of them are either a step in the process for finding the correct answer or can result from using a wrong operation. The Praxis Core uses such distractors, so be ready to reason through them. Use your academic street smarts at all times.

A proportion can have more than two ratios set equal to each other. When you encounter such a problem, you can work with any two of the ratios at a time because they're all equal to each other. With the following ratio, you can solve for both *u* and *w*.

$$\frac{4}{u} = \frac{2}{5} = \frac{w}{15}$$

$$\frac{4}{u} = \frac{2}{5}$$
$$4 \cdot 5 = 2 \cdot u$$
$$20 = 2u$$
$$\frac{20}{2} = \frac{2u}{2}$$
$$10 = u$$
$$u = 10$$

That process revealed the value of u. Now you can use another two-ratio proportion to solve for w.

$$\frac{2}{5} = \frac{w}{15}$$
$$2 \cdot 15 = w \cdot 5$$
$$30 = 5w$$
$$\frac{30}{5} = \frac{5w}{5}$$
$$6 = w$$
$$w = 6$$

Word problems can ask about proportions and the quantities in them. For such word problems, set equal ratios equal to each other. Like with other algebra word problems, use variables to represent unknown quantities and solve for the variables.

EXAMPLE

Samantha built a dog house, using bricks and wooden boards. For every 12 bricks she used to construct the dog house, she added 7 wooden boards. The finished dog house has 72 bricks in its structure. All of the bricks and boards are still intact. How many wooden boards are part of the composition of the dog house?

To answer the problem, you can use a variable to represent the unknown quantity, the number of wooden boards. You can call it w, for example. With the variable, set up a proportion. Then, solve for the variable.

$$\frac{12}{7} = \frac{72}{w}$$
$$12w = 72 \cdot 7$$
$$12w = 504$$
$$\frac{12w}{12} = \frac{504}{12}$$
$$w = 42$$

The dog house's structure contains 42 wooden boards.

Systems of equations

Equations that have two variables can be solved if they're accompanied by a second equation that has at least one of the variables. When presented with such sets of equations, or *systems of equations*, the trick is to use the information to get an equation that has one variable. Two major methods exist for accomplishing this: the substitution method and the elimination method.

Solving by substitution

The *substitution* method involves finding the value of one variable in terms of the other variable in one equation. Then, you can substitute that expression for the variable in the second equation. The result is an equation that has one variable, and you can solve an equation that has one variable by using the techniques discussed in the section "Solving for x and other variables," earlier in this chapter.

$$4x + 2y = 22$$
$$x + y = 8$$

The concept is that x has the same value in both equations, and so does y. To solve the system of equations by using the substitution method, you state either what y equals in terms of x or what x equals in terms of y. You can use either equation to make the determination, but the second equation is easier to work with in this case because neither variable has a pesky coefficient.

$$x + y = 8$$
$$x + y - y = 8 - y$$
$$x = 8 - y$$

Because x has exactly the same value as $8 - y$, you can substitute $8 - y$ for x in the other equation. Then you have an equation with just one variable.

$$4x + 2y = 22$$
$$4(8 - y) + 2y = 22$$
$$32 - 4y + 2y = 22$$
$$32 - 2y = 22$$
$$-2y = -10$$
$$y = 5$$

You can solve the equation to determine that $y = 5$. Then, you can substitute 5 for y in either equation and solve for x, which is 3.

WARNING When using the substitution method to solve a system of equations, make sure you don't substitute a variable expression for the other variable in the equation you used to determine the expression. You must use the other equation; otherwise, the result will be an equation that has no variable. An equation that has no variable can't be solved.

Solving by elimination

Another method used for solving systems of equations is *elimination*. It's based on the fact that adding the same value to or subtracting the same value from both sides of a true equation results in another true equation. In this case, the added or subtracted value is what's represented by both sides of one of the given equations. Check out this example:

$$3x + 4y = 34$$
$$-3x + 5y = 29$$

Because both sides of a true equation have the same value, the second equation can be added to the first equation. When you have a true equation and add a true equation to it, you're adding the same value to both sides of the first equation. The sides of the equation remain equal because the same amount was added to both of them. The result is a third equation that's also true. Because like terms can be combined, equations of like forms can be combined. Adding the equations is an ideal thing to do here because both equations are in the form. Adding $3x$ and $-3x$ gets rid of x, leaving you an equation with only one variable, y. The coefficients of x have the same absolute value, so elimination can work immediately. (You may sometimes have to subtract.)

$$3x + 4y = 34$$
$$-3x + 5y = 29$$
$$\overline{\phantom{-3x + {}}9y = 63}$$
$$y = 7$$

Knowing that $y = 7$, you can put 7 in for y in either equation to determine that $x = 2$. Substituting a variable with its numerical value in any equation does not create the problem caused by substituting a variable with a variable expression in the substitution method.

To use elimination when neither variable has coefficients with the same absolute value, you can multiply both sides of an equation by the same number and get a new equation. In some cases, you must do that to both equations. Consider the following equations:

$$3j + 5p = 29$$
$$2j + 4p = 22$$

Neither variable has coefficients with the same absolute value, but you can multiply both sides of the top equation by 2 and both sides of the bottom equation by 3 to give j the same coefficient. Then you can subtract one equation from the other and get an equation with one variable.

$$2(3j + 5p) = 2(29)$$
$$3(2j + 4p) = 3(22)$$

$$\begin{array}{r} 6j + 10p = 58 \\ 6j + 12p = 66 \\ \hline -2p = -8 \\ p = 4 \end{array}$$

Now that you know $p = 4$, you can substitute 4 in for p in either equation and solve for j, which has a value of 3.

TIP

Substitution is the ideal method to use when at least one of the variable terms has a coefficient of 1 (understood). Elimination is the generally preferred method to use when every variable term has a coefficient other than 1.

Solving for variables in terms of other variables

The substitution method of solving systems of equations requires finding the value of a variable in terms of another variable. Questions on the Praxis Core could ask you to do only that. You may also be asked to solve for a variable in terms of more than one other variable. Suppose you're given the equation $4p - q = r + 3$, and you're asked to solve for p in terms of the other variables. You can follow the same procedure you use to solve for a variable in terms of a number. The goal is to get p by itself on one side of the equal sign. What's on the other side of the equal sign will be the value of p.

$$4p - q = r + 3$$
$$4p - q + q = r + 3 + q$$
$$4p = r + 3 + q$$
$$\frac{4p}{4} = \frac{r + 3 + q}{4}$$
$$p = \frac{r + 3 + q}{4}$$

Because p is by itself on one side of the equation and isn't on the other side, the value of p in terms of q and r is on the other side. Notice that the answer could be presented in other forms, such as $\frac{q + r + 3}{4}$ and $\frac{3 + q + r}{4}$. Those, too, would qualify as correct answers.

Solving Inequalities

All men and women are created equal, but not all expressions are. An *inequality* is a mathematical statement in which one side is (or may be) greater than or less than the other side. Some inequalities also suggest that the sides may be equal.

The signs used in inequalities are

» < (which means "less than")

» > (which means "greater than")

» ≤ (which means "less than or equal to")

» ≥ (which means "greater than or equal to")

REMEMBER

The underlining of < and > to create ≤ and ≥ means "or equal to." Those signs indicate that the sides may be equal.

The following table shows examples of inequalities and what they mean.

$2x + 14 < 24$	"$2x + 14$ is **less than** 24."
$y + 6 > 11$	"$y + 6$ is **greater than** 11."
$9w - 20 \le 34$	"$9w - 20$ is **less than or equal to** 34."
$8b \ge 48$	"8b is **greater than or equal to** 48."

TIP

An inequality sign always points to the side that is (or may be) the one that's less. You can also think of it as a mouth that's trying to eat the greater side.

Like equations, inequalities can be solved when they involve only one variable of unknown value. For the most part, you solve inequalities the same way you do equations, but a couple of the rules change. We cover those rule changes in the following section.

Following two more rules when solving inequalities

To solve an inequality, you use exactly the same rules that you use to solve equations (flip back to the section "Solving for x and other variables," earlier in this chapter, for those rules). However, unlike an equal sign, an inequality sign can change directions. Because of this potential change, you must follow two extra rules when you solve inequalities. The sign in an inequality must change direction when either of the following happens:

» Both sides are multiplied or divided by a negative number.

» The sides are switched.

Consider the following:

$3 < 7$

You have a true inequality. However, what happens when you multiply both sides by a negative number?

$3(-1) < 7(-1)$
$-3 < -7$

The resulting inequality is false; −3 is not less than −7. However, if the sign were to change direction, the resulting inequality would be true.

$-3 > -7$

The example illustrates that when both sides of an inequality are multiplied or divided by a negative number, the sign must change direction.

Now consider what happens when the two sides of an inequality are switched.

$3 < 7$
$7 < 3$

It's true that 3 is less than 7, but 7 is not less than 3. Because the sides were switched, the direction of the sign has to change.

$3 < 7$
$7 > 3$

So, 3 is less than 7, and 7 is greater than 3.

Follow these steps to solve the inequality $47 \geq -10x - 3$:

1. **Isolate the term that contains the variable.**

   Add 3 to both sides to undo subtracting 3 from 10x.

   $47 + 3 \geq -10x - 3 + 3$

2. **Combine like terms and simplify each side.**

   $50 \geq -10x$

3. **Divide both sides of the equation by whatever number (coefficient) is in front of the x.**

   Divide both sides by –10 to undo multiplying x by –10.

4. **Simplify each side, and switch the direction of the sign because the sides were divided by a negative number.**

   $-5 \leq x$

5. **Switch the sides to make x the subject of the sentence (as a formality) and also change the direction of the sign (because the sides were switched).**

   $x \geq -5$

The solution to the inequality is $x \geq -5$, which represents –5 and all numbers greater than –5. Any number that's –5 or greater will make the original inequality true.

Graphing inequalities

Inequalities that have one variable can be graphed on the number line.

To graph an inequality on the number line, place a circle on the line at the point representing the boundary of the solution. If the number used in the solution is included by the inequality, darken in the circle. This happens when ≤ or ≥ is used. When < or > is used, the number used in the solution only marks the boundary of what makes the inequality true, and it's not included in the set of numbers that make the inequality true. In those situations, make the circle hollow, not darkened. Next, darken in the part of the number line that includes the solution.

For example, if $g \geq 3$, a $\geq$ sign is used, so g can be 3. Therefore, darken in the circle on the number line to show that 3 is included. Then, darken the part of the number line that includes everything greater than 3. If $x < 4$, x cannot be 4. 4 would only be the boundary for what x can be, so you wouldn't darken in the circle on the number line.

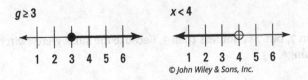

© John Wiley & Sons, Inc.

Describing solution steps

Thus far, we have shown you various types of algebraic statements and how to solve them. Questions on the Praxis Core that require knowledge of how to solve equations and inequalities may not ask for solutions. They may instead ask what steps are involved, with the choices being English descriptions of steps instead of mathematical forms of equations or inequalities. Some questions may ask about the reverse process.

EXAMPLE

Sarah correctly solved the equation $9u - 4 = 7u + 2$. If she checks her solution, which of the following could be the reverse operation of one of the steps used to solve the problem? Select **all** that apply.

(A) Subtract $7u$ from both sides.

(B) Divide both sides by 2.

(C) Add 4 to both sides.

(D) Multiply both sides by 2.

(E) Subtract 4 from both sides.

The correct answers are Choices (D) and (E). You can examine the situation by solving the equation and then looking at your steps.

$$9u - 4 = 7u + 2$$
$$9u - 4 - 7u = 7u + 2 - 7u$$
$$2u - 4 = 2$$
$$2u - 4 + 4 = 2 + 4$$
$$2u = 6$$
$$\frac{2u}{2} = \frac{6}{2}$$
$$u = 3$$

The final step is the equation that states the solution, $u = 3$. If the process is worked in the reverse, the second step after writing $u - 3$ is going from $\frac{2u}{2} = \frac{6}{2}$ to $2u = 6$. That's a matter of multiplying both sides by 2 (Choice D). You also see in the fourth step down that 4 is being added to both sides; the reverse would be to subtract 4 from both sides (Choice E).

Questions on the Praxis Core may also ask about reversing the steps of random operations performed with variables that aren't in equations. The same methodology applies to answering those kinds of questions.

Factoring in Algebra

In Chapter 4, we review factoring numbers. Factoring algebraic terms involves the same general concepts, but variables can be involved. On the Praxis Core exam, you may be asked to factor expressions that have varying numbers of terms.

Factoring terms out of bigger terms

To factor an expression that has more than one term, first see whether you can combine like terms. After that, take the greatest common factor of all the terms and put it on the outside of a set of parentheses. Then write what the factor has to be multiplied by to get each term in the expression. Don't forget to take signs into account.

$$6x^4y^2 + 15x^3y^2 - 3xy = 3xy(2x^3y + 5x^2y - 1)$$

An exam question may also ask you about factors of a single term.

EXAMPLE

Which of the following is a factor of $90a^2b^5c^3$?

(A) $90a^2b^6c^3$

(B) $80abc$

(C) $9a^3b$

(D) $10ac^2$

(E) $180a$

The correct answer is Choice (D). $10ac^2$ is the only term listed that can be factored out of $90a^2b^5c^3$. To determine this, write out the factorization of $90a^2b^5c^3$:

$$90a^2b^5c^3 = 3 \cdot 3 \cdot 2 \cdot 5 \cdot a \cdot a \cdot b \cdot b \cdot b \cdot b \cdot b \cdot c \cdot c \cdot c$$

$10ac^2$ is the only factor among the five answer choices because $5 \cdot 2 \cdot a \cdot c \cdot c$ can be taken out of the factorization.

Choice (A) is incorrect because b^6 can't be factored out of $90a^2b^5c^3$ because b^6 has an exponent greater than the exponent in b^5. Choice (B) is incorrect because 80 is not a factor of 90. Choice (C) is incorrect because a^3 is not a factor of a^2 because the exponent of a^3 is greater. Choice (E) is incorrect because 180 is not a factor of 90. It's a multiple of it.

Using reverse FOIL

Although FOIL (first, outer, inner, last) can be used for multiplying two-term expressions, *reverse FOIL* can take you in the opposite direction from one expression to two-term expressions times each other. It's a form of factoring.

Many types of expressions that can be factored through reverse FOIL exist, but the ones you'll typically see on the Praxis Core have three terms and one variable: for example, $w^2 + 2w - 15$.

TIP

If you need to factor a three- or four-term expression in which a variable has an exponent of 2, checking to see whether the expression can be factored through reverse FOIL is worthwhile.

To use reverse FOIL, create two sets of parentheses in which the first terms contain the variable that's squared in the expression you're factoring, if the expression has only one variable. If more than one variable is in the expression, you'll need to try combinations of first terms until you find the one that works. Then, think of the numbers that can be multiplied to get the final term of the factored expression. One of the combinations will form the last terms (the "L" in FOIL) in the parentheses. If the coefficient of the variable squared is understood to be 1 and the factored expression has one middle term, you have it made. All you have to do is pick the combination that adds up to the middle term coefficient. Otherwise, use trial and error. What matters is that the product of the two-term expressions in the parentheses is the factored expression. You can always test that.

Here's how the earlier expression would be factored using reverse FOIL:

$$w^2 + 2w - 15 = (w+5)(w-3)$$

In some cases, the coefficient of the term that has the variable squared will not be 1. With those expressions, the coefficients of the first terms of the factors have to be considered, as in this example:

$$3q^2 + 14q + 8 = (3q+2)(q+4)$$

A *difference of perfect squares* is a quadratic expression in which a perfect square is subtracted from another perfect square. Terms that are *perfect squares* have square roots that are whole numbers, positive fractions, variables, products of variables, or products of whole numbers or positive fractions and variables. Terms such as x^2, 64, $j^2 p^2$, and $81y^4$ are perfect squares. There's a shortcut that you can use to factor a difference of perfect squares. It's a quick way to use reverse FOIL. Consider the following quadratic expression:

$$4x^2 - 25$$

That's a difference of perfect squares because the square root of $4x^2$ is $2x$, a product of a whole number and a variable, and the square root of 25 is 5, a whole number. To factor a difference of perfect squares such as that one, put in parentheses the square root of the first perfect square minus the square root of the subtracted perfect square. Multiply the resulting two-term expression by the sum of the square roots of the original expression's terms. In other words, multiply the difference of the square roots by the sum of the square roots.

$$4x^2 - 25 = (2x-5)(2x+5)$$

You can FOIL the factorization to see that the product is the original expression.

REMEMBER

Always multiply what you determine to be the factors after you perform reverse FOIL to make sure they are the real factors.

In some cases, you can use reverse FOIL to solve quadratic equations, which can be written as quadratic expressions set equal to 0. Quadratic expressions can be written in the form $ax^2 + bx + c$. The expressions that we factor in this section by using reverse FOIL are quadratic expressions. The expression $7x^2 + 4x - 8$ is a quadratic expression, and $7x^2 + 4x - 8 = 0$ is a quadratic equation. The Praxis Core may require you to solve simple quadratic equations, such as $x^2 + 9x + 20 = 0$. That equation and other quadratic equations can be solved through factoring the quadratic expression and working with the two possibilities that the factoring illustrates. The method is rooted in the fact that the only way to multiply and get 0 is to multiply by 0. In other words, for $x^2 + 9x + 20$ to equal 0, at least one of its algebraic factors has to have a value of 0.

$$x^2 + 9x + 20 = 0$$
$$(x+5)(x+4) = 0$$

If $(x+5)(x+4)=0$, then either $x+5$ is 0 or $x+4$ is 0. If neither were 0, their product could not possibly be 0. You can work with both possibilities to find the solutions to the equation.

$$x+5=0$$
$$x+5-5=0-5$$
$$x=-5$$

$$x+4=0$$
$$x+4-4=0-4$$
$$x=-4$$

Both -5 and -4 make the equation true, so they're the two solutions to the equation. You can substitute both numbers in for x in the original equation and see that they work.

Some quadratic equations are even simpler. The equation $x^2=49$ is a quadratic equation because it can be written in the quadratic form $x^2+0x-49=0$. You can put the original equation in that quadratic form and use reverse FOIL to solve it. Drop $0x$ because it has a value of 0, and you get a difference of perfect squares. Then factor by using the shortcut: The only numbers that can be squared to get 49 are 7 and -7. Those are the solutions to the equation.

Decoding Algebra Word Problems

Algebra can be used to represent and figure out situations that are described with words. Variables can be used to represent quantities that aren't yet known, and every equation and inequality makes a statement. Using a variable in a mathematical statement can sum up what has been described with words, and mathematical statements that have one variable can usually be solved.

Translating English into mathematical language

Whenever you're given a description of a scenario that involves a number you don't know, you need to represent that number with a variable. That's always the first step. If another number isn't known, it may be possible to represent it by using the same variable after you do something to the variable, such as adding something to it or multiplying it by something. Think about the following description:

7 more than twice a number

The first step in representing the description mathematically is to use a variable to represent the unknown number. Just pick a letter, such as x. Write down how the number is represented so that you can keep up with it.

x: the number

Now, think about what's being done to the number. The description involves twice the number, which can be represented by $2x$. "7 more than" indicates that 7 is added to the amount, so the result is $2x+7$. "7 more than twice a number" and "$2x+7$" have the same meaning. However, "$2x+7$" is much easier to use in algebraic equations.

Algebraic word problems

Algebraic word problems can look complicated, but they simply involve representing a quantity with a variable (see the preceding section), writing a statement about it, solving for the variable, and using the variable's value to answer the question. Sometimes, you have to figure out the values of other numbers after the value of the variable has been determined. For example, a word problem might ask for a number that's 2 more than the number you represent with a variable. To solve the problem, you would need to determine the value of the variable and then add 2 to it. The problem might also ask for the value of a number 2 greater than the number 2 greater than the variable value, so you need to add 2 to the variable-plus-2 number. Here's an example of an algebraic word problem:

3 times a number is decreased by 5. The result is 25. What is the number?

To solve the problem, first use a variable to represent the number.

n: the number

Next, write a mathematical statement about the number by translating the word problem into mathematical language. "Decreased by" means "minus (−)," and "the result is" means "equals (=)." So, the word problem can be directly translated into mathematical language with this equation:

$$3n - 5 = 25$$

From there, you can simply solve the equation. The value of n, the number, is 10.

In some word problems, more than one quantity is described, but only one variable needs to be used. These problems work like the one that was just demonstrated, but you need to represent more than one quantity. Let a variable represent one unknown quantity, and let a more detailed expression involving the same variable represent another quantity.

Two consecutive even integers have a sum of 34. What are the integers?

Use a variable to represent one of the integers and use a longer expression to represent the other integer. Because consecutive even integers are always 2 apart, one is 2 greater than the other.

y: the first integer

$y + 2$: the second integer

Now just directly translate the word problem into mathematical language. A sum is the result of adding, so add the expressions and show that the result is 34.

$$y + y + 2 = 34$$

You can combine like terms to get the equation $2y + 2 = 34$ and then solve the equation. In this case, $y = 16$, so the first integer is 16 and the second integer is 2 more than that, which is 18. The two integers are 16 and 18. You can check the answer by adding 16 and 18. Their sum is 34.

REMEMBER

When solving algebraic word problems, make sure you know exactly what the question is. Don't make the mistake of assuming the question. The preceding word problem could have asked for just the first integer, just the second integer, or both integers. You need to take careful note of what the question is asking because it won't always be what you may automatically assume.

Thinking Outside the Algebra Box

The information reviewed so far in this chapter covers the basics of working algebra problems, but some of the problems in the Praxis Core math section require basic algebra skills plus an extra degree of critical thinking. Understanding patterns of relationships between quantities and the basic rules of reasoning will help you get the solutions to such problems.

Recognizing relational patterns

For some problems, you need to determine how a pattern works and represent it algebraically. This is another example of translating English into mathematical language, but the translating isn't as direct as it may be in other situations.

Direct variation

If a word problem involves a number of 18-wheeler trucks and the question is how many wheels there are in all, you need to understand that there are 18 wheels for every truck. In other words, the number of trucks multiplied by 18 equals the number of wheels. This is an example of *direct variation*, which is a relationship pattern in which one quantity increases while another one increases, though they may increase at different rates. Every time a number of 18-wheeler trucks is increased by 1, the number of wheels increases by 18. While one quantity increases, so does the other. The number of wheels increases 18 times faster than the number of trucks. If the number of trucks is represented by x, the number of wheels needs to be represented by $18x$.

Inverse variation

Inverse variation is a relationship pattern in which one quantity decreases while another one increases. The two quantities don't increase together, like they do with direct variation. With inverse variation, the greater one quantity is, the smaller the other one is. For example, the amount of time it takes to travel a certain distance decreases with increased rate. Suppose you're traveling a distance of 10 miles. The faster you travel, the less time it will take. The distance formula is $d = rt$, in which d = distance, r = rate, and t = time. From that formula, it can be concluded that $r = \frac{d}{t}$ and $t = \frac{d}{r}$. The relationship between t and r is one of inverse variation.

TIP

Any time a formula, such as $d = rt$, is used in algebra, simply write the formula with every variable's value filled in except for the variable that still has an unknown value. Then, solve for that variable. Word problems that require using formulas look more difficult than that on the surface, but they really are that simple.

Algebraic reasoning

Some of the math questions on the Praxis Core exam involve *conditional statements*, also known as "if-then statements." They state that if one given fact exists, another given fact exists. This is an example of a conditional statement:

If $p - 4 = 5$, then $p + 8 = 17$.

You may be asked whether a certain conditional statement is true. In many cases, you can solve an equation or inequality and then determine whether the conclusion is true. By solving either of the preceding equations, you can determine that $p = 9$. You can then put 9 in for p in the other equation and see whether the equation is true. In this example, it is. If p did not have the same value in both equations, the statement would be false.

If you're in doubt about how to figure out the full nature of a conditional statement, there's an effective method you can use. If you can come up with even one example of a situation where the conditional statement fails, the conditional statement is false. An exception to a conditional statement is a *counterexample*. Just one counterexample to a conditional statement proves that the statement is false. Think about this conditional statement:

If $y^2 > 64$, then $y > 8$.

All you have to do is look for one example of a number that makes the statement fail. If you can find any such number, the statement is false. When testing numbers, try using some positive integers, some negative integers, 0, and some fractions between 0 and 1. Sampling those sections of the number line goes a long way toward covering the numerical principles that need to be put to the test. Numbers that make both of the preceding inequalities true include all numbers that are greater than 8, but no number less than −8 works for both inequalities. If you put any number less than −8 in for y, you can see that it doesn't work and is therefore a counterexample. As soon as you find that one exception, you can truthfully conclude that the conditional statement is false.

Practice Questions about Algebra

These practice questions are similar to the algebra questions you'll encounter on the Praxis Core exam.

1. If $10x - 8 = 17$, what is the value of $7 + 4x$?

   (A) 17

   (B) 107

   (C) $10\frac{3}{5}$

   (D) 25

   (E) 41

2. If the value of $\frac{u}{3}$ is the same as the value of w^3, which of the following is equal to w^6?

   (A) $\frac{u}{w^2}$

   (B) $9u$

   (C) $\frac{u^2}{9}$

   (D) u^3

   (E) $\frac{u^2}{18}$

3. Which of the following is NOT a factor of the product of $9p^2q^5ru^7$ and $6p^2q^2r^2u^4$?

   (A) $-6p^4q^7r^3u^{11}$

   (B) $9q^8r^3$

   (C) $-27u$

   (D) $-18pqru^{11}$

   (E) $2p^4q^7r^3u^{11}$

4. Two consecutive even integers have a sum of 42. What is the higher of the two integers?

   (A) 20

   (B) 26

   (C) 18

   (D) 24

   (E) 22

5. Which of the following is a true statement if $-8x + 7 \geq 39$?

   (A) $x < -4$

   (B) $x \leq -5.75$

   (C) $x \leq -4$

   (D) $x > -5.75$

   (E) $x \geq -4$

Answers and Explanations

Use this answer key to score the practice algebra questions in this chapter.

1. **A. 17.** You can solve the first equation and determine the value of x.

$$10x - 8 = 17$$
$$10x = 25$$
$$\frac{10x}{10} = \frac{25}{10}$$
$$x = 2.5$$

Because the value of x is 2.5, you can substitute 2.5 for x in the expression $7 + 4x$ to determine the value of the expression. $7 + 4(2.5) = 7 + 10$, or 17.

Choice (B) is the value of $7 + 4(25)$, and 25 is the value of the right side of the equation before you divide both sides by 10. Choice (C) results from subtracting 8 from both sides instead of adding it. Choice (D) is the value of the right side of the equation after you add 8 to both sides. Choice (E) is just wrong.

2. **C.** $\frac{u^2}{9}$. For problems like this, first think about what can be done to one of the expressions that are stated to be equal to each other in order to get the expression to which one of the choices is equal. In this case, you can square w^3 to get w^6. That's a clue that you can try squaring $\frac{u}{3}$ and considering the result.

$$w^6 = \left(w^3\right)^2$$
$$= \left(\frac{u}{3}\right)^2$$
$$= \frac{u^2}{3^2}$$
$$= \frac{u^2}{9}$$

3. **B.** $9q^8r^3$. First, find the product of $9p^2q^5ru^7$ and $6p^2q^2r^2u^4$.

$$9p^2q^5ru^7 \cdot 6p^2q^2r^2u^4 = 9 \cdot 6 \cdot p^{2+2}q^{5+2}r^{1+2}u^{7+4}$$
$$= 54p^4q^7r^3u^{11}$$

Next, determine which choice is not a factor of $54p^4q^7r^3u^{11}$. For $9q^8r^3$, the variable q has an exponent of 8, which makes $9q^8r^3$ not a factor of $54p^4q^7r^3u^{11}$ because 8 is higher than the exponent of q in $54p^4q^7r^3u^{11}$. All the other choices are factors because their coefficients are factors of 54 and they have the same variables with exponents that are whole numbers that aren't greater than the corresponding exponents in $-54p^4q^7r^3u^{11}$.

4. **E. 22.** You can use x to represent the first integer. Because the next number is the next even integer, it's 2 higher, so you can represent it with the expression $x + 2$. The sum of the two consecutive even integers is 42, so you can represent the situation with the equation $x + x + 2 = 42$.

$$x + x + 2 = 42$$
$$2x + 2 = 42$$
$$2x + 2 - 2 = 42 - 2$$
$$2x = 40$$
$$\frac{2x}{2} = \frac{40}{2}$$
$$x = 20$$

Because the value of x is 20, the first even integer is 20. The next one is 2 higher, so it's 22.

Choice (A) is the lower of the two integers. The other choices are randomly incorrect.

5. **C.** $x \leq -4$. All of the choices have x followed by an inequality sign and then a number. That's one proper form of a solution to a single inequality. If you find the solution to the inequality in the question, you can determine which answer choice is a true statement. Solving this inequality involves reversing the sign because you have to divide by a negative number.

$$-8x + 7 \geq 39$$
$$-8x + 7 - 7 \geq 39 - 7$$
$$-8x \geq 32$$
$$\frac{-8x}{-8} \leq \frac{32}{-8}$$
$$x \leq -4$$

Choice (A) has the < symbol, not the ≤ symbol. Choice (B) results from adding 7 to both sides of the inequality rather than subtracting it. Choice (D) results from adding 7 to both sides of the inequality, not changing the direction of the inequality sign when dividing both sides by a negative number, and leaving out the "or equal to" mark. Choice (E) results from not changing the direction of the inequality sign when dividing both sides by a negative number.

IN THIS CHAPTER

» Getting the lowdown on points, lines, planes, and angles

» Defining and combining shapes

» Focusing on geometric formulas

» Understanding the *xy* coordinate plane

» Putting your geometry knowledge into practice

Chapter **6**

Grasping Geometry Concepts

The time has come for you to review America's favorite subject, geometry. Well, it's America's favorite subject according to a recent survey of one person — a geometry teacher. Okay, never mind that. *Geometry* is basically the study of the nature of shapes and where shapes exist. The subject begins with points and goes all the way to three-dimensional figures.

Like other areas of math, geometry involves principles from areas that typically precede its study. Algebraic expressions, for example, are commonly used in geometry, and using geometric principles to solve for variables is very common. So, make sure you have a good grasp of geometry concepts because you never know when one may appear on the Praxis Core — or in real life. The math test of the Praxis exam is about 12 percent geometry. Because the math test has 56 questions, you'll have about 7 geometry questions to answer.

Understanding the Building Blocks of Geometry

A few elements in geometry make up all the others, even the most complex geometric figures. You need to understand these elements to truly understand the more complicated figures and properties in geometry. The starting point for understanding geometric elements is the point. (The starting point would automatically have to be a point. It's not a starting prism.) And then you move onto lines, planes, and angles.

Getting to the point

The most basic building block of geometry is the *point,* which is an exact and infinitely small location. Points make up all the physical realities studied in geometry. Points are named by capital letters that are placed near them. These are Point A and Point B:

A   **B**
●   ●

© John Wiley & Sons, Inc.

Points aren't always represented by dots. Dots are generally used when the location of a point would otherwise be unclear.

Defining lines and parts of lines

Any two points, anywhere in the universe, are on the same line. A *line* is a continuous set of an infinite number of points extending infinitely in two directions. Lines are one-dimensional.

A line can be named by any two points on it in any order, with a line symbol on top. Three of the points on the following line are labeled. The line can be called $\overleftrightarrow{AB}$, $\overleftrightarrow{AC}$, $\overleftrightarrow{BA}$, $\overleftrightarrow{BC}$, $\overleftrightarrow{CB}$, or $\overleftrightarrow{CA}$.

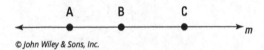

© John Wiley & Sons, Inc.

A line can also be named by a single italicized letter that isn't a point on it. For example, the preceding line can be called Line *m*.

Parts of lines that serve as building blocks of geometry include rays and segments. A *ray* is like a line, but it has one endpoint and extends infinitely in only one direction. A ray is named by its endpoint and any other point on it, with a ray symbol on top. The following ray can be called $\overrightarrow{DE}$ or $\overrightarrow{DF}$.

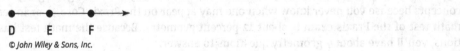

© John Wiley & Sons, Inc.

A line segment, more commonly called just a *segment,* is a part of a line that has two endpoints. Segments are named by their two endpoints, in either order. A segment symbol can be placed on top of the letters, but it isn't necessary. This line segment is $\overline{PQ}$ or $\overline{QP}$ and can also be written as just PQ or QP:

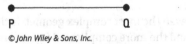

© John Wiley & Sons, Inc.

Moving along planes in space

You have now entered the second dimension on a plane. A *plane* is a flat surface that's infinitely thin and goes forever in all directions two-dimensionally. Any two intersecting lines exist on one plane. Planes are usually named by three points that are within the plane and not all on the same line.

They can also be named by a single italicized letter. The following plane can be named Plane RST, but it can also be called Plane *p*.

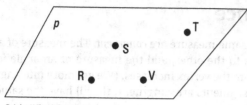
© John Wiley & Sons, Inc.

If two lines are on the same plane and never intersect, they are *parallel*. They remain the same distance from each other, infinitely. Parallel lines can be indicated with the same number of arrow-head marks on each line.

Getting the right angles on angles

An *angle* is a shape formed by two sides, with each side being either a line or part of a line. The point at which the two sides meet is called the *vertex*. An angle can be named by three points on it in the order of any point on either side, the vertex, and a point on the other side. You can change the order as long as the vertex stays in the middle. If the vertex is presented as the vertex of just one angle, that angle can be named by the vertex alone. The following angle can be called ∠B, ∠ABC, ∠CBA, or ∠3.

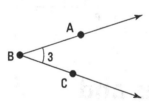
© John Wiley & Sons, Inc.

WARNING

If a point is the vertex of more than one angle shown, you can't name the angle by the vertex. That would be confusing because the angle named wouldn't be clearly identified. The name could apply to any of the angles that have that vertex. In the following illustration, which angle would be ∠J? Nothing indicates which angle it is.

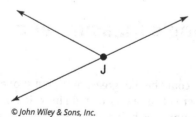
© John Wiley & Sons, Inc.

REMEMBER

An angle named by three of its points must be named with the vertex in the middle. Otherwise, a different angle is indicated.

Recognizing congruence

Two segments or angles that have the same measure are *congruent*. The measure of a segment is the distance from one of its endpoints to the other, and the measure of an angle is the rate at which the sides separate as distance from the vertex increases. (We get more into angle measurement in the following section.) If two segments are congruent, they'll have the same number of marks on them, if such marks are used.

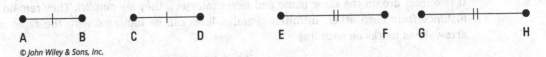

© John Wiley & Sons, Inc.

The congruence symbol is ≅. If AB has the same measure as CD, then AB ≅ CD. The single mark in each segment indicates that they're congruent. The congruence of EF and GH is also indicated, but they're not congruent to AB and CD, so they have two marks each.

Angles that have the same number of arcs are congruent. In the following illustration, ∠J is congruent to ∠M, but ∠P is not congruent to either.

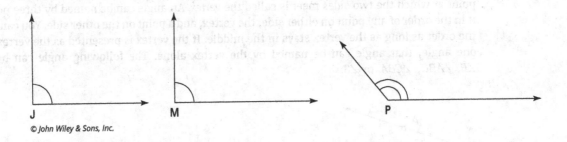

© John Wiley & Sons, Inc.

Understanding Angle Measures and Relationships

Angle sizes vary, so units are used to distinguish the different sizes. The unit of measure that's most commonly used — and the only one used on the Praxis Core exam — is the *degree*, and it's represented by the symbol °.

Distinguishing degrees of angle measure and naming angles

An angle in which both sides are merged together could be 0 degrees, or 0°, but if one side completes a full circle, the angle it forms with the other side is 360°. An angle in which the two sides are part of the same line is 180° because one side completes half a circle with the other side.

Angles are classified according to their general sizes. An angle that is between 0° and 90° is an *acute angle*. If an angle is exactly 90°, it's a *right angle*. An angle that has a measure between 90° and 180° is an *obtuse angle*, and a 180° angle is a *straight angle*. Right angles are often symbolized by a small square at the vertex.

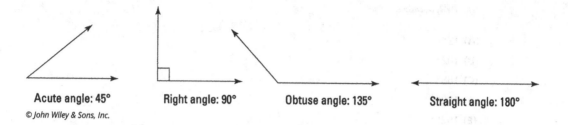

Acute angle: 45°   Right angle: 90°   Obtuse angle: 135°   Straight angle: 180°

© John Wiley & Sons, Inc.

Working with angle relationships

If two angles have measures that add up to 180°, they are *supplementary*. For example, a 130° angle and a 50° angle are supplementary. Because straight angles are 180°, two angles that share a side and form a straight angle together are automatically supplementary. They make what is called a *linear pair* because they are a pair of angles that together form a line.

Complementary angles are like supplementary angles, except two angles that are *complementary* have measures that add up to 90°. A 37° angle and a 53° angle are complementary. Two angles that share a side and form a right angle together are complementary.

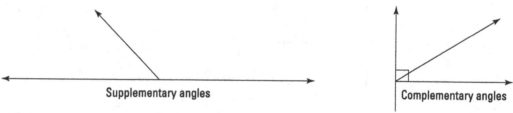

Supplementary angles   Complementary angles

© John Wiley & Sons, Inc.

Another major type of relationship is that of *vertical angles*, which are formed by two intersecting lines. Vertical angles are opposite each other, and if you have two intersecting lines, you always have two pairs of vertical angles. Vertical angles are always congruent; that is, they have the same measurement.

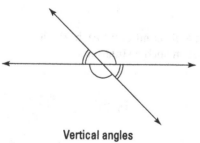

Vertical angles

© John Wiley & Sons, Inc.

EXAMPLE

The measure of ∠ABD is 168°. What is the measure of ∠DBC?

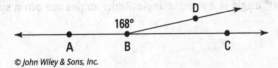

© John Wiley & Sons, Inc.

(A) 12°

(B) 102°

(C) 168°

(D) 180°

(E) 192°

The correct answer is Choice (A). ∠ABD and ∠DBC form a linear pair, so they're supplementary. That means their measures have a sum of 180°. 180 − 168 is 12, so the measure of ∠DBC is 12°. Choice (E) is the result of adding 12 to 180. Choice (C) is the same measure as that of ∠ABD, Choice (D) is merely the measure of a straight angle, and Choice (B) is the difference of 270° and 168°.

If two lines intersect and form four right angles, the lines are *perpendicular* to each other. The lines run straight into each other. Also, parts of lines can be perpendicular to lines and parts of lines. For example, a segment can be perpendicular to a segment.

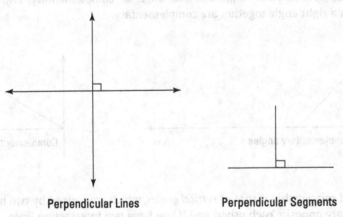

Perpendicular Lines   Perpendicular Segments

© John Wiley & Sons, Inc.

Although such situations involve more than one right angle, generally only one angle is marked as right because it's understood that any angle supplementary to or vertical to a right angle is also a right angle.

When two lines are intersected by a third line at a different point each, the intersecting line is a *transversal*. Various angle relationships are formed in such a situation.

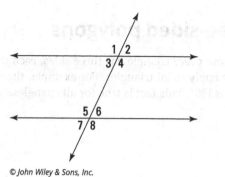

Angles 4 and 5, as well as angles 3 and 6, form a pair of *alternate interior angles* because they are on alternate sides of the transversal and interior to the given intersected lines. Angles 2 and 7 are *alternate exterior angles*. *Corresponding angles* are in the same type of position, but formed by two different lines that are intersected by the transversal. An example of a pair of corresponding angles is the pair of angles 1 and 5. Angles 4 and 6 form an example of a pair of *same-side interior angles*, also known as *consecutive angles*. They are on the same side of the transversal and interior to the lines it intersects to form the angle relationship.

If two lines intersected by a transversal are parallel, these are facts:

>> Each pair of alternate interior angles is congruent.

>> Each pair of alternate exterior angles is congruent.

>> Each pair of corresponding angles is congruent.

>> Each pair of same-side interior angles is supplementary.

Also, if any one of the preceding statements is a fact, it's complete proof that the lines intersected by the transversal are parallel. The rules work in both directions.

Knowing Common Shapes and Their Basic Properties

Understanding segments and the angles they form helps you analyze many of the geometric shapes you may be asked about on the Praxis Core exam. This includes the basic shapes such as squares and other rectangles, triangles, and even circles because segments exist inside circles. In the following sections, we review basic shapes.

Defining polygons in general

A *polygon* is an enclosed figure formed on one plane by segments joined at their endpoints. Rectangles, triangles, and some other shapes are types of polygons. The polygons primarily focused on in geometry — and more particularly on the Praxis Core exam — are *convex polygons*, which basically are polygons that don't point inward anywhere.

Polygons are also classified according to the number of sides they have. The number of sides a polygon has is also the number of *interior angles* (inside angles formed by sides that are next to each other) it has.

Analyzing triangles: Three-sided polygons

A *triangle* is a polygon with three sides. Because every triangle has three sides, each triangle has three interior angles also. Certain properties apply to all triangles. For example, the sum of the measures of the interior angles of a triangle is 180°. This fact is true for all triangles.

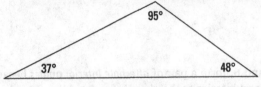

Sum of three angles = 180°

© John Wiley & Sons, Inc.

Another rule that applies to all triangles is that if two sides of a triangle are congruent, the angles opposite (across from) those sides are congruent. The rule also works in the other direction. If two angles of a triangle are congruent, the sides opposite those angles are congruent, too. A triangle with two congruent sides, thus two congruent angles, is an *isosceles* triangle. For an *equilateral* triangle, all three sides are congruent, and therefore all three angles are congruent. Because the three angles are congruent, an equilateral triangle is also *equiangular*. With a *scalene* triangle, no sides are congruent, so none of the angles are congruent.

 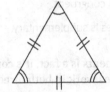 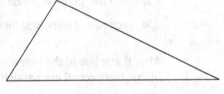

Isosceles Triangle   **Equilateral/Equiangular Triangle**   **Scalene Triangle**

© John Wiley & Sons, Inc.

Questions on the Praxis Core exam can involve more than one rule regarding triangles and sometimes more basic rules in addition to them. You may need to use multiple rules to reach a conclusion. Many combinations of principles can be involved.

EXAMPLE

According to the diagram, what is the measure of ∠1?

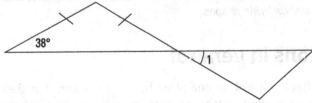

© John Wiley & Sons, Inc.

(A) 1

(B) 38°

(C) 52°

(D) 142°

(E) 322°

The correct answer is Choice (B). Two sides of the triangle on the left are congruent, so the angles opposite them are congruent. They are therefore both 38°. ∠1 is vertical to a 38° angle, so it too is 38°. Choice (A) involves the name of the angle in question, but 1 is not given as the measure of the angle. It has no ° beside it. Choice (C) is the complement of 38°. Choice (D) is the supplement of 38°. Choice (E) results from subtracting the given angle measure from 360°.

For three segments to come together, join endpoints, and form a triangle, the sum of the measures of any two segments must be greater than the measure of the third segment. Also, the third segment measure must be greater than the positive difference of the other two segment measures. The third segment has to be able to join the endpoints of the other two segments and form angles with them, so it can't have a measure that's equal to the sum or positive difference of their measures. Very simply put, if two segment measures are given, the third segment measure has to be between (not equal to) the sum and the positive difference of the other two segment measures. Imagine trying to form a triangle with these three segments.

© John Wiley & Sons, Inc.

It would be impossible. The two shorter segments couldn't join together, form an angle with a measure between zero and 180 degrees, and reach the endpoints of the third segment. The sum of the measures of the two shortest segments is less than the measure of the longest segment. Also, the longest segment measure minus either one of the other segment measures is greater than the remaining segment measure. There's no way for a segment measure to be between the sum and positive difference of the other two segment measures. That makes forming a triangle with the segments impossible.

If you're given two segment measures and asked within what range the third segment measure must be, you can find the sum and difference of the two given measures. The third must be within those. If you're given three segment measures and asked whether the segments can join at endpoints to form a triangle, the shortcut to the answer is to take the two shortest segments and see whether the sum of their measures is greater than the longest. If their sum is greater, then the segments can form a triangle. That's because if the sum of the two shortest segment measures is greater than the third segment measure, the other sums of two segment measures will have to be greater than the third. If it works with the two shortest, it has to work with the other combinations. Plus, the longest segment measure can't possibly be less than the positive difference of the two shortest segment measures. That one test covers all bases. (No pun intended.)

Consider a 3 m segment, a 9 m segment, and a 7 m segment. Can they form a triangle? The two shortest segments are the 3 m and 7 m segments. The sum of those measures is 10 m, which is greater than 9 m. That means the segments can form a triangle. Because the segments pass that test, they pass the other tests.

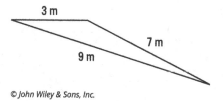

© John Wiley & Sons, Inc.

Identifying facts about quadrilaterals

Triangles (discussed in the preceding section) are three-sided polygons, and quadrilaterals are four-sided polygons. Squares and other rectangles are quadrilaterals, but they're not the only types. The sum of the interior angles of a quadrilateral is always 360°.

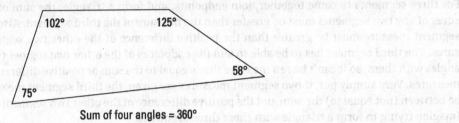

Sum of four angles = 360°

© John Wiley & Sons, Inc.

A quadrilateral in which both pairs of opposite sides are parallel is a *parallelogram*. For any parallelogram, both pairs of opposite sides are also congruent, and both pairs of opposite angles are congruent. Also, any quadrilateral in which both pairs of opposite sides are congruent is a parallelogram, and any quadrilateral in which both pairs of opposite angles are congruent is a parallelogram. A *rectangle* is a quadrilateral in which all four interior angles are right angles, and all rectangles are parallelograms, so their opposite sides are congruent. The diagonals of a rectangle are also congruent. A *square* is a rectangle in which all four sides are congruent. A quadrilateral in which all four sides are congruent is a *rhombus*. Every square is a rectangle and a rhombus.

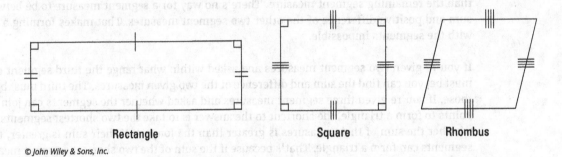

Rectangle   Square   Rhombus

© John Wiley & Sons, Inc.

A *trapezoid* is a quadrilateral that has just one pair of parallel sides. The two parallel sides are the *bases* of the trapezoid. The bases in the following trapezoid are indicated by arrows, which are used in geometry to suggest that lines and parts of lines are parallel.

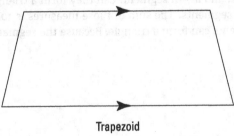

Trapezoid

© John Wiley & Sons, Inc.

Working with other types of polygons

No limit exists for the number of sides a polygon can have. Many names are used for types of polygons based on the number of sides they have. For example, a five-sided polygon is a *pentagon*, and an eight-sided polygon is an *octagon*. However, the Praxis Core exam doesn't focus on the major rules concerning polygons that have more than four sides. What you need to be able to do is recognize what is inside such polygons. Rules you need to know may apply to segments, angles, triangles, quadrilaterals, and other formations that are within them.

EXAMPLE

According to the diagram, what is the measure of ∠1?

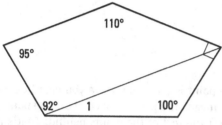

© John Wiley & Sons, Inc.

(A) 63°

(B) 27°

(C) 180°

(D) 88°

(E) 53°

The correct answer is Choice (E). The pentagon is divided into a quadrilateral and a triangle. Because the interior angle sum of a quadrilateral is 360°, the interior angle without a given measure in the quadrilateral is 63°. That angle is complementary to an angle in the triangle, so that angle in the triangle has a measure of 27°. Because another angle in the triangle is 100° and the interior angle sum of a triangle is 180°, ∠1 has to be 53°. The other choices can result from the wrong uses of formulas.

Knowing the basic facts about circles

A circle is a shape like the others covered so far, but a circle has no sides. A *circle* is the set of all points in one plane that are a given distance from a point called the *center*. The distance that all the points are from the center is the *radius* of the circle. A radius is also an actual segment that connects the center to a point on the circle. The *diameter* of a circle is the distance across the interior through the center, and it is also the name of a segment that covers the path. The diameter of a circle is always twice the radius. Because the radius of the following circle is 3 centimeters, the diameter is 6 centimeters. A circle is named by its center, so this circle is Circle K.

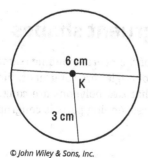

© John Wiley & Sons, Inc.

Two major types of angles exist within circles. A *central angle* has a vertex that is the center of the circle. An *inscribed angle* has a vertex that's a point on the circle. In the following diagram, ∠ABC is a central angle, and ∠ADC is an inscribed angle.

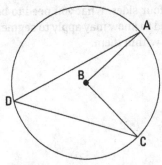

© John Wiley & Sons, Inc.

A line that intersects a circle at exactly one point is a *tangent*. Have you ever heard of someone going off on a tangent in a conversation? It means the person touched on one point in the conversation and kept talking but completely left the rest of the points behind. That's pretty much what a tangent line does to a circle, except it does not necessarily have conversations. It goes through one point on the circle and keeps going far away from the circle. The point intersected by a tangent is the point of tangency. A radius that goes to the point of tangency is perpendicular to the tangent.

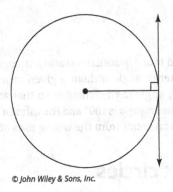

© John Wiley & Sons, Inc.

Working with Shapes that Are Alike

Polygons can be alike in certain ways, and so can circles. Polygons that have the same number of sides don't necessarily have the same shape, but they do if they are *congruent* (identical) or *similar* (the same shape).

Forming conclusions about congruent shapes

When two polygons have the same number of sides and all of their corresponding (same position, different polygons) pairs of sides and corresponding pairs of angles are congruent, the polygons themselves are congruent. Also, if you're given the fact that two polygons are congruent, you have enough information to conclude that every pair of corresponding parts is congruent.

The two following triangles are congruent. Notice that every side and angle of one triangle is congruent to its corresponding part in the other triangle. They are the same triangle in two different places, exact copies of each other. As a result, all of their corresponding parts are congruent.

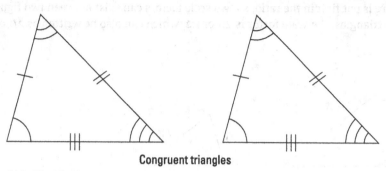

Congruent triangles

All other types of polygons can be congruent. Circles can be congruent too. If two circles have the same radius, they're congruent. They have the same diameter and other measures. We get into circumference and area in the section "Figuring out Geometric Formulas," later in this chapter, but for now it's enough to say that congruent circles have the same circumference (distance around the circle) and the same area. The following two circles are congruent.

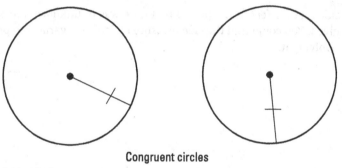

Congruent circles

Working with similar shapes

Similar shapes are exactly the same shape but not necessarily congruent. Imagine magnifying or reducing a picture of a quadrilateral. The resulting image would look identical to the original except that it would be a different size. The two shapes would be similar.

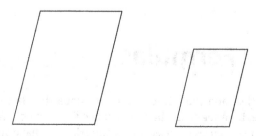

Similar quadrilaterals

Polygons that are similar have congruent corresponding angles. They also have side measures that are *proportional*, which means that the ratio of the measure of a side in one polygon to the measure of the side that corresponds to it in the other polygon is always the same ratio. Recall that a proportion is an equation in which one ratio is equal to another. The ratio of one side measure to its corresponding side measure is the *scale factor* of the similarity relationship. Scale factor depends on which figure is put first in the ratio, so two scale factors can exist between two figures. For the following two triangles, the scale factor is 2:1 or 1:2, which can also be written as 2/1 or 1/2.

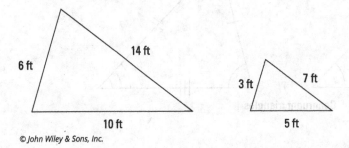

© *John Wiley & Sons, Inc.*

The way to determine the measure of a side of a polygon that's similar to another polygon is to compare ratios of corresponding sides within the two polygons. You can do that by writing a side measure over its corresponding side measure and setting it equal to another such ratio. Make sure you are consistent in the way you write the ratios. If you put the first polygon measure on top in one ratio, the first polygon measure has to go on top in the other ratio.

Suppose the triangle side that's 7 feet in the preceding figure was of unknown measure, but the other measures were given. You could find the side measure by letting a variable represent it and solving a proportion involving it.

$$\frac{6}{3} = \frac{14}{x}$$
$$6x = 14(3)$$
$$6x = 42$$
$$\frac{6x}{6} = \frac{42}{6}$$
$$x = 7$$

Corresponding angles of similar polygons are congruent.

REMEMBER You can apply these principles of shape similarity to maps of geographical regions, floor plans of houses, and other representations of places in reality. Such representations are called *scale models*, and they're shaped like the places they represent. You can use similarity principles to determine distances in real-world places based on distances in the scale models that represent the places. Finding the answers to such problems generally requires use of a given scale factor, usually presented in a sample ratio.

Figuring out Geometric Formulas

Geometric figures have certain properties, and the number of dimensions they have is part of what decides what properties they have. Line segments have a distance that can be referred to as length, width, or height. Two-dimensional figures such as circles and triangles have area, as well as parts that have one-dimensional measurements. Three-dimensional geometric figures have the preceding properties plus volume.

REMEMBER

Formulas are provided on the Praxis Core, but you'll need to know what the variables in them represent. You should also practice using the formulas before you take the exam to make sure you know what you're doing and help avoid errors.

Finding the perimeter

The perimeter of a two-dimensional figure is the distance around it. To determine the perimeter of a polygon, you can add all the side measures. The following rectangle has a perimeter of 28 meters.

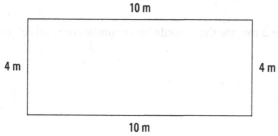

© John Wiley & Sons, Inc.

Because the opposite sides of a rectangle are congruent, a formula makes calculating the perimeter simpler than adding up all the side measures. Two of the sides have the same length (l), and two sides have the same width (w), so adding twice the length and twice the width gives the perimeter:

Perimeter of rectangle = $2l + 2w$

TIP

Because the length and width of a square are the same, you can get the perimeter by multiplying the measure of one side by 4.

Circling the circumference

The perimeter of a circle is the circle's *circumference.* The formula for circumference involves π, which is the ratio of a circle's circumference (C) divided by its diameter (d). Because all circles are *similar* (meaning they have the same shape), the ratio is the same for all circles.

$$\frac{C}{d} = \pi$$

π is an irrational number, so it never terminates or repeats in decimal form, but its value can be rounded to 3.14159. Because circumference divided by diameter is π, circumference is diameter times π.

$$\frac{C}{d} = \pi$$
$$\frac{C}{d}(d) = \pi(d)$$
$$C = \pi d$$

The diameter of a circle is twice the radius, so $d = 2r$. Therefore, $C = \pi(2r)$. The formal way to write a term is with numbers before variables, and π is a number, so the official formula for the circumference is this:

$$C = 2\pi r$$

Remember that within a formula, any variable can represent an unknown in a problem. To find the value of the variable, fill every known number into the formula and solve for what's not yet known.

What is the radius of a circle that has a circumference of 10π units?

EXAMPLE

(A) 10

(B) 5

(C) 100

(D) 5π

(E) 10π

The correct answer is Choice (B). You can use the formula for circumference and solve for r.

$$C = 2\pi r$$
$$10\pi = 2\pi r$$
$$\frac{10\pi}{2\pi} = \frac{2\pi r}{2\pi}$$
$$5 = r$$
$$r = 5$$

The other choices result from incorrectly using the circumference formula or using the wrong formula.

TIP

If a question involves π, the symbol π may or may not appear as part of the answer choices. If it's not part of the answer choices, then it has probably been calculated in approximated decimal form. In that case, you need to use 3.14159, the approximation for π, and do the calculation. The number 3.14159 is not exactly π, but you can use it to get really close approximations.

Getting into the area

A two-dimensional figure exists on a plane. The area of a two-dimensional figure is the amount of plane it contains. In other words, area is a measure of how much room is inside a two-dimensional shape. Different shapes have different area formulas.

The area of a parallelogram is its base times its height. The base can be any side, but the height has to be the measure of a segment that is perpendicular to it and its opposite side.

area of parallelogram = bh

The area of the following parallelogram is its base times its height, or (7 cm)(10 cm), which equals 70 cm².

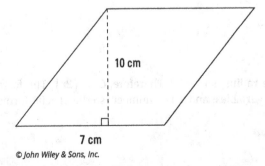

10 cm

7 cm

© John Wiley & Sons, Inc.

TIP

Any combination of base and height for a rectangle, which is a type of parallelogram, is a combination of length (l) and width (w), so the area of a rectangle is lw. Length and width are the same for a square because all four sides are congruent, so to get the area of a square, all you have to do is multiply a side measure by itself. In other words, square a side measure.

If a parallelogram is cut at the vertices (discussed in the section "Getting the right angles on angles," earlier in this chapter), the result is two congruent triangles. Also, any triangle can be put together with a congruent triangle to form a parallelogram. Because of this, every triangle has half the area of the parallelogram that can be formed by putting the triangle with an exact copy of itself. Therefore, the area of a triangle isn't base times height, but half that.

$$\text{area of triangle} = \frac{1}{2}bh$$

The area of the following triangle is $\frac{1}{2}bh$, or $\frac{1}{2}(8\text{ ft})(11\text{ ft})$, which is 44 ft^2.

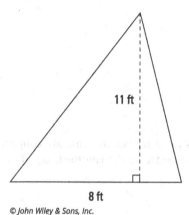

11 ft

8 ft

© John Wiley & Sons, Inc.

Table 6-1 shows the formulas for finding the areas of common shapes. Make sure you're very familiar with these formulas because you'll probably be asked at least one question about area on the Praxis.

If two-dimensional figures are *similar* (meaning the same shape), the ratio of their areas isn't the same as their scale factor. Because an extra dimension is involved in area, the ratio of their areas is the square of their scale factor. For example, if the sides of Triangle A are 3 times longer than the sides of Triangle B, the area of Triangle A is 3^2, or 9, times greater than the area of Triangle B. The ratio of the volumes of three-dimensional figures is the cube of the scale factor of their sides.

TABLE 6-1 ## Area Formulas for Common Shapes

Figure	Area
Parallelogram	bh
Rectangle	lw
Square	s^2
Triangle	$\frac{1}{2}bh$
Trapezoid	$\frac{1}{2}h(b_1 + b_2)$
Circle	πr^2

Finding the right volume

The Praxis Core may ask you to make a calculation concerning the volume of a *rectangular prism*, which is a three-dimensional figure made up of six rectangles joined together by their sides. Each rectangle is a *face*. All of the angles of a rectangular prism are right angles, and all pairs of faces that are across from each other are parallel. A rectangular prism is basically a box.

Volume is a three-dimensional measure. It's the amount of space inside a three-dimensional figure. For rectangular prisms, the volume can be found by multiplying the base area by the height. The volume is more specifically *lwh* because *lw* is the base area. Any face can be considered a base, but the height must be the measure of a side that connects the face considered the base to the face across from it. You can measure volume in cubic units, or units to the third power. For example, if the length, width, and height of a rectangular prism are presented on the exam in cm, the volume will be presented in cm^3.

Rectangular prism volume = *lwh*

Rectangular prism

A *cube* is a type of rectangular prism in which all six faces are squares that are congruent to each other. For any cube, the length, width, and height are equal, so the volume is equal to the cube of a side measure.

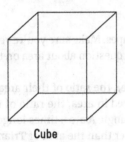

Cube

Combining Shapes

The Praxis Core exam may ask you about areas or volumes of figures created by joining figures of the types covered in the section "Knowing Common Shapes and Their Basic Properties," earlier in this chapter. In some situations, the combining of figures add area or volume, and in others, you may be asked for the area or volume of a shaded region that exists outside of another figure, in which cases, area or volume is reduced.

Coming together: Shapes that have joined without an invasion

When shapes join without one intruding on the other, you can find the total area or total volume of the figure they form together by adding the areas or volumes of the figures that form it.

For example, a triangle may share a side with a square, or a rectangular prism might share part of a base with another rectangular prism. Just add the areas or volumes of the figures to find the total area or volume.

The figure shown has a height of 14 cm and is composed of a square and a triangle that share a side. What is the area of the figure that they form?

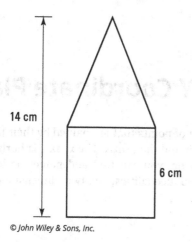

14 cm

6 cm

© John Wiley & Sons, Inc.

(A) 60 cm²

(B) 232 cm²

(C) 84 cm²

(D) 20 cm²

(E) 220 cm²

The correct answer is Choice (A). One side of the square is 6 cm, so all of its sides are 6 cm. That means the base of the triangle is also 6 cm. Because the height of the overall figure is 14 cm and a side of the square is 6 cm, the height of the triangle is 8 cm. The area of the square is s^2, or 36 cm², and the area of the triangle is $\frac{1}{2}bh$, or $\frac{1}{2}(6\text{ cm})(8\text{ cm})$, which is 24 cm². The sum of the areas of the square and the triangle is 36 cm² + 24 cm², or 60 cm². The other choices can result from incorrect calculations involving measures in the diagram.

Preparing for invasion: When one shape invades another

If a question on the Praxis Core exam involves a shape that exists within another one and you're asked to find the area or volume of the shape region that's outside of the intruding shape, subtract the area or volume of the intruding shape from that of the shape upon which it's intruding.

To find the area of the shaded region of the rectangle that follows, you can get the area of the rectangle and then subtract the area of the triangle. The remaining area is the area of the shaded region. The area of the rectangle is (12 mi)(5 mi), or 60 mi². The height of the triangle is the same as the width of the rectangle, so the area of the triangle is $\frac{1}{2}(12\text{ mi})(5\text{ mi})$, or 30 mi². 60 mi² − 30 mi² = 30 mi², so the remaining shaded region has an area of 30 mi².

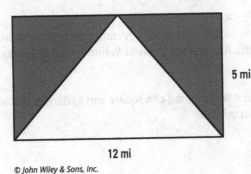

5 mi

12 mi

Knowing the Ways of the XY Coordinate Plane

The coordinate plane is a two-dimensional system of points that are named by their positions in regard to two intersecting number lines, the *x-axis* and the *y-axis*. The *x*-axis is horizontal, and the *y*-axis is vertical. Using the *xy* coordinate plane, you can find and name the locations of points, lines, parts of lines, graphs of equations and inequalities, and two-dimensional figures.

Naming coordinate pairs

Every point on the coordinate plane is named by two numbers, the first of which is an *x*-coordinate, which indicates a point's position along the *x*-axis, and the second of which is a *y*-coordinate, an indication of a point's position along the *y*-axis. The point of intersection of the *x* and *y* axes is called the *origin*, and its coordinates are (0, 0).

To determine the coordinates of a point, first locate the origin. Then determine which number on the *x*-axis the point is on (or directly above or below). That's the *x*-coordinate of the point. Then determine the number on the *y*-axis that the point is on or next to; that's the *y*-coordinate. To think about it another way, the number of horizontal units you move from the origin is the *x*-coordinate, and the number of vertical units you move from the origin is the *y*-coordinate. Several points and their corresponding ordered pairs are shown on the following coordinate plane.

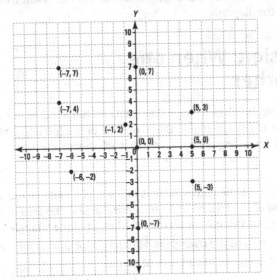

Up and right are positive directions on the coordinate plane, and down and left are negative directions.

Identifying linear equations and their graphs

Every line on the coordinate plane is the graph of a *linear equation*. The word *linear* is an adjective derived from the word *line*. Thus, a linear equation is the equation of a line. Every point on a line represents an ordered pair that makes a linear equation true. In other words, if the *x*-coordinate is put in for *x* in the equation and the *y* value is put in for *y*, the equation is true. The graph represents all the ordered pairs that make the equation work or that are solutions to the equation. So the variable values in each ordered pair make the sides of the equation equal. Every point on a line on the coordinate plane represents an ordered pair that is a solution to the equation. Also, every solution to the equation is represented on its linear graph.

Not all equations are linear. Equations that are linear have certain characteristics. The variables *x* and *y* are generally used in linear equations. Also, some linear equations have only one variable. At least one variable is necessary for the equation to be linear. Also, no variable has an exponent other than 1, which is generally understood and not shown. The variables are never exponents or multiplied by each other in linear equations. For example, $3x - 2y = 5$, $y = -7x + 4$, and $x = 12$ are all linear equations. The following graph represents $3x - 2y = 5$. Notice how every point on the graph represents an ordered pair that makes the equation true.

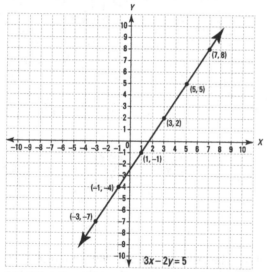

© John Wiley & Sons, Inc.

The *slope* of a line is an indication of the line's steepness and direction. It's a ratio of the rate of change in *y* to the rate of change in *x*. With any two points on a line on the coordinate plane, you can find the slope of the line. The change in *y* is the difference of the *y*-coordinates, and the change in *x* is the difference of the *x*-coordinates.

$$\text{slope} = \frac{y_2 - y_1}{x_2 - x_1}$$

In the formula for slope, (x_1, y_1) is one point and (x_2, y_2) represents the other point. Which point you call which doesn't matter, but make sure you are consistent. In other words, subtract in the same direction both times.

CHAPTER 6 Grasping Geometry Concepts   113

Another way to determine the slope of a line is to write the equation in slope-intercept form, $y = mx + b$, where m represents slope and b represents *y-intercept*, which is the y-coordinate of the point where the line intersects the y-axis. For example, the equation $2y - 10 = 8x$ can be rewritten as $y = 4x + 5$, which shows that the slope of the graph is 4 because it is the coefficient of x when the equation is in slope-intercept form. Just get y by itself on the left side and put the x term first on the right side. (If you need a review of how to isolate variables, flip back to Chapter 5.) Once the equation is in that form, the coefficient of x is the slope of the graph of the line.

When a linear equation is in slope-intercept form, the number that's added after the x term is the y-intercept. For the graph of $y = 4x + 5$, the y-intercept is 5. Because the point on the y-axis that's intersected by the line is at 5 on the y-axis, the point is (0, 5). Every point on the y-axis has an x-coordinate of 0 because there's no horizontal change from the origin. That's why you can always determine the y-intercept of a graph by figuring out what y equals when x is 0.

$$y = 4x + 5$$
$$y = 4(0) + 5$$
$$y = 0 + 5$$
$$y = 5$$

Similarly, you can find the x-intercept of a graph, or where the graph intersects the x-axis, by seeing what x is when y is 0. When y is 0, x equals $-\frac{5}{4}$, so the x-intercept of the graph of the equation is $-\frac{5}{4}$. That means the line intersects the y-axis at (0, 5) and intersects the x-axis at $(-\frac{5}{4}, 0)$.

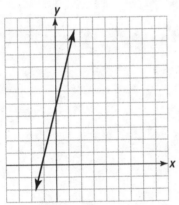

The graph of $y = 4x + 5$

If you know the slope and y-intercept of a line, you can use the slope-intercept formula to write the slope-intercept form of the equation of the line. For example, if the slope of a line is 7 and the y-intercept is 12, you can put 7 in for m and 12 in for b to form the equation.

$$y = mx + b$$
$$y = 7x + 12$$

If you don't know the slope and y-intercept of a line, you can still determine the equation of the line if you're given or can figure out two things: a point on the line and the slope of the line. If you have that information, you can use the point-slope formula to get an equation. The point-slope formula is this:

$$y - y_1 = m(x - x_1)$$

In the formula, m is the slope of the line, and x_1 and y_1 are the coordinates of a point on the line. That's all of the information you need to write an equation. Like with the slope-intercept formula, the name of the formula includes the two key pieces of information in it. The x and y without the subscript 1 next to them are the x and y that will end up in the final equation. You don't need to replace them with numbers. You may need to use the slope formula or other information to determine the slope of the line, but a point and the slope are the only two things you need to plug into the formula. Suppose the slope of a line is 8 and the line passes through (6, 11). You can use the point-slope formula to determine the equation of the line.

$$y - y_1 = m(x - x_1)$$
$$y - 11 = 8(x - 6)$$

The preceding equation is in the point-slope form. You can use that form of the equation to find the slope-intercept form.

$$y - 11 = 8(x - 6)$$
$$y - 11 + 11 = 8(x - 6) + 11$$
$$y = 8x - 48 + 11$$
$$y = 8x - 37$$

TIP

To determine whether a graph represents an equation, you can test the points on the graph. Every ordered pair represented by the graph must make the equation true. For a linear equation, testing two points is sufficient because only one line can pass through two points.

Using the distance and midpoint formulas

The distance between two points on the coordinate plane is given by the formula for distance: $\sqrt{(x_2 - x_1)^2 + (y_2 - y_1)^2}$. The formula is based on x and y changes and the Pythagorean theorem, which we cover in the section "Knowing what Pythagoras discovered," later in this chapter. The distance between the points (5, 7) and (9, 4) is

$$d = \sqrt{(5 - 9)^2 + (7 - 4)^2} = \sqrt{(-4)^2 + (3)^2}$$
$$d = \sqrt{25}$$
$$d = 5$$

The distance between the points is 5.

The *midpoint* between two points is the point halfway between them. Its x-coordinate is halfway between the two points' x-coordinates, and its y-coordinate is halfway between the two points' y-coordinates. The number that is halfway between two other numbers is the average of the two numbers. Thus, the midpoint between two points is the average of the x-coordinates followed by a comma, and then the average of the y-coordinates.

Midpoint: $\left(\dfrac{x_1 + x_2}{2}, \dfrac{y_1 + y_2}{2} \right)$

The midpoint between (−2, 7) and (4, 3) is

$$\left(\frac{-2 + 4}{2}, \frac{7 + 3}{2} \right) = \left(\frac{2}{2}, \frac{10}{2} \right)$$
$$= (1, 5)$$

REMEMBER

The distance between two points is a single number, but the midpoint between two points is a point, represented by an ordered pair.

Finding meaning in intersecting graphs

Because every point on the graph of an equation represents an ordered pair that's a solution to the equation, a point on two different equation graphs is a solution to both equations. Therefore, when two graphs intersect, their point of intersection represents a solution to both graphs' equations. The following graphs represent the equations $x + y = 7$ and $2x - y = 8$. They intersect at (5, 2), so (5, 2) is the solution to both equations. In other words, if you put 5 in for x and 2 in for y in either equation, you get an equation that's true.

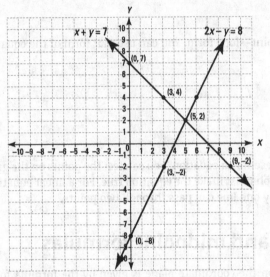

© John Wiley & Sons, Inc.

Transforming coordinate plane figures

Points on the coordinate plane can be the vertices of figures such as triangles and quadrilaterals. (You can flip back to the section "Getting the right angles on angles," for the lowdown on vertices.)

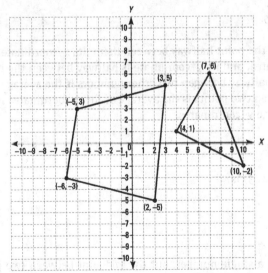

© John Wiley & Sons, Inc.

The figures can be altered in various ways by changing the locations of their vertices. Such changes are called *transformations*. Four major types of transformations can be covered on the Praxis Core exam. One type of transformation is a *translation*, which involves simply moving the figure from one location to another. Translating a figure involves sliding it a number of units horizontally and a number of units vertically. The number can, of course, be 0 for one of the changes.

In the following graph, a triangle has vertices $(-2, -3)$, $(0, 0)$, and $(4, -5)$. If it is translated 3 units left and 2 units up, 3 is subtracted from each x-coordinate and 2 is added to each y-coordinate to get the coordinates of the vertices of the new triangle. Thus, the new vertex coordinates are $(-5, -1)$, $(-3, 2)$, and $(1, -3)$.

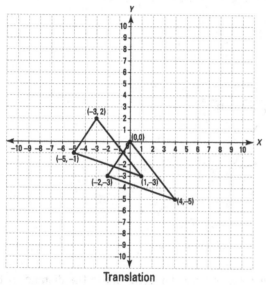

Translation

Reflections involve flipping figures over lines and creating new images that are like mirror reflections. To reflect a figure over the x-axis, change the y-coordinates of its points to their opposites. If the figure is a polygon, changing the vertices is enough. To reflect a figure over the y-axis, change the x-coordinates of the points to their opposites to get the new points. The following graph shows a reflection of a quadrilateral over the y-axis.

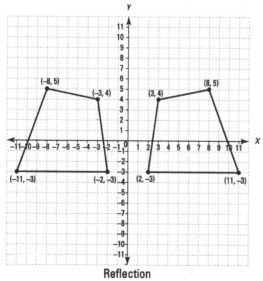

Reflection

Dilations are simply changes in the sizes of figures. The origin is usually the *center of dilation*, the point from which distances in a dilation are measured. Dilating a figure with the origin as the center of dilation is to dilate the figure *about the origin*. To dilate a figure about the origin by a certain scale factor, multiply both coordinates of the points by that number. The triangle in the graph that follows is dilated by a scale factor of 3, which makes each side of the resulting triangle 3 times longer than its corresponding side in the original triangle. This is achieved by multiplying all of the original triangle's vertex coordinates by 3 to get the new coordinates.

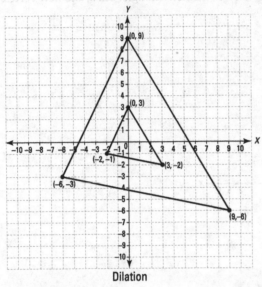

Dilation

Rotations involve the moving of figures along circular paths while the distance between every point and the center of the circular path stays the same. The types of rotations you are likely to see on the Praxis Core exam are 180° and 90° counterclockwise around the origin. To rotate a figure 180° around the origin, get the opposite of each coordinate. Those will be the new coordinates. To rotate 90° counterclockwise around the origin (or "about the origin"), switch the coordinates of each point and get the opposite of the resulting *x*-coordinate. In the following figure, a line segment is rotated 90° counterclockwise and 180° around the origin.

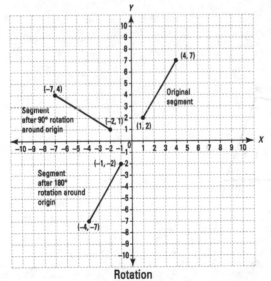

Rotation

To rotate a figure 90° clockwise around the origin, switch the coordinates of each point and get the opposite of each new y-coordinate. Making such determinations with the vertices or the other key points will be enough to graph the new figures.

Touching on Right Triangles

You can expect to see some questions about right triangles on the Praxis Core exam. A *right triangle* is a triangle that contains one right angle. A triangle can have no more than one right angle because the sum of the angles is 180°, and two right angles meet that number, not allowing for a third angle. By the same logic, an *obtuse triangle*, a triangle that has an angle with a measure greater than 90 degrees and less than 180 degrees, can't have a right angle and therefore can't be a right triangle. An *acute triangle* has three *acute* angles, angles that have measures between 0 and 90 degrees, so it's automatically not a right triangle.

The two sides of a right triangle that form the right angle are the *legs*, and the side across from the right angle is the *hypotenuse*.

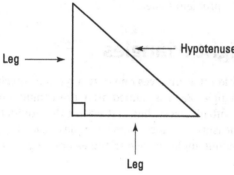

© John Wiley & Sons, Inc.

Knowing what Pythagoras discovered

Pythagoras was a Greek philosopher and mathematician who discovered a principle that became known as the Pythagorean theorem, which states that the sum of the squares of the two leg measures of a right triangle is equal to the square of the measure of the hypotenuse. The theorem is often represented by the equation $a^2 + b^2 = c^2$, where a and b are the measures of the legs of a right triangle and c is the measure of the hypotenuse.

Questions on the Praxis Core exam can ask for the measure of the hypotenuse when both leg measures are given, but they can also involve the measures of the hypotenuse and one leg being given when you are asked for the measure of the other leg. To determine the answer to any such question, use the formula $a^2 + b^2 = c^2$, fill in the known values, and solve for the unknown value. Really, that's how all formulas should be used.

EXAMPLE

If a leg of a right triangle is 3 cm and the hypotenuse is 5 cm, what is the measure of the other leg?

(A) 16 cm

(B) 8 cm

(C) 2 cm

(D) 4 cm

(E) 15 cm

The correct answer is Choice (D). Take the information you know, plug it into the formula, and solve for the information the question asks for:

$$a^2 + b^2 = c^2$$
$$3^2 + b^2 = 5^2$$
$$9 + b^2 = 25$$
$$b^2 = 16$$
$$b = 4 \text{ cm}$$

TIP

If a geometric figure is described but not illustrated, draw the figure so that you have a visual representation. That will make working the problem easier.

Working with special right triangles

The Praxis Core exam may ask you a question that involves one of two types of special right triangles — a 45-45-90 or a 30-60-90 triangle. Each is named after the combination of angle degree measures. (They both sound like football cheers, but that wasn't the original idea.) Both types have special rules concerning side measures because every example of each type of triangle is similar. Recall that when the corresponding angles of two triangles are *congruent* (identical), the triangles are *similar* (the same shape).

All 45-45-90 triangles are isosceles, which means they have two congruent sides. A 60-60-60 triangle is *equilateral*, which means all three of its sides are congruent. All 45-45-90 triangles are similar, all 30-60-90 triangles are similar, and all 60-60-60 triangles are similar. However, 60-60-60 triangles aren't right triangles. A right triangle has one 90° angle.

For every 45-45-90 triangle, the two legs are congruent because the angles opposite them are congruent. The hypotenuse is always $\sqrt{2}$ times the measure of a leg.

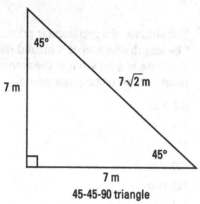

45-45-90 triangle

© John Wiley & Sons, Inc.

For every 30-60-90 triangle, the hypotenuse measure is twice that of the shorter leg (which is opposite the 30° angle), and the longer leg is $\sqrt{3}$ times the measure of the shorter leg.

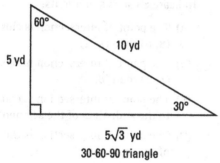

30-60-90 triangle

© John Wiley & Sons, Inc.

Practice Questions about Geometry

These practice questions are similar to the geometry questions that you'll encounter on the Praxis.

1. The hypotenuse of a 30-60-90 triangle is 12 meters. What is the measure of the longer leg?

   (A) $6\sqrt{3}$ meters

   (B) 24 meters

   (C) $6\sqrt{2}$ meters

   (D) 6 meters

   (E) $12\sqrt{2}$ meters

2. In the diagram, what is the value of x?

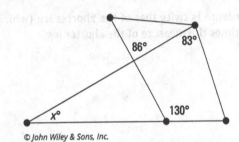

© John Wiley & Sons, Inc.

   (A) 86

   (B) 130

   (C) 24

   (D) 44

   (E) 50

3. What is the circumference of a circle that has an area of 25π cm²?

   (A) 5 cm

   (B) 12.5 cm

   (C) 12.5π cm

   (D) 10π cm

   (E) 10 cm

4. The volume of a rectangular prism is 60 m³. The length of a base is 5 m, and the width of that base is 4 m. What is the accompanying height of the rectangular prism?

   (A) 1 m

   (B) 3 m

   (C) 5 m

   (D) 7 m

   (E) 11 m

5. A segment on the coordinate plane has endpoints (8, 6) and (4, 2). If a line intersects the segment at (6, 4), which of the following statements is true?

   Indicate **all** such statements.

   (A) The point of intersection is closer to (8, 6) than (4, 2).

   (B) The point of intersection is closer to (4, 2) than (8, 6).

   (C) The point of intersection is equally close to the endpoints of the segment.

   (D) The point of intersection is the midpoint of the segment.

   (E) The proximity of the point of intersection to the endpoints of the segment cannot be determined.

Answers and Explanations

Use this answer key to score the practice geometry questions in this chapter.

1. **A. $6\sqrt{3}$ meters.** The hypotenuse is 12, and the shorter leg is half that measure, or 6. The longer leg is the shorter leg measure times $\sqrt{3}$, so the measure of the longer leg is $6\sqrt{3}$. Choices (C) and (E) involve the use of $\sqrt{2}$, which is part of a formula for the measure of the hypotenuse of a 45-45-90 triangle. Be careful. Choices (B) and (D) can result from careless errors involving the given information.

2. **D. 44.** The triangle that has an angle measure of $x°$ has an angle that's a vertical angle to an 86° angle, and vertical angles are congruent. The third angle of the same triangle is supplementary to a 130° angle because they form a linear pair, so that third angle is 50°. The sum of 86 and 50 is 136. The interior angle sum of a triangle is 180°, and $180° - 136° = 44°$. Therefore, x is 44. The other choices can result from using false principles involving the measurements in the diagram.

3. **D. 10π cm.** To solve this problem, you must use what you know to find the value of the radius, which is needed for the circumference formula. Because the area of a circle is πr^2, $r^2 = 25$. That means $r = 5$. The circumference of a circle is $2\pi r$. So $2\pi(5) = 10\pi$. The other choices can result from misuse of operations involved in the necessary steps.

4. **B. 3 m.** The volume of a rectangular prism is equal to a base area times the height that goes with the given base. In short, the volume is length $\times$ width $\times$ height, or lwh. For this problem, l and w are given. You can plug their values into the formula and solve for the unknown, h.

$$V = lwh$$
$$60 = (5)(4)h$$
$$60 = 20h$$
$$\frac{60}{20} = \frac{20h}{20}$$
$$3 = h$$
$$h = 3$$

The height is 3 m.

5. **C and D. (C) The point of intersection is equally close to the endpoints of the segment, (D) The point of intersection is the midpoint of the segment.** The best place to start is getting the midpoint between the endpoints of the segment. That point is the midpoint of the segment. Determining it will help you figure out where the point of intersection is in relation to the endpoints of the segment. The midpoint between two points is $\left(\frac{x_1 + x_2}{2}, \frac{y_1 + y_2}{2} \right)$, or the average of the x-coordinates and the average of the y-coordinates separated by a comma. The average of 8 and 4 is 6, and the average of 6 and 2 is 4, so the midpoint is (6, 4). That's also the point of intersection, so the point of intersection is the midpoint of the segment and is therefore equally close to the endpoints of the segment.

IN THIS CHAPTER

» Creating and analyzing visual representations of data

» Determining the probability of an event

» Writing numbers in scientific notation

» Trying out some practice questions and reviewing the answers

Chapter 7

Statistics and Probability

The probability of you becoming a statistician immediately after you finish this chapter is about one out of infinity; meaning it's not very likely to happen. *Statistics* is the study of simple, real-life facts and figures — such as the number of students who passed or failed a math quiz or the number of people who access Facebook on their cellphone versus their computer. *Statistical data* can be thought of as data that's analyzed, averaged, and displayed in tables and graphs.

The review in this chapter also focuses on *probability*, which deals with how likely something is to happen. So, we can easily say that you're likely to be asked to solve probability problems on the Praxis Core exam, given that we know that there are about 18 questions on the exam that deal with statistics and probability.

Representing Data

It's time to plan a date with a collection of a lot of pieces of information called *data*. On your date, you'll find that data are honest, true-life, and based on facts of everyday life. A collection of data is known as a *data set*.

While you get familiar with data, make a point of looking for patterns within the data. Looking for patterns allows you to predict what new data may come later on and then use that prediction to make important real-life decisions.

For the Praxis Core exam, you need to become familiar with many ways to display or represent your data. Using lists, tables, graphs, charts, and plots to represent data is a surefire way to make sure you aren't tricked by the data. These methods of organizing data can also help you see patterns more readily. In the sections that follow, you can become skilled at dissecting and interpreting different types of data representations.

Tables

When you have gobs of data about a particular subject, you can sort, analyze, and display your data in a table. Tables work only if you have at least two sets of data to be organized into columns and rows.

REMEMBER

When working with tables, make sure to pay attention to the title of the table; it helps you understand what data to analyze. Next, notice the column and row titles.

In the following table, the data for the types of flowers and the number of each type of plant in Mary's flower bed are listed. Make sure to read your question carefully and dissect the data accordingly.

EXAMPLE

Which ratio compares the number of rose plants to the number of daffodil plants?

Mary's Flower Bed

Type of Flower	Number of Plants
Roses	8
Tulips	10
Daffodils	12
Total	30

© John Wiley & Sons, Inc.

(A) 3:2

(B) 2:3

(C) 4:3

(D) 5:6

(E) 3:4

The correct answer is Choice (B). The ratio of roses to daffodils is 8:12; when simplified, the ratio is 2:3. The Praxis Core exam will expect answers in the simplest form.

Bar graphs and line graphs

A bar graph uses the length of vertical or horizontal bars to represent numbers and compare data. Bar graphs are good to use when your data is in categories. Bar graphs must contain a title, axis labels for the horizontal and vertical axes, scales, and bars that represent numbers.

The following bar graph shows the number of canned goods collected by homerooms at Cardozo Middle School.

Canned Goods Collections by Homeroom

[Bar graph with y-axis "Number of Canned Goods Collected" scaled 0 to 70, and x-axis homerooms: Jackson, Thomas, Lewis, Davis, Reed, Smith, Daniels, Young]

© John Wiley & Sons, Inc.

Mr. Smith's homeroom collected more cans than how many other homerooms?

(A) 3

(B) 4

(C) 5

(D) 6

(E) 7

The correct answer is Choice (A). Use the graph to compare the number of cans collected by each homeroom. According to the lengths of the vertical bars, Mr. Smith's homeroom collected more cans than Mr. Lewis's, Mr. Davis's, and Mrs. Reed's classes.

Line graphs are graphs that show data that's connected in some way over a period of time. Suppose you're preparing for a statistics test and each day you take a short online quiz to see how you're progressing. These are the results:

Day 1	30 percent
Day 2	20 percent
Day 3	50 percent
Day 4	60 percent
Day 5	80 percent

After you've created a table from your results, display them in a line graph. You can then decide, based on your progress on the practice quizzes, how likely you are to pass your statistics test. What trends do you see in the following graph?

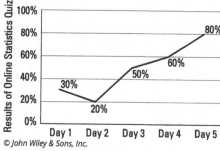

© John Wiley & Sons, Inc.

The graph indicates that while the days of practicing the online quizzes increase, your score increases; so you will, more than likely, pass your statistics test.

Pie charts

Are you ready for a slice of pie? Pie charts are also known as *circle graphs*. These graphs focus on a whole set of data that's divided into parts. Each category represented in a pie chart is represented by a part, called a *sector*, of the interior of the circle. The portion of the circle interior that a category's sector takes up is part of what represents the portion of the whole (population, number of items sold, and so on) that the category makes up. For example, if a pie chart represents categories of county government spending and 10 percent of the county government spending goes to road maintenance, the category of road maintenance would be labeled in a sector that takes up 10 percent of the interior of the circle. The sector would also have "10%" presented in it, and the sector would be labeled with "Road Maintenance."

The following table shows the conversion of raw data to information that can be used to create a pie chart. The resulting pie chart is shown in the example question.

Favorite Fruit of 170 People					
Type of Fruit	Number	Fraction	Decimal	Percent	Degrees
Apples	45	$\frac{45}{170}$	0.26	26%	95
Bananas	20	$\frac{20}{170}$	0.12	12%	42
Strawberries	50	$\frac{50}{170}$	0.29	29%	106
Peaches	55	$\frac{55}{170}$	0.32	32%	116
Total	170	$\frac{170}{170}$	0.99*	99%*	360

*Due to rounding, amounts total less than 100 percent.

© John Wiley & Sons, Inc.

REMEMBER When reading a pie chart, the larger the value, the larger the piece of pie!

Use this graph to answer the following questions.

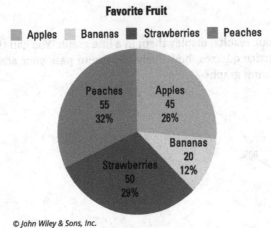

Favorite Fruit

■ Apples   ■ Bananas   ■ Strawberries   ■ Peaches

© John Wiley & Sons, Inc.

EXAMPLE What are the two favorite fruits of the people surveyed?

(A) Strawberries and apples

(B) Peaches and strawberries

(C) Peaches and apples

(D) Strawberries and bananas

(E) Peaches and bananas

The correct answer is Choice (B) Peaches and strawberries. Out of 170 people, 55 chose peaches. When $\frac{55}{170}$ is converted to a decimal and rounded to the nearest hundredth, it becomes 0.32 or 32 percent. Out of the same 170 people, 50 chose strawberries. When $\frac{50}{170}$ is converted to a decimal, it becomes 0.29, or 29 percent. These are the two largest pieces of the pie.

EXAMPLE

What percentage of the people chose strawberries or bananas?

(A) 41%

(B) 47%

(C) 53%

(D) 59%

(E) 61%

The correct answer is Choice (A) 41%. Out of 170 people, 50 chose strawberries. When $\frac{50}{170}$ is converted to a decimal, it becomes 0.29 or 29 percent. Out of the same 170 people, 20 chose bananas. When $\frac{20}{170}$ is converted to a decimal, it becomes 0.12, or 12 percent. Adding these percentages together, 29% + 12% = 41%.

Stem-and-leaf plots

A stem-and-leaf plot blossoms into a useful graph when analyzed properly. You usually use this type of graph when you have large amounts of data to analyze. You can analyze data sets such as classroom test results or scores of the basketball team using a stem-and-leaf plot.

Based on place value, each value in your data set is divided into a stem and leaf. What each stem and leaf represents is indicated by a key. Draw a vertical line to separate the stem from the leaf. The leaf is always the last digit in the number. The stem represents all other digits to the left of the leaf. To divide 105 into stem-and-leaf format, you draw a line to separate the stem from the leaf, 10|5, which indicates a stem of 10 and a leaf of 5.

Say you have the following numbers:

50, 65, 65, 60, 50, 50, 55, 70, 55

The first step is to arrange your data in least-to-greatest order, as follows:

50, 50, 50, 55, 55, 60, 65, 65, 70

Now arrange these numbers vertically in a table:

Math Test Results

Stem	Leaf
5	0 0 0 5 5
6	0 5 5
7	0

Key: 5|0 means 50

This arrangement allows you to quickly identify your stems. Your stems in the data set are 5, 6, and 7. You have five data values in the list in the 50s: 50, 50, 50, 55, and 55. The leaves that go along with the 5 stem are 0, 0, 0, 5, and 5. You have three data values in the 60s: 60, 65, and 65. The leaves that go with the 6 stem are 0, 5, and 5. Finally, you have one leaf of 0 to accompany the stem of 7, so you have one data value of 70.

When using a stem-and-leaf plot, you can quickly identify the least and greatest values in the data set (50 and 70), calculate the range ($70 - 50 = 20$), and calculate the *median*, meaning the middle number (55).

EXAMPLE

The following data show the number of people visiting a particular frozen yogurt shop per hour across a 12-hour day.

Hourly customers: 4, 17, 22, 31, 39, 40, 25, 43, 35, 40, 38, 13.

When this data is arranged in a stem-and-leaf plot, you get the following diagram. Use it to answer the question that follows.

Hourly Customers

Stem	Leaf
0	4
1	3 7
2	2 5
3	1 5 8 9
4	0 0 3

Key: 4|0 means 40

What was the largest number of people who entered the shop during an hour?

The correct answer is 43. Based on the diagram, the highest stem is 4 and the highest leaf in that stem is 3.

Box-and-whisker plots

Box-and-whisker plots, also known as *box plots*, show different parts of a data set, using a line of numbers that are in order from least to greatest.

A box-and-whisker plot allows you to divide your data into four parts using *quartiles*. The *median*, also called the *middle quartile* or *second quartile*, divides the data into a lower set and an upper set (for more on finding the median, see the section "Marking the middle with the median," later in this chapter). The median of the lower set is *the lower quartile* or *first quartile*. The median of the upper set is the *upper quartile* or *third quartile*. Your data set will contain the following five parts:

>> **The least value:** The smallest value (number) in the data set.

>> **The lower quartile:** The median of the lower set of the data set.

>> **The median:** The second (middle) quartile. This divides the data into a lower set and an upper set. The median is the number in the center of the data set when the data is in numerical order (or the average of the two numbers in the center if there are an even number of numbers).

>> **The upper quartile:** The median of the upper set of the data set.

>> **The greatest value:** The largest value in the data set.

The following diagram shows how data is dissected by using a box-and-whisker plot. To create a box-and-whisker plot, follow the diagram below.

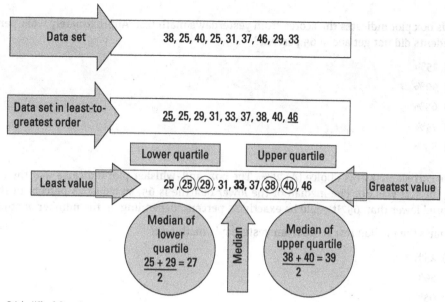

© John Wiley & Sons, Inc.

The diagram begins with the data set. The data set needs to first be put in least-to-greatest order. The next step is to find the median, which is either a single middle number or an average of two middle numbers. The median of the entire set of data (called the *second quartile or middle quartile*, abbreviated Q_2) divides the data set into the lower set and higher set. You must then find the median of the lower set. That's the *lower quartile* (also called the *first quartile*, abbreviated Q_1). You must also find the median of the upper set. That median is the *upper quartile* (also called *the third quartile*, abbreviated Q_3). If you have to get the average of two numbers to find Q_2, those two numbers are still included in the sets of numbers used to determine Q_1 and Q_3. They are not to be discarded from consideration just because they were used in finding Q_2. The word *quartile* can also be used to refer to a division of numbers marked off by Q_1, Q_2, and Q_3.

After dissecting the data into the five values, graph the five values on a number line. Draw a box from Q_1 to $Q3$. Draw a vertical line inside the box at Q_2. The lines connecting the least and greatest values to the box are called the *whiskers*.

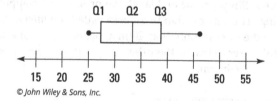

© John Wiley & Sons, Inc.

EXAMPLE

Use the following graph to answer the following questions.

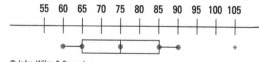

© John Wiley & Sons, Inc.

This box plot indicates the scores from yesterday's math test. Approximately what percent of the students did not get above 65 percent?

(A) 25%

(B) 50%

(C) 65%

(D) 75%

(E) 85%

The correct answer is Choice (A) 25%. The box-and-whisker plot indicates that the lowest score on the test was 60. The median of the lower quartile is 65, so about 25 percent of the students scored lower than 65. It could be exactly 25 percent, depending on the number of students.

What's the median test score from yesterday's math test?

(A) 25%

(B) 50%

(C) 65%

(D) 75%

(E) 85%

The correct answer is Choice (D) 75%. The median of the box-and-whisker plot is indicated by a line drawn through the center of the box. The value graphed at this point is 75.

The *interquartile range* (IQR) of a set of data is the numerical distance from the first quartile (Q_1) to the third quartile (Q_3). You can find the interquartile range by subtracting Q_1 from Q_3. For the set of data in the preceding example, the interquartile range is 20.

$$Q_3 - Q_1 = 85 - 65$$
$$= 20$$

Venn diagrams

"Venn" you need to picture relationships between different groups of things, use a Venn diagram. A *Venn diagram* is an illustration in which individual data sets are represented by using basic geometrical shapes, such as ovals or circles. Simply draw and label two or more overlapping shapes to represent the sets you're comparing. The sets overlap in an area called the *intersection*. When an item is listed in both sets, it goes in the intersection. If an item appears in only one set, it falls into the part of the shape that doesn't intersect with the other shape. If an item doesn't fit in either set, it falls outside the shapes you've drawn.

Use the following graph to answer the following questions.

EXAMPLE

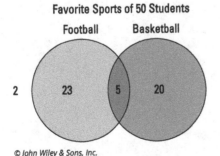

Favorite Sports of 50 Students

© *John Wiley & Sons, Inc.*

Football is the only favorite sport of how many students in the Venn diagram?

(A) 2

(B) 5

(C) 23

(D) 25

(E) 48

The correct answer is Choice (C) 23. In the Venn diagram, 23 students picked football as their favorite sport. This is the only portion of the diagram reserved for football *only*.

How many students chose both football and basketball as their favorite sports?

(A) 2

(B) 5

(C) 23

(D) 25

(E) 48

The correct answer is Choice (B) 5. Five students in the Venn diagram picked football and basketball. This is the portion of the diagram that football and basketball have in common.

How many students did not choose football or basketball?

(A) 2

(B) 5

(C) 23

(D) 25

(E) 48

The correct answer is Choice (A) 2. There are two students who did not fall inside the Venn diagram's circles; therefore, they chose neither football nor basketball.

Scrambling around scatter plots

If you want to determine the strength of your relationship, use a scatter plot. Scatter plots are graphical representations of two variables that help determine whether a positive, a negative, or no correlation exists between those variables. A *correlation* is a relationship between two variables in which, while one increases or decreases, the other one tends to increase or decrease. There's a correlation between time studying and test scores, for example. While time studying increases, test scores tend to increase.

Data from two sets are plotted in scatter plots as ordered pairs (x, y). You can draw three conclusions from scatter plots:

>> If the coordinates are close to forming a straight line that rises up from left to right, then a positive relationship or correlation exists.

>> If the coordinates are close to forming a straight line (line of best fit) with one variable increasing while the other decreases, then a negative relationship or correlation exists.

>> If the coordinates don't come close to forming a line and are all over the place, then *no relationship or correlation exists!* Hence, the name "scatter plot."

This figure shows the three types of correlations.

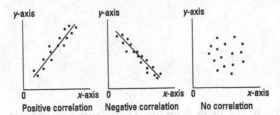

REMEMBER

Make sure that you give your plot a title and label your axes when you create a scatter plot.

Correlation alone doesn't prove causation. If a variable tends to increase while another variable increases, for example, it doesn't mean that the tendency is caused by the other variable. The number of mud puddles tends to become greater when the occurrence of lightning increases. Does an increase in the occurrence of lightning cause the number of mud puddles to get higher? Do the additions of mud puddles cause more lightning? The correlation between the two doesn't prove that one causes the other, and in fact, neither causes the other. Over time, an increase in rain causes both.

Also, even when a change in one variable does cause a change in another, that alone doesn't prove which variable change is causing which. Studies have shown that changes in the closeness of the moon cause shifting of the tides, but the correlation by itself isn't the proof. If correlation worked that way, we could just as easily conclude that the shifting of the tides causes major changes in the closeness of the moon.

Loitering around line plots

If you want to see your *mode* (the value that occurs the most) pop up quickly, use a line plot. A line plot, also known as a dot plot, allows you to identify the range, mode, and outliers in your data set. Follow these simple steps:

1. Put your data in order from least to greatest.

2. Arrange your data on a number line.

3. Mark each value in the data set with an *x* or a dot.

EXAMPLE

Using the following line plot, determine the mode of the data set.

Mrs. Tates' test scores: 50, 50, 60, 90, 90, 50, 70, 90, 80, 90

Line Plot of Mrs. Tates' Test Scores

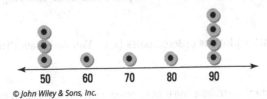

(A) 50

(B) 60

(C) 70

(D) 80

(E) 90

The correct answer is Choice (E) 90. The score of 90 appears in the data set the most.

Analyzing Data

After you create a visual representation of your data (which we talk about in the section "Representing Data," earlier in this chapter), the next phase is to analyze and interpret the data by making comparisons; calculating the mean, median, and mode; determining the range; and finding out what variables affect your data set. After you analyze, interpret, and display these pieces of information, you can use them to make important decisions. The following sections prepare you to analyze data sets in a variety of ways.

Combing through comparisons

When you're working data analysis problems on the Praxis Core exam, it's wise to comb your data set, looking for the smallest and largest values to calculate the range. Then you need to find the mean, median, or mode — which are all known as measures of central tendency — of the data set. A *measure of central tendency* tells you where the middle of a data set lies. You have to be clear on which measure is appropriate for the data you have. Then you can use your data analysis to make important, real-life decisions.

Homing in on the range

When preparing for the Praxis Core exam, you need to know how to calculate the range of a data set. The *range* is the difference between the largest (maximum) and smallest (minimum) values in your data set. If your range is small, most values in the data set are alike; however, if you have a large range, the values in the data set are very different from each other. Whether you have 14 or 14,000 pieces of data in your set, simply take the difference between the largest and smallest values in the data set to find the range.

EXAMPLE

Brit went bowling with her classmates. She bowled five games with the following scores: 193, 190, 149, 146, and 183. What is the range of her bowling scores?

(A) 3

(B) 44

(C) 46

(D) 47

(E) 149

The correct answer is Choice (D) 47. The range is calculated by subtracting the smallest number in the data set from the largest number in the data set: $193 - 146 = 47$.

Measuring arithmetic mean, median, or mode

Who do you think is the most popular in the measures of central tendency clique: mean, median, or mode? The measures of central tendency are all types of centers of data sets. When preparing for the Praxis Core exam, you need to be able to decide a data set's central-tendency value that best describes the entire data set.

Mastering the mean

For a data set that has no high or low numbers that stand out as abnormally high or low compared to the rest of the data set, the *mean*, also known as the *average*, is the most popular measure of central tendency. To find the mean of a set of values, use the following formula:

$$\frac{\text{Sum of all values in the data set}}{\text{Number of values in the data set}}$$

Marking the middle with the median

When the data set has any values much higher or lower than the others, the *median* (the middle value in the sequential list of values) is the most popular measure of central tendency. When finding the median of a data set, you must first ensure that the data is in order from least to greatest. Use the cross-out method to mark out values until you get to the center. If you're left with one number, that's your median. If two values are left in the center, take the average of them.

Median: ~~45, 65, 65,~~ 70, 75, ~~77, 80, 250~~

$$\frac{70+75}{2} = \frac{145}{2}$$
$$= 72.5$$

Making the most of the mode

When your data set has many instances of the same data value and also has a small range, then the *mode* (the value that appears most often) may win as the most popular value. In the following data set, the mode is 23 because it appears most often.

15, 20, **23, 23, 23,** 40

EXAMPLE

The following table contains Kelsey's FaceTime usage for one week (in minutes).

Amount of Daily Face Time Usage for 1 Week (in minutes)						
Sun	Mon	Tue	Wed	Thur	Fri	Sat
65	250	75	65	45	77	80

© John Wiley & Sons, Inc.

Find the mean, median, and mode of the data set. Write your answers in the boxes provided. Which measure best describes the amount of time spent on FaceTime?

(A) Mean

(B) Median

(C) Mode

The mean (93.86 when rounded to the nearest hundredth) and mode (65) are close to only a few data points; the median (75) is close to most data points, so the best measure of central tendency for this data set is the median. You can say that Kelsey spends about 75 minutes per day on FaceTime.

Here's how to calculate each of the three measures of central tendency:

» Mean = $45 + 65 + 65 + 75 + 77 + 80 + 250 = 657$; $657 \div 7 \approx 93.86$

» Median = $\cancel{45}, \cancel{65}, 65, 75, 77, \cancel{80}, \cancel{250} = 75$

» Mode = 65 (because it appears most frequently in this set of data)

Looking for outliers

When you work with data analysis, variables often affect the data. Did you ever have a test score that was exceedingly better or worse than your other scores? In statistics, this piece of data is known as the *outlier*, which drifts way out at the end of a data set. Outliers can affect how your data is interpreted.

You can tell whether your data set has outliers by putting your numbers in least to greatest (ascending) order. Check each number to see whether it's much less or much greater than the number following or preceding it.

The following data set contains the math test scores for a student. Plot the data set on a line plot.

Math test scores: 40, 45, 50, 55, 90

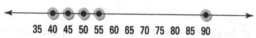

35 40 45 50 55 60 65 70 75 80 85 90

© John Wiley & Sons, Inc.

After you see the test data displayed on a line plot, you can see that 90 is a loner, an *outlier*, in the data set. To decide what best measure of central tendency to use, calculate the mean, median, and mode of the data set.

The most technical definition of *outlier*, a definition you most likely won't need to deal with on the Praxis Core exam, involves specific calculations. By that definition, an *outlier* is a data element that's more than 1.5 interquartile ranges less than Q_1 or greater than Q_3.

Measuring the spread of data

To analyze how spread out the items in a set of data are, you can find the variance of the set. The *variance* is the average of the squares of the differences from the mean. In other words, you can find the variance by finding the mean, calculating each element's distance (positive or negative) from the mean, squaring each distance (the result of which is positive even if the distance that is squared is negative), and then determining the average (or mean) of those squares. Take the square root of the variance (that average you just calculated) to get the *standard deviation* of the set of data. In summary, the *variance* is the average of the squares of the distances from the mean, and the *standard deviation* is the square root of the variance.

EXAMPLE

The following table shows the scores of five participants in a skydiving acrobatics competition.

Participant	Score
Frederick	8
Bernard	10
Wilma	9
Dean	10
Bethany	8

What's the standard deviation, rounded to the nearest hundredth, of the set of data?

(A) 0.89

(B) 0.91

(C) 2.46

(D) 4.01

(E) 7.28

The correct answer is Choice (A).

To determine the standard deviation of the data, first find the mean.

$$\frac{8+10+9+10+8}{5}=\frac{45}{5}$$
$$=9$$

The mean is 9. Now, subtract every item in the data set from the mean of the data (9).

$$9-8=1$$
$$9-10=-1$$
$$9-9=0$$
$$9-10=-1$$
$$9-8=1$$

Next, find the mean of the squares of those differences.

$$\frac{1^2+(-1)^2+0^2+(-1)^2+1^2}{5}=\frac{1+1+0+1+1}{5}$$
$$=\frac{4}{5}$$
$$=0.8$$

The variance is 0.8. The standard deviation is the square root of the variance, so it's the square root of 0.8. The square root of 0.8, rounded to the nearest hundredth, is 0.89.

Scrutinizing samples for data analysis

What if you were collecting data about the favorite food of middle-school students? It would be difficult to interview every student in the middle-school group or population, so you'd take a *sample*, which is a depiction of the entire group.

The sample you choose must represent the whole group or population. You wouldn't collect data from only the football team or the math classes. An ideal sample would be to randomly select five students from each class period or to randomly select students from the school directory. From the sample, you can infer data about the entire population. If 10 kids out of 100 like pizza for lunch, then about 100 kids out of 1,000 probably like pizza for lunch, too.

A *random sample* is a select group that represents the entire population. If you're studying middle-school students, you can't just survey your sibling's middle-school friends. You need to randomly select students from the middle-school directory — including all ages and all grades taught at the school.

Interpreting linear models

You can use data in a table to make a graph. The graph and the table both present the same data but in different ways. If the graph of the values in a table forms a line when graphed, then it can be called a *linear function*. First graph the data points, and then connect the points with a line. If you can connect them with a line, the relationship is linear.

Linear models simply use patterns to explore relationships. Say that the honor society is selling mugs as a fundraiser. The daily sales and income are recorded in a table. The mugs sell for $10 each.

First, identify your input (x) and output (y) variables. The income or money you make depends on how many mugs are sold, so the number of mugs you sell (x) will determine how much money you make at $10 a mug ($y = 10x$). Next, record the mug sales in a table.

Number of Mugs Sold (x)	Income (10x)
1	10
5	50
10	100
30	300

Then, plot your table values as a line graph. Now you're ready to analyze your data. Make sure you study the shape of the following graph; use your finger to trace the x and y values. You can say that the number of mugs sold (x) determines the income (y), or $\$10x = y$. The more mugs sold, the more income made. The table shows that if you sell one mug, you'll make $10; if you sell 10 mugs, you'll make $100.

© John Wiley & Sons, Inc.

Calculating Probability

The review in this section focuses on probability of an event, also known as P (event), which deals with how likely something is to occur. You can record the probability of an event as a fraction, decimal, or percent.

A chance action, such as tossing a number cube, is also called an *experiment*. Each observation of the experiment is called a *trial*, and what happens at the end of the trial is the *outcome*. One or more outcomes are called *events*.

When you throw a single die, there are six possible outcomes: 1, 2, 3, 4, 5, or 6. The probability of any one of them occurring is 1/6.

Determining the likelihood of an event

When you throw a single die, there are six sides and six possible outcomes. The following table indicates that the even outcomes are half and the not-even outcomes are half; therefore, the likelihood of rolling an even number is as likely to happen as not — you have a 3/6 (read, three in six) or 50-50 chance.

Even	Not Even
2, 4, 6	1, 3, 5

What's the likelihood that you'll roll a 6 on the single die? When a single die is rolled, either a 6 will be rolled or it won't be rolled. There is only one 6 on the single die, so the likelihood that it will be rolled is 1 out of 6.

Using complements

Are you ready for a complement? The *complement* of an event is the set of all outcomes that aren't the event itself. Analyze the situation that's occurring and find your total possible outcomes.

For example, you have 16 total marbles in a bag, and the marbles are different colors. Write each color as a fraction, decimal, or percent of the total number.

The bag contains nine blue marbles, four red marbles, two green marbles, and one black marble. The probability of randomly picking a blue marble is 9/16. What's the probability of not drawing a blue marble? The probability of not picking a blue marble would be 7/16, the sum of the numbers of remaining marbles in the bag $(4+2+1=7)$ divided by the total number of marbles (16). The (P) of not picking blue is the complement.

Blue	Red	Green	Black	Total
8/16	4/16	2/16	1/16	16/16 or 1

Pointing Out Scientific Notation Facts

Scientific notation is a shortcut for writing very large or very small numbers. The decimal point is moved about in such a way as to make the numbers easier to write and read.

The goal is to write the scientific notation number as a product of two factors: The first factor is a decimal number that has an absolute value equal to or greater than 1 but less than 10, and the second factor is a power of 10. So, to write 3,000 in scientific notation, you'd write 3.0×10^3. The major focus is on the decimal point.

Exponents tell you how many times to use the base as a factor. A positive exponent indicates a number that has a large absolute value (10 or greater), and a negative exponent indicates a small number (less than 1).

EXAMPLE

Light travels 1 meter in 0.0000000025 seconds. Write the number for the speed of light (in meters per second) in scientific notation.

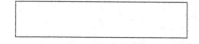

The correct answer is 2.5×10^{-9}. Focus on the decimal point. You have to move the decimal point nine places to the right to reach 2.5. Why would you decide to stop the decimal at 2.5? Because that number's absolute value is equal to or greater than 1 and less than 10. Write the number in scientific notation as 2.5×10^{-9}. Needing to move the decimal point in the original number form (not in scientific notation) to the right indicates that the number is less than 1 and must be written in scientific notation with a negative exponent.

EXAMPLE

Light travels 18,000,000,000 meters per minute. Write the number in scientific notation.

The correct answer is 1.8×10^{10}. Focus on the decimal point.

REMEMBER

If the decimal point isn't visible in the first number in a scientific notation expression, it's understood to be at the end of it. Your task is to count how many places you have to move the decimal point to get to a number equal to or greater than 1 and less than 10. The number in this example problem written in scientific notation is 1.8×10^{10}.

Practice Questions about Statistics and Probability

These practice questions are similar to the questions about statistics and probability that you'll encounter on the Praxis.

1. There are 9 yellow counters and 15 red counters in a bag. What is the probability of picking a yellow counter from the bag?

   (A) 5/8

   (B) 1/2

   (C) 2/5

   (D) 2/3

   (E) 3/8

2. Using the following line plot, what is the mean of the data set?

   Mrs. Tates' test scores: 50, 50, 60, 90, 90, 50, 70, 90, 80, 90

   Line Plot of Mrs. Tates' Test Scores

   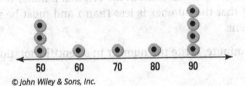

   © John Wiley & Sons, Inc.

   (A) 65

   (B) 72

   (C) 75

   (D) 80

   (E) 82

3. The heights from a group of 20 students include 7 that are 4 or less feet tall and 8 that are 5 or more feet tall. What is the probability that a student selected will be between 4 and 5 feet tall?

   (A) $\frac{1}{2}$

   (B) $\frac{1}{4}$

   (C) $\frac{2}{5}$

   (D) $\frac{2}{3}$

   (E) $\frac{1}{20}$

4. Find the range, mean, median, and mode for the following data set:

   1, 3, 3, 3, 3, 4, 6, 6, 6, 8, 12

   Range

   Mean

   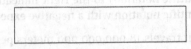

   Median

   Mode

5. Using the stem-and-leaf plot that follows, find the median number of people who entered a frozen yogurt shop during a given hour.

Hourly Customers

Stem	Leaf Top row, left side in red should be 0, not 1.
1	4
1	3 7
2	2 5
3	1 5 8 9
4	0 0 3

Key: 2|5 = 25

(A) 22

(B) 29

(C) 33

(D) 40

(E) 43

6. Which of the following represents 57,590,000 in scientific notation?

(A) 57.59×10^6

(B) 5.759×10^{-7}

(C) 57.59×10^{-7}

(D) 5.759×10^7

(E) 57.59×10^7

7. Which is the best way to survey a random sample of students from your school about their favorite radio station?

(A) Survey 5 students in each first-period class.

(B) Survey 12 students in the band.

(C) Call 25 friends.

(D) Survey each student in your math class.

(E) Survey the football team.

Answers and Explanations

Use this answer key to score the practice questions in the preceding section.

1. **E. 3/8.** There are 24 counters in the bag. Nine of the 24 counters, or 9/24, are yellow, which reduces to 3/8.

2. **B. 72.** The mean of the line plot is identified by taking the average of the numbers: $\frac{720}{10} = 72$

3. **B. $\frac{1}{4}$.** If the total number of students is 20, and 15 of the students aren't within the described height range while the rest are, then 5 students are within the described height range. Five of the 20 students have heights between 4 and 5 feet because 15 don't.

$$\frac{5}{20} = \frac{1}{4}$$

4. **Range = 11; mean = 5; median = 4; and mode = 3.**

   Using the data set 1, 3, 3, 3, 3, 4, 6, 6, 6, 8, 12, the range is $12 - 1 = 11$. You find the range by subtracting the smallest data value from the largest.

   The mean is $55 \div 11 = 5$. You find the mean, also known as the average, by adding the numbers in the data set and dividing the total by the number of items in the data set.

   The median is 4. The median is the center or middle number in the data set. If there are two numbers in the center of the data set, find the average of them.

   The mode is 3. It's the number that occurs the most frequently in the data set.

   Please note: You won't usually see this many separate requests for information in one question on the Praxis Core; however, you may have to calculate all of these to answer a single question.

5. **C. 33.** Because there are 12 data points, take the middle two numbers and get the average.

$$31 + 35 = 66$$
$$\frac{66}{2} = 33$$

6. **D. 5.759×10^7.** 57,590,000 written in scientific notation is 5.759×10^7. Move your decimal point to the left until you reach a whole digit number from 1 to 9. It takes 7 places to the left to reach 5.759; therefore, your answer should be 5.759×10^7.

7. **A. Survey 5 students in each first-period class.** Surveying five students in each first period class will give a more diverse sample than the other methods presented in the other answer choices.

Chapter **8**

Test-Taking Strategies for Core Math

Mathematical knowledge and practice are very important for taking the Praxis Core exam's math section, but the arsenal you take into battle doesn't have to stop there. Test-taking strategies can make your weapons even more effective. What you know is extremely important, but so is what you do with what you know. This chapter is about making the best of the knowledge you have.

WARNING

If you decide to use only one bit of advice on test-taking strategies, let it be this: Never stay on a question that looks like it will take an extreme amount of time to answer. You can save it for after you answer the questions that don't take long to answer. This advice applies to any type of question. You can write down the number of the question in the hope of going back to it later. Some people get so caught up in a challenge to answer a time-consuming question that they use up time they could have used to answer four or five other questions.

REMEMBER

All the Praxis Core exam math questions are worth the same number of points, so make sure you don't treat any one of them as if it's more important than the others. Whether you're asked to solve a simple equation or find the volume of a remaining region of a rectangular prism, the question is worth as many points as the other 55. Timing is part of the challenge, so use it well.

Using Helpful Shortcuts

Getting answers that are correct on the Praxis Core exam is really important. However, coming up with the right answers isn't your only concern. You must consider something else of major relevance: The exam is timed. You have 90 minutes to answer 56 problems. Any methods you can use to reduce the time you take to answer questions without sacrificing accuracy will help you. The methods we outline in the following sections are real, and they work. We encourage you to give them a trial run as you take the practice tests in Part 5 and online.

Solving equations versus determining what must be solved

You'll almost definitely have word problems that require setting up and solving algebraic equations when you take the Praxis Core exam. Solving these problems requires more than the ability to solve equations. You also need to determine what information the problem is asking you for — that is, what needs to be solved. You can use a variable to represent the unknown quantity that must be determined.

TIP

If the problem has more than one unknown, see whether you can represent the others in terms of the first. For example, if Bob's score in bowling is in question and the problem says that Frank scored 10 points higher than Bob, you can use x to represent Bob's score and $x + 10$ to represent Frank's score.

The next step is to put the algebraic expressions into an equation and solve the equation. The solution to the equation will be the value of the first unknown. After you know the value of the first unknown, you can find the values of any other unknowns by putting the value of that variable into the expressions that you used to represent the values you haven't yet determined.

EXAMPLE

John is four years older than Adam. John was twice Adam's age 33 years ago. What is John's age now?

(A) 42

(B) 8

(C) 25

(D) 41

(E) 37

The correct answer is Choice (D). The question asks for John's age, so you can make John's age the first unknown and represent it with a variable, such as x. Because John is four years older than Adam, you can represent Adam's age with the expression $x - 4$. The next step is to write an equation with the two expressions. Just translate the information in the word problem into mathematical language. John was twice Adam's age 33 years ago. Their ages 33 years ago can be represented by subtracting 33 from their current ages:

John: $x - 33$

Adam: $x - 4 - 33$

"Twice Adam's age 33 years ago" can be represented by 2 multiplied by 33 less than Adam's current age.

Adam: $2(x - 4 - 33)$

Then set up an equation that shows their ages 33 years ago with John's being twice as much as Adam's:

$$x - 33 = 2(x - 4 - 33)$$

Notice the direct translation of worded information in that equation. It says exactly the same thing in a different way. The solution to the equation is 41. (For a review of how to solve algebraic equations, turn to Chapter 5.) John's age is therefore 41.

TIP

Be extremely careful in making sure you know precisely what question you're being asked. It's not always what you may assume it is. In the preceding example, for instance, you could have been asked Adam's current age or even the sum of John's and Adam's ages. Don't assume that the first unknown is the answer to the question. The need to use caution in identifying the exact question you're being asked is often even greater on geometry questions.

Using estimation and approximation

Estimation is the act of using known information to get a number that is close to the answer to a question although it may not be the actual answer. This can be helpful on the Praxis Core exam because most of the test is multiple choice. When you estimate, you have a good chance of getting the answer right by choosing the one that's closest to your estimate. Because the test is timed, estimation may be handy for a few last answers before time's up.

Estimation can also help you eliminate choices that are definitely wrong, and it can help you make sure the answer you get is not something beyond the fringe of reason or the result of a miscalculation. However, don't spend too much time estimating for just that purpose. You'll be performing a juggling act with time and caution.

Approximation is using numbers that are very close to numbers given in a problem for the purpose of making calculating easier. This, too, can save you time when time is running short, and it can also help you eliminate wrong answers. If you have to make a wild guess, your chances of guessing the correct choice increase when you can eliminate some of the choices.

When you multiply with irrational numbers in decimal form, you often have to approximate. An *irrational number* is a number that can't be represented as a ratio of two integers. An irrational number in decimal form doesn't terminate or repeat. In other words, the digits after the decimal don't have a pattern and continue infinitely. Because you don't have time to calculate with an infinite number of digits, approximation can often help.

For example, the number 7.32960584965105 . . . is an irrational number. You may come across a number like that when you use your calculator. Rounding such a number to four decimal places should be sufficient to get a correct result in almost all cases. Rounding also saves time, and time is precious on the Praxis Core exam. In some cases, you can just leave a number in your calculator and do the necessary operation with it.

Using the calculator

An on-screen calculator is provided for you on the math section of the Praxis Core exam. That makes computation easier and saves time over doing calculations on paper. The calculator's keypad includes keys for all the digits, the four basic operations (adding, subtracting, multiplying, and dividing), square roots, making numbers negative, a decimal, parentheses, memory, clearing, transfer display (which can transfer your answers to the answer box on constructed response questions), and, of course, the highly important equal sign. The calculator is also programmed to follow the order of operations. However, you still need to know the order of operations for solving variable equations.

Identifying calculations you can make in your head

We highly encourage caution when making calculations for the Praxis Core exam. That involves writing out work on scratch paper and using the calculator, but only when you actually have time to do those things. You should write and use the calculator even for the calculations you're sure you can do in your head when you're keeping a good pace, although we don't recommend using the calculator for calculations that can come from pure memory.

However, when time becomes a major issue, you need to know what more complex calculations you can do in your head relatively safely. The first category to consider is problems for which writing and using the calculator don't actually help you figure out the answer. For these calculations, the paper and calculator will only help you avoid careless errors. Suppose you have to calculate $2 + 2$. We recommend using paper even for that when you're good on time. Using paper allows you to write out every step of the calculations, better ensuring that you avoid careless errors. But when you're way behind on time, you should speed up by making such a calculation only in your head. Timing is important, but so is caution.

Make sure you can add and subtract all combinations of two single-digit numbers purely by memory. This will help you add numbers with more than one digit in your head when necessary. For example, if you know that $9 + 8 = 17$, you can quickly conclude that $59 + 8 = 67$. Also, make very sure that you know all the multiplication tables for 2 through 12.

Although we believe in writing every step involved in answering a math question, we don't think the calculator should be used for every single calculation. The more you have in your brain's memory, the faster your pace will be.

The art of guessing as a last resort

If time really wears thin on the exam and you only have time to make wild guesses, go ahead and make nothing but wild guesses. A point may come where you don't even have time to estimate, approximate, or do quick calculations in your head. That's when you need to just start hitting answers as fast as you can.

If you make all of your choices randomly, you have some probability of getting all of them right. However, the flip side to that coin is that you have equal probability of getting all of them wrong. Still, you'll most likely get some right if you answer enough of them that way.

We recommend choosing the same option every time. The Praxis Core exam tends to distribute answer choices close to evenly. Because of this, if you pick the third choice every time, for example, you'll almost surely get an answer right if you pick it enough times.

In the examples used in this book, the choices are lettered. That's only for the purpose of being able to easily identify the choices when discussing them. On the actual Praxis exam, the choices aren't lettered. They have elliptical figures beside them. With that being the case, you should pick a certain number in the order of choices and stick with it when you're in wild guess mode. You could pick the first choice, second choice, third choice, and so on, and stick with it every time. However, if you get a quick enough peek to have any reason at all to think any choice is even slightly better than the others, you should choose that one.

A small number of questions tell you that more than one answer choice may apply. If you notice one of those during a pure guessing phase, you should mark at least two answers of the choices presented.

A few of the questions don't have choices presented with them. You should answer those last if you're in a guessing phase. When you get around to guessing on them, see how much time you have left. Quickly look at the problem and give the best guess you can give. If you still have a few more seconds to actually think about the answer, do all of the thinking you have time to do, and then give the best answer you can.

Working backward

When you're in doubt about how to answer a math problem by using the conventional calculation methods, you can increase the probability of getting the correct answer by *working backward*. This approach can be used in various situations and in different ways. For example, if an end result is given and you're asked about what was involved in getting the result, you can start at the end and work toward the beginning. This technique can be used for age problems, problems concerning final amounts of money, final locations, and other types of problems. The technique is sometimes the only one that will work.

EXAMPLE

Robert went for a walk on a trail that runs north and south after getting a ride on a four-wheeler. At the end of his walk, he was 14 miles north of his campsite. He had previously walked 10 miles south, and before that he walked 20 miles north. How far north of his campsite was Robert when he began his walk?

(A) 24 miles

(B) 0 miles

(C) 4 miles

(D) 44 miles

(E) 6 miles

The correct answer is Choice (C). You can answer this problem by using positive and negative numbers and adding them, with north distances being positive and south distances being negative. However, you can also work backward from the final distance and trace Robert's travel back to the beginning of the hike. If Robert was 14 miles north and had previously walked 10 miles south, he was 24 miles from his campsite before the final part of the walk. If he got to that point by walking 20 miles north, he was 20 miles back, which is 4 miles from the campsite. Choice (A) is the distance Robert was from his campsite before changing directions, but not the initial distance. Choice (D) results from adding 20 to 24, rather than subtracting it.

Narrowing Down Answer Choices

You improve your chances of choosing the right answer — and choosing it quickly — by eliminating choices that you know are wrong. This narrows the set of choices to consider and helps lead you to the right answer. We discuss this process of elimination in the section "Using estimation and approximation," earlier in this chapter, to make a case for increasing the probability of getting the right answer, but another advantage is that it helps lead you to better considerations.

Eliminating obviously wrong answer choices

If a choice is so outrageous that it couldn't possibly be the correct answer, you should eliminate it from consideration. For example, the length of a rectangle can never be greater than the rectangle's perimeter. A person's age years ago can't be greater than their current age. The mean of a set of data can never be greater than the highest number. These are just some examples of impossibilities you can readily notice.

EXAMPLE

If $3j = 90$, what is the value of j?

(A) 270

(B) 30

(C) 60

(D) 120

(E) 3

The correct answer is Choice (B). You can find the answer by solving the equation.

$$3j = 90$$
$$\frac{3j}{3} = \frac{90}{3}$$
$$j = 30$$

To help ensure you get the correct answer, you can eliminate Choices (A) and (D) because both of those choices are greater than 90. You have to multiply 3 by a positive number to get 90, and no positive number is greater than 3 times itself. Eliminating those choices leaves you with three choices to consider instead of five. Choices (C) and (E) are randomly incorrect.

Avoiding the most common wrong answers

Other choices to watch out for and be ready to eliminate are the ones that result from the most common calculation mistakes. Memorizing the rules for all the math topics you'll face on the Praxis is important for avoiding these common mistakes.

For geometry questions, some of the most common mistakes involve getting formulas confused, such as area and circumference. If you have a question about the area or circumference of a circle, you may have an answer choice that gives you the number involved in a measure about which you're not being asked. Be ready to avoid such answers.

Also, remember the difference between the interior angle sums of triangles and quadrilaterals. Choices may be the result of using the wrong number. Confusion between supplementary and complementary angles is common, and so is confusion between formulas for surface area and volume. Forgetting the formulas for the volume of pyramids and cones also happens often. (Take a spin through Chapter 6 if you need a refresher on any of these geometry topics.)

As for algebra and number and quantity questions, losing track of the fact that a number is negative is one of the most common mistakes. The distributive property is very frequently used improperly. Remember that the term right before the parentheses is supposed to be multiplied by every term in the parentheses, not just the first one. $5(x + 3)$ is equal to $5x + 15$, not $5x + 3$.

The rules for switching between decimals and percents can be easily confused. Keep in mind that moving a decimal two places to the right is equivalent to multiplying by 100 and moving the decimal two places to the left is the same as dividing by 100. Adding a percent sign is the same as dividing by 100 because a percent is "out of 100." For that same reason, removing a percent sign is multiplying by 100 (it undoes the percent's dividing by 100).

For statistics and probability questions, be careful about confusing mean, median, and mode. People often forget that the median of a set of data can be found only when the numbers are in order. When using scientific notation, be careful about the direction in which you move decimals. Numbers resulting from wrong decimal directions may be in the choices.

EXAMPLE

Which of the following has the same value as 35.937 percent?

(A) 3,593.7

(B) 3.5937

(C) 0.35937

(D) 35,937

(E) 0.035937

The correct answer is Choice (C). To convert a percent to a decimal number, drop the percent symbol (which can be % or the word "percent") and move the decimal two places to the left. Choice (A) results from dropping the percent symbol and moving the decimal two places to the right. The other choices result from moving the decimal points something other than two places to the right or left. The main lesson here is that Choice (A) can be reached through a very common mistake in converting percents to decimals. You want to avoid such wrong choices. They're lurking, so be ready.

EXAMPLE

45 17 90 28 17

What is the median of the preceding set of data?

(A) 28

(B) 90

(C) 17

(D) 39.4

(E) 45

The correct answer is Choice (A). When the numbers are in order, the middle number is 28. It is therefore the median. Interestingly, Choice (A) also happens to be the range of the set of data. Hopefully, you didn't reach the correct answer because you mistook median for range. Sometimes, mistakes lead to the right answers, but we don't advise counting on that method. Choice (B) is the middle number in the set of data as it is presented, but not when the data is in order. Choice (C) is the mode and the lowest number. Choice (D) is the mean. Choice (E) is just one of the numbers in the set of data.

Tackling the Constructed Response

Some of the questions on the Praxis Core exam's mathematics section aren't multiple choice. You'll be asked to type the answer in a box for this type of question. These are called constructed-response questions. Test designers can change how many of these types of questions you will see, so you should be familiar with how they work and what's expected in your answers. Because you won't have the benefit of being able to look at any answer choices, you need to be aware of the requirements for submitting answers in the correct forms.

Tips for preparing responses and answering questions

The first thing to make sure of before you submit a constructed response is that the answer you typed is the answer you actually got. Leaving out a decimal, a digit, π, or something else essential to a correct answer will result in a wrong answer and no points for that question. Figuring out a correct answer is not the final step in a constructed-response question. Submitting the correct answer is the only thing that counts.

Also, make sure you're very clear on the instructions. A question may ask something like what measure of an angle is represented by $(2x+3)°$, in which case you would have to figure out the value of a variable to determine the answer. For such a question, make sure your answer is the measure of the angle and not the value of the variable. That is one example of when paying close attention to the question is necessary.

You also need to be careful about subtle parts of instructions. A question may ask for an exact answer, an answer rounded to the nearest hundredth, or an answer in terms of π. If you're asked to answer in terms of π, your answer should have π in it. That means you do not want to use 3.14 in your calculation. 3.14 is not π; it is a rounded approximation of it. Neglecting to follow the instructions exactly can cause an answer to be incorrect.

Some constructed-response questions ask for more than one answer. If you're given such a question, make sure you give all the required answers. People are so used to answering each question with one answer submission on a test that they can easily overlook the need for more than one answer to a constructed-response question on the Praxis exam. Again, you need to follow instructions very closely.

Some proper ways of representing answers

REMEMBER

The instructions for constructed-response questions tell you how you're required to answer them if more than one possibility would otherwise exist. If an answer includes a unit of measurement, you need to submit it. If you're asked to answer something in terms of some kind of unit, variable, or other representation, including it in your answer is a must.

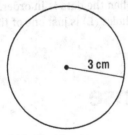

3 cm

© John Wiley & Sons, Inc.

EXAMPLE

What is the area of a circle that has a radius of 3 centimeters? Give your answer in terms of π.

The correct answer is 9π cm^2. The area of a circle is πr^2.

$$A = \pi r^2$$
$$= \pi (3)^2$$
$$= \pi (9)$$
$$= 9\pi$$

The unit used for the radius is centimeters, so the unit used for area must be square centimeters (cm²). The answer to the problem has to involve a number times π and also cm². The proper answer is therefore 81π cm^2, not just 81π or the result of multiplying 81 by 3.14. You should force your constructed responses to pass a major inspection that you conduct.

Avoiding careless errors

Careless errors are one of the major obstacles that stand between people and high levels of math success. The problem seems to apply especially to algebra students. To avoid careless errors, you must be cautious in all aspects of working through the math problem. Several methods can be used to defeat this menace:

» **Work every step of a problem on scratch paper.** Even if you feel like you can make a calculation correctly in your head, you should work it out completely so that you have a visual account of what you're doing. This greatly helps you avoid going in a wrong direction.

» **Always be on the lookout for errors.** Try to catch them before they would otherwise happen. Think about how careful surgeons are when they perform surgery. One false move can be tragic. Missing a problem on the Praxis Core exam isn't quite as tragic, but it is unfortunate. Be careful and aware of potential mistakes, just like a surgeon.

» **Talk problems out in your head while you work them.** This process adds one more level of attention, in addition to thinking about the problems and seeing them worked out on paper.

» **Go back over problems if you have time.** If you finish the test before your time runs out, don't pass up the opportunity to review your answers and possibly push up your score. Every minute you can spend reviewing your answers is valuable.

» **Be especially careful when working with negative numbers.** They are the number one area for careless errors. If you see a negative sign, think of it as a wet-floor sign telling you to be extra cautious.

» **Don't assume that not noticing a careless error means you didn't make one.** Careless errors are sneaky. Most of them aren't caught in the act, but the damage they cause is almost always revealed.

3

Refining Your Reading Comprehension Skills

IN THIS CHAPTER

» Surveying the parameters of the reading test

» Answering questions about short passages and long passages

» Interpreting image-based questions

» Working on reading comprehension

» Reviewing the right (and wrong) answers

Chapter 9

Reading Comprehension: Finding Meaning and Identifying Purpose

I f you've looked at Chapter 12, you already know that the Praxis "writing" test is mainly a grammar test, and that the point of that test is to make sure you have your grammatical rules straightened out. But why is there a Praxis reading test? After all, if you're even taking the test (or reading this book), then you obviously already know how to read. The answer is that, as Sherlock Holmes is so fond of telling people, there's a difference between *seeing* and *observing*: Anyone who has a pair of eyes can look around a room and see what's there, but only a clever sleuth will discern the difference between what's an important clue and what's not.

Educational Testing Service (ETS) knows perfectly well that you can read all the words in the little paragraphs it gives you. What you're being tested on is whether you can pick out the details that are most important or relevant when it comes to answering a specific question.

Previewing the Praxis Reading Test

An important thing to keep in mind while taking the Praxis reading test is that you aren't being tested on prior or outside knowledge. The subject matter of the passages may be history, science, the arts, or anything at all, but the test isn't a history, or a science, or an art test. The information you need to answer the question correctly is always contained in the passage that precedes the question. In fact, outside knowledge of a particular subject could even be a disadvantage because you're expected to answer the questions based *solely* on the arguments and details contained within the passages provided. This is why questions typically begin with the phrase "*According to* the passage" or "According to the author" (in the rare cases where the question doesn't specify this, remember to answer based solely on the passage anyway). You're expected to comprehend claims and follow arguments about a wide variety of topics; you're being tested on your comprehension ability, not your familiarity with those topics.

Knowing what the test contains

The passages on the test can be about absolutely anything. There's no point in worrying about what the subject matter will be for a couple of reasons: One, there's no way to predict it because every test is different, and two, it doesn't — and more importantly, it *shouldn't* — matter. If you walk into the Praxis reading test hoping that there will be passages about *this* or you're concerned that there may be passages about *that*, you're thinking about the test the wrong way. You want to train yourself to let go of the instinct to react to a passage by thinking "Yay! This one is about elephants, and I like elephants!" or "Oh, no! This one is about submarines, and I don't know the first thing about submarines!" You're only being tested on your ability to follow what the passage is saying, so it really doesn't matter what the passage is about.

The Praxis reading test lasts for 85 minutes (there will be a countdown clock in the upper-right corner of your computer screen to help you manage time), and in that time, you're given 56 selected-response questions. The Praxis reading test contains four types of questions, as follows:

>> Paired passages of about 200 words total, followed by four to seven questions

>> Long passages of about 200 words, followed by four to seven questions

>> Short passages of about 100 words, followed by two or three questions

>> Brief statements followed by one question; may include visual representation questions based on charts and graphs, many containing numeric information

Technically, we suppose there are different question types on the Praxis reading test, but the way we see it, this is what philosophers would call "a distinction without a difference." Don't be discouraged or intimidated by a big, Goliath passage. Chop down the giant one sentence at a time. Aside from the visual- and quantitative-information questions, which are about charts and graphs, and the paired passages, on which you're expected to compare one author's argument to another's, the rest of the test is the same basic thing over and over: You read a paragraph, and you answer one or more questions about it. Sometimes the paragraph is a little shorter, and sometimes it's a little longer. Sometimes there's only one question about the paragraph, and sometimes there are three or four. But you never have to actually do anything differently based on these differences, so there's no point in worrying about them. On every single question, your mission is identical: Read the paragraph and answer the question(s) based on the information it contains. (And as for the intimidation factor of a "long" passage, this paragraph you're reading now contains about 200 words — did it seem terribly "long" to you?)

Applying a general strategy

Like most of the major standardized tests, the Praxis has one section about grammar and another section about reading comprehension. Grammar involves rules that can be memorized; reading comprehension is a bit trickier.

Because grammar is rule-based, even if you think you're bad at grammar, you can improve your skills quickly by memorizing a list of rules and practicing them (even if doing so isn't necessarily the most fun you've ever had).

But how do you study for the reading comprehension section of the test that's not so cut and dried? You apply strategies to correctly answer the questions. A strategy is basically just a rule that depends on circumstances. Whereas a rule says "Do this," a strategy says "If this happens, then do this." (We give you more details about these if…then concepts in the section "Getting the hang of 'If' questions," later in this chapter.)

No matter what the question asks, you're mostly faced with exactly four wrong answers and one right answer (except on those "check all that apply" questions, of which there are usually only one or two, or boxes that ask you to fill in an exact answer, usually numerically based). Concentrating on this simple idea — that only one answer is right — is the most important step in becoming a whiz at reading comprehension tests. Just keep these points in mind:

>> On most questions, there are always four wrong answers and one right answer. As of the writing of this book, ETS notes that there are 56 reading selected-response (multiple-choice) questions. This convention can change at any time, however.

>> A choice that isn't right is wrong, and a choice that isn't wrong is right.

>> When you select an answer as right, you are *implicitly declaring that the other four are wrong.*

>> If one of the other choices *isn't wrong,* then it *must be right,* so you should have picked that one instead.

>> In short, you aren't looking for the *right* answer so much as you are looking for the *not-wrong* answer.

Mastering Short-Passage Questions

The most common type of question in the reading portion of the Praxis exam is what's called a short-passage question. You're given a selection of text, usually only three or four sentences in length, and you're asked one question about it. The question is unique to the passage, and the passage is unique to the question.

In the following sections, we outline the types of information the questions focus on and give you pointers on how to figure out what the correct answer is.

Ferreting out the main idea

The most common — and the most straightforward — type of short-passage question is a "main idea" question. The wording of the question is usually along the lines of "The main idea of the passage is . . ." or "The primary purpose of the passage is . . ." And your mission is to select the answer choice that best completes the sentence. Basically, phrases such as "main idea" and "primary purpose" are just fancier ways of asking

>> "What's this about?"

>> "What's the point of this?"

>> "What is this paragraph trying to say?"

Although such questions may seem easy after you've had a bit of practice with them, they can be difficult in the sense of being deceptively simple if you're not used to them. Questions such as these can be challenging because the wrong answers appear flashier or more attractive than the right one. They may have more details in them, or they may contain more exact words from the passage.

You're not looking for the statement about the passage that's the most detailed or the most specific — you're looking for the statement that is *true*. And there will be only one of those. The other four choices, for one reason or another, will be wrong. A common tactic the test-writers use on such questions is to make the right answer so vague or uninteresting that you barely notice it. The wrong answers stand out more. But never forget that all you're trying to do is pick the statement about the purpose of the passage that's *true* (in other words, *not wrong*) — no more and no less. Consider the following example.

EXAMPLE

Anyone who paid attention in grade-school science class could tell you that the five classes of vertebrates are mammals, reptiles, amphibians, birds, and fish. For centuries, these categories made sense to scientists because they represented clear distinctions based on what we were able to observe about the animal kingdom. But now that we know more about evolutionary history, the borders between these traditional and visually "obvious" classes are not so clear. A crocodile looks more like a turtle than a penguin, but the common ancestor of the crocodile and the penguin actually lived more recently than did the common ancestor of the crocodile and the turtle.

The primary purpose of the passage is to

(A) explain how penguins evolved from crocodiles.

(B) dispute some recent theories in the field of evolutionary biology.

(C) correct a misconception common in grade-school science curricula.

(D) discuss how a biological concept is more complicated than it looks.

(E) summarize a disagreement about vertebrates between two schools of zoologists.

The correct answer is Choice (D). To understand why Choice (D) is correct, consider: *Does* the passage "discuss how a biological concept is more complicated than it looks"? Yes, it does. In fact, it *indisputably* does — in other words, there's no reasonable way to argue that the passage does *not* do this. So (D) is the right answer because it *cannot possibly be wrong*.

As for the others, by now you've figured out that they're all wrong. But look at what they have in common: All the wrong answers stand out by repeating specifics or key words from the passage — but they also twist those specifics so the statements are no longer true.

Choice (A) is wrong because the passage technically doesn't say that penguins evolved *from* crocodiles; it says that penguins and crocodiles *have a common ancestor*. And even if the passage did say this, it wouldn't be the primary purpose of the passage because it's only one example given right at the end. The test-writers know that the example given at the end will be fresh in your mind, so they try to get you to jump the gun by making it the first choice.

Choice (B) is wrong because of the verb it uses. The author is indeed talking about "recent theories in the field of evolutionary biology," but he isn't *disputing* them, only *explaining* them (there is no indication that the author disagrees). Always remember that it only takes one false move to make an answer choice wrong.

Choice (C) is wrong because the passage technically never says that the vertebrate classes as explained in schools are incorrect (a "misconception"). The five classes of vertebrates are still mammals, amphibians, reptiles, birds, and fish. The passage discusses some interesting information that *seems as if* it *might lead* to scientists changing those categories somehow *in the future*, but it never says they've done so already.

As for Choice (E), did the passage say or imply anything about "two schools" of zoologists? No. The passage explains that *zoologists* (biologists that specifically study animals) nowadays have more information than zoologists did in the past, but it never hints at anything about a debate.

160 PART 3 Refining Your Reading Comprehension Skills

Discerning the author's tone and intent

The most common type of reading-comprehension question that students complain about — even dread — is the *authorial-intent* question. "I can answer questions about the information in the passage," they say, "but how am I supposed to know what the author *intended* to do? What am I, a mind reader?" But you don't have to be a mind reader to answer this type of question. You answer it the same way you answer any other question on the Praxis reading test — four of the choices are wrong, and you pick the one that isn't.

Look at it this way: If I showed you a picture of a man carrying a guitar, and I asked you what he was on his way to do, you wouldn't know. He might be on his way to band practice, he might be returning the guitar to a friend, or he might be an actor who's portraying a musician in a play. All of those answers are plausible. *However,* if it were a *selected-response* question, all you'd have to do is eliminate the four implausible choices and select the one that remains. If the man were on his way to build a porch, he would have a toolbox rather than a guitar; if he were on his way to help put out a fire, he'd have a bucket of water instead of a guitar; and so forth.

That's how you answer an authorial-intent question without needing to be psychic. Four of the choices are implausible, and the right answer is the one that's left.

EXAMPLE

The frequent complaint by horror-movie fans that their favorite genre is discriminated against at the Academy Awards is difficult to assess. The data would seem to back it up: After all, in the 85-year history of cinema's top prizes, only one horror film — 1991's *The Silence of the Lambs* — has taken home the Oscar for Best Picture. On the other hand, many critically respected scary movies have simply had very bad luck: *Jaws* and *The Exorcist* almost certainly would have won had they not been up against Oscar-magnets *One Flew Over the Cuckoo's Nest* and *The Sting* in their respective years. Some critics have suggested that the "horror movies never win awards" objection is a self-fulfilling prophecy: When a movie wins many prestigious awards, we stop thinking of it as a "horror movie," no matter how scary it is.

In the preceding passage, the author's intent is to

(A) analyze the idea that horror movies are discriminated against at the Oscars.

(B) rebut the assertion that horror movies seldom win prestigious awards.

(C) persuade Academy Awards voters to stop overlooking deserving horror films.

(D) satirize a silly idea about "discrimination" against a certain genre of films.

(E) predict whether more horror movies will win Oscars in the near future.

The correct answer is Choice (A). Why? Because there's no way that the correct answer *can't* be Choice A. The passage is about the idea that horror movies seldom win Oscars, and the author is indisputably analyzing that idea. Remember, *analyze* is just a fancy word for "look at closely and thoroughly." Because this is all that Choice (A) asserts to be the case, there's no room for it to be wrong.

Choice (B) is wrong because the author is not *rebutting* anything (to *rebut* means to "offer a counterargument"). Choice (C) is wrong because the author isn't trying to *persuade* anyone to do anything, only presenting information. Choice (D) is wrong because the author isn't *satirizing* anything (*satirizing* means "making fun of" — did you laugh?). Choice (E) is wrong because the author doesn't say one single word about what may or may not happen in the future, so the passage doesn't contain any *predictions*.

If you have a knack for this sort of thing, you may have noticed that the *initial verb* in each answer choice was pretty much all you needed to eliminate the four wrong answers: The author is not *rebutting, persuading, satirizing,* or *predicting,* but he *is analyzing* (because hey, how could he *not* be analyzing?). And even if you didn't pick up on that, don't despair — because you've picked up on it now.

We certainly don't mean to imply that you should only look at portions of the answer choices. A cardinal rule of selected-response test-taking is that you should always read all the choices in their entirety before making a decision. What we're saying is that sometimes the distinction between the right answer and the wrong ones doesn't depend equally on every single word the answers contain. It only takes one wrong word to make an answer choice wrong, so because Choices (B), (C), (D), and (E) are all wrong based on their first words, those first words are all you need to eliminate them, leaving only Choice (A), which must, therefore, be right.

As for questions about the author's tone, those are basically the same game. The only difference is that you deal with adjectives instead of verbs. For example, whereas the answer choices for an authorial-intent question may begin with the words *analyze, rebut, persuade, satirize,* and *predict,* the answer choices for a question about the author's tone may describe that tone alternately as *analytical, argumentative, persuasive, satirical,* or *speculative.* In either case, you should approach the question in the same way: Eliminate four wrong answers and pick the one that's left.

Putting vocabulary in context

Don't panic — if you've taken the SAT, you've seen this before! The Praxis reading test asks you a few *vocabulary-in-context* questions, wherein five proposed synonyms for a given word from the passage are offered as choices, and you're expected to select the one that works best.

You can answer these questions correctly by using the intuitive method of plugging all five choices into the place of the given word and seeing which one works best. There are just a few things you'll want to be careful of, however, and we go over those right after this sample question.

EXAMPLE

Though conspiracy theorists like to think of themselves as rebels whose ideas are too shocking to be accepted, the charge leveled at them by mainstream historians is not one of disrespect but rather of wishful thinking: There is almost never any aspect of the event in question that the conspiracy theory is necessary to explain, and it is almost always far less plausible than any number of less titillating theories.

As used in Line 2, "charge" most nearly means

(A) credit

(B) attack

(C) accusation

(D) content

(E) responsibility

The correct answer is Choice (C), simply because *accusation* is the word that works best if you plug it into the passage in place of *charge* (an *accusation* of wishful thinking is leveled at the conspiracy theorists by mainstream historians). None of the other words make anywhere near as much sense as *accusation* when substituted for the word *charge.*

Now, notice that all the answer choices can function as synonyms for the word "charge" in different contexts: To *charge* something is to put it on *credit* if we're talking about shopping; a *charge* is an *attack* if we're talking about a battlefield; in physics, *charge* can mean *content* (the noun with the stress on the first syllable, not the adjective with the stress on the second), as in whether an atom contains more protons than electrons or vice versa, giving the atom a positive or a negative charge; and a *charge* can be a *responsibility* in the sense that when you're in charge of something, you're responsible for it.

So the difficulty isn't that you may not know the meaning of the word in question. Rather, the difficulty is that you *do* know the words, all too well! The question is counting on the fact that most people will recognize all the choices as possible synonyms for *charge* under the right circumstances, and it's asking which one works as a synonym for it under *these particular* circumstances.

TIP

The trick, then, is to simply ignore the original word and everything you know about it. Don't think about what it means most of the time or attempt to psychoanalyze the question by determining what the "hardest" or "easiest" thing it might mean is. Just pretend that a blank exists instead of the original word and then pick the answer choice that works best in that blank. The original word doesn't even matter!

Looking at Long-Passage Questions

Although the Praxis reading test has many short-passage questions (which we talk about in the section "Mastering Short-Passage Questions," earlier in this chapter) that pair very brief paragraphs with generally broad questions in a 1:1 ratio (that is, one question per passage), the test also features long-passage questions, wherein several questions are asked about a single passage of two or three paragraphs in length.

Though there are no hard-and-fast rules about which types of questions can or will be asked about which types of passages (in other words, a main-point or vocabulary-in-context question *could* be asked in reference to a long passage), certain types of questions are more commonly paired with the long passages. A question dealing with support for an argument, for example, is more likely to pop up in reference to a long passage, simply because the short passages are usually too brief to contain much in the way of detailed support for (or attacks on) an argument.

So, although there's no reason why a long passage couldn't contain any of the types of questions discussed in the section "Mastering Short-Passage Questions," earlier in this chapter, long passages are far more likely than short passages to contain the types of questions discussed in the following sections.

Purpose and paraphrase

If there's one thing you can expect from a series of long-passage questions, it's that there'll be at least one question that identifies a little detail or factoid from somewhere in the passage and asks you "What's the point of this?" The question won't be phrased that way, of course. It will be more drawn out, along the lines of one of the following:

>> When the author writes that "this, that, or the other," he most nearly means that . . .

>> It can be inferred that the author views the "such-and-such" as a type of . . .

>> It is implied that the "blah blah blah" is significant because . . .

Although a "What's the point of this part?" question can be phrased in any number of ways, it always basically comes down to the same thing: The question quotes a portion of the passage (it may be an entire sentence or a small detail comprised of two or three words), and it essentially asks, "Why did the author mention this right here?"

This question type may sound similar to authorial intent and mind reading (see the section "Discerning the author's tone and intent," earlier in this chapter, for more about that), but it's not. Just like with authorial-intent questions, the best method of answering a "What's the point of this part?" question is to eliminate wrong answers until only one choice is left.

In theory, an author may use a particular phrase or reference a particular detail for any number of reasons — just like a piece of writing may be about any topic under the sun or written with any of a host of intentions. In practice, however, Praxis reading questions tend to ask about only a finite number of points that a particular phrase may have. With reference to the types of questions referred to in the preceding bullet points, for example, the most likely explanations are as follows:

>> If a question asks you "what the author most nearly means by" a particular phrase, you're simply being asked for a paraphrase of the quoted text. A good strategy is to rephrase the quotation to yourself in your own words before looking at the choices, and then pick the answer choice that is the closest to what you just said.

>> If a question asks you to "infer how the author views" the quoted detail, the quoted detail is probably a particular example of some general category that is referenced elsewhere in the passage (for example, if the passage as a whole is about mythical animals and the author mentions Bigfoot, he does so because Bigfoot is a type of mythical animal).

>> If the question asks "Why is this significant?" about a quoted detail, the point of the detail is likely that it impacts the meaning of something else. Perhaps it's an important example of some general principle that the passage is trying to prove or explain, or perhaps it's a notable exception to that principle.

Arguments and support

A typical *argumentation/support* question on the Praxis reading test quotes a statement from the passage back to you — usually a detail or factoid — and then asks you why the author made mention of that detail or factoid at that particular juncture. Usually, the detail in question is being used to support a particular assertion, and you're being asked what assertion or viewpoint it's being used to support.

The best analogy here is to the vocabulary-in-context questions (see the section, "Putting vocabulary in context," earlier in this chapter). Why? Because there's no point in trying to answer the question without looking back at the passage. Just like the word in a Praxis vocabulary question is meaningless out of context, the detail in a Praxis argument/support question is meaningless out of context, too.

TIP

Just like you should answer the vocabulary questions by plugging the five answer choices back into the passage to see which suggested word works as a synonym, you should approach the argumentation/support questions by plugging the five answer choices into the passage to see which suggested concept *relates to* the context surrounding it.

After all, even though a piece of argumentative writing can be about anything, it's still going to be arranged in a logical fashion. You wouldn't offer a detail to support one idea when you're right in the middle of talking about something else!

Getting the hang of "If" questions

"If" questions (so called because they usually begin with "If it were found that . . .") are like argumentation/support questions, only instead of asking how a detail from the passage is used to support the author's argument, they ask how a detail or fact that is *not* in the passage *would* affect the author's argument *if* it were found to be true. The point of such questions is that they demonstrate advanced logical thinking — that is, they show that the test-taker fully understands the weight and implications of the argument being made on an abstract level, rather than merely showing that the test-taker comprehends the passage's exact words.

For example, consider a question like "*If* it were found that the defendant in a murder trial has a twin brother, how badly would this weaken the prosecution's case?" The answer would be that the prosecution's case would be weakened if it relied solely on eyewitness testimony but that it would not be weakened if they had fingerprint evidence, because twins look alike but don't have identical fingerprints. Don't worry — questions on the test don't involve outside knowledge; they deal only with the information provided to you in the passage and the questions themselves. (So if, in the example given here, they wanted you to base your answer on the fact that twins don't have identical fingerprints, the passage would tell you this.) This is just an example of what is meant by an "if" question.

If you're good at logical reasoning, you may be excited about answering "if" questions. But if you're not so hot at logical reasoning, rest assured that there are simple, step-by-step ways to eliminate wrong answers to an "if" question, just like there are for the other types of questions.

"If" questions come in two basic types. In the first kind, the question gives you a detail, and the answer choices are possible ways that the detail may affect the argument. Keep in mind that there are only *three* ways in which a given detail can possibly affect an argument:

>> It can support it.

>> It can undermine it.

>> It can have no effect.

However, the question needs to have *five* choices, so the choices can involve questions of degree: "The given fact completely proves the argument," "The given fact supports the argument slightly," "The given fact completely disproves the argument," "The given fact undermines the argument slightly," and "The given fact has no effect on the argument."

"If" questions also often pop up in reference to passages that compare excerpts from two authors, in which case, the answer choices may be something like "The given fact supports the author of Passage 1," "The given fact undermines the author of Passage 1," "The given fact supports the author of Passage 2," "The given fact undermines the author of Passage 2," and "The given fact has no effect on the argument of either author."

The second type of "if" question reverses this dynamic. Instead of providing you with a single detail and giving you five choices about how the detail affects the argument, this type of "if" question asks you to identify which of five possible details supports or undermines the argument.

The way to approach such a *reverse if* question is to begin by understanding that a detail has to be *about the same thing* as the argument in order to have any effect on it one way or the other. So, your first step is to eliminate all the choices that are unrelated (for example, if the author's argument is that Babe Ruth is the greatest baseball player of all time, then a factoid about basketball's Michael Jordan or football's Jerry Rice neither supports nor undermines it). After you eliminate the answer choices that have no effect one way or the other (unless you're being asked to identify the detail that has *no* effect on the argument, which is rare, but possible), the next step is to look for points that are either consistent with or mutually exclusive to the author's viewpoint. A detail or factoid that is *consistent with* the author's viewpoint (a detail that would or could be true if the author is right) supports that argument, and a detail or factoid that is *mutually exclusive to* (that is, couldn't be true at the same time as) the author's viewpoint undermines it.

Sample questions for long passages

In this section, you get a chance to practice some "purpose" questions, "support" questions, and "if" questions by looking at a long passage followed by an example of each.

EXAMPLE

"Did King Arthur really exist?" may seem like a fairly straightforward question, but the only possible answer to it is, "It depends on what you mean by 'King Arthur.'" Though virtually all adults now understand that the existence of a historical English king by the name of Arthur wouldn't involve his possessing a magical sword called Excalibur or being friends with a wizard named Merlin, far fewer people realize how tricky it would be to call him a king, or even to call him English.

Every first-millennium history book that makes mention of Arthur indicates that he lived during the late 5th and early 6th centuries and agrees that he played a role in the Battle of Badon in approximately 517. We know that the Battle of Badon was a real event, but what a historical Arthur might have done besides participate in this battle is anyone's guess. The earliest source that mentions Arthur, the *Historia Brittonum* of 828, links him with Badon but refers to him only as a *dux bellorum*, or war commander — not as a king (the fact that no British historical text composed between 517 and 828 mentions Arthur, even though they all mention Badon, is not terribly convenient for those who wish to believe in his existence).

Indeed, there wouldn't even have been a "king" in that place at that time. The Roman Empire had only recently pulled out of Great Britain, and the power vacuum quickly reduced the region to a free-for-all of warring tribes. If Arthur held political power, it wasn't over very many people, and it certainly wasn't over all England. And as for the English? Ironically, those were the people he was fighting against. The people who spoke the language that became English and were the ancestors of the people we now think of as English were the Anglo-Saxons, who invaded Great Britain from mainland Europe during Arthur's purported lifetime. Arthur himself, if he existed, was a Briton, one of the original inhabitants who had been conquered by the Romans and subsequently resisted (unsuccessfully) the Anglo-Saxons. The descendants of Arthur's people would be today's Welsh, not the English.

When the author writes "We know that the Battle of Badon was a real event, but what a historical Arthur might have done besides participate in this battle is anyone's guess" (Line 9), he means to say that

(A) Arthur must have existed, because he is linked by multiple sources to a battle we know to have occurred.

(B) Arthur probably did not exist, because if he did, then he would have been mentioned in earlier sources about this battle.

(C) Although it is likely that Arthur fought at Badon, we don't know what rank he held or even which side he fought on.

(D) It is not impossible that there were two Arthurs, one who fought at Badon and another who was a king.

(E) Even if Arthur did exist, we don't know anything about him besides the fact that he supposedly fought in one battle.

The correct answer is Choice (E). The construction "*a* historical Arthur" (as opposed to "*the* historical Arthur") implies uncertainty about whether Arthur existed. Saying that what he "might have done besides participate in this battle is anyone's guess" is another way of saying that his participation in the Battle of Badon is the only fact about Arthur asserted by any of the primary historical texts. The pertinent information here is that Arthur may or may not have existed, and that if he did exist, all we know about him is that he fought at Badon. This is simply a paraphrase question, and Choice (E) is simply a paraphrase of the quoted sentence from the passage.

Choice (A) is wrong because, although both the quoted sentence and the passage as a whole indicate that *if* Arthur existed, *then* he fought at Badon, neither the quoted sentence nor the passage as a whole ever asserts that he *must have* existed.

Choice (B) is wrong because, although the passage as a whole does imply that Arthur's existence is unlikely based on his absence from texts composed shortly after Badon, this fact is not a paraphrase of the quoted sentence, which is what the question is asking for.

Choice (C) is wrong because the passage as a whole establishes which side Arthur fought on at Badon (if he existed), and because, in any case, this question is not what the quoted sentence is addressing (the question is asking for a paraphrase of the quoted sentence).

Choice (D) is wrong because, while it may be possible that there were two Arthurs, this is not what the quoted sentence is addressing, and the question is asking for a paraphrase of the quoted sentence.

When the author describes early 6th-century Britain as "a free-for-all of warring tribes" (Line 17), he most likely does this in order to support the idea that

(A) a historical Arthur almost certainly did not exist.

(B) a historical Arthur would not have spoken English.

(C) the historical Arthur probably didn't hold political power.

(D) a historical Arthur couldn't have been a king.

(E) Great Britain had formerly been controlled by the Romans.

The correct answer is Choice (D). The context makes it clear that what is in question here is the concept of Arthur as a "king." The characterization of early 6th-century Britain as "a free-for-all of warring tribes" is meant to support the assertion that the people were not all ruled by one man.

Choice (A) is wrong because, although the passage as a whole does seem to indicate that the existence of a historical Arthur is unlikely, the context of the quoted phrase concentrates specifically on the implausibility of anyone (be it Arthur or anybody else) being a "king" in any recognizable sense in this particular place and time.

Choice (B) is wrong because, although the passage as a whole definitely establishes that a historical Arthur would not have spoken English, the context of the quoted phrase concentrates specifically on the implausibility of anyone being a "king" in any recognizable sense in this particular place and time.

Choice (C) is wrong because, although the passage as a whole does cast doubt on the idea that Arthur held political power rather than merely a military rank, the context of the quoted phrase concentrates specifically on the implausibility of anyone being a "king" in any recognizable sense in this particular place and time. This section of the passage *doesn't* establish that Arthur couldn't have held *any* political office, just that he wasn't a king.

Choice (E) is wrong because, although the passage does state that Great Britain had been controlled by the Romans, this is not the assertion that the "free-for-all of warring tribes" concept is being used to support; we already know it is true, and the "free-for-all of warring tribes" is what happened afterwards.

Which of the following discoveries, if such a discovery were made, would provide the most compelling new evidence for the existence of a historical Arthur?

(A) a text composed in 855 that definitively calls him a king

(B) a text composed in 925 that states he was born in 482

(C) a text composed in 595 that says he fought at Badon, but was not a king

(D) a monument erected soon after Badon and dedicated to an unidentified king

(E) a painting from 835 that includes a figure clearly labeled as King Arthur

The correct answer is Choice (C). The question doesn't ask you to identify a finding that would support the existence of a historical *King* Arthur, just the existence of Arthur as a historical figure who lived at all (the passage already explains that it was virtually impossible for him to have been a king). The end of the second paragraph establishes that the biggest problem for historians who support the existence of a historical Arthur is that he is not mentioned in any source for about 300 years after he supposedly lived. A source that mentions Arthur and was written closer to his own lifetime would be a marvelous find for those who want to argue his existence (and a text from 595 would be much closer to Arthur's reputed lifetime than any text we currently have).

Choice (A) is wrong because the passage states that the earliest source we have that mentions Arthur is from 828, so a source from 855 would not be earlier (and therefore more persuasive). It would be interesting that it called him a king (because the text from 828 does not), but this wouldn't be very good evidence — it could easily be an embellishment based on the 828 text.

Choice (B) is wrong because, although specifics like a birth year are good to have, the sudden assertion of a birth year in a text from 925 would be highly suspect. If no texts from the previous 400 years mentioned the year that Arthur was born, where would a writer in 925 suddenly have gotten this information?

Choice (D) is wrong because the mere existence of an early 6th-century monument to *some* king wouldn't mean that the king was Arthur.

Choice (E) is wrong because, although a painting of "King Arthur" from 835 would be the earliest reference to Arthur as a king, it wouldn't be evidence that he existed. Like with the hypothetical text from 855 in Choice (A), this rendering could just be an embellishment of the text from 828.

Visual- and Quantitative-Information Questions

Questions about vocabulary and authorial intent — the types of Praxis reading questions we cover in the sections "Mastering Short-Passage Questions" and "Looking at Long-Passage Questions," earlier in this chapter — probably aren't terribly different from what you remember encountering on tests you had to take in school. The most unusual thing about the Praxis reading test (don't worry — we said *unusual*, not *difficult*) is that it also includes what are referred to as *visual- and quantitative-information* questions, which is the Praxis's fancy term for questions about charts and graphs. Most reading and writing tests don't do this.

There aren't a ton of visual- and quantitative-information questions on the Praxis exam. There may only be two or three. Depending on the exam you happen to take, you may see three questions all about the same graph, or you may see one or two questions each about a couple of different graphs. But every point helps, so the following sections tell you about these questions.

Rethinking charts and graphs

If charts and graphs make you nervous because they seem more like math and science stuff than reading and writing stuff, the first step for you is to think about visual- and numeric-representation questions differently. The fact that visual- and quantitative-information questions are on the Praxis reading portion of the exam isn't a mistake or the result of someone's bizarre whim — it proves that, regardless of appearances, these questions really are reading-comprehension questions at heart.

REMEMBER

A graph — or any kind of picture — can be thought of as a visual depiction of information that could also be presented verbally. Just like you could represent an idea by *either* composing the sentence "A horse jumps over a fence" *or* drawing a picture of a horse jumping over a fence, a bar graph, line graph, pie chart, or any other type of chart or graph can be thought of as verbal information presented in pictorial form.

So, relax. The visual- and quantitative-information questions *are* reading-comprehension questions. They're just different.

Getting graphs

The most common type of a graph is a line graph. A line graph represents the relationship between two variables: an independent variable plotted along the *x* (horizontal) axis and a dependent variable (a variable that *depends on* the first one) plotted along the *y* (vertical) axis. The line running through the quadrant formed by their intersection is what you look at to figure out what value for one variable is paired with what value for the other. So say you had a line graph that plotted the relationship between "hours spent studying" and "score on the Praxis reading test" (as though everyone who studied for the same amount of time got the exact same score, which would certainly be nice). The "hours spent studying" would be plotted with hatch marks along the horizontal axis, and the various possible "scores on the Praxis reading test" would be plotted along the vertical axis, because this is the variable that depends on the other one. If you want to know the score someone who studied for, say, five hours, would get, you'd just proceed upward from the five-hour hatch mark on the bottom until you hit the line representing the actual data, then turn and go left until you hit the corresponding score on the side of the graph.

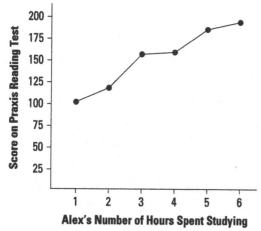

© *John Wiley & Sons, Inc.*

See Chapter 7 for more on line graphs.

Another type of graph commonly found in Praxis visual- and quantitative-information questions is a bar graph. Rather than depicting the relationship between an independent and a dependent variable like a line graph does, a bar graph represents how different categories stack up against each other with respect to some particular idea. For example, you might use a bar graph to compare the number of World Series won by various baseball teams. The names of all the teams would be plotted along the horizontal with a bar above each name, and the heights of the bars would indicate the number of World Series each team had won, with the vertical axis of the graph hatch-marked to indicate how many championships were represented by a given bar height. The bar representing the New York Yankees would be very high (some might say unfairly high); the bars representing the St. Louis Cardinals, Oakland Athletics, and Boston Red Sox would be lower, but still respectably high; and the San Diego Padres and Texas Rangers wouldn't have bars over their names at all (at least not as of this writing, since neither team has yet won a World Series).

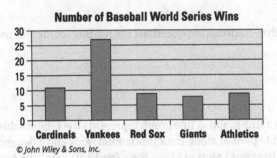

Number of Baseball World Series Wins

© John Wiley & Sons, Inc.

You could also plot that same information with another common type of graph called a pie chart. The difference between a pie chart and a bar graph is that a pie chart represents percentages of a total, so it looks like a circle with different-sized triangle-like pieces marked off inside it (hence its name). On a World Series pie chart, the Yankees' slice of the pie would be nearly one-fourth of the whole pie, as there have been 115 World Series and the Yankees have won 27 of them. The Cardinals' slice would be about one-tenth of the pie (11 World Series victories out of 115). Because a pie graph represents percentages of a total, the teams that have never won a World Series wouldn't appear on the pie at all.

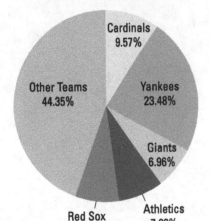

Baseball World Series Wins

Cardinals 9.57%
Yankees 23.48%
Giants 6.96%
Athletics 7.83%
Red Sox 7.83%
Other Teams 44.35%

*Each presented percentage is rounded to the nearest hundredth of a percentage.

© John Wiley & Sons, Inc.

But really, there's no sense in trying to memorize every type of chart or graph in the world. There are far too many ways to represent data visually for it to be in your interest to try to guess which types of charts or graphs will make an appearance when you take the exam. The best approach is to identify key words from the question, connect them to information represented in the graph, and then analyze the answer choices.

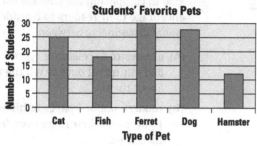

© John Wiley & Sons, Inc.

EXAMPLE

Based on the preceding graph, the biggest drop-off in popularity between consecutively ranked pets is between

(A) the most popular pet and the second most popular pet.

(B) the second most popular pet and the third most popular pet.

(C) the third most popular pet and the fourth most popular pet.

(D) the fourth most popular pet and the fifth most popular pet.

(E) The drop-offs in popularity between the first and second most popular pets, and between the third and fourth most popular pets were equally large.

The correct answer is Choice (B). In order to answer this question correctly, you have to think about the pets in order of most popular to least popular — that is, rank them *consecutively* as the question states. The biggest drop-off in popularity between consecutively ranked pets by a fairly wide margin is between cats (the second-most-popular pet, chosen by 25 students) and fish (the third most popular pet, chosen by about 17 or 18 students), with a drop-off of 7 or 8 votes. Note that the bar graph doesn't allow you to judge perfectly how many students voted for fish, but that doesn't matter. Whether fish got 17 or 18 votes, the biggest drop-off in popularity is still between cats and fish.

Choice (A) is wrong because cats got only two or three fewer votes than dogs, so this isn't the biggest drop-off in popularity. Choice (C) is wrong because ferrets got only three or four fewer votes than fish, so this isn't the biggest drop-off in popularity. Choice (D) is wrong because hamsters got only one or two fewer votes than ferrets, so this isn't the biggest drop-off in popularity.

Choice (E) is wrong because, although it is *true* that the gap between dogs and cats and the gap between fish and ferrets are equally large, neither of them is the largest drop-off in popularity. It doesn't matter that they were equally large because the question was asking for the largest drop-off. Be careful!

Practice Reading-Comprehension Questions

These practice questions are similar to the reading-comprehension questions that you'll encounter on the Praxis.

Questions 1 through 3 are based on the following passage.

Perhaps more so than that of any other man, his name is synonymous with incalculable brilliance in the hard sciences, and yet it is far from accurate to view Sir Isaac Newton as a model of rationalism. True, he invented calculus, laid the foundations for the science of optics, and — most famously — formulated the laws of motion and the principles of gravitation. Yet his myriad discoveries are more accurately seen as the byproducts of his boundless and obsessive mathematical mind than as the result of what today we would deem a scientific worldview: Privately, Newton spent as much time on alchemy and the search for the Philosopher's Stone as on legitimate empirical science, and he was consumed with efforts to calculate the date of Armageddon based on a supposed secret code in the Bible. Rather than being the human embodiment of the secular Enlightenment, Isaac Newton the man was a superstitious mystic whose awe-inspiring brain still managed to kickstart the scientifically modern world almost despite himself.

1. The central idea of the passage is to set up a contrast between

   (A) Newton's brilliant scientific successes and his embarrassing scientific failures.

   (B) Newton's secret private life and his false public image.

   (C) scientific methodology before Newton and scientific methodology after Newton.

   (D) Newton's scientific achievements and his unscientific worldview.

   (E) how Newton is viewed today and how he was viewed in his own time.

2. As it is used in context, the word "empirical" seems most nearly to mean

   (A) evidence-based.

   (B) mystical.

   (C) awe-inspiring.

   (D) outdated.

   (E) ironic.

3. It is fair to assume that part of the author's goal in composing the passage was to encourage their readers to consider the occasional disconnects between

   (A) our desire to celebrate "great" minds and our moral duty to tell the truth about them.

   (B) modern public images of historical figures and their more complex real identities.

   (C) humanity's ability to reason and our dark and chaotic emotional lives.

   (D) what some people are mistakenly credited with doing and what they actually did.

   (E) the greatness of our modern scientific worldview and the horrors of our superstitious past.

Questions 4 through 6 are based on the following passage.

Nathaniel Essex is a serious scientist born into a comic-book world. Toiling obsessively to prove his theories, shunned by the scientific establishment for his unorthodox experiments, he stands on the brink of enlightenment or, perhaps, corruption. A fateful encounter with Apocalypse provides both. When offered genetic knowledge from outside his own timeline, Essex accepts transformation at Apocalypse's hands, refashioning his body and mind to eliminate mortal weakness — and with it, his essential humanity. Casting off his identity as Essex, he becomes the diabolical figure known as Mister Sinister. In decades to come, he will emerge as a geneticist of unparalleled brilliance and daring, a witness to great discoveries and travesties of medical history, and one of the most dangerous opponents the X-Men will ever face.

4. The passage uses the term "corruption" to refer to all of the following actions of Nathaniel Essex except

(A) losing his identity.

(B) giving up his essential humanity.

(C) ridding himself of mortal weakness.

(D) becoming one of the most dangerous opponents of the X-Men.

(E) turning into a diabolical and sinister figure.

5. What life experience does the author imply may have been the basis for Essex's decision to be transformed?

(A) failing to impress Apocalypse.

(B) suddenly appearing in a comic book world.

(C) doubting his own scientific theories.

(D) changing his name.

(E) struggling to establish himself as a successful and respected scientist.

6. Which of the following best describes the organization of the passage?

(A) A story is told, and the author's view on the nature of what happens in it is presented.

(B) A drastic change is described, but it is also illustrated as beyond the possibility of judgment.

(C) A wish to be like a certain comic book figure is expressed.

(D) A scientific theory about a fictitious change is supported by details of a character's life.

(E) A comic book story is reviewed with both praise and criticism.

Questions 7 through 9 are based on the following passage.

After the Gadsden Purchase of 1853, the United States needed to find an efficient way of exploring the territory newly acquired from Mexico, much of which was desert. The idea of purchasing camels and forming a U.S. Army Camel Corps for the purpose was initially scoffed at, but finally approved in 1855, and a herd of 70 camels was subsequently amassed by Navy vessels sent off to Egypt and Turkey. Ironically,

however, the Camel Corps was stationed in Texas, a state that seceded from the Union upon the outbreak of the Civil War in 1861. With a war to fight and no need or desire to explore territory that now belonged to another nation, Texas simply set the camels free and shooed them off into the desert. The lucky camels thrived and bred, and a feral camel population survived in the southwestern United States until well into the 20th century, occasionally causing havoc when one or more camels would wander into a town and spark a riot among the horses. The last such incident recorded took place in 1941.

7. The author's tone in the passage can best be characterized as

(A) primarily explanatory but subtly critical.

(B) largely theoretical but consistently open-minded.

(C) primarily informative and somewhat humorous.

(D) largely analytical and mildly biased.

(E) primarily skeptical but ultimately forgiving.

8. In context, the "another nation" referred to in Line 13 is

(A) the United States.

(B) the Confederacy.

(C) Mexico.

(D) Egypt.

(E) Turkey.

9. The primary purpose of the final sentence of the passage is presumably to

(A) emphasize how large the population of feral camels eventually became.

(B) surprise the reader by linking the content of the passage to living memory.

(C) provide a hint about what finally killed off the wild camel population.

(D) definitively answer a question posed at the beginning of the passage.

(E) imply that some wild camels might still be alive in the American Southwest.

Questions 10 through 12 are based on the following passage.

Even the poorest of history students could tell you that it was *Marie* Antoinette who issued the oblivious response, "Let them eat cake," upon being informed that the peasants had no bread — except that it wasn't. The famous anecdote so frequently used to underscore how out-of-touch the very wealthy can be appears in Jean-Jacques Rousseau's *Confessions*, written in 1765, when the future and ill-fated queen of France was only nine years old and still living in her native Austria. Far from making any claims to historical accuracy, Rousseau attributes the pampered faux pas only to an anonymous "great princess" and presents it as a yarn that was old and corny even then. Presumably, the legend had been repeated about any number of European royal women for generations — but since Marie Antoinette ended up being the *last* queen of France, the version in which she says it was the one that stuck.

10. According to the passage, the most likely reason that the phrase "Let them eat cake" has become associated with Marie Antoinette is that

(A) she may have actually said it, although this cannot be proven.

(B) her life happened to overlap with that of Jean-Jacques Rousseau.

(C) she was the final person to have her name inserted into an old joke.

(D) food shortages among the peasants reached an apex during her reign.

(E) she is the only queen of France that the average history student can name.

11. Which of the following questions is directly answered by the passage?

(A) From what nation was Marie Antoinette originally?

(B) In what nation did the "Let them eat cake" legend first start?

(C) Who lived longer, Jean-Jacques Rousseau or Marie Antoinette?

(D) Whom did Rousseau himself believe had said "Let them eat cake"?

(E) What point was Rousseau trying to make with the "Let them eat cake" anecdote?

12. Which of the following phrases from the passage is used most nearly as a synonym for *oblivious*, as it appears in the first sentence?

(A) "ill-fated"

(B) "pampered"

(C) "anonymous"

(D) "old and corny"

(E) "out-of-touch"

Answers and Explanations

Use this answer key to score the practice reading-comprehension questions in the preceding section.

1. **D. Newton's scientific achievements and his unscientific worldview.** The passage establishes that Isaac Newton was personally superstitious and a religious fanatic, and this "unscientific worldview" is contrasted with the brilliant scientific achievements he made despite this.

    The right answer is not Choice (A) because the passage never alludes to any "embarrassing scientific failures" of Newton — only to private beliefs and endeavors that were unscientific. The right answer is not Choice (B) because the passage never implies that Newton deliberately cultivated a "false public image," only that he privately believed superstitious things.

    The right answer is not Choice (C) because, although science after Newton was certainly different as a result of the many landmark innovations he made, the passage is concerned only with Newton himself, not with the difference in the sciences before and after him. The right answer is not Choice (E) because while the passage points out inaccuracies in the way Newton is often viewed today, it doesn't address how he was viewed in his own time.

2. **A. evidence-based.** Both in the passage and in most contexts, "empirical" means "evidence-based."

    The right answer is not Choice (B) because "empirical" doesn't mean "mystical," either in the passage or in most contexts (in fact, it means very nearly the opposite). The right answer is not Choice (C) because "empirical" doesn't mean "awe-inspiring" (this is just another unrelated phrase from the passage, used as a red herring).

    The right answer is not Choice (D) because although the passage characterizes some of Newton's personal beliefs as "outdated," the word "empirical" does not mean or appear to mean "outdated" in context. The right answer is not Choice (E) because although the contrast between Newton's achievements and his personal beliefs is "ironic," this is not what the word "empirical" means or appears to mean in context.

3. **B. modern public images of historical figures and their more complex real identities.** The passage is primarily — indeed, almost exclusively — concerned with highlighting the difference between our modern idea of Isaac Newton as an Enlightenment rationalist and the more complex truth of his status as a superstitious mystic.

    The right answer is not Choice (A) because the passage doesn't hint at anything like a "moral duty to tell the truth" about famous figures like Newton; it corrects a misconception, but it's not an exposé, as such. The right answer is not Choice (C) because the passage is about Newton specifically, not the human race in general, and it doesn't characterize Newton's private life as "dark and chaotic," only "superstitious."

    The right answer is not Choice (D) because the passage never addresses anything that Newton is "mistakenly credited with doing." The right answer is not Choice (E) because while the passage characterizes Newton as superstitious, it never brings up anything resembling any collective "horrors" of the superstitious past of humanity in general.

4. **C. ridding himself of all mortal weakness.** The passage discusses major changes Nathaniel Essex went through. One of the mentioned changes is presented as positive, and the others are described as negative. The two words that refer to the changes before they are described are "enlightenment" and "corruption." The author says both took place, but mentions "corruption" as what would seem to be just a negative possibility at the time Nathaniel

made his decision to change. It is mentioned as a possible downside that ended up coming true. The positive change that is discussed must therefore be the "enlightenment," and it is Nathaniel's ridding himself of all mortal weakness. That alone is an improvement, a positive change.

Choices (A), (B), (D), and (E) are changes that are presented as problematic, so they are parts of the downside of the situation. They are therefore aspects of the "corruption," not "enlightenment."

5. **E. Struggling to establish himself as a successful and respected scientist.** In the second sentence, the author describes Nathaniel's failures at being a scientist. The author also describes how hard Nathaniel was working to overcome those failures, suggesting frustration and a need to try something different. The author then immediately explains Nathaniel's opportunity to drastically change as a scientist, indicating that Nathaniel made the decision because it would give him what he had been working "obsessively" to achieve during a period illustrated by the author to be frustrating. That is how the author connects desire and resulting frustration to a decision to majorly transform.

Choice (A) is incorrect because nothing in the passage suggests that Nathaniel had any desire to impress Apocalypse. Choice (B) is wrong because the passage does not indicate that Nathaniel suddenly ended up in a comic book world after being somewhere else. The first sentence merely describes a character who was created for comic books. It is not about a place in reality where characters can end up after some time. Nothing in the passage suggests that it is. Even if it were, it would not mean that such an unmentioned change of location had anything to do with Nathaniel's decision to drastically change his identity, humanity, morality, name, or level of dangerousness. Choice (C) is incorrect for the same type of reason. The passage does not indicate in any way that Nathaniel ever doubted his own theories. He was working with great effort to get others to believe his theories by proving them, but that suggests he believed his theories since he thought he could prove them. Also, nothing the author says implies that there was any connection between self-doubt and the will to change. Choice (D) is wrong because Nathaniel's name change happened in a way that described what he had become as a result of the changes Apocalypse gave him the ability to undergo. Nothing suggests that the name change caused anything. The passage says that Nathaniel became somebody else with a different name, not that he became somebody else because he had a different name.

6. **A. A story is told, and the author's view on the nature of what happens in it is presented.** The passage gives the story of Nathaniel Essex's change into someone very different with a different name, so a story is told. The author provides his view on what happened by saying the change involved enlightenment and corruption. The author therefore tells a story and presents his view on what ends up happening in it.

Choice (B) is wrong because the author does not ever suggest that what happens in the story is beyond the possibility of judgment. He never indicates in any way that it cannot be judged. In fact, he judges it. Choice (C) is incorrect because the author never expresses a wish to be like Nathaniel. He never even mentions or hints at his own desires at all. Choice (D) is wrong since the passage is not about any scientific theories that exist in reality. The passage mentions the scientific theories of a fictitious scientist character, but it does not even say what those theories are, and they are just part of a fiction story. The story does not mention or suggest any scientific theories, so it could not support any, and it does not support any. Choice (E) is incorrect because the author does not indicate how much he likes or dislikes the story. He just tells it and says what he thinks it means without giving his view of the intellectual or artistic quality of it.

7. **C. primarily informative and somewhat humorous.** The passage is indisputably informative, and it is, on occasion, slightly humorous. Because both these things are true, there's no real way that this answer choice can be wrong.

The right answer is not Choice (A) because though the passage is explanatory, it's never critical. The right answer is not Choice (B) because the passage merely relates historical events; there's nothing "theoretical" about it, and "open-mindedness" isn't an issue.

The right answer is not Choice (D) because the passage merely relates information without analyzing anything; by extension, it can't be biased because it doesn't present an opinion. The right answer is not Choice (E) because the passage deals only with historical facts, not opinion or theory, so there's nothing for it to be either "skeptical" or "forgiving" about.

8. **A. the United States.** From Texas's point of view, the United States was "another nation" because Texas had seceded to join the Confederacy.

The fact that Texas itself was part of the Confederacy eliminates Choice (B). Mexico, Choice (C), is the nation to which the Gadsden Purchase land originally belonged. Egypt and Turkey, Choices (D) and (E), respectively, are merely nations from which the camels were purchased.

9. **B. surprise the reader by linking the content of the passage to living memory.** The author's intent in the last sentence is to shock and amuse the reader, who will presumably be surprised to hear that wild camel "incidents" were still taking place in the United States in 1941 (in other words, in *living memory* — a phrase used to mean "within the memory of at least some people who are still alive").

The right answer is not Choice (A) because the final sentence of the passage doesn't imply anything about the size of the wild camel herd at any point. The right answer is not Choice (C) because, although it presumably implies that the camels didn't survive too long past 1941, the final sentence of the passage doesn't imply anything about how they actually died.

The right answer is not Choice (D) because there is no question at the beginning of the passage that the final sentence answers. The right answer is not Choice (E) because the final sentence doesn't imply that some camels may have survived — if they had, there presumably would have been camel incidents after 1941.

10. **C. she was the final person to have her name inserted into an old joke.** The ending of the passage offers the theory that the "Let them eat cake" joke was repeated about royals for years, and that the version with Marie Antoinette's name is the version that "stuck" because there were no more French queens after her.

The right answer is not Choice (A) because the passage definitively establishes that Marie Antoinette couldn't have said "Let them eat cake" (the joke appears in a book written when she was a child). The right answer is not Choice (B) because, while it's true that the life of Marie Antoinette overlapped with that of Jean-Jacques Rousseau, the passage doesn't imply that this is the reason the "Let them eat cake" story is associated with her. (Why would it be?)

The right answer is not Choice (D) because, although it may be true that food shortages among the peasantry reached an apex during Marie Antoinette's reign, the passage does not state or imply that this is the main reason why the "Let them eat cake" story is associated with her. The right answer is not Choice (E) because, while it may be true that Marie Antoinette is the only queen of France that the average student can name (in America, at least), the passage doesn't state or imply that this is the main reason why the "Let them eat cake" story is associated with her.

11. A. From what nation was Marie Antoinette originally? The middle of the passage makes reference to Marie Antoinette's "native Austria."

The right answer is not Choice (B) because the passage never answers the question of what nation the "Let them eat cake" story originated in — it implies that the story was told about "any number of *European* royal women for generations." The right answer is not Choice (C) because the passage never states or suggests whether Jean-Jacques Rousseau or Marie Antoinette lived longer.

The right answer is not Choice (D) because the passage never implies that Rousseau had any belief about who "really" said "Let them eat cake"; if he presented the story as an old joke, then he likely believed that no one really said it. The right answer is not Choice (E) because, although the passage states that the "Let them eat cake" story is often used to emphasize the cluelessness of the rich, it never explains what point Rousseau himself was using it to make in the context of his *Confessions*.

12. E. "out-of-touch." In both the context of the passage and most of the time, "oblivious" means "clueless" or "out-of-touch," a term used in the next sentence to clarify the meaning of the word "oblivious" as it is used in the passage.

Nothing in the passage implies that it means "ill-fated," "pampered," "anonymous," or "old and corny," either in the context of the passage or elsewhere, ruling out Choices (A), (B), (C), and (D), respectively.

Chapter **10**

Test-Taking Strategies for Core Reading

C hapter 9 covers the structure of the Praxis reading test and the types of questions you can expect to see. But that chapter is principally an overview of the types of reading skills you'll want to hone before the exam. In this chapter, we take more of a "game theory" approach to the task at hand, helping you to crack the code of the test and earn a great score by any down-and-dirty means necessary (aside from cheating, of course).

Which to Read First: The Passage or the Question

The same question seems to arise first whenever the subject of answering questions about reading passages comes up: Should you read the passage first and then look at the question(s), or should you scan the question(s) first and then look back for the answers in the passage?

The majority of students who struggle with reading comprehension find that it's best to start by reading the passage.

So *why* is it better to read the passage first? Wouldn't a more commonsense approach be to glance at the question beforehand so that you know what you're supposed to be looking for? That thinking is understandable, but the question-first method is less desirable for a few reasons.

On most reading tests, there are multiple questions about a single passage, so if you start with the questions and then look back, you end up reading certain bits and pieces of the passage over and over instead of reading the whole thing only once. Reading the passage once saves time.

Now, granted, the Praxis reading test has a good number of one-to-one pairings — brief passages about which only one question is asked — and reading the questions first doesn't cause as many problems in these instances. However, because you encounter a variety of reading passages on the Praxis — long passages, short passages, one-to-one pairings — you don't want to continually change your strategy based on the type of question that pops up on the screen. Getting into the habit of reading the question first only on the brief passages means you have to switch up your strategy when a long passage that has multiple questions appears. You run the risk of getting thrown off your game. (Whatever your method is, practicing it and sticking to it is always a good idea.)

When you look at the question before reading the passage, having the question on your mind while reading has a tendency to get in the way. You're unable to really consider what the passage is saying because you're mentally hearing the question over and over and nervously scanning the text for one sentence that explicitly states the answer. But right answers often aren't found in one particular sentence. Sometimes they involve making an inference based on considering several of the author's points together; other times, you may be dealing with a "tone" or "purpose" question that requires you to take a step back and consider the passage as a whole.

REMEMBER

As a general rule, focusing on the task before you is always easier when nothing is distracting you. It's why you can easily walk across a balance beam that's 1 foot off the ground, whereas walking across the same beam when it's 50 feet off the ground is terrifying. Having the question running through your head while you're trying to make sense of the passage is like trying to walk the balance beam while you're freaking out about how high off the ground it is. Just take the passage on its own terms. If you do that well, when it comes time to look at a question, the answer should be obvious.

What about those questions that ask you what the author means by a specific phrase or give you a specific line number? You're just wasting time reading the whole passage if the question is only about one measly little line or sentence in it, right? Wrong! One of the most dangerous pitfalls of the question-first method is that it can instill you with a false sense of confidence about where you need to look. Just because the question asks you what the author means in Line 17 doesn't necessarily mean that the best way to answer the question is to jump straight to Line 17 and read it again and again. Often, the purpose of a given sentence is best clarified by contextual clues found elsewhere in the passage.

REMEMBER

Having a good sense of what the passage as a whole means is always an advantage, even if the question ends up asking about only one specific part of the passage. Reading the whole passage before you see the question allows you to process the flow of the text as a whole, rather than as merely a series of statements and details, as you'd see it if you were scanning for one single point.

But the most important reason not to look at the question first is that looking at the question will probably also tempt you to look at the answer choices. And the answer choices were *designed* to confuse you.

Having the wording of the answer choices in your head while you're reading the passage is a recipe for disaster. The writers of the test design the wrong answer choices by taking details or groups of words from the passage that are memorable or seem important, and then inserting them into answer choices that don't answer the question. So, having those phrases in your mind while you read causes you to linger over red herrings, possibly ignoring the right answer in the process.

Examining Strategies for the Various Passages

Most people who take the Praxis don't mind brief statements that are accompanied by one question. Where folks get a little nervous is when they have to read a longer passage (100 to 200 or so words) and then answer a couple of questions about what they just read. Many people aren't too fond of the paired passages either, where they have to read two passages of about 200 words total and then answer a handful of questions.

In the following sections, we reveal what types of questions usually correspond to each type of passage. Armed with these details, you can face any passage with confidence.

Approaching long and short passages

When a new question first pops up on your computer screen, you can easily tell whether it's going to be a one-to-one pairing of a brief passage and a single question or a long passage about which there will be several questions. A one-to-one question appears as a centered paragraph with a question below it, whereas a long passage is narrower, with the question (which is the first of several) off to the side. Often, the lines in the passage are also numbered so that questions can specifically refer to "Line 5" or "Line 13." Also, each question has specific directions in bold at the top of the screen. Single passage questions will direct the user to answer the question listed below, while multiple question passages will tell the test-taker how many questions are based on the passage, such as "Questions 5 and 6 refer to the following passage."

REMEMBER

On the long passages, sticking to the method of reading the passage before the questions is doubly important because repeatedly scanning a long passage for several answers that are only revealed one at a time adds up to a lot of time wasted. But aside from sticking to the system of reading the passage first, what *else* should you keep in mind while reading the long passage?

A long passage often asks about the meaning or purpose of specific details or sentences, as opposed to asking you about the tone or the purpose of the passage as a whole. Of course, the test *might* ask you about the overall tone in a long passage, just like it might pair a vocabulary question with a short passage — there aren't really any rules stipulating that certain types of questions have to be paired with certain passage lengths. But the fact remains that certain types of questions are more commonly found on the long passages.

Questions for long passages often examine the relationship between the passage's main idea and its supporting points. So when you see a long passage pop up, be prepared for questions along the lines of "The author mentions *[some factoid]* in order to support the assertion that . . ." Long-passage questions tend to be about how the parts form the whole: The questions ask you about the parts, but getting the answers involves comprehending the whole.

WARNING

Be careful of the trick where a minor detail from the end of a passage is purported to be the "main idea" or "primary purpose" of the passage in an early answer choice. The question writers do that to try to trick you into jumping on that answer merely because it's fresh in your mind. Remember, something that wasn't even brought up until the end of the passage is unlikely to be the main idea.

Short passages tend to ask more fact-based questions. When you see a short passage, be prepared to answer questions along the lines of "The passage is primarily concerned with [some factoid]" or "Which of the following is an unstated assumption made by the author of the passage?"

REMEMBER

The long and the short passages really aren't that different. The long passages have more questions about them because, well, they're *longer*, so the test writers have more text to ask questions about. But honestly, that's about it. Aside from the fact that a long passage is more likely to be argumentative (and therefore lend itself to questions about main and supporting points), whereas a short passage is more likely to be purely informative, you don't need to approach either one of them in some essentially "different" way. Answering four questions about four paragraphs is more or less the same as answering one question about one paragraph four times.

Approaching the paired passages

Some of the passages on the Praxis reading test involve a side-by-side comparison of two passages by two different authors on the same topic. They may explicitly disagree with each other and present two arguments that are *mutually exclusive* (that is, can't be true at the same time), or they may just analyze the same issue from two different angles. The questions concentrate on the differences between the two passages. (If this sounds like a pain, keep in mind that you *usually* see only one passage like this on a given Praxis reading test, although no rule says that there can't be more than one.)

You know you're facing a question like this when the first paragraph is designated as "Passage 1" and the second as "Passage 2" (they both pop up on your computer screen at the same time, one above the other). When you have two passages like this before you, expect to see questions about the differences between the two authors' viewpoints.

Now, the strategy to successfully dealing with paired passages is to avoid going straight from reading the passage to reading the question like you would for other reading questions. Instead, take a few seconds to *anticipate* the question. Formulating an expectation in your head about what the question may be is actually a good idea, and when it comes to paired passages, it's a *very* good idea. Trying to anticipate questions can inspire you to think more about what the passages say and to analyze them more deeply. Enhanced attention and analysis are especially helpful when you have to compare or contrast two different passages. Finding parallels and distinctions between two bodies of writing requires an extra level of understanding their fine details and complexities. After you read the two paired passages, stop for a moment before looking at the questions and ask yourself: *What are the similarities and differences between the two authors' viewpoints?* Then, think of what the questions about the passages may be, and reflect further before answering the questions.

Your goal with this approach is to look at two brief, mutually exclusive, thesis-driven paragraphs and explain the difference between them in your own words. You probably wouldn't have any trouble writing a short sentence that would accurately explain the essence of the two authors' disagreement. However, when you're asked to choose from among five prospective explanations written by someone else, discerning the difference between the authors' points gets tricky.

The solution to this problem is easy: Consider what the difference is in your own words *before* you look at the question and the answer choices, and then pick the answer choice that presents the nearest paraphrase of what you just said.

Of course, "What is the difference between the two authors' arguments?" isn't the *only* question that the Praxis reading test can ask you about a set of paired passages. A version of this question is almost certain to be *one* of the questions that follows the paired passages, but there will be others, too (as a type of "long passage," a paired passage is always followed by multiple questions). Another common question asks something along the lines of "Which of the following devices is used by the author of Passage 1 but not by the author of Passage 2?" The answer choices then present you with five options along the lines of rhetorical questions, similes, flashbacks, pop-culture references, and personification. There's really no shortcut to answering a question like this: You just have to look back at the passages and see which of the devices is used by the first author but not the second. (Don't worry — the two passages are brief enough that you can do this without eating up a whole lot of time.)

These questions may also ask the reader to apply the ideas in the texts to other situations, to predict based on what has been read, and to analyze the stylistic structure of a text, such as the difference in the organization of the texts.

The real trick is not getting confused or turned around. When a question asks something like "Which of these devices is used by Author 1 but not Author 2?" there's often a wrong answer choice that names a device that is used *by Author 2 but not Author 1* to try and trip you up. So, stay sharp and remember what the question asks. ("I got it backwards" is a common head-slapping exclamation on tests like this — so, seriously, watch out.)

Approaching Questions about Charts and Graphs

As Chapter 9 explains, the visual- and quantitative-information questions are where the Praxis reading test breaks the mold of most reading-comprehension tests. People simply aren't used to encountering charts and graphs on a reading test, so these questions can make even very sharp English majors nervous because they seem like something that escaped from a math or science test. But the best way to think about the visual- and quantitative-information questions (of which you'll see only a few) is to remember that they *are*, in fact, reading-comprehension questions — you just "read" pictures instead of words. They are still testing for literacy, but it's a form called *visual literacy*, which is the ability to make meaning from information and images as opposed to just the written word.

So, the good news about the charts and graphs questions is that they really aren't any harder than any of the other questions on the Praxis reading test. The bad news is that there's no trick for answering them correctly. You just have to read the question and then look at the chart or graph to find the answer.

Just because there isn't a trick, though, doesn't mean that there isn't an advantage that can be exploited. There's actually a big advantage ripe for exploitation on these questions, and that's the fact that they invariably appear toward the very end of the test. The Praxis reading exam usually has about 56 questions, and the visual- and quantitative-information questions usually appear in the late 40s or early 50s. So, if you're the sort of person who gets nervous around charts and graphs, you'll at least be in a good position to calculate how much time it's wise to spend on them.

TIP

In short, the best advice about the visual- and quantitative-information questions for people who aren't comfortable around charts and graphs is to look at the clock, realize how much time you have, and be meticulous in selecting your answer. For example, rather than just reading the question and looking at the graph to see what you think the answer is, take the extra time to plug in the other four answer choices and make sure they're all wrong. Maybe you made a silly mistake on the first glance that this process will help you catch.

Eliminating Wrong Answers

When you're taking the Praxis reading test, remember a piece of advice that was actually the brainchild of a student many years ago: "Don't answer the questions; question the answers."

What in the world does that mean? Well, it all comes back to the advice from Chapter 9 about how there are almost always four wrong answers and one right answer, and any answer choice that isn't wrong must be right. No matter what kind of question you're looking at, no matter how long or short the passage is, you are always fundamentally dealing with the same situation: You're given five statements about the passage, and only one of them is 100 percent true. So, look each answer choice straight in the eye and ask it "Are you 100 percent not wrong?" The answer can be "yes" to only one of them.

We can't stress this enough: You're not looking for the most interesting statement about the passage, the most detailed one, the one with the biggest words in it, the one that's the most different from the others, the longest one, or the shortest one. You are looking for the one that has nothing in it that isn't true. The right answer may be vague, boring, or unremarkable, but that doesn't matter. All that matters is that *everything in it is true.*

That's what *questioning the answers* means. If you train your test-taking head to examine the answer choices this way, you'll almost always be able to eliminate at least three of them pretty quickly. If you can eliminate four, well then, problem solved. But sometimes, you may find that the question-the-answers method leaves you with a 50/50 conundrum — two remaining choices that you can't seem to choose between because they both look plausible.

When that happens, ask yourself: *Which of these statements about the passage could be true without the other one also automatically being true?* For example, if Choice (B) says "the passage is about an elephant" and Choice (D) says "the passage is about a mammal," the answer must be Choice (D). Why? Because elephants are mammals, so if Choice (B) is true, then so is Choice D. An animal can be a mammal without also being an elephant, but an animal can't be an elephant without also being a mammal.

The "Which of these statements can be true by itself?" method won't solve every 50/50 dilemma, but you'll be surprised by how many of them it does end up solving. If you do find yourself in a 50/50 bind that you just can't seem to crack, pick one, even if it's just a wild guess. Unlike some other standardized tests, you don't lose points for a wrong answer (as opposed to a blank one) on the Praxis. Because there's no difference between "blank" and "wrong," you have no reason not to guess.

TIP

If the true-by-itself razor doesn't help, try looking out for red-flag words such as "always" and "never" (pick the choice that doesn't have them). If this tip doesn't apply, then just pick the broader or less detailed of the two answers, on the grounds that an answer choice with less detail in it has a lesser chance of any of the details being wrong.

4
Fine-Tuning Your Writing Skills

IN THIS PART . . .

Discover the differences between the two essays you have to write, and get tips for writing a solid essay in just 30 minutes.

Review the essential grammar rules you're tested on when you take the Praxis.

Get insights on the most logical ways to approach sentence-correction, passage-revision, and research-skills questions.

Chapter **11**

Acing the Essay

I n your career as a teacher, success depends on your being clearly understood, not only by your students, but also by their parents, your colleagues, the school administration, and your community. The Praxis tests this ability by requiring you to write two essays. One directs you to respond to a statement by writing an essay that agrees or disagrees with a particular point of view. This essay is referred to as the *argumentative essay*, and you draw on your own observations and opinions to complete this writing assignment.

The other essay gives you a statement about a general topic that's familiar to all adults and asks you to write an essay about that topic, using two provided sources. This is the *informative/explanatory essay.* You don't need any special knowledge to write the essay. In addition to using information from the source material, you can also support the topic with examples from your own personal experience and general knowledge.

You have 30 minutes to produce each essay, so the essays don't have to be long. But they do need to be organized, logical, and supportive of the main ideas. Additionally, in the informative/ explanatory essay, you must demonstrate that you can extract information from the provided sources and cite the sources correctly.

This chapter gives you details about how to write a strong essay, explains how your essay will be scored, and gives you several essay prompts so that you can practice your writing skills.

Perusing the Types of Prompts: "Picking a Side" versus "Exploring an Idea"

The Praxis presents a prompt for writing the essay, and this prompt directs you to address the topic in a particular manner. You're directed to write either an *argumentative essay,* in which you argue for or against the stated idea, or an *informative/explanatory essay,* in which you write about a topic and explain why it's important. Understanding the writing prompt is essential for writing a successful essay. Take time to analyze the prompt before you begin the drafting process. Restate the topic in your own words.

The following sections explain how to write an argumentative essay and how to write an informative/explanatory essay.

Writing persuasively in the argumentative essay

A persuasive essay is written to convince the reader to accept your view or your opinion. A good persuasive essay is forceful, well-organized, and carefully reasoned.

The prompt may concern an issue about which you feel strongly. If so, your job in writing your essay is to persuade the reader to accept your view. Conversely, the prompt may be one about which you have no strong feelings. In this case, you can address the topic by exploring both sides of the idea. In either case, you must make your position clear. The scorer should not have to guess where you stand.

The directions for the first essay will be similar to this example:

> Discuss the extent to which you agree or disagree with this opinion. Support your views with specific reasons and examples from your own experience, observations, or reading.

Read the prompt carefully. Think about it. Do you agree or disagree? Maybe you're not sure of your opinion. In that case, which stance is easier for you to take? For which side of the issue can you generate the most support? For which side of the issue can you produce the best essay? Take that side.

Sticking to the facts in the informative essay

The second essay requires you to read passages from two sources and draw on the information in both sources, as well as your own experiences, to write the essay. You must correctly cite the sources.

The directions for the second essay will be similar to this example:

> The following assignment requires you to use information from two sources to discuss the most important concerns that relate to a specific issue. When paraphrasing or quoting from the sources, cite each source by referring to the author's last name, the title, or any other clear identifier.

The Praxis doesn't test the depth of your knowledge of a topic. The Praxis tests your ability to analyze information, write well, and incorporate outside sources while citing correctly. So, you don't need to be a *Jeopardy!* champion to write this essay.

REMEMBER

The Praxis scorers want just the facts in your essay. Don't waste their time and endanger your good score with unnecessary descriptions or comments that don't contribute to your main point, your *thesis*.

Creating a Solid Essay

The standard five-paragraph essay structure is an excellent way to organize an essay, and this method is the most frequently taught form of writing in the classroom. Even though this method isn't the only way to produce an essay, for most test-takers, the five-paragraph essay form is a good choice for the Praxis essay. You may find, however, that only one or two middle paragraphs are sufficient to fully develop your thesis.

Making an outline: Essential or overrated?

Although a formal outline isn't necessary, getting organized is essential. After you've read the directions and the prompt, restate the prompt in your own words. Be sure you understand what the prompt is asking you to do.

If you're writing the argumentative essay, think about your viewpoint. If you're working on the informative/explanatory essay, read the source material. Then, for either essay, formulate a rough thesis. Next, take a mental inventory. What examples or experiences can you relate to the topic? Write them down. In what order will you arrange these supporting details? Number them. Reread the prompt. Are your supporting details relevant? Make adjustments and rewrite your thesis, if necessary. You should spend no more than five to seven minutes on these tasks.

TIP

A common maxim regarding essay writing is, "Tell them what you are going to tell them, tell them, and then tell them what you told them." Although a bit simplistic, this is still good advice to keep in mind when you're organizing your writing.

Dividing up your essay into sections

Keep in mind that good writing of any kind requires an excellent thesis, topic sentences, and well-organized supporting details, as well as a strong conclusion.

Here's a breakdown of how to structure each paragraph in your essay:

» First paragraph

- Craft a short introduction.

- State your position, which is your thesis. (Here's your chance to make a good first impression. Best foot forward!)

» Middle paragraphs

- Begin with a topic sentence related to your thesis.

- Provide specific examples, details, and/or experiences. Explain why these are important and how they relate to your thesis. If you're working on the argumentative essay, what benefits can occur as a result of your point of view?

- End each paragraph with a strong final sentence relating to the thesis.

TIP

Read the prompt again to be sure everything you wrote relates to it. You don't want the thought "So what?" to enter the minds of your readers.

» Conclusion

- Put a bow on it. Tie up your ideas into one neat package. Avoid merely summarizing.

- Restate your position if this is the argumentative essay.

- Sum up the supporting details.

- Drive your point home.

» Works Cited

- Only for the essay requiring the use of sources.

- Be sure to format your sources properly.

After you organize your thoughts, begin writing your essay. Be sure to save the last four or five minutes to proofread, correcting spelling and grammar.

Don't box yourself in: Theses aren't set in stone

After you've written your thesis and begun to develop it in your middle paragraphs, you may find that an adjustment is in order. You may discover while writing your examples or experiences that your thesis statement has evolved and could be better.

Write your revised statement. After you've completed your essay, revisit your revised thesis and reread the prompt. If your revised thesis is better, change it.

Citing the sources

When you write the informative/explanatory essay, you must cite any outside sources you quote or paraphrase. You can cite sources within the body of the text several different ways:

>> You can cite a source by including the author's name in the sentence you are writing. Be sure to use quotation marks when quoting directly:

- According to Mary Lucas, "Children learn best by doing."

If you paraphrase, you must still cite your source:

- Mary Lucas believes that children can learn best by doing.

>> You can cite a source by writing the last name of the author in parentheses at the end of the sentence before the period:

- Children learn best by doing (Lucas).

Some additional writing pointers

Here are some general, but important, tips to keep in mind while you write your essays (see Chapter 13 for some additional strategies):

>> **Be careful to address only the assigned topic.** Don't wander off course — no sudden left turns.

>> **Don't leave anything out.** Address every point, but be concise. Be specific; make every word count.

>> **Provide clear support for your points.** Imagine that for every point you make, someone asks, "So what?" Be sure you have an answer. Doing this keeps your writing relevant.

>> **Pay attention to grammar, usage, and mechanics.** Errors here will cost you points.

>> **Use transitions.** Make your words flow from idea to idea and paragraph to paragraph.

>> **Vary the length and structure of your sentences.** Variety adds style that helps prevent monotony, thereby working to gain the interest and attention of the reader. Also, long sentences can be ideal for presenting a lot of information, and short sentences can be effective at adding emphasis.

Turning a Good Essay into a Great One

The Praxis essay scorers are looking for the complete package. They want a well-written, interesting essay. If you want a top score, you need to do more than organize your essay well and have good support for your thesis. You should also provide anecdotes when applicable, choose your words carefully, and acknowledge the other side of the argument when writing a persuasive essay. The following sections touch on these tactics.

Adding interesting anecdotes

Experienced writers and speakers often relate an anecdote to make a point. An *anecdote* is a very short story and can be an excellent way to support your essay's thesis. Personal stories are particularly memorable and, consequently, make your point memorable, too.

Consider this prompt for an argumentative essay:

> Because students have so many extracurricular activities and so little time outside the school day, the majority of school hours should be limited to academic courses only.

What could be better to support your view than a brief anecdote about your own experience in juggling extracurricular activities and academics?

The anecdote is simply a suggestion and not a requirement when writing your essay. It helps to illustrate your main ideas by using a real-life situation.

Although the Praxis is no place to practice your stand-up comedy routine, an amusing anecdote to illustrate your point is certainly allowed and can add energy and personality to your essay. Just be sure that the anecdote clearly supports your thesis and doesn't distract the reader.

Painting a picture with words

The old saying "A picture is worth a thousand words" applies to the essay. Even though you can't literally place a picture into your essay, your words can paint a picture to support your point. Create an image, a "word picture," by being very specific. Consider the following descriptions:

Vague: a nice day

Specific: bright sunshine and marshmallow clouds in a brilliant blue sky

By revising the vague statement of a nice day, the specific, detailed adjectives and nouns create a detailed image of a nice day in the reader's brain.

Vague verbs are too weak to create an image. Instead, use strong, active verbs. For example, instead of "walk," use a more specific verb — "amble," "stroll," or "trot."

REMEMBER

Use specific words in your essay to appeal to the five senses: sight, hearing, touch, taste, and smell. Doing so gives the reader the sense that they're there and can experience what you're describing.

However, using specific words also comes with a caveat. You should know the words that you use. "Big words" won't earn you extra points.

The big word isn't necessarily preferable to the simple word, nor is the unusual word preferable to the everyday word. Clarity is your goal. Don't confuse the reader by "overwriting." Big words used inappropriately can mean fewer points for your essay. Use words with which you're comfortable.

WARNING

Finally, avoid jargon — language that's so specialized that it may be misunderstood. You may know, for example, the specialized language that computer techies use every day, but assume that your reader doesn't.

Anticipating objections against your position

When you write the argumentative essay, consider what could be said against your view and prepare a strong retort. Recognizing opposing views strengthens your own. By refuting the opposite view, you make yours much stronger.

Ignoring a major opposing view weakens your position. Suppose, for example, you're writing in favor of banning certain books in the school library. Think about the opposing views and decide how you can refute them. Including counterarguments actually makes your own points stronger, not weaker, because it shows you clearly thought about the topic and are organized in your approach.

Understanding How the Essay Is Scored

Your essay will be evaluated by two scorers. Each will assign a point value of 1 to 6. If the points vary widely, your essay will be reviewed by a third evaluator.

The scorers issue points based on the following factors:

>> **A 6-point essay demonstrates a high degree of competence.** This is a winner! It takes into consideration all the advice given in this chapter. It doesn't have to be perfect, but it does make the writer's position clear, and it's well organized. In addition, a 6-point essay uses strong supporting details, displays sentence variety, and exhibits excellent grammar, competent word usage, and almost flawless mechanics.

>> **A 5-point essay is just a step below the 6.** Although it's strong and displays some of the characteristics of the 6-point essay, the ideas don't flow as logically, the sentence variety isn't as effective, and the language use may not display as much facility.

>> **A 4-point essay demonstrates competence.** Although it's adequate, it's not as well-written as higher-scoring essays. The thesis may not be stated as clearly as the higher-scoring essays. Relevant supporting details, examples, and reasons are not as well explained.

>> **A 3-point essay is blemished but demonstrates some competence.** The thesis and supporting ideas may only be implied instead of clearly stated. It may display errors in language use, grammar, and mechanics.

>> **A 2-point essay has serious flaws.** The thesis may be weak or nonexistent. The organization may be weak with few supporting details. It may have frequent errors in grammar, word usage, and mechanics.

>> **A 1-point essay is sorely lacking coherence and development.** No clear thesis or support is mentioned. This essay completely misses the mark.

The Praxis scorers are a diverse lot, but they have one thing in common: They're looking for good writing. They don't score essays based upon their own personal views, so don't worry about writing your essay based on what you think the scorers want to hear. Although you never want to write anything that could offend anyone, you need not concern yourself with taking a particular view to please the scorer. Praxis scores are holistic, based on an overall assessment of your work.

Checking Out Some Practice Prompts

To better prepare for the essay-writing section of the Praxis, try writing an essay using one or all of these practice prompts. Remember to organize first. Then write. Time yourself.

Prompts for argumentative essays

Directions: Discuss the extent to which you agree or disagree with the presented opinion. Support your views with specific reasons and examples from your own experience, observations, or reading.

Because students have so many extracurricular activities and so little time outside the school day, the majority of school hours should be limited to academic courses only.

The technology included in the latest model automobiles — weather reports, email access, GPS, and so forth — distracts the driver and should be eliminated.

Although learning to eat nutritious food is important, some leaders in our society have taken the matter of eating healthy too far.

Television reporting of news in the United States has begun to rely too heavily on ratings, leading networks to strive for entertainment and sensationalism rather than unbiased reporting.

All high-school and college students should be required to take regular drug tests.

Students with poor academic performance should be barred from all extracurricular activities.

Prompts for informative/explanatory essays

Prompt #1

Directions: The following assignment requires you to use information from two sources to discuss the most important concerns that relate to a specific issue. When paraphrasing or quoting from the sources, cite each source by referring to the author's last name, the title, or any other clear identifier.

Source 1:

Adapted from: Fitzpatrick, John R. "House and the Virtue of Eccentricity," *House and Philosophy*. Hoboken, NJ: John Wiley & Sons, Inc. 2009. Print.

Diogenes of Sinope (404–323 BCE) was the most famous of the cynics. He distrusted the written word, and if he did write anything, none of it survived. But he was influential enough for others to record his life and views. Diogenes's philosophy stressed living an ethical life, a life as nature intended. Thus, the conventional life of Athens was far too soft, and the polite life of civil society was far too dishonest. Diogenes believed that one's private persona and public persona should be identical — what one says and does in private should be what one says and does in public. Diogenes is perhaps best known for walking the streets with a lit torch "looking for an honest man." We are all aware of modern politicians who preach family values in public while privately divorcing their spouses, abandoning their children, or soliciting prostitutes. For Diogenes, if you're going to talk the talk, then you'd better walk the walk; only by "walking your talk" can you live ethically and happily.

Source 2:

Adapted from: Malloy, Daniel P. "Clark Kent Is Superman: The Ethics of Secrecy," *Superman and Philosophy: What Would the Man of Steel Do?* Hoboken, NJ: John Wiley & Sons, Inc. 2013. Print.

The essential difference between secrecy and privacy is that privacy is often thought of as a right, whereas secrecy is a method. There are certain things we all have a right to keep to ourselves that do not require secrecy. The right to privacy has been somewhat controversial. Legally, at least in America, it has been established through precedent and interpretation, but cannot actually be found anywhere in the U.S. Constitution. Contemporary philosopher Judith Jarvis Thompson, along with some other philosophers, has argued that the right to privacy isn't a moral right either. Instead, Thompson argues that what we take to be the right to privacy is actually an amalgam of rights that a person has over herself and her property. Still, privacy does have some moral grounding. Secrecy, on the other hand, is not morally grounded. We have no right to keep secrets. Secrecy, then, is morally neutral. It is not presumed to be immoral, as lying is. Nor is it presumed to be a moral right. Secrecy is a tool, and just like any other tool, its rightness or wrongness depends on the use to which it is put.

Prompt #2

Directions: The following assignment requires you to use information from two sources to discuss the most important concerns that relate to a specific issue. When paraphrasing or quoting from the sources, cite each source by referring to the author's last name, the title, or any other clear identifier.

Source 1:

Adapted from: Nielsen, Carsten Fogh. "World's Finest Philosophers," *Superman and Philosophy: What Would the Man of Steel Do?* Hoboken, NJ: John Wiley & Sons, Inc. 2013. Print.

In *Leviathan*, one of the most influential books on political philosophy ever written, the British philosopher Thomas Hobbes claimed that human beings neither do nor should trust each other, and described the natural state of human association as a war "of every man against every man." Hobbes recognized that many people might not agree with this somewhat depressing analysis, and that some might claim that human beings are not nearly as bad as Hobbes portrays them. In response to this, Hobbes asked those who disagreed with him to take a closer look at how they themselves actually behave: "Let him therefore consider with himself, when taking a journey, he arms himself, and seeks to go well accompanied; when going to sleep, he locks his doors; when even in his house, he locks his chest . . . Does he not there as much accuse mankind by his actions as I do by my words?"

Source 2:

Adapted from: Finkelman, Leonard. "Superman and Man," *Superman and Philosophy: What Would the Man of Steel Do?* Hoboken, NJ: John Wiley & Sons, Inc. 2013. Print.

The human-nature optimist believes that the essence of humanity is selflessness. To quote philosopher Jean-Jacques Rousseau (1712–1778), "men, being wild rather than wicked, and more intent to guard themselves against the mischief that might be done them, than to do mischief to others, were by no means subject to very perilous dissensions." . . . Rousseau wrote that mankind is "born free, and everywhere is in chains." In the state of nature, you have compassion for your neighbor; however, your desire for compassion from her will compel you toward vanity, or the attempt to elevate yourself and diminish others.

Reviewing a Sample Essay

Take a look at a highly competent essay based on the following prompt: "Because students have so many extracurricular activities and so little time outside the school day, the majority of school hours should be limited to academic courses only":

So much to do. So little time. The school day is packed with activity, much of it unrelated to academic coursework. Assemblies, pep rallies, class meetings, and the myriad of other activities packed into a school day break students' concentration and fragment the day. Even so, most of these activities provide students with valuable learning experiences and hours of fun. To better serve students, the school day should strictly separate academics and extracurricular activities.

A typical school day lasts from 8 a.m. until 3 p.m. During that school day, approximately five hours are devoted to academics, and those five hours are typically interrupted several times by nonacademic activities. For example, on a typical day at my school, the academic day is interrupted at least half a dozen times by announcements, guest speakers, club and class meetings, bake sales, pep rallies, assemblies . . . The list goes on and on. Consequently, students often lose their concentration and focus. Students are continuously shifting from academics to non-academics and back.

In addition, the time that students spend dashing to and from the classroom to extracurricular activities in the gym, auditorium, or other areas is time that could be better spent. Separating academics from extracurricular by moving all extracurricular activities to the end of the day would reduce transition time, and valuable minutes would be added to study. Any appointments or obligations students might need to schedule outside of school could be attended to during the nonacademic hours, further increasing the time devoted to study. Once the academic portion of the day has ended, students would be free to enjoy the other side of school life: socializing, building relationships, attending events, listening to speakers, and, in general, participating fully in the school community. Students could catch their breath, stretch, smile, and look forward to the next few hours with friends, knowing the day's most important work was behind them.

While five straight hours of academics would be quite grueling and certainly not the answer, these "academic hours" could be broken by short, nonstructured breaks and lunch. By placing uninterrupted academic study first, academics become top priority. With no extended interruptions and less time spent in transition, students would be more focused and academic performance would increase. Numerous studies show that emphasizing the importance of academics in the school day leads to increased student performance.

The typical school day can overwhelm students with the volume and variety of activities to which they must attend. They sprint from one activity to another, barely stopping to catch their breath or assimilate the impact of the last class. Simply rearranging and compartmentalizing the many activities will add productive time to the school day, increase students' concentration and focus, and lead not only to better academic performance but also to more enjoyment of extracurricular activities.

Here is why this essay would receive a score of 6:

>> **Introduction:** The introduction catches the reader's attention: "So much to do. So little time." The introduction also sets the stage for what's to come by mentioning the many activities in a school day and why these activities are a problem. The paragraph ends with a strong statement, a thesis.

>> **Middle paragraph 1:** Notice that the first paragraph begins to build the case for a separation of academic and nonacademic activities. The argument is strengthened through the use of a personal anecdote. Note the transition words like "for example" and "consequently" that move the reader smoothly through the paragraph.

>> **Middle paragraph 2:** The second paragraph continues to build the argument by presenting another benefit to the separation of academic and nonacademic activities: time saved. This idea is presented in the first sentence, the topic sentence. Notice the active verb, "dashing." Notice the "word picture" created in the last sentence, "Students could catch their breath . . ." Also notice that the final sentence is a strong one, further stressing the benefit.

>> **Middle paragraph 3:** In this paragraph, the writer recognizes and addresses an opposing argument: Five hours of academics would be too grueling. The writer continues to present further benefits to their suggested plan and ends with a strong sentence.

>> **Conclusion:** The conclusion sums up the argument, restates the thesis, and brings closure.

Evaluating Your Essay

After you write your essay by using one of the prompts in the section "Checking Out Some Practice Prompts," earlier in this chapter, use the following list to help you evaluate your writing:

>> **Have you constructed a strong, narrow thesis that directly addresses the prompt?** Does your essay proceed logically from paragraph to paragraph and idea to idea? Does the introduction lead smoothly to the conclusion? If your thesis isn't clear, you'll lose points. If your essay contains anything that doesn't pertain to your thesis, you'll lose points.

>> **Does your introductory paragraph anticipate the rest of your essay?** Does it easily hook to the thesis statement and link to the supporting details?

>> **Are your supporting details relevant to the topic and closely aligned to your thesis?** Be sure your evidence is specific. General, vague statements will cost you. Be sure each middle paragraph has a sentence (preferably at the end) that clearly connects to your thesis.

>> **Do you use transitions to move logically from one idea to another?** Examples of transitions include "consequently," "in addition," "however," "conversely," "in contrast," and "similarly."

>> **Is your essay well organized?** Make sure it contains an introduction, your thesis, supporting details, and a conclusion. It should consist of a clear beginning, middle, and end.

>> **Have you paid attention to action verbs and specific language?** Is your language natural, or have you tried to impress by using language with which you're not comfortable? Watch out for overuse of the verb "to be." Try to substitute strong, active verbs wherever possible. Create "word pictures" with specific language.

>> **Have you used a variety of sentences?** Vary the length and structure. Use some short sentences and some long ones. Use some with introductory clauses and some without. Use simple sentences as well as complex and compound sentences.

>> **Does your conclusion bring closure and drive your point home?** The reader should leave with a clear understanding of your position and should completely understand why you hold that position.

>> **Have you used correct grammar, spelling, and punctuation?** Be sure you save a few minutes of the allotted time to proofread for careless errors. If you have two or three mistakes in punctuation, spelling, or grammar, they may cost you.

>> **Have you correctly cited any outside sources?** Be careful to cite any sources, whether you quote directly or paraphrase. If you have any doubt about whether to cite or not, err on the side of citing.

How many points does your essay deserve? Read your essay again, placing yourself in the scorer's shoes (refer to the section "Understanding How the Essay Is Scored," earlier in this chapter, for more details on scoring).

TIP

Write, write, write. You *can* improve your score by practicing. Have others read your essay and make suggestions. The more you write, the more comfortable you'll be on test day. Read your essay out loud. Doing so will help you notice areas where your thoughts may not flow smoothly. If possible, use grammar/spell check in your word processor program to help you catch any errors and learn from them.

IN THIS CHAPTER

» Identifying the purposes of the parts of speech

» Putting together various sentence structures

» Reviewing the rules regarding punctuation and capitalization

» Watching out for misplaced modifiers, redundancy, and double negatives

» Homing in on homophones

Chapter **12**

Giving Grammar a Glance

You probably wince when you hear the word "grammar." That's okay; so do most people. Folks tend to run screaming when they hear the word because they imagine "grammar" as a set of "rules for the sake of rules" that some highfalutin' person imposes on them in an effort to force them to speak "properly."

Grammar rules aren't rules "because someone says so." Rather, grammar refers to the internal logic by which words in English — or any other language — connect to one another in speech or writing. This chapter reviews the rules you need to know to ace the Praxis Core exam, featuring selected-response questions that cover standard English usage, revision in context, and sentence correction.

Getting a Grip on the Parts of Speech

The parts of speech are the categories into which different words are organized. English has eight of them: nouns, verbs, adjectives, adverbs, pronouns, prepositions, conjunctions, and interjections. These terms probably sound familiar to you from elementary school (with the possible exception of "interjections," which refer to stand-alone exclamations like "Wow" — but interjections don't come up on the Praxis, so this is the only time twe mention them).

Like most grammar tests, the Praxis writing test doesn't ask you directly about the parts of speech — you aren't asked to identify what part of speech a particular word within a sentence is. But because it's impossible to discuss grammar without using the terms for the different parts of speech, we review them here. Along the way, we alert you to different types of Praxis questions that involve the various parts of speech so that you know what to look out for.

REMEMBER

Bear in mind that a given word doesn't always act as the same part of speech. What part of speech a word is depends on its function in the sentence in which it appears. For example, "purple" is an adjective in the sentence "I like purple lollipops," but it's a noun in the sentence "Purple is my favorite color."

Finding nouns as subjects and objects

A noun is a person, place, or thing. It's important to clarify that "things" don't necessarily have to be physical objects — for our purposes here, concepts and ideas are also "things." Thus, words like "justice," "honor," "hunger," and "love" (when they're not acting as verbs or adjectives, of course) can also be used as nouns. Three types of objects that you may see on the Praxis that function as nouns are direct objects, which receive the action of action verbs; indirect objects, which receive the action of the verb when the sentence also contains a direct object; and objects of the preposition, which follow the preposition in a prepositional phrase. (We explain objects in more detail in the section "Subjective versus objective pronouns," later in this chapter.)

Every sentence must have a noun or pronoun (a word that replaces a noun) and also a verb. (Commands that consist solely of verbs — such as "Help!" or "Stop!" — are still complete sentences because the subject is implied to be whomever the speaker is addressing.)

Although nouns are the bedrock of any language, we don't need to talk too much about them because the Praxis doesn't try to trip you up where nouns are concerned.

There's really only one noun-related trick or difficulty that you need to watch out for: Although the subject of a sentence is always a noun or pronoun, and you may be used to thinking of "the subject" as meaning "whoever or whatever the sentence is about," that's actually not the most efficient way to locate the subject of a sentence in grammatical terms. For example, in the sentence "One of my best friends is a lawyer," the subject isn't "friends" or "lawyer" — it's "one." (For more tips on this issue, consult the section "The sentence skeleton: Identifying the main subject and verb," later in this chapter.)

Putting verbs to work

Verbs are "action words" and "being words." Along with nouns or pronouns that replace nouns, they're one of the parts of speech that you absolutely need in order to have a complete sentence (and in a command, a verb can be a complete sentence all by itself because the subject is understood).

Making verbs agree with other words

The order of the day when it comes to verbs on the Praxis (or any other grammar test) is agreement. A verb has to *agree* with the noun or pronoun that performs the action or has the state of being. A verb also has to agree with the other verbs in the sentence.

As far as agreement between verbs and nouns (or pronouns) is concerned, the main issue is number agreement, as in singular versus plural. A singular noun needs to govern a verb in its singular form (as in "the elephant dances"), and a plural noun needs to govern a verb in its plural form (as in "the elephants dance"). Number-agreement issues are easy to spot when the noun and verb are right next to each other, but a favorite trick of grammar tests is to give you a sentence where the noun and verb *aren't* right next to each other. (See the section "The sentence skeleton: Identifying the main subject and verb," later in this chapter, for more details about finding the subject and verb when they aren't side by side.)

The other type of agreement you need to look out for is *tense* agreement, which concerns the agreement of one verb with another verb. For example, you can't say "I ran to the store and *buy* cat food" or "I *run* to the store and *bought* cat food"; it has to be "I *ran* to the store and *bought* cat food" or "I *run* to the store and *buy* cat food." Just like with number agreement, problems with tense agreement are easy to spot when the words concerned are close to each other in the sentence, but the Praxis tries to trick you by writing a long sentence in which the words concerned are far apart.

You should also be aware that, under certain circumstances, not every verb in a sentence has to be in the same tense: For example, it's just fine to say, "I ran to the store *to buy* cat food" (this time, *buy* is in the infinitive, so it doesn't have to agree with the past-tense *ran*). Mixing verb tenses is also perfectly alright if the actions in question were performed at different times. For instance, in the sentence "I *got* a good grade on the test because I *had studied* that book in high school," the verb *got* is in the past tense and the verb *had studied* is in the past-perfect tense, but the sentence is correct because one action was performed more recently than the other.

You don't have to know the different tense names on the Praxis Core, but you should be familiar with their various forms. Check out the progression of the verb "run" in the following list:

>> **Present:** I run

>> **Present progressive:** I am running

>> **Present perfect:** I have run

>> **Past:** I ran

>> **Past progressive:** I was running

>> **Past perfect:** I had run

>> **Future:** I will run

>> **Future progressive:** I will be running

>> **Future perfect:** I will have run

WARNING

Watch out for the trick where the test gives you a sentence containing a noun whose singular and plural forms are identical (such as "sheep" or "fish") or a verb whose present- and past-tense forms are identical (such as "read"). In these cases, look for context clues elsewhere in the sentence to determine the number intended for the noun or the tense intended for the verb.

Some verbs have *transitive* and *intransitive* forms: The verb is different depending on whether it takes an object. "Rise/raise" is a good example: Compare the sentences "I *rise* from my chair (no object = intransitive) and "I *raise* the window" (object = transitive). In the first sentence, you yourself are *rising*, and in the second, you are *raising* something else. This rule is the explanation to the allegedly difficult (but not really so difficult once you know the rule) "lie/lay" conundrum: "lie" is intransitive and "lay" is transitive, so it's "I *lie* down" but "I *lay* the book down on the table."

Parallel phrasing

If you just felt a heart attack coming on when you saw the word "parallel" because you remember it from math class rather than English class, don't worry — this rule doesn't involve any geometry (nor is it as difficult as parallel parking, in case what you just experienced was actually a driver's ed flashback). *Parallel phrasing* simply means that when you have a sentence with multiple verb phrases, the verbs in those phrases all need to be in the same form. (And if you actually enjoyed geometry, then I hope we never meet. Get it? Parallel? "Never meet?" Oh, forget it!)

Verbals are words, or groups of words, that were originally verbs but are used as or in other parts of speech. The three types of verbals, which grammar tests like to mix up when creating parallel-phrasing questions, are the

>> **Infinitive:** With "to" in front of a word that started out as a verb, like "to be" or "to go," used as a noun, adjective, or adverb

>> **Participle:** Word that was originally a verb but is used as an adjective

>> **Gerund:** Word that was just a verb at its creation but is used as a noun and ends with "ing"

None of these forms is more correct than the others — they just have to match. So, for example, it's fine to say either "I like to swim and to bike" or "I like swimming and biking," but you can't say "I like to swim and biking" or "I like swimming and to bike."

There are other, less blatant violations of parallel phrasing, as well. For example, the sentence "Nobody cares about what I say or my actions" should be revised to read either "Nobody cares about what I say or what I do," or "Nobody cares about my words or my actions." See how the second two sentences flow better? This sort of parallel phrasing, however, is more about style than grammar, so standardized tests almost always limit mix-ups to infinitives and participles.

EXAMPLE

Which of the following choices presents the best revision of the following sentence?

The time to compose outlines has passed, so you should begin writing your essay, making sure to use persuasive arguments and inspiring quotations.

(A) The time to compose outlines has passed, so you should begin writing your essay, making sure to use persuasive arguments and inspiring quotations.

(B) The time for composing outlines has passed, so you should begin to write your essay, to use persuasive arguments, and to inspire with quotations.

(C) The time to compose outlines has passed, so you should begin to write your essay, to be sure to use persuasive arguments and inspiring quotations.

(D) The time to compose outlines has passed, so you should begin to write your essay, in which you should use persuasive arguments and inspiring quotations.

(E) The time for composing outlines has passed, so you should begin writing your essay, making sure of using persuasive arguments and inspiring quotations.

The correct answer is Choice (D). "To compose" and "to write" are both in the infinitive, the infinitive/participial choice in the next clause is avoided through the use of an "in which" clause, and the word "inspiring" doesn't have anything to do with the parallel-phrasing issue because it's being used as an adjective. Choice (A) is the best of the incorrect choices, but it could be better; the juxtaposition of the infinitive ("to compose") and the gerund ("writing") is a bit messy. Choice (B) seems like it might be right at first because all the verbs forms in the second independent clause are in the infinitive, but the list-like structure make it seem as if writing the essay, using arguments, and using quotations are three *different* activities, when what the sentence *wants* to imply is that the second two are a part of the first (don't simply look at verb forms without paying attention to the flow of the sentence as a whole). Also, the first verb form ("composing") is a gerund. Choice (C) is simply messy and confusing: The "to be" infinitive that follows the last comma makes it sound like a list is coming, but then the sentence stops short. Choice (E) may seem right at first, because all the verb forms are parallel, but the alteration of "to use" to "of using" is extremely awkward — there is more at stake in a sentence than whether the verbals match.

Gerunds: Verb forms that act as nouns

Some words may appear to be verbs but are actually nouns, and they're called gerunds. A *gerund* ends in "ing" and is a verb form that works as a concept in the sentence, rather than as an action performed by, or state of being of, a noun or pronoun. Check out these examples:

<u>Boxing</u> is a sport that has been around for a long time.

<u>Standing</u> in a busy road is not wise.

<u>Looking</u> for gerunds is fun.

None of the underlined words are verbs, though they can be used as verbs. They are nouns. In fact, they're the subjects of the sentences. A gerund doesn't always need to be the subject of a sentence, however. In the sentence "Dancing is fun," the gerund is the subject, but in the sentence "I like dancing," the gerund is the object. In short, the key to recognizing gerunds is to look out for verb forms that are being *referred to as ideas*, rather than being *performed by nouns or pronouns*.

There are other cases where a word that's normally a verb can be a noun, such as *run* in the sentence "I'm going to go for a run" or *dance* in the sentence "The big dance raised a lot of money for the school," but these aren't examples of gerunds — they're just words that can be nouns as well as verbs. In general, there's a lot of overlap between nouns and verbs.

Because they're technically nouns, gerunds can be possessions, so if a noun or pronoun "owns" the gerund, the noun or pronoun should be in the possessive: "*Nina's* singing is lovely," "I appreciate *your* answering the telephone," "Please excuse *my* spilling that drink," and so on.

Using adjectives to describe people, places, and things

Adjectives modify nouns and pronouns. You probably don't have too much difficulty spotting an adjective when you see one, and in any case, the Praxis doesn't ask you to simply pick out all the adjectives in a given sentence, so we can get right to discussing the adjective-related tricks that the test *does* use.

When it comes to the Praxis writing test, the most common adjective-related trick is to substitute an adjective for an adverb, or vice versa, in an effort to see whether you catch the mistake. Look out for this trick, especially on those "no error" questions wherein four portions of a given sentence are underlined, and you have to indicate which portion contains an error or select "no error" if the sentence is correct. Anytime you see an adjective or an adverb underlined by itself on such a question, you should always double-check to ensure that the word in question is being used correctly.

The reason this trick is possible to play, of course, is that most (but not all) adjectives can be turned into adverbs with the addition of "–ly." Examine, for example, the roles of the adjective *quick* and the adverb *quickly* in the similar sentences: "The quick dog ran up the hill" and "The dog ran quickly up the hill." True to their respective functions, the adjective modifies a noun (*dog*), and the adverb modifies a verb (*ran*).

The Praxis tries to trick you by giving you a sentence in which the words that are supposed to agree are not right next to each other. If, for example, you encountered the sentence "The dog ran up the hill quick," it may be less immediately noticeable that *quick* should be *quickly*. (Even though *quick* is next to the noun *hill*, the intent of the word is still to modify the verb; therefore, it must be an adverb because adjectives can't modify verbs.)

And if the Praxis *really* wants to get tricky, it will throw a participial verb form into the mix, so that you have to figure out whether the "–ing" word is a noun (in which case it should be modified by an adjective) or a verb (in which case it should be modified by an adverb). Consider the differences between these two correct sentences:

Constant dancing has worn out my shoes.

My shoes are worn out because I am constantly dancing.

In the first sentence, *dancing* is a gerund (and the subject of the sentence), so it is modified with the adjective *constant*. In the second sentence, *dancing* is a verb in the present-progressive tense, so it's modified with the adverb *constantly*. Pretty sneaky, huh?

REMEMBER

Not all adverbs end in "–ly," not all adjectives can be turned into adverbs by adding "–ly," and some words that end in "–ly" are adjectives (adverbs are discussed in more detail in the following section). Take adjectives of number, for example. *Five* is an adjective in the sentence "There are *five* cupcakes on the table" (it modifies a noun, after all), but there's no such word as *fively*. *Old* is an adjective in "The *old* forest is beautiful," but the forest can't do something *oldly*, because no such word exists. *Elderly* is a word, but guess what? It's an adjective — as is *elder*, making *elder/ elderly* one of the few cases where a word and the same word with "–ly" attached are both adjectives, albeit ones with different meanings: The first is a comparative adjective meaning "older (than someone else)," and the second just means "old." If that isn't enough to blow your mind, note that "beautiful" in the sentence about the forest is, of course, also an adjective, despite the fact that it comes next to the verb *is*.

WARNING

Don't try to determine whether a word is (or should be) an adjective or an adverb based on how it's spelled or what it looks like. Instead, look at the job it is doing in the sentence — that is, whether it's modifying a noun/pronoun or a verb.

The last bit of adjective-related funny business concerns punctuation. In the sentence "The four young French girls are charming," you may notice something odd: There are no commas in the sentence, even though the noun *girls* has three adjectives in front of it. You've presumably been taught that you need commas when multiple adjectives modify the same noun (as in "The hairy, hungry, faithful dog ran up the hill"), so what's going on here?

Certain types of adjectives don't need to be separated by commas when they appear in a series before a noun — in this case, our exceptions are "articles," "adjectives of number," "adjectives of age," and "adjectives of nationality." Adjectives of size are another exception: You wouldn't put a comma between *big* and *American* in "the big American ship," would you? (Nor, for example, would you ever say "the American big ship," because another convention dictates that adjectives of nationality must immediately precede the noun.) You need to separate adjectives with commas only when adjective order doesn't matter. When adjectives indicating age, nationality, size, and other characteristics are used, order does matter, so commas shouldn't be used to separate them.

REMEMBER

Trust your ear. Although memorizing rules certainly has its place when it comes to grammar, it's not always the most efficient strategy. You may not have known that there were any rules about adjective order, but if you had heard someone say, "the Japanese old five cars," it would have sounded wrong to you, right? You would have simply *sensed* that it should be "the five old Japanese cars," for some reason you couldn't explain. When you have an instinct like that, following it is usually more reliable than racking your brain for a rule. Speakers of a language — especially native speakers — often sense rules that may never have been explained to them. Cool, huh?

Calling on adverbs to describe actions and conditions

Adverbs can modify verbs, adjectives, or other adverbs — and they don't need to be anywhere near the words they modify to get the job done. All things considered, adverbs are probably the most versatile part of speech. They can look many different ways, they can perform many different jobs, and they can appear just about anywhere in the sentence. In short, whenever you find yourself looking at a word and wondering "What the heck part of speech is this word?" the safe bet is that it's an adverb.

Just consider the following three correct sentences:

I studied tirelessly all night. (*Tirelessly* is an adverb modifying the verb *studied.*)

The movie was very sad. (*Very* is an adverb modifying the adjective *sad.*)

I handled the dynamite extremely gently. (*Extremely* is an adverb modifying the other adverb *gently,* which is modifying the verb *handled.*)

In those examples, two of the adverbs end in "–ly," and the one that doesn't is still fairly easy to spot as an adverb because *very* means the same thing as *extremely.*

But adverbs can disguise themselves much more confusingly than that. They can even look like nouns. For example, in the sentence "I'm going to a concert tonight," the word *tonight* is an adverb. Why? Because it is doing the job of an adverb. If I asked you to describe what the word *tonight* is doing in that sentence, you'd probably say that it's modifying (or adding more information to) the word *going* (namely, it answers the question of *when* the speaker is going). And because *going* is a verb, the word that modifies it must therefore be an adverb.

REMEMBER

When it comes to adverbs, be aware that they are masters of disguise. Never try to pick out adverbs based on what they look like. Instead, look at what the word in question is modifying. If it's modifying a verb, an adjective, or another adverb, it's an adverb, no matter what it looks like.

TIP

In cases where the word looks so little like an adverb that you simply can't believe it is one, a good way to double-check is to substitute a word that *does* look like an adverb and see whether it can do the same job. For example, if you alter the sentence "I'm going to a concert tonight" to read "I'm going to a concert excitedly" or "I'm going to a concert cheerfully," you can see that all three sentences are grammatically correct and that *excitedly* and *cheerfully* are clearly adverbs. Therefore, *tonight* must be an adverb, too, because it occupies the space in the sentence that needs to be occupied by an adverb.

Getting the lowdown on pronouns

A *pronoun* is a word that takes the place of a noun. Pronouns were created to avoid repetition of nouns. Think about the repetitive nature of the following sentence:

Richard went to the store and bought Richard some bread, and then Richard drove to another store where Richard often shops.

Now look at what pronouns can do:

Richard went to the store and bought himself some bread, and then he drove to another store where he often shops.

The words "himself" and "he" are pronouns, and they take the place of the noun "Richard" three times in the preceding sentence. The most common pronouns — and the ones that are probably the most familiar to you — are the *personal pronouns*. Basically, personal pronouns represent specific people and things and work as substitutes for their specific names.

When it comes to pronouns on the Praxis, there are two tricks you have to watch out for: singular versus plural, and subjective case versus objective case. Table 12-1 summarizes these properties, and we go into these properties in more detail in the following sections.

TABLE 12-1 Pronouns and Their Properties

	Subjective Case		Objective Case	
	Singular	Plural	Singular	Plural
First person	I	we	me	us
Second person	you	you	you	you
Third person	he, she, it	they	him, her, it	them

Singular versus plural pronouns

One of the most important issues with pronouns is that they agree in number with their antecedents (*antecedent* is the fancy word for "the noun that a pronoun takes the place of," but although the word literally means "comes before," it's important to note that a pronoun doesn't *always* come after the word it's standing in for in the sentence).

Take, for example, the following correct sentence:

If a student wants to drop a class, he or she must visit the Registrar's office.

You don't know who this hypothetical student is, but regardless, you still know there is only *one* hypothetical student, so you need a singular pronoun. Although it's now very common to use *they* in spoken English as a gender-neutral singular pronoun (to avoid the labor of constantly saying "he or she" or the sexism of just saying "he" when gender is unknown), be advised that the Praxis and virtually all grammar tests do *not* yet consider this to be correct. Inclusive and time-saving as it is, "they" is still plural and *only* plural as far as most tests are concerned. Although there is a growing acceptance of "they" as singular, not everyone has caught on yet. So, it's better to be safe than sorry.

As an example, consider the following correct sentence:

If students want to drop a class, they must visit the Registrar's office.

This time, of course, the pronoun's antecedent ("students") is actually plural, so *they* is correct. You only have to watch out for mismatches like the following:

Incorrect: If a *student* wants to drop a class, *they* must visit the Registrar's office.

Incorrect: If *students* want to drop a class, *he or she* must visit the Registrar's office.

Subjective versus objective pronouns

Aside from singular versus plural (see the preceding section), the most common pronoun-related trick that the Praxis uses involves subjective versus objective case. If those terms aren't familiar to you, don't worry: You already know what they mean, even if you don't know the fancy terms.

The difference between subjective and objective case is the difference between "I" and "me," or "we" and "us," or "he/she" and "him/her," or "they" and "them." Namely, the difference is that you use the second word (the *objective* case) when the pronoun is the *object* of a verb or a preposition. A pronoun doesn't have to be the *subject* of the sentence for you to use the first word, or *subjective* case — you use it whenever the pronoun is *not* the object of anything.

Even if you've never heard the terms "subjective case" and "objective case" before, you probably still sense that it's wrong to say, "He hit I" or "Throw the ball to I." As an English speaker, situations where you should say "me" instead of "I" (or "us" instead of "we," and so on) are simply something you sense. You've probably been using subjective and objective pronoun cases correctly 99 percent of the time all your life, even if nobody has ever taught you the rule for doing so.

What you need to be concerned about for the Praxis is that 1 percent of cases where you *don't* automatically sense what the correct usage is. Also, predictably, the way a test tries to trip you up with pronoun case is the same way it tries to trip you up with anything else: by putting other words in between the two words that are supposed to agree with each other.

Look at the following four sentences, all of which are incorrect, but some of which are more obviously incorrect than others:

> **Obviously incorrect:** Please take I home now.
>
> **Obviously incorrect:** Throw the ball to I.
>
> **Less obviously incorrect:** Please take Taryn and I home now.
>
> **Less obviously incorrect:** Throw the balls to my friends and I.

The error in all four of those sentences is that the pronoun should be in the objective case rather than the subjective case — in other words, it should be "me" instead of "I." In two of the sentences, the pronoun is the object of a verb ("take"), and in the other two, it's the object of a preposition ("to"). But putting another noun in between the verb or preposition and the pronoun makes it a lot less obvious that the wrong pronoun case is being used, doesn't it?

WARNING

The verb "be" doesn't take an objective case for its object, because it can't have an object. It's used for connecting subjects to words that rename them and adjectives that modify them. The subject for "be" is the same person or thing as the subject of the clause: That's why it's correct to say, "This is *she*" instead of "This is *her*" when you answer the telephone and someone asks to speak to you. It's never grammatically correct to use the objective case of a pronoun when it's not an object.

EXAMPLE

Which version of the underlined portion makes the sentence correct?

Before you take the photograph of <u>Deloris and I, let</u> us adjust our lights.

(A) Deloris and I, let

(B) Deloris and me, let

(C) Deloris and myself, let

(D) Deloris, and I let

(E) Deloris, and me let

The correct answer is Choice (B). The pronoun is one of the objects of the preposition *of*, so it should be the objective-case *me*, not the subjective-case *I*. The comma should be placed between that pronoun and the verb *let*, because that's the point at which the introductory subordinate clause ends and the main independent clause (which is a command) begins.

The right answer is not Choice (A) because the pronoun is one of the objects of the preposition *of*, so it should be the objective-case *me*, not the subjective-case *I*.

The right answer is not Choice (C) because the speaker has not yet appeared in the sentence and is not reflexively performing any verb upon himself, so there's no need to use *myself* instead of *me*.

The right answer is not Choice (D) because the pronoun is one of the objects of the preposition *of*, so it should be the objective-case *me*, not the subjective-case *I*. Additionally, the comma should be placed between that pronoun and the verb *let* because that's the point at which the introductory subordinate clause ends and the main independent clause (which is a command) begins.

The right answer is not Choice (E) because the comma should be placed between the pronoun and the verb *let*. That's the point at which the introductory subordinate clause ends and the main independent clause (which is a command) begins.

The dreaded "whom" made easy

Perhaps no single word in the English language strikes more terror into the hearts of those who are about to take a grammar test than *whom*. Hardly anyone who isn't an English teacher has any confidence whatsoever in his or her ability to use it correctly, and most people just avoid using it altogether. But believe it or not, *whom*'s bark is much worse than its bite. Its usage is really not all that difficult to understand.

Just like "me" is the objective case of "I" or "us" is the objective case of "we," "whom" is simply the objective case of "who." The rules for *who/whom* are no different from the rules for *I/me, he/him, we/us,* or *they/them*. So where did its fearsome reputation come from? Well, *who/whom* is made a bit more complicated than the other pronouns by the fact that *who* is frequently used as an *interrogative* pronoun, meaning that it's used to ask questions. The arrangement of words in a question is different from the arrangement of words in a statement. For example, in a question, the pronoun may be the first word, whereas the verb of which it is the object may be the last word. So, a question like "*Who* do you love?" should actually be "*Whom* do you love?" because the pronoun is the object of the verb *love*.

Most of the time, if a question on the Praxis involves *whom*, it employs *whom* as a relative pronoun rather than an interrogative one. Consider the following sentence, which uses *whom* correctly but as a relative pronoun (that is, it's used to link clauses rather than to ask a question):

My grandmother, from whom I inherited my green eyes, lives in Wisconsin.

You remember the simple grade-school rule about how you're supposed to use *who* when you're talking about a person, but *that* or *which* when you're talking about an animal or a thing, right? Okay, so the sentence you just examined is structurally no different than

This book, from which I learned grammar, was well worth the price.

In both cases, the relative pronoun is right next to the preposition *from*, so it's easy to spot it as the object. In the first sentence, you use *who/whom* instead of *which* because you're talking about a person, and the form is *whom* instead of *who* because it's the object of a preposition. If *whom* comes up on the Praxis, it will probably be in a situation like that.

Reflexively using intensive and reflexive pronouns

Reflexive and intensive pronouns are the same words, but they're used differently. They end with "self" and include words like "myself," "yourself," and "herself." "Himself" and "themselves" are pronouns, but "hisself" and "theirself" are not. It is important to be careful not to use those. Remember that a group of people cannot be just one self.

Reflexive pronouns are necessary to the meanings of sentences, but intensive pronouns are not. Intensive pronouns just intensify sentences. For example, in the sentence "John himself organized the party," "himself" is an intensive pronoun. It's not vital to the meaning of the sentence, but it does add effect. However, "John saw himself in the mirror" uses the word "himself" as a word that is needed for making the point. It's a reflexive pronoun.

The major rule concerning reflexive pronouns is that they should never be used when personal pronouns can be used instead.

> Incorrect: I saw Jenny, and she said that *herself* is moving to Florida.

> Correct: I saw Jenny, and she said that *she* is moving to Florida.

Considering conjunctions

Conjunctions link parts of a sentence together (think *conjoin*), be they individual words (as in "I bought bread *and* eggs") or entire clauses (as in "I went cycling on Saturday, *and* I went swimming on Sunday"). In addition to the "big three" conjunctions — *and*, *but*, and *or* — some other common ones are *so, yet,* and *nor.* (*For* can also be a conjunction, but most of the time, *for* is a preposition, as in "The telephone call was *for* you.")

The seven words discussed in the preceding paragraph are the only seven *coordinating* conjunctions, which you can remember with the mnemonic FANBOYS (**f**or, **a**nd, **n**or, **b**ut, **o**r, **y**et, **s**o). But there are many more *subordinating* conjunctions (*because, since, although, when, unless, while,* and *until* are just a few).

So, what's the difference? When two clauses are linked with a coordinating conjunction, the conjunction can *only* go in the middle, whereas a subordinating conjunction may appear at the beginning of a sentence or between two clauses in a sentence.

In terms of taking the Praxis writing test, why do you need to know this? The answer is "commas." Questions on the Praxis writing exam expect you to know where commas do or don't go. In fact, in the questions that underline four portions of a sentence and instruct you to pick the portion that contains an error (or select "no error" if there are no errors), occasionally *a single comma by itself* is underlined as one of the four choices, so you need to know whether a comma belongs in that spot. And knowledge of conjunction rules plays a big part in knowing where commas should or shouldn't go.

So, say you have two independent clauses: "I studied hard" and "I aced the test." Now say you want to link them with a conjunction. If you want to link them with a coordinating conjunction, there's only one way to do that: Put the coordinating conjunction between the independent clauses and place a comma before the conjunction ("I studied hard, so I aced the test").

WARNING

It's incorrect to place a comma before a coordinating conjunction unless the coordinating conjunction links two independent clauses (compare "I like watching TV and playing video games" and "I like watching TV, and I like playing video games") or precedes the last item in a series (compare "I invited James, Tom, Scott, and Brian").

If, on the other hand, you feel like linking the two clauses with a subordinating conjunction, you have two options: Put the subordinate clause second and don't use a comma ("I aced the test because I studied hard"), or put the subordinate clause first and use a comma ("Because I studied hard, I aced the test"). Keep in mind that if you include the comma when the subordinate clause comes second or omit the comma when the subordinate clause comes first, the sentence is incorrect.

Perusing prepositions

You hear a lot about prepositions in the section "Getting the lowdown on pronouns," earlier in this chapter, because it talks about how pronouns should be in the objective case when they're the objects of either verbs or prepositions. Of course, that knowledge isn't much help if you don't know a preposition when you see one.

So, what is a *preposition*? It's a word that provides information about the relationship of words to each other in time and space: *before* and *after* are prepositions, for example, as are *over* and *under*. (The "time and space" rule is not absolute, however. *About* is one example of a preposition that does not relate to relationships in time and space, as in "The movie was *about* skateboarders." Oh, and be aware that *about* can also be an adverb meaning *approximately*, as in "The movie was *about* two hours long.")

There are too many prepositions for you to simply memorize all of them, but a handy, short list includes the following: *aboard, about, above, around, at, before, behind, below, beneath, beside, between, beyond, but* (when used like *except*, as in "I want everything *but* anchovies on the pizza"; the rest of the time, it's a conjunction), *by, down, during, except, for, from, in, inside, into, like* (when used to mean *similarly to* or *such as*, as in "He looks *like* my cousin" or "Some countries, *like* Switzerland, are landlocked"), *near, of, off, on, over, past, since* (when used to signify the last time something occurred, as in "I haven't seen him *since* Monday"), *through, throughout, to, toward, under, underneath, until, up, upon, with, within,* and *without.*

TIP

Many people find it helpful to refer to prepositions as "squirrel words," meaning that they represent things a squirrel can do: The squirrel ran *around* the room; the squirrel ran *under* the table; the squirrel jumped *over* the chair; the squirrel crawled *inside* my desk; the squirrel ran *down* the hallway, *past* the water fountain, and *through* the door; and so on.

Most preposition-related questions on the Praxis writing exam involve determining whether the pronoun should be in the subjective or objective case. The only other common type of preposition question on the Praxis concerns preposition selection itself. Occasionally, a "no error" question will have a preposition underlined by itself, and you're expected to know whether the preposition is being used correctly in that context or whether another preposition would be better. Consider these examples:

> **Correct:** I'm obsessed *with* grammar.
>
> **Incorrect:** I'm obsessed *on* grammar.
>
> **Correct:** The movie was based *on* the book.
>
> **Incorrect:** The movie was based *about* the book.

So, whenever you see a preposition underlined by itself on a "no error" question, make sure it's the best one to use in that context. Unfortunately, preposition usage in English is largely *idiomatic,* which is the fancy word for "you say it that way because you just do." Think about it: Why do you say "*in* the morning" but "*at* night?" or "get *in* the car" but "get *on* the plane?" You just do.

REMEMBER

Many prepositions can also function as other parts of speech, so the mere presence of a word that, in some instances, can be a preposition doesn't necessarily mean that the pronoun following it should be in the objective case. (Compare "I get to use the bike *after* him," in which *after* is a preposition, to "*After* he is done using it, I get the bike," in which *after* is a subordinating conjunction.) The words *but* and *since* can be either prepositions or conjunctions, and the incredibly versatile word *like* can actually function as any part of speech except a pronoun.

TIP

If you want to memorize many of the most common prepositions, do an Internet search for "prepositions Jingle Bells." There's a song setting a list of prepositions to the tune of the song "Jingle Bells," which is incredibly helpful and quite easy to memorize.

Making Sense of Sentence Structure

Now that you've reviewed the parts of speech and how to put them together (see the preceding sections), it's time to brush up on how groups of words fit together to make sentences. When it comes to "groups of words," there are two types: *clauses* and *phrases*. Without getting unnecessarily technical, the difference is that a *clause* has both a subject and a verb whereas a *phrase* does not.

Now, you probably know that the definition of a *sentence* is that it has both a subject and a verb. So, you're probably wondering what the difference is between a *clause* and a *sentence*. Well, the best analogy is that it's like the difference between a home and a building. If you live in a house, then your home and your building are the same thing. But if you live in an apartment, then your building contains other homes in addition to yours. To qualify as a home, a given space needs to contain a few essential elements: a bedroom and a bathroom, for example. A big fancy house may have multiple bedrooms and bathrooms, but it's still just one home. Conversely, an apartment building can contain many bedrooms and bathrooms but be divided up into many different homes, each of which contains one bedroom and one bathroom.

A sentence, then, may only contain one clause — in this case, the clause and the sentence are the same thing. A longer sentence, on the other hand, can contain multiple clauses. It also may contain one or more *phrases* — bits of extra information that are nice to have, but not necessary to make a complete sentence. To continue with the "home" analogy, you can say that a phrase is like a den: It's nice to have a den in your home, but you don't need to have one for your home to count as a home; at the same time, a den all by itself cannot be said to constitute a home.

To turn now to punctuation, you can say that punctuation marks are like walls. Periods are the outer walls that separate your home from other people's homes, and commas (or semicolons, dashes, and so forth) are the inner walls that separate the rooms in your home from one another. Sometimes these inner walls are absolutely necessary (it would certainly be odd if your bathroom were not separated from the other rooms by any walls), and other times, they're not (the kitchen and the dining room may just be two separate areas within one big room). Most of the time, clauses and phrases are separated from one another by punctuation marks such as commas, but under certain circumstances, they may not be. We review punctuation in the section "Pondering Punctuation," later in this chapter. The following sections focus on sentence structure.

Independent clauses versus everything else

Independent clause is the fancy name for a group of words that can stand as a complete sentence by itself. Some sentences consist of a single independent clause, but others consist of an independent clause joined to one or more phrases or subordinate clauses. Still others consist of two or more independent clauses joined to one another, or of two or more independent clauses joined to one or more phrases or subordinate clauses, and so on. From a strictly grammatical standpoint, you can combine as many clauses and phrases as you like into a single sentence, as long as you combine them according to the rules.

Take the sentence "I eat popcorn." It's both an independent clause and a complete sentence. But say you want to make this sentence a little more interesting, so you change it to "I eat popcorn at the movies." *At the movies* is a prepositional phrase (which you can tell by the fact that *at* is a preposition). It's not divided from your initial independent clause with commas, and you can say that it's now part of your independent clause, even though it's not an essential part — you can get rid of it and still have a complete sentence. Now suppose you expand the sentence yet again, to read "Every Tuesday, I eat popcorn at the movies." Now you have an *adverbial phrase* at the beginning, followed by a comma, because it precedes the independent clause. Now say you expand the sentence even further, to read "Every Tuesday, if I'm hungry, I eat popcorn at the movies." This time, you've added a *dependent clause*: "I'm hungry" *could* be a complete sentence by itself, but here, it's bonded to the subordinating conjunction *if*, so the clause is dependent. You now have multiple subjects and verbs in the sentence, but the main subject and verb of the whole sentence are still "I eat," from your initial independent clause. Anything that isn't an independent clause is considered a fragment, which doesn't generate a complete thought.

The sentence skeleton: Identifying the main subject and verb

Don't worry: You don't actually need to know the difference between one type of phrase and another to answer any questions on the Praxis writing test. You *do*, however, need to be pretty good at quickly identifying the main subject and verb of a sentence. The ability to do this is useful when it comes to answering all sorts of grammar questions, and being familiar with the terms *independent clauses*, *dependent clauses*, and *phrases* makes the task easier (the preceding section gives you the lowdown on these terms).

In other words, you *don't* technically need to know the fancy names for all the different types of "extra stuff" that can be in a sentence, but you *do* need to be able to tell the difference between the things that need to be there in order to have a complete sentence and the things that don't.

So, okay, say you're asked to identify the main subject and verb of this sentence:

According to biologists, one of the most endangered animals is the Javan rhinoceros.

If you correctly discerned that the subject is *one* and the verb is *is*, good job! The nouns in the sentence that jumped out at you were probably *biologists, animals,* and *Javan rhinoceros*, but none of these is the main subject. Why not? Well, *biologists* can't be the subject of the sentence because it's part of an introductory phrase rather than the main independent clause. *Animals* can't be the subject because it's part of a prepositional phrase (specifically, the one governed by *of*). And *Javan rhinoceros* can't be the subject because it's a *predicate nominative*, which means that it is a particular entity the subject is said to be. If a being verb is used to say that a word is also something that has already been mentioned, the word cannot be the subject. A subject is not a renaming via a being verb, but it can be something that is renamed by a predicate nominative through the use of a being verb.

The use of the word *one* can sometimes be confusing in this case because it's sometimes used as a numerical expression. However, *one* is an indefinite pronoun in the sentence, and it has a predicate nominative *Javan rhinoceros*. Other indefinite pronouns, such as *all, many,* or *some* could be substituted in its place, and the sentence would still make sense.

As for the verb, not only is *is* the main verb, but it's actually the *only* verb in the whole sentence! *According to* is a two-word preposition, and *endangered* here is an adjective modifying *animals*.

TIP

No matter what sort of grammar question you're dealing with, it's always a good idea to ground yourself by first identifying the main subject and verb — what I call the "sentence skeleton" — because everything else in the sentence is constructed around it. You can get rid of everything in a sentence except the main independent clause (or, for that matter, the subject and verb of the main independent clause) and still have a complete sentence. The sentence won't be as informative, but it will still be grammatically correct. And no word that's located in one of the parts of the sentence that you can get rid of can possibly be the main subject or main verb. For example, if you were to take all the words that are not the subject or verb from the sentence about the rhinoceros, you'd be left with the sentence *One is*.

Run-ons and comma splices

Although you probably remember the term *run-on* from school, you may not be 100 percent sure what it means. Many people mistakenly believe that a run-on sentence is just a sentence that is too long, but that's not actually what the term means.

A *run-on sentence* is a sentence wherein two (or more, in especially messy cases) independent clauses have been placed next to each other without being joined. A *comma splice*, the run-on sentence's ugly cousin, is a situation in which two independent clauses are joined with only a comma, when more than just a comma is necessary.

In short, both run-ons and comma splices are grammatical errors, and very similar ones — the difference is that a comma splice has a comma in it and a run-on doesn't.

In case all that was about as clear as mud, here are some examples. Start by examining the correct, complete sentence "Shakespeare is my favorite writer, and his characters are the most memorable." This sentence consists of two independent clauses ("Shakespeare is my favorite writer" and "his characters are the most memorable"), joined with the conjunction *and* and a comma before the conjunction. Using a comma and a conjunction is the most common way to correctly join two independent clauses. A comma splice is when the writer puts in just the comma without the conjunction, and a run-on is when the writer puts nothing at all between the two clauses.

>> **Comma splice:** Shakespeare is my favorite writer, his characters are the most memorable.

>> **Run-on:** Shakespeare is my favorite writer his characters are the most memorable.

TIP

Most grammar tests for older students or adults don't bother throwing in too many run-ons because they're easy to spot. But test-writers just *love* to throw comma splices at you! Figure out how to spot a comma splice from a mile away, and your score will shoot up significantly solely due to your acquiring that one skill!

EXAMPLE

Which of the following sentences is *not* grammatically correct?

(A) Before your friends get here, we should pick up some snacks.

(B) That movie was too long, I almost fell asleep.

(C) If I don't get this question right, I'm going to be deeply ashamed.

(D) I'm afraid of that dog, so I'm going to walk the long way home.

(E) The sun is warm, the sky is blue, and I'm happy.

The correct answer is Choice (B). That sentence presents two independent clauses joined with only a comma, making it a comma splice and the only one of the five choices that is *not* a correct sentence. Choice (A) presents an independent clause preceded by a dependent clause, with a comma between the two, which is correct. Choice (C) links a subordinate clause to an independent clause by placing a comma between them and using the subordinate conjunction "if" at the beginning of the first clause, which is correct. Choice (D) links two independent clauses with a comma and a coordinating conjunction, which is correct. Choice (E) presents three independent clauses as a list. That is why the use of a comma between the first two, and the use of a comma and a conjunction between the second and last, is correct.

Pondering Punctuation

Just as road signs or traffic signals are placed wherever streets intersect with one another, punctuation marks appear at the junctures where different parts of a sentence come together. After you know all about phrases and clauses (check out the section "Making Sense of Sentence Structure," earlier in this chapter), it's time to review how punctuation marks are used to mark their intersections. You already know that a period (or a question mark or an exclamation point) comes at the end of a sentence, so we don't need to talk about periods. Instead, the following sections are mainly concerned with commas, as well as with the other, less common, punctuation marks that may come up on the Praxis writing test.

Commas

It may be a little gross, but you may find it helpful to think of commas as the scars that are left when a sentence is operated on. The "operation" may be a "transplant," wherein a portion of the sentence is moved elsewhere (for example, placing a subordinate clause before the main independent clause rather than after it). Or it may be a "graft," wherein two elements of a sentence are spliced together (for example, making two independent clauses into one sentence or adding extra information to an independent clause).

Comma placement is determined by what is happening at a given point in the sentence. There are six situations in which commas are necessary, which we outline in the following sections.

Joining two or more independent clauses

A comma is always necessary if there's more than one independent clause in the sentence (unless another punctuation mark, such as a semicolon, colon, or dash, does the job):

> "There was no school" and "I went to the beach"

> There was no school, so I went to the beach.

Note: A coordinating conjunction is absolutely required after the comma. In cases where more than two independent clauses are being combined, a comma is still required after each one, but the coordinating conjunction is only necessary before the last, as in "Ben plays guitar, Brian plays bass, and Scott plays drums."

Following an introductory clause or phrase

When the sentence opens with a subordinate clause that functions as an adverb or adjective, a comma is required after the introductory clause:

> If you want to pass the test, you must study.

When an introductory clause functions as a noun, it shouldn't be followed by a comma:

Whether you pass the test will depend on how much you study.

When a sentence begins with a phrase, following the phrase with a comma is required in some cases but only recommended in others. If a sentence opens with a prepositional phrase, following the phrase with a comma is a requirement if the phrase has more than four words. Otherwise, use of a comma following an introductory prepositional phrase is merely recommended. An introductory participial phrase should be followed by a comma in every case. So should every introductory infinitive phrase that functions as an adverb or adjective:

To make money, Al mowed yards.

That's because the infinitive phrase functions as an adverb that modifies "mowed." However, no comma is necessary for following an infinitive phrase that functions as a noun:

"To be happy is what I wish."

In the preceding sentence, "To be happy" is the subject of the sentence. There's no reason to follow it with a comma.

In summary, commas must follow introductory clauses and phrases that function as adverbs or adjectives, except commas aren't required to follow introductory prepositional phrases with four or fewer words. Commas are still optional in those cases. Commas should not follow introductory noun clauses or introductory noun phrases.

REMEMBER

Whether a clause is independent or subordinate, as well as whether a comma is required, has nothing to do with the length of the sentence. You can have a long independent clause preceded by an introductory phrase as brief as two words in length ("Very Relieved, he called his friends and family to tell them how well he did on the test"), or you can have a brief independent clause preceded by a fairly lengthy subordinate/dependent one ("Although he tried not to be saddened by all the sorrow and confusion in this crazy, modern world of ours, he wept").

Before an "afterthought"

An "afterthought" is like an introduction, but it comes after the independent clause rather than before or within it:

I don't need a tune-up, just an oil change.

I saw my two favorite animals at the zoo, lemurs and red pandas.

On both sides of an "interrupting" clause, phrase, or word

Usually, when a subordinate clause or a phrase comes in the middle of an independent clause, it needs to be set off with commas on both sides. For example, the second sentence in the preceding section could also have taken the form of "I saw my two favorite animals, lemurs and red pandas, at the zoo." The phrase "lemurs and red pandas" is an example of an *appositive phrase* because it gives more specific details of what is referred to by a previous word, "animals." "Lemurs" and "pandas" are the *appositives* in the appositive phrase because they specify which animals are referred to by "animals." Like other interrupting phrases, appositive phrases used within independent clauses need to be separated from the rest of their sentences by commas.

However, an interrupting appositive that comes alone, not in a phrase, needs commas beside it only if it is the only thing that can rename the previous word. If Adam is John's only brother, John could write correctly, "My brother, Adam, lives in my neighborhood." If John has more than one brother, he should not use commas around the appositive. He can write, "My brother Adam lives in my neighborhood." Use commas when only one of what is named exists. There's no rhyme or reason to which part of the sentence *has* to be the interrupting phrase or clause; it all depends on how you feel like writing it: You can say either "Abraham Lincoln, the 16th president, was the first president with a beard" or "The 16th president, Abraham Lincoln, was the first president with a beard."

Participles and participial phrases also need to be separated by commas when they interrupt independent clauses. Commas are necessary for separating the participial phrase in the sentence "William, still really surprised, accepted his trophy." Even if the participle were not part of a phrase, it would need to be separated by commas. The sentence would be "William, surprised, accepted his trophy."

Although, for the sake of your sanity, this book avoids using all the fancy names for the many types of interrupting clauses, phrases, and words, there are some other types that don't technically involve appositives or participles but still need to be set off with commas. A *which* clause is a good example, as in "Halloween, which was called Samhain by the Celts, is my favorite holiday." Other types of interrupting clauses, phrases, and words can be used, like *for example* or *however* (as in "This sentence, for example, has a very short interrupting phrase in the middle" or "This sentence, however, has just an interrupting word"). It is the interruption that calls for commas.

Separating items in a list

When three or more words or phrases are listed, commas are used to separate the items in the list. You may be listing individual words:

I bought cheese, milk, bread, pasta sauce, and fireworks.

You may be listing phrases or concepts several words long:

I bought a book with a green cover, an umbrella with purple stripes, six leopards that can dance the tango, and fireworks with which to scare the leopards if they won't stop dancing.

The comma preceding the *and* before the last item in the list — the so-called *Oxford comma* — is considered optional by grammarians. It is correct either to include or omit it, and the Praxis doesn't ask you questions about this rule.

Separating multiple adjectives before a single noun

"The brave, popular, wizened, sleepy, jocular elephant taught the leopards to tango" is an example of a sentence containing multiple adjectives that all modify the same noun. Accordingly, they are separated by commas. As explained in the section "Using adjectives to describe people, places, and things," earlier in this chapter, certain types of adjectives don't require commas even when they appear in series, but grammar tests very rarely test on this.

Semicolons

As far as the Praxis writing test and virtually all other grammar tests are concerned, semicolons do one thing and one thing only: Namely, they separate two independent clauses within a single sentence. We've already talked about how two independent clauses can be joined by a comma and a coordinating conjunction; the semicolon takes the place of both the comma and the coordinating conjunction. So, you can write either of the following sentences:

I fed the cats, and now they like me.

I fed the cats; now they like me.

When it comes to semicolons, that's about it. If you see a semicolon on the test, check to make sure that the words both before and after it constitute independent clauses. If they do, the semicolon is being used correctly; if they don't, it probably isn't. (This doesn't necessarily mean that an answer choice that uses a semicolon correctly is the right answer, because it may be wrong for some other reason. It just means that the semicolon isn't the reason it's wrong.)

Apostrophes

Unlike the other punctuation marks discussed in this section, apostrophes don't separate parts of a sentence. Rather, they're used within individual words for two reasons: to show contraction (as in "cannot" becoming "can't") and to indicate possession (as in "my friend's car"). When it comes to contractions, the apostrophe goes where the missing letter or letters would be. The only tricky thing about this is distinguishing certain contractions from similar-sounding words that don't have apostrophes (we discuss that in the section "Homophones: 'They're in there with their bear,'" later in this chapter).

As for using apostrophes to indicate possession, that's a little more complicated, but not exactly difficult. Here's what you need to know:

>> To make a singular word (not ending in "s") possessive, add both an apostrophe and an "s," with the apostrophe coming before the "s," as in "I borrowed my cousin's guitar."

>> To make a singular word ending in "s" possessive, put an apostrophe after the "s," and put an "s" after the apostrophe, as in "I like the bus's windows."

>> To make a plural word ending in "s" possessive, add an apostrophe after the "s," as in "My parents' house is in the suburbs."

>> To make a plural word that does not end in "s" possessive, add both an apostrophe and an "s," with the apostrophe coming before the "s," as in "That room is where we keep the children's toys."

WARNING

Perhaps the most important apostrophe rule concerns what apostrophes are *not* used to do: Namely, they are *never* used to indicate pluralization. So, remember, it's *not* "My friend's brought their guitar's," because *friends* and *guitars* in that sentence are simply plural and not possessive. Yes, the friends own the guitars, but the words themselves are not indicating possession from a grammatical perspective.

Misplaced Modifiers

Depending on when you went to school, you may be familiar with the rules in this section under a different name. Once upon a time, misplaced modifiers were called *dangling participles*. Then they were called *dangling modifiers* for a while. Then someone decided that the "dangling" business just sounded silly, so now grammarians call them *misplaced modifiers*.

A *modifier* is a word, phrase, or clause that provides detail to another part of the sentence. Modifiers can be adjectives, adverbs, or groups of words functioning as adjectives or adverbs. Some modifiers open sentences in ways that require them to be followed by commas. If such a modifier functions as an adjective, what it modifies (describes) must be the first noun or pronoun after the comma. When that rule is not followed, confusion can be created.

For example, take the sentence "Tired of the parade, Taryn went home." "Tired of the parade" is a participle phrase (the participle *tired* plus a prepositional phrase that modifies the participle), so it functions as an adjective. It describes, and therefore modifies, "Taryn." That is why "Taryn" has to be the first noun or pronoun (a noun in this case) after the comma.

The sentence in the preceding paragraph is correct, but if someone were to write "Growing tired of the parade, we found out that Taryn went home," that would be an example of a misplaced modifier. A reader might be able to intuit from the context that Taryn is the one who left, but as written, the sentence means that *we* are the ones who got tired of the parade rather than Taryn because *we* is the pronoun that immediately follows the modifying clause (and is the subject of the independent clause).

EXAMPLE

Which of the following sentences is correct?

(A) Needing to make an urgent call, Megan's search for her phone charger was frantic.

(B) While playing football in the house, the lamp was broken.

(C) Confused by the directions, the gang drove around aimlessly.

(D) Never having met him before, I'm amazed you got along so well with Danny.

(E) Unlike some people, you can always depend on Gabriel.

The correct answer is Choice (C). "The gang" is who or what was "confused," so this sentence places its subject in correct relation to its modifier (the fact that "the" precedes "gang" doesn't matter). Choice (A) is wrong because, although the name "Megan" comes right after the comma, it's possessive, so the entire noun phrase is "Megan's search" — and Megan's *search* didn't need to make a call; Megan *herself* did. Choice (B) is wrong because, although what the writer means to say is clear, the sentence as written means that the *lamp* was playing football, which it obviously wasn't doing. Choice (D) is wrong because it's clear from context that the person being addressed is the one who has never met Danny before, not the speaker, so "I'm" should not immediately follow the comma. Choice (E) is wrong because, although it's clear from the context that reliable Gabriel is the one who is "unlike some people," the sentence as written means that the person being addressed is the one who is "unlike some people," which is presumably not what the speaker means to say.

Redundancy and Double Negatives

You should never repeat yourself or say the same thing twice. In other words, you should avoid doing what the previous sentence just did! In the grammar game, that's known as *redundancy*. Redundancy can take the form of an entire phrase that repeats information provided by an earlier phrase (like in the little joke that opened this paragraph), or it can come down to something as simple as an unnecessary adjective, as in "the tree-filled forest" (by definition, a forest is filled with trees, so pointing this out is hardly necessary).

Grammar tests like to throw in some redundancy questions now and then because the test-writers know that most people are too concerned with grammar to stop and think about what a sentence actually *means*. (The first sentence in this section, for example, is *grammatically* correct in the sense that it doesn't break any rules about clauses, agreement, punctuation, or anything like that, but it's still undesirable, because you could chop the sentence in half and each half would mean the same thing.)

Double negatives are a special type of redundancy that occurs when two words that both indicate the negation of an idea are inserted into a sentence when only one is necessary, as in the sentence "Nobody gave me nothing." Either "Nobody gave me anything" or "People gave me nothing" would be correct, but you don't need to use a "negating" word twice. Doing so results in the opposite meaning from what's intended because the two negatives cancel each other. If nobody gives a person nothing, then everybody gives the person something. Singing "I can't get no satisfaction" made the Rolling Stones a lot of money, but it wouldn't have been a correct response on the Praxis or any other test.

Homophones: "They're in there with their bear"

As you probably remember from elementary school, *homophones* are words that sound the same but are spelled differently. Two things about homophones are likely to trip you up when you take the Praxis: the differences between words that are spelled the same, when one has an apostrophe; and the meanings of words that sound the same but have different spellings.

Which one has the apostrophe?

The types of homophones that give the average person the most trouble are the ones where one word is a contraction (that is, it has an apostrophe) and the other word is a possessive pronoun — for example, "it's/its," "you're/your," "they're/their (and there)," and "who's/whose." In all of those cases, the one with the apostrophe is the contraction. Possessive personal pronouns shouldn't have apostrophes. This concept is confusing because the first thing you learn about apostrophes is that they show possession, and now suddenly the word without the apostrophe is the possessive one. But hey, that's the rule (don't look at us — we didn't invent the English language).

TIP

The easiest way to keep all this straight (and get the questions right on the Praxis) is simply to get in the habit of reading the words with the apostrophes as though they were two separate words: "it's" means "it is," so say/think "it is" whenever you see "it's." Say "you are" whenever you see "you're," say "they are" whenever you see "they're," say "who is" whenever you see "who's," and so on. If the sentence no longer makes sense, then the word in question should be the one *without* the apostrophe. Incorrect use of apostrophes can cause confusion because it can make words look like contractions when that's not what they are. For example, "Who's backpack is this?" could be interpreted to mean "Who is backpack is this?" The second meaning does not make sense.

Spelled and used differently, but sound the same

If the homophone you have trouble with is *their* versus *there*, you can remember that *their* is the possessive because it contains the word *heir*, and that *there* is the one about places because it contains the word *here* (that's not actually *why* the words are spelled that way; it's just a good way to remember which is which). When it comes to homophone trouble in cases where neither word has an apostrophe, here are the most common pairs of words that give people grief and how to remember which is which:

- **Then/than:** *Then* is an adverb indicating order ("I aced the test, and then I went straight to the bar"), and *than* is a subordinating conjunction used for comparison ("I know grammar better than my friends do, thanks to this book") or a preposition ("Indianapolis is larger than Jackson"). Getting into the habit of pronouncing them differently helps a lot, but if there's no time for that, then just use the "e" and "a" themselves as clues and think *then* = *order* and *than* = *comparison*.

- **Affect/effect:** Ninety-nine percent of the time, the difference is that *affect* is a verb and *effect* is a noun: "His insults did not *affect* me" versus "His insults had no *effect* on me." Unfortunately, there's more. *Effect* can also be a verb meaning "to bring about," as in "You'll need to do more than sign petitions if you really want to *effect* change." And just to make sure your day is completely ruined, *affect* can also be a noun. *Affect* as a noun is a word that has to do with a person's behavior. For the purposes of the Praxis, just remember that, in the vast majority of cases, *affect* is a verb and *effect* is a noun, but there are exceptions.

- **To/too:** *To* is a preposition that can be used in all sorts of ways. *Too* is an adverb that can mean either "extremely" or "unacceptably" ("The music is *too* loud"), or "also" ("I'm coming *too*"). The best method for keeping them straight is to remember that one word is used *way* more than the other: There probably isn't a single paragraph in this book that doesn't use *to*. So rather than trying to memorize the million different things that *to* can do, just remember that if it means "unacceptably/very" or "also," it's *too*, and if not, then it's *to*." (There's also *two*, which means the whole number between one and three, but most people don't have any trouble with that.)

- **Compliment/complement:** The one with the "i" means saying something nice about somebody, and the one with the "e" means that two things go together well ("He *complimented* me on the fact that my shoes *complement* my dress").

- **Whether/weather:** The first one means that something is in question, and the second one refers to what it's like when you go outside ("I don't know *whether* the *weather* will improve"). As with *than/then*, it helps to get into the habit of pronouncing them differently. Your friends may think it's obnoxious of you to start pronouncing the "h" in "whether," but you can stop after the test.

- **Farther/further:** These words aren't technically homophones because they're pronounced differently, but they still give people a lot of trouble. The difference is that *farther* relates to actual physical distance, whereas *further* indicates extent ("I don't want to have any *further* discussion about whether you can long-jump *farther* than I can").

Capitalization: What You Need to Know

When you first began looking into what is or isn't tested on the Praxis writing exam, your reaction to finding out that there were questions about capitalization was probably something like "There are questions about *capitalization* on this test?! What am I, in third grade?"

Yes, you almost certainly already know that the first letters of the first words of sentences are capitalized, as are people's names; the names of proper places like cities, states, or countries; the names of companies, such as Facebook; the names of sports teams and bands; and the words in the titles of books, movies, and so on.

You may not, however, know some of the trickier rules about capitalization, and those are the ones that the Praxis writing test will ask about. Here's a rundown of the most common capitalization-related tricks:

>> **Titles, such as "president":** Titles, such as "president," "mayor," and so forth, are only capitalized when they are placed before the name of, or used to indicate, a *specific* president or mayor or what have you. So, you should write "Abraham Lincoln was the 16th president," but "Everyone knows that President Lincoln wore a stovepipe hat."

The same rule applies for God versus a god: You capitalize "God" when referring to a/the deity with the proper name God, but not when you're talking about deities in general: "I prayed to God that I would pass the test" versus "Apollo was one of the Greek gods."

>> **The names of seasons:** Many people are unclear about this, but the rule is that the names of seasons are only capitalized if you are addressing the season directly, as you might in a poem. So, you say "I love the way the leaves change color in the fall," but "Oh, my beloved Fall, how I love it when your leaves change color!"

>> **The names of specific regions, even if they are not actual countries:** You should capitalize the names of all proper nouns, and that includes geographical areas that are not technically specific countries, cities, and the like: "My uncle frequently travels to the Far East." You should *not,* however, capitalize the names of cardinal directions when they're just used to indicate directions rather than areas: "My uncle has to fly east to get to the Far East." You should also not capitalize the "cardinal direction" part of a name when a suffix is attached to it, because that involves a comparison rather than a proper name, with the exception of cases where the cardinal direction with a comparative suffix is part of an actual proper noun: "Many people don't realize that northern Brazil lies in the Northern Hemisphere."

>> **Specific eras in history:** The title of a specific period in history, even a slang or unofficial one, is a proper noun and should be capitalized accordingly: "The Disco Era was mercifully short-lived."

Practice Questions about Grammar

These practice questions are similar to the questions about grammar that you'll encounter on the Praxis.

1. Which version of the following sentence is correct?

   The childrens' toys, are all over the floor, so you'd better watch your step.

   (A) The childrens' toys, are all over the floor, so you'd better watch your step.

   (B) The childrens' toys are all over the floor, so you'd better watch you're step.

   (C) The children's toys, are all over the floor, so you'd better watch you're step.

   (D) The children's toys are all over the floor, so you'd better watch your step.

   (E) The childrens toys, are all over the floor, so you'd better watch your step.

2. Which version of the following sentence is correct?

   I wouldn't eat that sandwich if I were you, I'm not sure how long its been in the refrigerator.

   (A) I wouldn't eat that sandwich if I were you, I'm not sure how long its been in the refrigerator.

   (B) I wouldn't eat that sandwich if I were you, I'm not sure how long it's been in the refrigerator.

   (C) I wouldn't eat that sandwich if I were you; I'm not sure how long its been in the refrigerator.

   (D) I wouldn't eat that sandwich if I were you, I'm not sure how long; it's been in the refrigerator.

   (E) I wouldn't eat that sandwich if I were you; I'm not sure how long it's been in the refrigerator.

3. Which version of the following sentence is correct?

   That hotdog restaurant, was a village land-mark, I can't believe it closed!

   (A) That hotdog restaurant, was a village landmark, I can't believe it closed!

   (B) That hotdog restaurant, it was a village landmark, and I can't believe it closed!

   (C) That hotdog restaurant — as a village landmark — I can't believe it closed!

   (D) That hotdog restaurant was a village landmark — I can't believe it closed!

   (E) That hotdog restaurant being a village landmark, so I can't believe it closed!

4. Which version of the following sentence is correct?

   The album containing all my birthday pictures is missing!

   (A) The album containing all my birthday pictures is missing!

   (B) The album containing all my birthday pictures are missing!

   (C) The album contains all my birthday pictures are missing!

   (D) The album contains all my birthday pictures is missing!

   (E) The album containing all my birthday pictures, which is missing!

5. Which version of the following sentence is correct?

She was running late for work, Megan locked herself out of her apartment.

(A) She was running late for work, Megan locked herself out of her apartment.

(B) Because she was running late for work, and Megan locked herself out of her apartment.

(C) Running late for work, Megan locked herself out of her apartment.

(D) Running late for work, and Megan locked herself out of her apartment.

(E) Running late for work; Megan locked herself out of her apartment.

6. Which version of the underlined portion makes the sentence correct?

Although we've had a rough couple of seasons, because I think this might be our year.

(A) seasons, because I think

(B) seasons, I think

(C) seasons, but I think

(D) seasons, however, I think

(E) seasons: I think

7. Which version of the following sentence is correct?

The affects of the anesthesia has begun to wear off.

(A) The affects of the anesthesia has begun to wear off.

(B) The affects of the anesthesia have begun to wear off.

(C) The effects of the anesthesia have begun to wear off.

(D) The effects of the anesthesia has began to wear off.

(E) The effects of the anesthesia have began to wear off.

8. How many commas are needed to correctly punctuate the following sentence?

The fastest two-legged animal the ostrich may be found in Australia and zoos all over the world.

(A) None

(B) One

(C) Two

(D) Three

(E) Four

9. Which version of the underlined portion of the following sentence makes the sentence correct?

When I was young, I won a year supply of pretzels in a radio contest.

(A) a year supply

(B) a year's supply

(C) a years' supply

(D) yearly a supply

(E) a year of supplies

10. The problem with the following sentence is that it contains a

As someone whom I have known for years, I'd expect you not to take his side over mine.

(A) comma splice

(B) misplaced modifier

(C) parallel-phrasing error

(D) redundancy

(E) misuse of "whom"

11. Which version of the underlined portion makes the sentence correct?

Don't let any of the cats' toys slide under the stove, it will whine all night.

(A) stove, it

(B) stove, or it

(C) stove, they

(D) stove, or they

(E) stove; it

12. How many of the words in the following sentence are capitalized when they should *not* be?

Neither my Father nor I could believe that Coach Collins wanted me to start in center field for the Brooklyn Beavers this Spring.

(A) None

(B) One

(C) Two

(D) Three

(E) Four

13. Which version of the underlined portion makes the sentence correct?

It's going to take more than one person to get this couch upstairs.

(A) It's going to take more than

(B) Its going to take more then

(C) It's going to takes more than

(D) Its going to takes more then

(E) It's going to take more then

14. Which version of the underlined portion makes the sentence correct?

Before you take the picture of Sam and I, let us fix our hair.

(A) Sam and I, let

(B) Sam and me, let

(C) Sam and myself, let

(D) Sam, and I let

(E) Sam, and me let

15. A sentence that contains a colon is definitely grammatically incorrect *if*

(A) the colon does not precede a list or quotation.

(B) the sentence does not also have a comma in it.

(C) the portion of the sentence after the colon is longer than the portion before it.

(D) the colon is not preceded by an independent clause.

(E) the colon is not both preceded by and followed by independent clauses.

Answers and Explanations

Use this answer key to score the practice grammar questions in the preceding section.

1. **D. The children's toys are all over the floor, so you'd better watch your step.** The sentence is two independent clauses joined by the coordinating conjunction "so," so you need only one comma, placed right before the conjunction. The possessive of the word *children* is *children's*, and the possessive second-person pronoun is *your*.

    The right answer is not Choice (A) because there's no such word as *childrens'* (with the apostrophe after the "s"), and because no comma is needed between the subject and the verb. The right answer is not Choice (B) because there's no such word as *childrens'* (with the apostrophe after the "s"), and because the possessive form is *your*, not *you're*.

    The right answer is not Choice (C) because no comma is needed between the subject and the verb and because the possessive form is *your*, not *you're*. The right answer is not Choice (E) because there's no such word as *childrens* (with no apostrophe) and because no comma is needed between the subject and the verb.

2. **E. I wouldn't eat that sandwich if I were you; I'm not sure how long it's been in the refrigerator.** The two independent clauses are correctly separated by a semicolon, and the correct *it's* (the one with the apostrophe, which means *it is*, or in this case, *it has*) is used.

    The right answer is not Choice (A) because this sentence contains a comma splice and because the wrong *its* is used (you need the one with the apostrophe, which means *it has* in this case). The right answer is not Choice (B) because this sentence contains a comma splice.

    The right answer is not Choice (C) because the wrong *its* is used (you need the one with the apostrophe, which means *it is* or *it has*). The right answer is not Choice (D) because the punctuation is misplaced: You need a semicolon in place of that comma, and no punctuation at all in the place where the semicolon currently appears.

3. **D. That hotdog restaurant was a village landmark — I can't believe it closed!** This sentence correctly presents two independent clauses separated by a single dash (a semicolon would also have been correct, but that's not one of the options).

    The right answer is not Choice (A) because the first comma, which appears between the subject and the verb, is unnecessary and because the second comma results in a comma splice.

    The right answer is not Choice (B) because there's no need to repeat the subject by inserting a comma and a pronoun *(it)* before the verb. That portion of the sentence should simply read "restaurant was," rather than "restaurant, it was." (The inclusion of *and* after the second comma avoids creating a comma splice, but the sentence is already incorrect for the aforementioned reason.)

    The right answer is not Choice (C) because double dashes are only appropriate when the portions of the sentence outside the dashes work together to form a complete sentence (in other words, the dashes work like parentheses). The right answer is not Choice (E) because *being* can't work here as the main verb of the sentence; it should say *was*.

4. **A. The album containing all my birthday pictures is missing!** The main verb of the sentence is the singular *is* (because the subject is the singular *album*), and the word *containing* functions as a participle here.

    The right answer is not Choice (B) because the subject of the sentence is *album*, so the verb should be the singular *is*, not the plural *are*. The right answer is not Choice (C) because *contains* is not meant to be the verb; you need the participle *containing*, not *contains*. Additionally, the subject of the sentence is *album*, so the verb should be the singular *is*, not the plural *are*.

The right answer is not Choice (D) because *contains* is not the verb; it's meant to work as a participle here, so you need *containing*, not *contains*. The right answer is not Choice (E) because the sentence has no main verb. The use of *is* following *which* makes *is* part of a subordinate clause, so the sentence would have to keep going after the *which* clause to form a main verb clause.

5. **C. Running late for work, Megan locked herself out of her apartment.** This sentence correctly presents an independent clause preceded by a participial phrase and a comma.

The right answer is not Choice (A) because it contains a comma splice. The right answer is not Choice (B) because a comma that immediately follows an introductory dependent clause should not be immediately followed by a conjunction. A comma not immediately followed by a conjunction should be used instead. A comma that is followed immediately by a conjunction is used to separate two independent clauses, not a dependent clause and an independent clause. If *because* (which makes the first sentence a dependent clause) or *and* were omitted, the sentence would be correct.

The right answer is not Choice (D) because the second clause is the independent clause, and no conjunction is necessary. The right answer is not Choice (E) because the introductory phrase is not an independent clause, so you need a comma instead of a semicolon.

6. **B. seasons, I think.** The presence of the subordinating conjunction *although* means that the first clause is not independent, so the second of the two clauses should be an independent clause with no conjunction (this is the "although trick").

The right answer is not Choice (A) because the presence of both *although* and *because* means that both clauses are subordinate — in other words, the sentence contains no independent clause. The right answer is not Choice (C) because, although the sentence would be correct with *either* "although" in the first clause *or* "but" in the second, it is incorrect to include both.

The right answer is not Choice (D) because *however* with commas on either side properly interrupts a single independent clause; it doesn't join two clauses (in other words, *however* is not a conjunction). In any case, the presence of *although* in the first clause means that this sentence would still be incorrect, even if *however* were a conjunction.

The right answer is not Choice (E) because the clause that precedes a colon must be independent (which this clause isn't because it's subordinated to *although*).

7. **C. The effects of the anesthesia have begun to wear off.** *Effects* is the subject of the sentence and a noun, so it should be spelled with an "e." It is also plural, so the verb should be *have*, not *has*. Finally, the present perfect plural form of *begin* is *have begun*, not *have began*.

The right answer is not Choice (A) because *effects* is the subject of the sentence and a noun, so it should be spelled with an "e." It's also plural, so the verb should be *have*, not *has*. The right answer is not Choice (B) because *effects* is the subject of the sentence and a noun, so it should be spelled with an "e."

The right answer is not Choice (D) because *effects* is plural, so the verb should be *have*, not *has*, and because the present perfect plural form of *begin* is *have begun*, not *have began*. The right answer is not Choice (E) because the present perfect plural form of *begin* is *have begun*, not *have began*.

8. **C. Two.** Only two commas are needed, one on either side of the appositive phrase *the ostrich*. The main sentence works as a single independent clause if *the ostrich* is lifted out. No comma is needed for the series of adjectives that precede *animal* because they limit or modify each other. And no comma is needed before the *and* because the verb *found* extends to both places.

9. **B. a year's supply.** Even though the pretzels belong to the speaker and not literally to the year, the word *year* must still be possessive: "a *year's* supply," "a *year's* worth," and so on.

The right answer is not Choice (A) because the word *year* must be possessive. The right answer is not Choice (C) because you are talking about one year's supply of pretzels, so you need the singular possessive (with the apostrophe before the "s"), not the plural possessive.

The right answer is not Choice (D) because it's difficult to discern what this sentence is trying to say; the syntax is awkward in a way that impedes comprehension. The right answer is not Choice (E) because, although it is possible to discern what the sentence means to say, it's unnecessarily wordy. Why say "a year of supplies of pretzels" rather than simply "a year's supply of pretzels"?

10. **B. misplaced modifier.** The sentence contains a misplaced modifier. The initial modifying clause reads "As someone whom I've known for years," which means that a word referring to the person whom the speaker knows (either a proper name or pronoun) must immediately follow the comma.

The right answer is not Choice (A) because both clauses are not independent, so the sentence doesn't contain a comma splice. The right answer is not Choice (C) because there's no parallel-phrasing issue with this sentence.

The right answer is not Choice (D) because there's no example of redundancy in this sentence. The right answer is not Choice (E) because *whom* is used correctly in this sentence (the pronoun is the object of *known*, so it should be in the objective case).

11. **D. stove, or they.** The plural possessive form *cats'* in the non-underlined portion of the sentence establishes that you are dealing with more than one cat, so the pronoun should be *they* rather than *it*. A conjunction (in this case, *or*) is also needed to avoid a comma splice.

The right answer is not Choice (A) because it's a comma splice and because the pronoun should be *they*, not *it*. The right answer is not Choice (B) because the pronoun should be *they*, not *it*.

The right answer is not Choice (C) because it's a comma splice. The right answer is not Choice (E) because the pronoun should be *they*, not *it*.

12. **C. Two.** Neither *father* nor *spring* should be capitalized, because they're not being directly addressed. The other capitalized terms, *Coach Collins* and *Brooklyn Beavers*, are proper nouns and are appropriately capitalized.

The right answer is not Choice (A) because there are words in the sentence that are incorrectly capitalized. The right answer is not Choice (B) because more than one word in the sentence is incorrectly capitalized.

The right answer is not Choice (D) because fewer than three words in the sentence are incorrectly capitalized. The right answer is not Choice (E) because fewer than four words in the sentence are incorrectly capitalized.

13. **A. It's going to take more than.** The sentence is correct as it is because it appropriately includes the contraction *it's* (for *it is*), the infinitive to *take*, and the preposition *than* (spelled with an "a"). The right answer is not Choice (B) because you need the contraction *it's* (for *it is*), not the possessive *its*, and because you need the preposition *than*, not the adverb *then*. The right answer is not Choice (C) because you need the infinitive to *take*, not to *takes*. The right answer is not Choice (D) because you need the contraction *it's* (for *it is*), not the possessive *its*; the infinitive to *take*, not to *takes*; and the preposition *than*, not the adverb *then*. The right answer is not Choice (E) because you need the preposition *than*, not the adverb *then*.

14. **B. Sam and me, let.** The pronoun is one of the objects of the preposition *of*, so it should be the objective-case *me*, not the subjective-case *I*. The comma should be placed between that pronoun and the verb *let* because that's the point at which the introductory subordinate clause ends and the main independent clause (which is a command) begins.

    The right answer is not Choice (A) because the pronoun is one of the objects of the preposition *of*, so it should be the objective-case *me*, not the subjective-case *I*. The right answer is not Choice (C) because the speaker has not yet appeared in the sentence and is not reflexively performing any verb upon himself, so there's no need to use *myself* instead of *me*.

    The right answer is not Choice (D) because the pronoun is one of the objects of the preposition *of*, so it should be the objective-case *me*, not the subjective-case *I*. Additionally, the comma should be placed between that pronoun and the verb *let* because that's the point at which the introductory subordinate clause ends and the main independent clause (which is a command) begins.

    The right answer is not Choice (E) because the comma should be placed between the pronoun and the verb *let*. That's the point at which the introductory subordinate clause ends and the main independent clause (which is a command) begins.

15. **D. the colon is not preceded by an independent clause.** The one hard-and-fast rule for colons is that the portion of the sentence preceding the colon must contain an independent clause.

    The right answer is not Choice (A) because a colon doesn't necessarily have to precede either a list or a quotation. Those are just the most common uses for colons. The right answer is not Choice (B) because there's no rule about any kind of relationship between the presence of a colon and the presence of a comma.

    The right answer is not Choice (C) because there's no rule about whether the portion of the sentence before or after the colon has to be longer. The right answer is not Choice (E) because a colon doesn't have to link two independent clauses to be used although it can in certain cases.

Chapter 13

Test-Taking Strategies for Core Writing

D o you have the writing skills you need for a successful career in education? The Praxis Core writing test is meant to determine exactly that. Whether you feel pretty confident about your writing skills or you're just starting to gear up for the Praxis, this chapter gives you the strategies you need to tackle the writing section.

Knowing the Types of Selected-Response Writing Questions

The selected-response portion of the Praxis writing test contains 40 questions with a 40-minute time limit. Some of the questions consist of a sentence or two followed by choices. Other questions involve reading a longer passage and selecting such choices as the best revision, best conclusion, or best version.

These questions address usage, research skills, sentence correction, and revision in context:

» **Usage:** The usage questions require you to recognize a variety of errors regarding mechanics, structure, grammatical relationships, and word choice. The questions test your ability to find errors in using adjectives and adverbs, subject and verb agreement, pronoun and antecedent agreement, verb tense, pronoun case, and the use of intensive pronouns. You're also expected to identify errors in punctuation and capitalization.

» **Research skills:** The questions concerning research test your ability to use reliable research strategies, to recognize the parts of a citation, and to judge the credibility and relevance of research sources.

» **Sentence correction:** In addressing questions concerning sentence correction, you choose the answer that best revises or restates a phrase or sentence by using standard written English. For some questions, you select Choice (A) if the sentence is correct as written. Errors you may encounter include problems with parallelism, run-on sentences, fragments, misplaced (also known as dangling) modifiers, coordinating and subordinating conjunctions, and errors in the placement of phrases and clauses.

» **Revision in context:** The revision-in-context questions test your ability to recognize the best way to improve a passage or a portion of a passage. These questions may address many different aspects: organization, word choice (precise and effective words), consistency in style and tone, and correct grammatical conventions. Some questions test your ability to recognize that some passages or portions thereof need no improvement.

The selected-response section of the writing test is scored separately from the essay section. Keep these points in mind:

» **Only one choice is correct.** No questions have more than one right answer.

» **Read the question carefully.** Try putting the question into your own words, if possible.

» **Read all the answer choices.** Only then make your choice.

» **Avoid reading too much into the questions.** There are no "trick" questions.

» **Skip questions that are difficult for you.** Come back to those questions later.

» **Pay attention to time.** Remember to leave a few minutes so that you can go back to the questions you skipped and also check your work. For unanswered questions, try to narrow your choices. If necessary, guess. Keep in mind that you are not penalized for wrong answers.

Type 1: Answering usage questions

Some of the selected-response questions consist of a sentence that contains underlined portions. You must decide whether any one of the underlined portions has an error in grammar, sentence construction, word use, punctuation, or capitalization. If so, you select the underlined portion that contains the error. If the sentence is correct as written, you select "No error." No sentence has more than one error.

You know you're looking at a usage question when one of the answer choices is "No error." The first thing to do in this situation is to read the question without paying attention to the underlined portions. You may find the error immediately. If you don't, look carefully at each underlined portion. Still nothing? Then, mark "No error."

TIP Put on your grammar policing outfit and watch out for these errors:

» Incorrect punctuation, particularly commas, semicolons, and apostrophes

» Pronoun usage, particularly pronoun/antecedent errors or vague pronouns

» Verb tense

» Subject/verb agreement errors

» Word choice, particularly words like *affect* and *effect,* which are often confused

Each of the following questions consists of a sentence with four underlined portions. Read each question and decide whether any of the underlined parts contains an element that would be considered incorrect or inappropriate in carefully written English. The error or concern may be in grammatical construction, word use, capitalization, or punctuation. Select the underlined portion that should be revised. If there are no errors, select "No error."

Because <u>writing a novel is</u> a long and involved process <u>requiring a great deal of patience</u> and
_A _B
perseverance, <u>the aspiring novelist must have</u> a quiet place to <u>work; a noisy environment is</u> not
_C _D
conducive to thought and creativity. <u>No error.</u>

EXAMPLE

Because the example question represents no problems in usage, structure, or word choice,
Choice (E) is the correct answer.

<u>When someone gives a speech</u>, however informative it may be, <u>they must be sure</u> to <u>engage</u>
_A _B
<u>the audience</u> for <u>its entire duration</u>. <u>No error.</u>
_C _D _E

EXAMPLE

The correct answer is Choice (B). The plural pronoun "they" refers to the pronoun "someone,"
which is singular. The error, then, is a disagreement between the pronoun and its antecedent.

<u>My parents have been living</u> in Europe <u>before I was born</u>, but <u>they came to America</u> in 1998 to
_A _B _C
join <u>my uncle's</u> business. <u>No error.</u>
_D _E

EXAMPLE

The correct answer is Choice (A). The verb phrase "have been living" is present-perfect tense,
which indicates something that began in the past and continues in the present. Because the
parents no longer live in Europe, the correct verb should be past tense, "lived."

<u>My best friend, as well as</u> my many associates <u>at work, think</u> that the local library <u>is both</u>
_A _B _C
poorly staffed and <u>utterly inefficiently</u> managed. <u>No error.</u>
_D _E

EXAMPLE

The correct answer is Choice (B). The subject of the sentence is "friend," a singular noun.
Therefore, a singular verb, "thinks," is correct. Remember that subjects and verbs must agree
in number. The intervening phase, "as well as my many associates at work," does not affect the
number of the subject. "Friend" is still singular.

Type 2: Showing your research skills

Some questions on the Praxis test your knowledge of basic research skills. Your task is to choose
the best answer from the choices given. You should be ready to answer questions about correct
citation, relevance and credibility of sources, and appropriate research strategies.

Smith, S. "Making Hay While the Sun Shines." *Hobbies.* 12 May 2002: 51–52.

In the preceding citation, which of the following is cited?

EXAMPLE

(A) a magazine article

(B) a book

(C) an interview

(D) a newspaper article

(E) a website

The correct answer is Choice (A). Citations are arranged in a specific order, and various
elements of the citation clue you in to the fact that the source cited is a magazine article. For
example, there are two titles, one in quotation marks (the title of the article) and one in italics
(the title of the magazine itself). The fact that the date of publication includes a month and day,
as opposed to just a year, is also evidence that this is a citation for a magazine article.

Which of the following is a secondary source on John Adams?

(A) A biography of John Adams

(B) A letter written by John Adams to his father

(C) A photograph of John Adams and his son

(D) A copy of a speech delivered by John Adams

(E) An essay written by John Adams

The correct answer is Choice (A). A secondary source contains information that has been interpreted by another scholar, as opposed to being an original discovery. The other choices represent primary sources because they are firsthand, original information that hasn't been subjected to interpretation.

Type 3: Making sentence corrections

In questions involving sentence correction, the Praxis presents a sentence in which some part of the sentence or the entire sentence is underlined. You're given five choices for rewriting the underlined section of the sentence (or the entire sentence). The first choice makes no changes; the other four are different ways of writing the sentence. Choose the first choice if you believe no change is necessary. Otherwise, indicate which of the remaining choices is best.

The correct answer will be clearly written and will most effectively express the idea presented in the original sentence. Be particularly mindful of word choice, sentence construction, correct grammar, and punctuation.

Annie, who won the blue ribbon for her apple pie, is a better cook than any contestant in the contest.

(A) Annie, who won the blue ribbon for her apple pie, is a better cook than any contestant in the contest.

(B) Annie won the blue ribbon for her apple pie; and is the best cook.

(C) Annie, who won the blue ribbon for her apple pie, had been better in comparison to anyone in the contest.

(D) Annie, who won the blue ribbon for her apple pie, is a better cook than any other contestant in the contest.

(E) Annie won the blue ribbon for her apple pie, she is a better cook than any other contestant.

The correct answer is Choice (D). Using the words "any other" is necessary so Annie (who is a contestant) isn't compared to herself.

Choice (A) compares Annie to herself. Because she is one of the contestants, she can't be better than all of the contestants; she can't be better than herself. Choice (B) uses a semicolon incorrectly. Choice (C) omits the word "other" and also has an error in verb tense. The verb "had been" creates inconsistent verb tense. Choice (E) contains a comma splice.

My best friend Jacob lately discovered that neither new clothes nor having the right kind of car would get him a date with Sophia.

(A) neither new clothes nor having the right kind of car

(B) neither how good his clothes were nor his car

(C) neither the right clothes or securing the right car

(D) neither new clothes and getting the right car

(E) neither new clothes nor the right car

The correct choice is (E). The correlative conjunctions "neither/nor" must link similar grammatical elements. Choice (E) links a noun, "clothes" to another noun, "car." Choices (A) and (B) both contain parallel-phrasing errors, and Choices (C) and (D) use incorrect conjunctions instead of using "neither's" partner, "nor."

Type 4: Regarding revision-in-context questions

Revision-in-context questions ask that you edit or revise a passage to make it better. The problem may be a clumsy or incorrect sentence or portion of a sentence. Your job is to make the choice that best improves the sentence. Improving the passage may require a change in word choice, style, tone, grammar, or organization. For some passages, no revision is necessary.

TIP

Think of the passage as your first draft of an assigned essay. Imagine that this essay will mean the difference between a B and a C as your final grade in the course (and your grade point average really could use a B). How can you make it better? Try to imagine what comments your instructor would make.

For each of the following three example questions, choose the best answer based on this passage:

⌐1⌐It's a cold, clear day in the neighborhood. ⌐2⌐It is a good day to go for a walk. ⌐3⌐I like walking because it is good exercise. ⌐4⌐It is a time to notice the change in seasons. ⌐5⌐It is a good time to stop and visit with neighbors. ⌐6⌐My dog really likes to walk with me, too. ⌐7⌐He doesn't know about exercise; he just likes the companionship.

EXAMPLE

Which would be the best revision, if any, of Sentences 1 and 2?

(A) It's a cold, clear day in the neighborhood, a good day for a walk.

(B) Being cold and clear, I like to walk.

(C) Walking is good on a cold, clear day.

(D) It's a cold, clear day in the neighborhood, and it is a good day to go for a walk.

(E) It's a cold and clear day, I feel like going for a walk around the neighborhood.

The correct answer is Choice (A). Because both sentences are short, joining them improves the passage. Although all the choices join the sentences, only Choice (A) preserves the original context and is also concise. Choice (B) contains a misplaced modifier. "Being cold and clear" appears to modify "I." Choice (C) leaves out the idea of walking in a neighborhood (which is important to the rest of the passage). Choice (D) joins the sentences but is less concise. Choice (E) contains a comma splice.

EXAMPLE

Which would be the best revision, if any, of Sentences 3, 4, and 5?

(A) No change.

(B) I like to exercise and to notice the change in seasons and visit the neighbors when I walk.

(C) Not only is walking good exercise, but walking also provides the opportunity to notice the change in seasons and to visit with neighbors.

(D) I can exercise, look at the change of season, and visit with neighbors while I walk.

(E) Walking is good because it makes me exercise. I can also notice the seasons and visit with neighbors.

The correct answer is Choice (C). This choice effectively uses the correlative conjunctions "not only" and "but also" to provide a transition and to link ideas concisely. The other choices provide no transition and are less effective in linking ideas. The goal in writing is to use the most effective words to convey meaning. This doesn't necessarily mean using the fewest words, but it does mean using the strongest choices.

EXAMPLE

Which would be the best revision, if any, of Sentences 6 and 7?

(A) No change.

(B) Another benefit to a neighborhood walk is the chance to take my dog; he enjoys the walk and the companionship, even though he knows nothing about exercise.

(C) My dog knows nothing about exercise; he enjoys the walk for the companionship.

(D) My dog likes the walk, he enjoys the companionship.

(E) However, my dog enjoys the walk and the companionship.

The correct answer is Choice (C). It maintains the essence of the two sentences in a concise way. Although Choices (A) and (B) are correct grammatically, they use more words than necessary to convey meaning. Choice (D) incorrectly joins independent clauses with a comma. Choice (E) uses an illogical transition, "however."

Identifying and Correcting Errors in Selected-Response Items

Correctly answering selected-response items on the writing portion of the Praxis requires that you read each question carefully. Where possible, put the question into your own words. Be sure to read every choice before you make your selection.

Eliminating the obviously wrong choices

The process of elimination can help you choose the correct answer in a selected-response question. Start by crossing off the answers that can't be right. Then spend your time focusing on the possible correct choices before selecting your answer. Doing so greatly increases the odds of your choosing correctly.

TIP

Pay special attention to answers that contain these words: *none, never, all, more, always,* and *only.* These words indicate that the answer is an undisputed fact and, consequently, isn't likely to be the correct choice. Conditional words such as *usually* or *probably* make the answer more likely.

REMEMBER

Be particularly careful of selected-response questions that use the words *not, least,* and *except.* These questions usually ask you to select the choice that doesn't fit. Stay alert! It's easy to misread these questions.

Don't be afraid to say it's right the way it is

Although it may seem counterintuitive, if a sentence is correct as written, "No error" is the correct answer. Fear not: Some tasks will be written correctly. Just be sure to consider all the choices before making your decision.

The art of guessing as a last resort

Your score is based on the number of correct answers. You're not penalized for incorrect answers. For this reason, you should answer every question.

TIP

If you face a difficult question, narrow your choices as much as possible and, if necessary, guess. Don't spend too much time considering a difficult question. Mark the question and come back to it. Answer the easy questions first.

You're not expected to answer all the questions correctly. In order to pass the Praxis, you must simply achieve the minimum passing score for your state.

A word of advice about trusting your ear

If you grew up in a family of English teachers who corrected your every incorrect utterance, complete with an accompanying grammar lesson, it's probably pretty safe for you to *trust your ear*, meaning whatever sounds right to you is likely right. However, if you're like most people, you grew up in a family that was considerably less interested in your grammar. Language that sounds right to you is simply language you're accustomed to hearing and may very well be incorrect. Play it safe and analyze the sentence carefully. It's easy to make a mistake when trusting your ear. Consider some examples.

Neither the boys nor the girl (is/are) paying attention.

While "are" may sound right, the correct answer is "is." The verb agrees with the closest subject when subjects are compound.

I will split the cost between you and (I/me).

You probably hear someone use the incorrect construction of "between you and I" pretty often. Just because you hear it spoken, though, doesn't mean it's correct grammar. Objects of the preposition must be objective case, so "me" is the pronoun to use here.

You and (I/me) should see that new movie.

In this example, the personal pronoun is being used as one of the subjects of the sentence. Subjects must be subjective case, so "I" is the correct choice here.

Mastering the Essay

The Praxis requires you to write two essays. One is an *argumentative essay,* which means you must support a particular position, giving clear and specific examples and reasons. The second essay, the *informative/explanatory essay,* requires you to read articles from two different sources, identify the main ideas and issues of both, and use them to construct your own essay. You have 30 minutes to write each essay.

Although you don't need any specific knowledge of the topics you're given, you are expected to draw from your own experience and observation to write an effective essay using appropriate organization, development, tone, style, word choice, and standard written English. Above all, write clearly and stay on topic. Be careful to address all the points presented.

For the informative/explanatory essay, it's important to use information from both sources and correctly cite the sources. Read the source material carefully and organize your thoughts before you begin to write. You're judged according to how well you synthesize the source material.

REMEMBER

Your essay should be clear, consistent, and forceful, paying careful attention to mechanics and usage, as well as diction and syntax. Keep the following pointers in mind:

» Read the prompt carefully. Think about what you must do to adequately address the prompt.

» Establish your point quickly. Make a strong first impression.

» Avoid long introductions.

» Organize each body paragraph around a strong topic sentence.

» Be sure every paragraph supports the thesis.

» Support for your thesis should include examples from your own experiences, reading, and observations.

» Pay attention to word choice: strong verbs, precise nouns.

» Use a variety of sentence types and lengths.

» Use clear transitions to aid the flow of your essay.

» Be concise.

» Strive for a strong conclusion that delivers a final punch.

TIP

How can you best prepare for essays? Write, write, write. For the argumentative essay, practice taking a side in a current issue you have read or heard about. How can you support your opinion? How can you organize? For the informative/informational essay, read about a topic from two or three sources and practice using this information in an essay.

5

Tackling Praxis Core Practice Tests

Chapter **14**

Practice Exam 1

N ow it's time to audition for the starring role in "Acing the Praxis Core." It's your chance to see how well you can perform on the practice exam in a mock test setting. Remember, Praxis makes perfect . . . we mean, "practice makes perfect." When you take the following practice test, try your best to create a setting that's similar to the one in which you'll take the real Praxis. That means

>> De-gadgetize! No cellphone, tablet, TV remote, and so on. However, you have access to an on-screen, four-function calculator when you take the Praxis math test, so you can keep a calculator handy when you reach the math practice test in this chapter.

>> Find a quiet place to take the practice test — somewhere free from disruptions.

After you create a testing environment, adjust your mind-set:

>> Make sure you're aware of the amount of time allowed for each section so that you don't spend too much time on one question.

>> Focus on the concept that you're being tested on and turn your radar on to identify key words that indicate the operation you need to solve the problem.

>> Don't leave any answers blank.

>> Stay focused on your goal — to ace the Praxis Core. Have self-confidence because now is your opportunity to shine!

When you finish this audition, there shouldn't be a need to call in an understudy. Make sure to go through the detailed explanations of the answers in Chapter 15. Pay close attention to the questions you missed. Go back and review the question, and then review the answer to make sure you understand it.

REMEMBER

If you want to practice taking the test electronically, like you'll do on test day, go to Dummies.com, then follow the steps outlined in this book's Introduction so that you can access this practice test online. This online practice is included with the book. There, you can answer the questions digitally, and the software records which questions you answered correctly and incorrectly. This summary provides you with a snapshot of which areas you excel in and which areas you may need additional review.

Answer Sheet for Practice Exam 1

Reading

1. Ⓐ Ⓑ Ⓒ Ⓓ Ⓔ
2. Ⓐ Ⓑ Ⓒ Ⓓ Ⓔ
3. Ⓐ Ⓑ Ⓒ Ⓓ Ⓔ
4. Ⓐ Ⓑ Ⓒ Ⓓ Ⓔ
5. Ⓐ Ⓑ Ⓒ Ⓓ Ⓔ
6. Ⓐ Ⓑ Ⓒ Ⓓ Ⓔ
7. Ⓐ Ⓑ Ⓒ Ⓓ Ⓔ
8. Ⓐ Ⓑ Ⓒ Ⓓ Ⓔ
9. Ⓐ Ⓑ Ⓒ Ⓓ Ⓔ
10. Ⓐ Ⓑ Ⓒ Ⓓ Ⓔ
11. Ⓐ Ⓑ Ⓒ Ⓓ Ⓔ
12. Ⓐ Ⓑ Ⓒ Ⓓ Ⓔ
13. Ⓐ Ⓑ Ⓒ Ⓓ Ⓔ
14. Ⓐ Ⓑ Ⓒ Ⓓ Ⓔ
15. Ⓐ Ⓑ Ⓒ Ⓓ Ⓔ
16. Ⓐ Ⓑ Ⓒ Ⓓ Ⓔ
17. Ⓐ Ⓑ Ⓒ Ⓓ Ⓔ
18. Ⓐ Ⓑ Ⓒ Ⓓ Ⓔ
19. Ⓐ Ⓑ Ⓒ Ⓓ Ⓔ
20. Ⓐ Ⓑ Ⓒ Ⓓ Ⓔ
21. Ⓐ Ⓑ Ⓒ Ⓓ Ⓔ
22. Ⓐ Ⓑ Ⓒ Ⓓ Ⓔ
23. Ⓐ Ⓑ Ⓒ Ⓓ Ⓔ
24. Ⓐ Ⓑ Ⓒ Ⓓ Ⓔ
25. Ⓐ Ⓑ Ⓒ Ⓓ Ⓔ
26. Ⓐ Ⓑ Ⓒ Ⓓ Ⓔ
27. Ⓐ Ⓑ Ⓒ Ⓓ Ⓔ
28. Ⓐ Ⓑ Ⓒ Ⓓ Ⓔ
29. Ⓐ Ⓑ Ⓒ Ⓓ Ⓔ
30. Ⓐ Ⓑ Ⓒ Ⓓ Ⓔ
31. Ⓐ Ⓑ Ⓒ Ⓓ Ⓔ
32. Ⓐ Ⓑ Ⓒ Ⓓ Ⓔ
33. Ⓐ Ⓑ Ⓒ Ⓓ Ⓔ
34. Ⓐ Ⓑ Ⓒ Ⓓ Ⓔ
35. Ⓐ Ⓑ Ⓒ Ⓓ Ⓔ
36. Ⓐ Ⓑ Ⓒ Ⓓ Ⓔ
37. Ⓐ Ⓑ Ⓒ Ⓓ Ⓔ
38. Ⓐ Ⓑ Ⓒ Ⓓ Ⓔ
39. Ⓐ Ⓑ Ⓒ Ⓓ Ⓔ
40. Ⓐ Ⓑ Ⓒ Ⓓ Ⓔ
41. Ⓐ Ⓑ Ⓒ Ⓓ Ⓔ
42. _____
43. Ⓐ Ⓑ Ⓒ Ⓓ Ⓔ
44. Ⓐ Ⓑ Ⓒ Ⓓ Ⓔ
45. Ⓐ Ⓑ Ⓒ Ⓓ Ⓔ
46. Ⓐ Ⓑ Ⓒ Ⓓ Ⓔ
47. Ⓐ Ⓑ Ⓒ Ⓓ Ⓔ
48. Ⓐ Ⓑ Ⓒ Ⓓ Ⓔ
49. Ⓐ Ⓑ Ⓒ Ⓓ Ⓔ
50. Ⓐ Ⓑ Ⓒ Ⓓ Ⓔ
51. Ⓐ Ⓑ Ⓒ Ⓓ Ⓔ
52. Ⓐ Ⓑ Ⓒ Ⓓ Ⓔ
53. Ⓐ Ⓑ Ⓒ Ⓓ Ⓔ
54. Ⓐ Ⓑ Ⓒ Ⓓ Ⓔ
55. Ⓐ Ⓑ Ⓒ Ⓓ Ⓔ
56. Ⓐ Ⓑ Ⓒ Ⓓ Ⓔ

Writing

1. Ⓐ Ⓑ Ⓒ Ⓓ Ⓔ
2. Ⓐ Ⓑ Ⓒ Ⓓ Ⓔ
3. Ⓐ Ⓑ Ⓒ Ⓓ Ⓔ
4. Ⓐ Ⓑ Ⓒ Ⓓ Ⓔ
5. Ⓐ Ⓑ Ⓒ Ⓓ Ⓔ
6. Ⓐ Ⓑ Ⓒ Ⓓ Ⓔ
7. Ⓐ Ⓑ Ⓒ Ⓓ Ⓔ
8. Ⓐ Ⓑ Ⓒ Ⓓ Ⓔ
9. Ⓐ Ⓑ Ⓒ Ⓓ Ⓔ
10. Ⓐ Ⓑ Ⓒ Ⓓ Ⓔ
11. Ⓐ Ⓑ Ⓒ Ⓓ Ⓔ
12. Ⓐ Ⓑ Ⓒ Ⓓ Ⓔ
13. Ⓐ Ⓑ Ⓒ Ⓓ Ⓔ
14. Ⓐ Ⓑ Ⓒ Ⓓ Ⓔ
15. Ⓐ Ⓑ Ⓒ Ⓓ Ⓔ
16. Ⓐ Ⓑ Ⓒ Ⓓ Ⓔ
17. Ⓐ Ⓑ Ⓒ Ⓓ Ⓔ
18. Ⓐ Ⓑ Ⓒ Ⓓ Ⓔ
19. Ⓐ Ⓑ Ⓒ Ⓓ Ⓔ
20. Ⓐ Ⓑ Ⓒ Ⓓ Ⓔ
21. Ⓐ Ⓑ Ⓒ Ⓓ Ⓔ
22. Ⓐ Ⓑ Ⓒ Ⓓ Ⓔ
23. Ⓐ Ⓑ Ⓒ Ⓓ Ⓔ
24. Ⓐ Ⓑ Ⓒ Ⓓ Ⓔ
25. Ⓐ Ⓑ Ⓒ Ⓓ Ⓔ
26. Ⓐ Ⓑ Ⓒ Ⓓ Ⓔ
27. Ⓐ Ⓑ Ⓒ Ⓓ Ⓔ
28. Ⓐ Ⓑ Ⓒ Ⓓ Ⓔ
29. Ⓐ Ⓑ Ⓒ Ⓓ Ⓔ
30. Ⓐ Ⓑ Ⓒ Ⓓ Ⓔ
31. Ⓐ Ⓑ Ⓒ Ⓓ Ⓔ
32. Ⓐ Ⓑ Ⓒ Ⓓ Ⓔ
33. Ⓐ Ⓑ Ⓒ Ⓓ Ⓔ
34. Ⓐ Ⓑ Ⓒ Ⓓ Ⓔ
35. Ⓐ Ⓑ Ⓒ Ⓓ Ⓔ
36. Ⓐ Ⓑ Ⓒ Ⓓ Ⓔ
37. Ⓐ Ⓑ Ⓒ Ⓓ Ⓔ
38. Ⓐ Ⓑ Ⓒ Ⓓ Ⓔ
39. Ⓐ Ⓑ Ⓒ Ⓓ Ⓔ
40. Ⓐ Ⓑ Ⓒ Ⓓ Ⓔ

Math

1. Ⓐ Ⓑ Ⓒ Ⓓ Ⓔ
2. Ⓐ Ⓑ Ⓒ Ⓓ Ⓔ
3. Ⓐ Ⓑ Ⓒ Ⓓ Ⓔ
4. Ⓐ Ⓑ Ⓒ Ⓓ Ⓔ
5. Ⓐ Ⓑ Ⓒ Ⓓ Ⓔ
6. Ⓐ Ⓑ Ⓒ Ⓓ Ⓔ
7. Ⓐ Ⓑ Ⓒ Ⓓ Ⓔ
8. Ⓐ Ⓑ Ⓒ Ⓓ Ⓔ
9. Ⓐ Ⓑ Ⓒ Ⓓ Ⓔ
10. Ⓐ Ⓑ Ⓒ Ⓓ Ⓔ
11. Ⓐ Ⓑ Ⓒ Ⓓ Ⓔ
12. Ⓐ Ⓑ Ⓒ Ⓓ Ⓔ
13. Ⓐ Ⓑ Ⓒ Ⓓ Ⓔ
14. Ⓐ Ⓑ Ⓒ Ⓓ Ⓔ
15. Ⓐ Ⓑ Ⓒ Ⓓ Ⓔ
16. Ⓐ Ⓑ Ⓒ Ⓓ Ⓔ
17. _____
18. Ⓐ Ⓑ Ⓒ Ⓓ Ⓔ
19. Ⓐ Ⓑ Ⓒ Ⓓ Ⓔ
20. Ⓐ Ⓑ Ⓒ Ⓓ Ⓔ
21. Ⓐ Ⓑ Ⓒ Ⓓ Ⓔ
22. Ⓐ Ⓑ Ⓒ Ⓓ Ⓔ
23. Ⓐ Ⓑ Ⓒ Ⓓ Ⓔ
24. _____
25. Ⓐ Ⓑ Ⓒ Ⓓ Ⓔ
26. Ⓐ Ⓑ Ⓒ Ⓓ Ⓔ
27. Ⓐ Ⓑ Ⓒ Ⓓ Ⓔ
28. Ⓐ Ⓑ Ⓒ Ⓓ Ⓔ
29. Ⓐ Ⓑ Ⓒ Ⓓ Ⓔ
30. Ⓐ Ⓑ Ⓒ Ⓓ Ⓔ
31. Ⓐ Ⓑ Ⓒ Ⓓ Ⓔ
32. Ⓐ Ⓑ Ⓒ Ⓓ Ⓔ
33. Ⓐ Ⓑ Ⓒ Ⓓ Ⓔ
34. Ⓐ Ⓑ Ⓒ Ⓓ Ⓔ
35. Ⓐ Ⓑ Ⓒ Ⓓ Ⓔ
36. Ⓐ Ⓑ Ⓒ Ⓓ Ⓔ
37. Ⓐ Ⓑ Ⓒ Ⓓ Ⓔ
38. Ⓐ Ⓑ Ⓒ Ⓓ Ⓔ
39. Ⓐ Ⓑ Ⓒ Ⓓ Ⓔ
40. Ⓐ Ⓑ Ⓒ Ⓓ Ⓔ
41. Ⓐ Ⓑ Ⓒ Ⓓ Ⓔ
42. Ⓐ Ⓑ Ⓒ Ⓓ Ⓔ
43. Ⓐ Ⓑ Ⓒ Ⓓ Ⓔ
44. Ⓐ Ⓑ Ⓒ Ⓓ Ⓔ
45. Ⓐ Ⓑ Ⓒ Ⓓ Ⓔ
46. Ⓐ Ⓑ Ⓒ Ⓓ Ⓔ
47. Ⓐ Ⓑ Ⓒ Ⓓ Ⓔ
48. Ⓐ Ⓑ Ⓒ Ⓓ Ⓔ
49. _____
50. Ⓐ Ⓑ Ⓒ Ⓓ Ⓔ
51. Ⓐ Ⓑ Ⓒ Ⓓ Ⓔ
52. Ⓐ Ⓑ Ⓒ Ⓓ Ⓔ
53. Ⓐ Ⓑ Ⓒ Ⓓ Ⓔ
54. Ⓐ Ⓑ Ⓒ Ⓓ Ⓔ
55. Ⓐ Ⓑ Ⓒ Ⓓ Ⓔ
56. Ⓐ Ⓑ Ⓒ Ⓓ Ⓔ

Part 1: Reading

TIME: 85 minutes for 56 questions

DIRECTIONS: Each statement or passage in this test is followed by a selected-response question or questions based on its content. After reading a statement or passage, choose the best answer or answers to each question from among the choices given. Answer all questions following a statement or passage on the basis of what is stated or implied in that statement or passage; you are not expected to have any previous knowledge of the topics presented in the statements and passages. Remember, try to answer every question.

This is a study of ancient sport, not ancient sports, a sport history or a history of sport rather than a sports history or a history of sports. Traditional sports history tends to be event oriented, concentrating on individual sports and providing chronological narratives by leagues, teams, or players. Treating data (e.g., records and statistics) as facts, it favors anecdote above analysis. Instead, sport history pursues the phenomenon of sport over time, identifying and trying to explain its changes and continuity both causally and in context. It approaches ancient sport and spectacle not as isolated pastimes but as essential elements in social, civic, and religious life. Serious interdisciplinary sport history uses sport as a lens to examine human nature, societies, and cultures, not as an end in itself.

Kyle, D.G. *Sport and Spectacle in the Ancient World*. John Wiley & Sons, Inc., 2015. (p. 3).

1. The author suggests which of the following concerning the difference between the terms *sport* and *sports*?

   (A) *Sports* is a modern term, while *sport* is a term that refers to historical examples of physical challenge.

   (B) The modern use of the term *sports* focuses on traditional views solely focused on physical competition, while the author proposes that the study of *sport* can be a gauge to measure other aspects of particular cultures and time periods.

   (C) The terms can be used interchangeably, but the author wants to refer to *sports* as those contests involving multiple competitors.

   (D) *Sport* encompasses more than just physical challenges, while *sports* focuses on the pursuit of physical competition.

   (E) Most studies of the subject will reveal only *sports* histories because only a few elevated examples can be considered *sport*, a phenomenon that transcends physical competition.

Assessing the value of Homer's accounts of games as historical evidence involves tackling the "Homeric question." Whether seen as one bard's composition or several writers' compilation, Homer's profession, patrons, and medium as an epic poet mandated that he applaud the heroic deeds of a greater age of men.

Kyle, D.G. *Sport and Spectacle in the Ancient World*. John Wiley & Sons, Inc., 2015. (p. 55).

2. The passage suggests which of the following about Homer's purpose in writing his works?

   (A) In order to satisfy the public, Homer appealed with tales of epic heroic deeds.

   (B) The Homeric question involves whether or not Homer the man wrote the vast volume attributed to him or whether such work was actually the work of many writers.

   (C) In order to write so many works that appeal to so many people, it was necessary that a great many people must have written what has since been attributed solely to Homer.

   (D) Qualities of a Homeric tale will involve a hero undertaking some struggle or fame in order to showcase the greatness of man.

   (E) Homer's works can best be viewed as heroic deeds involving both games and historical evidence that symbolize the overall greatness of man.

GO ON TO NEXT PAGE

Until recently, we viewed Greek antiquity through a haze of romanticism. Works illustrated with scenes of bucolic Olympia, or serene Delphi on the heights of Mt. Parnassus, or the Parthenon on the Acropolis, presented Greek culture as natural, graceful, inspiring, and uplifting. The people who gave us democracy, philosophy, and the beauty of classical art and architecture held their games out of vitality and devotion, not out of boredom and lust.

Kyle, D.G. *Sport and Spectacle in the Ancient World*. John Wiley & Sons, Inc., 2015. (p. 15).

3. In the context of the first sentence, "romanticism" most nearly means

   (A) idyllic.

   (B) typical of a rural life.

   (C) a movement that was a revolt against the view of neoclassicism.

   (D) thinking that involves an emphasis on an appreciation of nature and the common man.

   (E) something not clearly seen or evidenced.

The supposedly exceptionally negative case of Roman spectacles has suffered by comparison with the supposedly exceptionally positive case of Greek sport. Modern biases have entrenched the myth of an incompatible antithetical dichotomy between the wise world of Greek sport and the wild world of Roman spectacle. Greek sport elevated but Roman spectacles debased human nature.

Kyle, D.G. *Sport and Spectacle in the Ancient World*. John Wiley & Sons, Inc., 2015. (p. 15).

4. Which of the following conclusions is most consistent with the information in the passage?

   (A) Although modern viewpoints are more biased toward the Greeks as a positive cultural example, the Romans are more deserving of it.

   (B) The modern viewpoint of Greeks as the positive cultural example and Romans as the negative example have been borne out by evidence.

   (C) There are no inherent differences in Greek and Roman cultural evidence, but man has historically cast one in a more negative light.

   (D) One myth of the cultural sports spectacle is that Greek sports have been wiser and better, while Roman sports have debased man's nature.

   (E) Romans have long labored under a cultural myth that has lately proven to be untrue and unfounded.

Despite Hollywood, we should clarify what a gladiator was and was not. The earliest gladiators may have been slaves or prisoners of war forced to fight to the death at funerals, but by the later second century a gladiator (from *gladius*, the Spanish sword used by Roman soldiers), while still a slave or captive, was a skilled, trained, and armored weapons fighter who performed in public combats against another gladiator.

Kyle, D.G. *Sport and Spectacle in the Ancient World*. John Wiley & Sons, Inc., 2015. (p. 257).

5. Which of the following statements can best be inferred from the passage?

   (A) Hollywood has perpetrated a false image of gladiators that isn't supported by historical evidence.

   (B) Hollywood has supported the idea that gladiators have been Spanish slaves or prisoners of war.

   (C) Most people don't know that gladiators were skilled fighters instead of slaves or prisoners of war.

   (D) Gladiators were actually very highly skilled fighters who chose to perform in combat rather than being forced to.

   (E) Hollywood has supported the idea that gladiators have been skilled and trained fighters who performed for public acclaim and honor.

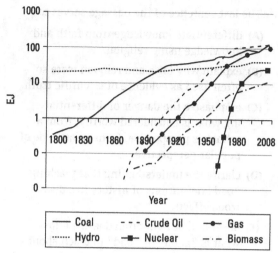

EJ

Year

— Coal   - - - Crude Oil   —●— Gas
····· Hydro   —■— Nuclear   —··— Biomass

Bradshaw, 2014 / John Wiley & Sons

6. Based on the information listed in the graph, which fuel has seen the most steady use of energy consumption?

(A) coal

(B) crude oil

(C) hydro

(D) nuclear

(E) gas

The rate of population growth is another key factor in determining future energy demand. At a simple level, more people means more demand; but it is obviously more complicated than that, as the future standard of living of each new citizen is vitally important. Jared Diamond calculated that the estimated 1 billion people who live in the developed world (which includes most of you reading) have a relative per capita consumption rate of 32. By comparison, most of the other 5–6 billion people living in the developing world have a relative per capita consumption well below 32, with most being close to one. Put another way, the average American consumes 32 times more resources than the average Kenyan.

Bradshaw, M. *Global Energy Dilemmas*. Polity Press, 2014. (p. 45).

7. Given the information provided in the passage, which of the following forecasts would adequately describe per capita consumption rates?

(A) Per capita consumption rates cannot be adequately forecast due to wildly varying population growth rates.

(B) Where future generations are born determines their per capita consumption rates.

(C) Per capita consumption rates will be greater in America than in the developing nations because Americans consume more energy.

(D) Per capita consumption rates will be greater in developing nations because those nations have higher population growth rates.

(E) Per capita consumption rates are largely determined by the standard of living within an area. A better standard of living translates to higher consumption of energy.

Sexism negatively affects not only women and girls, but also men and boys. While the former manifestation of sexism is widely acknowledged, few people recognize or take seriously the fact that males are the primary victims of many and quite serious forms of sex discrimination.

Benatar, D. *The Second Sexism*. Polity Press, 2012.

8. The evidence the author presents supports which of the following conclusions?

(A) Women and girls are negatively affected by sexism.

(B) Women and girls can be positively affected by sexism.

(C) Men and boys are negatively affected by sexism.

(D) Men and boys can be positively affected by sexism.

(E) Although one might expect sexism to negatively affect women and girls, men and boys can also be targets of this kind of discrimination.

GO ON TO NEXT PAGE ➤

Fathers might not be the only males to suffer disadvantage from post-divorce and other custodial arrangements, although the evidence on this is mixed. Many studies have found that sons fare less well than daughters following the separation of their parents. In one study, for example, divorced mothers showed their sons less affection than their daughters, "treated their sons more harshly and gave them more threatening commands — though they did not systematically enforce them." "Even after two years . . . boys in . . . divorced families were . . . more aggressive, more impulsive and more disobedient with their mothers than either girls in divorced families or children in intact families."

Benatar, D. *The Second Sexism*. John Wiley & Sons, Inc., 2012. (p. 51).

9. Which of the following statements would form the most logical conclusion of the passage?

   (A) In short, these and other studies suggest that boys tend to suffer more than girls as a result of divorce and of living with a single parent.

   (B) Surprisingly, the suffering of boys tends to last longer and be more detrimentally harmful than that of girls.

   (C) Of course, the study doesn't take into account the age of the boy. Likely, this would affect the studies.

   (D) Thus, the suffering and despair of mothers and fathers has been alleviated by the results of the study.

   (E) Sadly, the studies present no conclusions.

Definitions of what is good and bad throughout history have often been drawn from religion and faith. This is a delicate matter for historians. Today's scholars uphold a position of skepticism about things like divine intervention, miracles, the supernatural, or the paranormal. No good evidence exists that any of these things actually has changed history, except insofar as people have taken action on the basis of their personal or communal beliefs in them. Most notoriously, the witch hunts clearly happened because people believed that witches conspired with the Devil to overthrow Christian society, even though there was never any proof of a diabolic conspiracy, much less of the efficacy of curses and spells.

Pavlac, B. A. *Game of Thrones Versus History*. John Wiley & Sons, Inc., 2017. (p. 5).

10. The last sentence of the passage serves to

    (A) differentiate knowledge from faith and knowledge using religion.

    (B) explain why faith and religion were so often used as evidence of scientific truth.

    (C) emphasize the danger of differentiating what is considered worthy, from a scholar's perspective, from an attitude of popular perspective.

    (D) clarify the understanding that teaching "bad" definitions of history has disastrous effects.

    (E) observe that man often doesn't know what is "good" or "bad" to teach about history.

We are still learning how gender designations are generated and embodied; how they operate in the early modern period and our own; how sexual identities become attached to or disconnected from gender; and how gender intersects with all other aspects of culture and society. The operations of gender remain so naturalized that they are difficult to see, and even when made visible, they can all too soon again vanish from sight. Furthermore, some patriarchal ideas have a very long shelf life indeed. To give but one example, in her brilliant study *Marriage and Violence: The Early Modern Legacy*, Frances E. Dolan details the ways in which some of the most egregious notions about conjugal intimacy, specifically ones which physically endanger women, remain alive and well in the twenty-first century.

Callaghan, D. *A Feminist Companion to Shakespeare*. John Wiley & Sons, Ltd., 2016. (p. xvii).

11. Which of the following best describes the way in which the information in the passage is conveyed?

    (A) A metaphor is used in an explanation, and then an example is provided.

    (B) An objection is made to a claim, and a counterexample is given.

    (C) A dry point is enlivened by a comparison and contrast.

    (D) An image is made to illustrate a suspected claim.

    (E) A generalization is made followed by a specific example.

If woman-centered readings are often made to function as the scapegoat for the tendency to read Shakespeare's plays as political commentaries on present moments, that is in part because the articulation of women's concerns is only too readily understood as the special pleading of a "minority" interest. But it is also because women have themselves been prepared to frankly disavow attempts to produce generally valid readings of the plays. Mary Cowden Clarke understood her notorious book *The Girlhood of Shakespeare's Heroines in a Series of Fifteen Tales* (1850), as few have understood it since, as a work of fiction. "It was believed that such a design would combine much matter of interesting speculation, afford scope for pleasant fancy, and be productive of entertainment."

Callaghan, D. *A Feminist Companion to Shakespeare.* John Wiley & Sons, Ltd., 2016. (p. 27).

12. Which of the following inferences about feminist readers of Shakespeare can be made based on the passage?

   (A) Their viewpoints are welcomed and considered valid.

   (B) Their viewpoints have been treated scornfully in the past, with merit.

   (C) Critical readings and writings by this group have not been treated with serious academic respect.

   (D) Their ideas bring a new perspective to the subject that has opened up avenues of fresh study.

   (E) Such notions have been dismissed as no serious female academic Shakespeare expert has held up to the intense scrutiny required for the subject.

The Greeks had an equivalent to the lion-headed Sekhmet: Athena. In Classical Greece female warriors were limited to the realms of mythology. There was no Greek equivalent to the office held by Egyptian royal women. However, in Macedonia at the time of Alexander we see a very different type of woman emerging. As in Egypt women were used to cement political allegiances. Philip II of Macedon, Alexander's father, took a total of seven wives but divorced none. Philip's wives and his daughters were warriors who went into battle, arranged their own daughters' marriages and promoted their sons.

Ashton, S.A. *Cleopatra and Egypt.* Blackwell Publishing, 2008. (p. 10).

13. The author most probably uses the word "cement" to mean

   (A) harden.

   (B) enervate.

   (C) liberate.

   (D) strengthen.

   (E) vitalize.

Julius Caesar wrote an account of his meeting with Cleopatra in the more general sense of a narrative of his campaign. Nowhere in his accounts are there any personal references to the queen or his relationship with her. Caesar was a notorious womanizer. In Cleopatra he had found a woman who had power beyond even the imagination of Roman women at this time. We are entirely dependent upon largely later historical sources for descriptions of Caesar's relationship with Cleopatra and there are far fewer references on the subject than on Antony and Cleopatra. This is largely because of Octavian's campaign against the latter pair. Criticizing Julius Caesar, Octavian's adopted "father," was less likely to obtain imperial support.

Ashton, S.A. *Cleopatra and Egypt.* Blackwell Publishing, 2008. (p. 54).

14. The author mentions Julius Caesar's philandering most likely in order to

   (A) note an exception from Caesar's normal moral code of character.

   (B) suggest Caesar had finally met his match in Cleopatra.

   (C) provide a contrast with the accepted view of Caesar's historical reputation.

   (D) lend credence to the idea that Caesar cared more about Cleopatra's power than the idea of love.

   (E) indicate that past understandings about this famous love story are false historical understandings.

GO ON TO NEXT PAGE

The combination of record imports and record prices has created a trade deficit in energy greater than the much-ballyhooed one with China, and has poured vast sums of money into the oil-exporting countries. The amount of money involved is stunning: the United States is currently spending a billion dollars a day on imported fuel.

The United States cannot ignore the consequences of where the money to pay for its oil is going. The growing political clout of countries like Iran, Russia, and Venezuela rests on the explosion of world oil prices in recent years. If they take actions we disapprove of or money going to the Persian Gulf ends up in the hands of terrorists, we, as the world's greatest consumer of oil, pay (at least indirectly) for it.

Hakes, J. *A Declaration of Energy Independence.* John Wiley & Sons, Inc., 2015. (p. 4).

15. Which of the following best describes the organization of the passage?

(A) An unresolved question is pointed out, and then a possible answer to the question is put forth.

(B) A movement is defined, and then illustrations to enhance that definition are presented.

(C) A period in history is described, and then some pivotal events that occurred during the period are discussed.

(D) A political movement is summarized, and then its major contributors are discussed in detail.

(E) A controversial claim is presented, and then evidence and reasons are given to support one side of the controversy.

Annotation has outgrown footnote status so that "Long Notes" now appear at the end of volumes. The extent of, and detail in, annotation obviously depends on the intended audience. Any editor begins not by thinking about the text but about its audience. When an edition is to form part of a series, this audience has already been considered by the general editor and the editorial board. Most commercial editions are aimed at the high school and undergraduate markets — an impressionable audience by any standards, and often an enthusiastic one, eager to think about social values, critical methodology, and literary relevance; the editor has the opportunity therefore to function

as teacher and social worker, both proselytizer and poser of provocative questions.

Callaghan, D. *A Feminist Companion to Shakespeare.* John Wiley & Sons, Ltd., 2016. (p. 82).

16. According to the passage, the growth of annotation is based on which of the following?

(A) an outgrowth of footnote status in order to serialize volumes for broader commercial appeal

(B) the advent of editions and subsequent series in a volume of work

(C) the cultivation of critical methodology

(D) a desire to sell works to a specific audience

(E) the transformation of the publishing industry

Ptolemy XII was a prolific builder, a characteristic that ironically seems often to reveal a weak or threatened ruler. In Upper Egypt a gateway was added to the Ptah temple at Karnak. This small temple had received previous gateways from earlier rulers since its foundation. Its importance is probably due to its position — it is just south of the main temple enclosure wall, which dates to Thirtieth Dynasty or the early Ptolemaic period. The Ptah temple is placed on the main northwest *dromos* leading from the main temple of Amun, past a series of chapels and towards the gateway that led through to the Montu enclosure. The gateway is small and would not have cost a great deal of money to build.

Ashton, S.A. *Cleopatra and Egypt.* Blackwell Publishing, 2008. (p. 34–5).

17. The primary purpose of the passage is to

(A) suggest that Ptolemy should be remembered as a powerful king because of his prolific building of temples.

(B) explain that evidence bears out the understood assumption that Ptolemy was a weak ruler.

(C) contrast accepted knowledge with revealing archeological evidence.

(D) describe the changes that have occurred in understandings about Ptolemy because of recent archeological evidence.

(E) compare Ptolemy's accepted building projects with new evidence that can also be attributed to his reign.

The combination of record imports and record prices has created a trade deficit in energy greater than the much-ballyhooed one with China, and has poured vast sums of money into the oil-exporting countries. The amount of money involved is stunning: the United States is currently spending a billion dollars a day on imported fuel.

Hakes, J. *A Declaration of Energy Independence.* John Wiley & Sons, Inc., 2008. (p. 4).

18. The author most probably uses the word "ballyhooed" to mean

(A) excited commotion.

(B) attention-getting, but insubstantial.

(C) sensationally touted.

(D) disturbance.

(E) unrest.

There was one silver lining in the dark cloud of the gasoline shortage. In the first week of February, the National Safety Council reported that about 1,000 fewer people were killed in traffic accidents in the United States in 1973 than in 1972, the greatest reductions coming in December, when the energy shortage hit and many speed limits had been lowered. Several weeks later, the National Highway Safety Administration announced fatalities for the month of January were 853 (23 percent) below January of the previous year. The embargo was irritating motorists and dragging down the economy, but it was also saving lives.

Hakes, J. *A Declaration of Energy Independence.* John Wiley & Sons, Inc., 2008. (p. 34).

19. The author draws a direct correlation between the nationwide gasoline shortage of 1972–73 and

(A) fewer traffic accidents.

(B) lowering of speed limits.

(C) an overall energy shortage.

(D) a decrease in traffic-related fatalities.

(E) a fuel embargo.

[President Jimmy] Carter signaled in the early days of his presidency his intent to move quickly on "a comprehensive, long-range energy policy." His first fireside chat (wearing a camel-colored cardigan sweater now on display at the Carter Presidential Library in Atlanta) just two weeks after his inauguration emphasized the energy problem.

Following the reasoning of the 1974 Project Independence report derided by Ford's advisors, Carter proclaimed, "Our program will emphasize conservation. The amount of energy being wasted which could be saved is greater than the total energy that we are importing from other countries."

Hakes, J. *A Declaration of Energy Independence.* John Wiley & Sons, Inc., 2008. (p. 45).

20. According to evidence from the passage, why has President Carter's camel-colored cardigan sweater been preserved?

(A) It symbolized the conservatism of his presidency.

(B) It symbolized the stark contrast between Ford's wasteful practices in his presidency and Carter's more conservative one.

(C) It was worn during his first fireside chat.

(D) It was the first thing people saw him wearing after his inauguration two weeks prior.

(E) It came to symbolize the nation's energy problem and its reliance on Middle Eastern fuel.

The cost of the U.S. military presence in the Persian Gulf can be calculated in many ways. The heaviest toll comes, of course, from the loss of life. Early in 2008, U.S. military fatalities in the Iraq War surpassed 4,000. To this must be added the deaths of other coalition forces, contractors, journalists, and innocent Iraqis. There is also an immense burden placed on many survivors of the war, ranging from life-altering injuries to immense pressures on young families.

The cost can also be measured in dollars. Through the end of the 2007 budget year, Congress appropriated $602 billion for military operations in Iraq and Afghanistan, and other activities associated with the war on terrorism.

Hakes, J. *A Declaration of Energy Independence.* John Wiley & Sons, Inc., 2008. (p. 101).

GO ON TO NEXT PAGE ➡

21. Which of the following best states the main idea of the passage?

(A) When assessing how much it costs to fight terrorism in the Persian Gulf, consideration has to be made for multifaceted effects.

(B) More research needs to be done in order to understand fully the effects of the war in the Persian Gulf.

(C) More people were killed who were outside the military than those who were actively serving.

(D) While the Persian Gulf War was a huge national sacrifice, the attributive effects have proved the benefit of military action.

(E) Military presence in the Persian Gulf has benefited the area, and the money spent has lessened terrorist activities.

Questions 22 and 23 refer to the following passage.

However propagandistic, Leni Riefenstahl's film *Olympia* (1938) about the 1936 Olympics was a triumph of cinematography and an inspiration for later sport documentaries and photography. With striking camera angles, iconic forms, and ageless symbols, the film turned athletic intensity into aesthetic delight. With scenes of misty mythological times, an athletic statue coming to life and hurling a discus, robust maidens dancing outdoors, and ancient ruins of Athens and Olympia, the film evokes ancient glory. A torch relay of handsome youths brings the talismanic fire of Classical Greece across miles and millennia to sanction the "Nazi" Olympics. Almost seamlessly, the film transports the viewer from the supposedly serene pure sport of Ancient Greece to the spectacle of the Berlin Olympics with its colossal stadium, masses of excited spectators, Roman symbols (e.g., eagles and military standards) of the Third Reich, and, of course, the emperor Hitler as the attentive patron, beaming as athletic envoys of nation after nation parade through and salute him.

Kyle, D.G. *Sport and Spectacle in the Ancient World.* John Wiley & Sons, Inc., 2015. (p. 1).

22. This passage is primarily concerned with

(A) warning people that propagandistic films can have dire, adverse consequences.

(B) lamenting that the film classic *Olympia* has been inadvertently historically linked with Hitler.

(C) pointing out that the film *Olympia* gave credence to the Berlin Olympics through the propagandistic use of symbols featuring honor and glory.

(D) explaining that any connection between the film classic *Olympia* and Hitler's Berlin Olympics is only one of historical timing, not purposeful intent.

(E) encouraging readers to view the film classic *Olympia* in the same negative light as that of any other Nazi propagandization technique.

23. According to the passage,

(A) Hitler purposely designed the film to showcase German athletes in a light as directly compared to the ideals of physical perfection, as thought of earlier Olympic trials.

(B) while the film may have been made for nefarious reasons, *Olympia* has nevertheless changed cinematic history and inspired future sports films.

(C) the film *Olympia* was a shining example of how sports films should be made — with the view that athletic films should inspire feelings of glory that bring to mind feats of honor from times past.

(D) the film *Olympia* would likely not be remembered today if not for the connection to the infamous Berlin Olympics.

(E) the Berlin Olympics was the perfect place to unveil the film *Olympia* because it was a patriotic spectacle with masses of spectators and Hitler receiving the participants as a king receives his subjects.

Questions 24 and 25 refer to the following passage.

From schoolchildren to weekend quarterbacks, from doctors to lawyers, from entrepreneurs to politicians, from the YMCA to the World Cup, sport permeates modern society. Sport is encouraged as a good thing, but it is fraught with problems. Violence in modern sport ranges from brutality on the field to riots in the stands and the streets. Sport is big business for the media and the stars, and franchises and stadiums affect the political and economic life of cities. Our modern vocabulary is rich in sporting imagery: home run, strike out, knockout, air ball, fumble, hat trick, Hail Mary, and more. The annual calendar of the United States is marked by sporting seasons, by opening day and the playoffs, with the championships of major sports as high holy days. In an age of high-definition big screen televisions and satellite broadcasts, we still talk of traditions, legends of the game, and the good old days.

Kyle, D.G. *Sport and Spectacle in the Ancient World*. John Wiley & Sons, Inc., 2015. (p. 31).

24. This passage is primarily concerned with

   (A) proposing that sports should not be viewed from only a positive perspective.

   (B) refuting an argument that sports should only be viewed from a positive perspective.

   (C) explaining that sport permeates modern society and, while that is primarily viewed in a positive light, there are also many negative effects.

   (D) summarizing how sport is seen in modern society.

   (E) anticipating an argument against the viewpoint that the positives of sport outweigh the negative.

25. Which of the following best expresses the main idea of the passage?

   (A) Sport has no discernible effect on the development of modern culture.

   (B) While sport is seen in mostly a positive light, the negative side of the argument encompasses both violence and commercialization.

   (C) The negative aspects of sports should be overlooked for the traditions and legendary aspects that make people feel good about past accomplishments.

   (D) Modern culture disagrees considerably about whether sport influences society in a positive way.

   (E) How sport is viewed is left to the individual, and no real effect is seen on most of modern culture.

Questions 26–29 refer to the following passage.

Given what has been said about the relationship between energy consumption and economic development, it follows that the energy intensity of countries varies in large part in relation to the level of economic development (measured as GDP) or the UNDP's Human Development Index (HDI). Just as there are huge variations in the level of wealth and income across the globe, so there are variations in the level of energy consumption. According to Gaye, "on average, the poorest 2.5 billion people in the world use only 0.2 toe per capita annually, while the billion richest people use 5 toe per capita a year, which is 25 times more." At present, about 2.5 billion people, mostly in developing countries, still rely on traditional biomass fuels for cooking and 1.6 billion people lack access to electricity. Thus, the lack of access to energy services — energy poverty — is seen as a key aspect of the development challenge and it highlights the fact that the relationship between energy and development is very different across the countries and regions that comprise the global energy system.

Bradshaw, M. *Global Energy Dilemmas*. Polity Press, 2014. (p. 12).

26. Which of the following conclusions is best supported by the passage?

(A) Scientists and economics still disagree about the connection between energy consumption and economic development.

(B) The energy consumption of countries can be directly related to the wealth and income of the people who reside there.

(C) The variations between the GDP and the HDI are too great for any real correlations to be found.

(D) The people who live in the poorest areas of the world do not have access to proper energy systems.

(E) The richest people in the world extravagantly use the best forms of energy development while the poorest people across the globe suffer from energy poverty.

27. According to the passage, people in developing countries

(A) often lack access to electricity and have to rely on biomass fuel options.

(B) are energy poor because they do not spend money on proper energy development options.

(C) rely on the largesse of wealthier inhabitants of their country to provide for energy needs.

(D) will always be kept in energy poverty because the richest people have a monopoly on better energy options.

(E) rely on traditional energy methods more in line with cultural norms rather than embracing new options of energy development.

28. "Energy poverty" refers to

(A) a lack of interest in the development of alternative energy sources.

(B) a lack of resources for proper energy development.

(C) a lack of access to money that can bring about development of energy options.

(D) a lack of access to money that can purchase better energy options.

(E) a lack of access to energy.

29. The author talks about the energy intensity variations among countries in order to

(A) explain why so many of the world's poorest people have a lack of energy development.

(B) reinforce the idea that energy development will cost huge amounts of money.

(C) challenge the assumption that richer people have better lives.

(D) compare the huge discrepancies of energy consumption between the richest and poorest people in the world.

(E) dispel the notion that some parts of the world provide a better condition of living than others.

Questions 30–32 refer to the following passage.

In those times and places where the pressures on men to join the military have been social rather than legal, the costs of not enlisting have been either shame or ostracism. It may be hard for people in contemporary western societies to understand how powerful those forces have been in other contexts. However, young men, and even boys, have felt, and been made to feel, that their manhood is impugned if they fail to enlist. In other words, they would be cowards if they failed to respond to the call to arms. Women, oblivious to their own privilege in being exempt from such pressures and expectations, have sometimes taken a lead in shaming men who they thought should already have volunteered.

Benatar, D. *The Second Sexism*. John Wiley & Sons, Inc., 2012. (p. 27).

30. The passage provides information for answering most fully which of the following questions?

(A) At what times and places in history has there been the most pressure on men to join the military?

(B) Why is it so hard for people in contemporary western societies to understand a reluctance to serve in the military?

(C) What kinds of men are reluctant to join the military and why do others seem to relish the experience?

(D) How does not joining the military on a volunteer basis affect men?

(E) Why are women exempt from the same pressures put on men to join the military?

31. Which of the following best summarizes the main idea of the passage?

    (A) If men or boys choose not to join the military, there are clear effects from a societal and personal perspective.

    (B) Being a woman is a privilege because women don't have to be held accountable to the same standard as men in regard to military service.

    (C) Contemporary western society places great pressure on men and boys to join the military.

    (D) Men or boys who do not join the military will have a loss of self-esteem directly connected to their sense of "manhood."

    (E) Contemporary western military suffers because of a general reluctance of modern men and boys to voluntarily join the service.

32. Why does the author mention the treatment of women who choose not to join the military?

    (A) to provide further examples of bias against those who choose not to voluntarily enlist in the military

    (B) to suggest that women are held in a higher esteem than men

    (C) to identify reasons as to why men are held more accountable for voluntary military service

    (D) to explain why modern society places such a high value on heroism and military service

    (E) to illustrate key differences in the treatment of women and men in regard to voluntary military service

Questions 33 and 34 refer to the following passage.

The bodily privacy of females is valued more than the bodily privacy of males. In many places and times this imposes a disadvantage on females who are required to cover their bodies more extensively than men are. For example, in some places women are required to cover themselves from head to toe in a burqa, while no comparable restriction is placed on males. However, the greater value placed on the shielding of the female body from view has some significant disadvantages for males, who are more likely to be subjected by society to unwanted invasions of their bodily privacy. In other words, whereas females are sometimes forced to cover up

their bodies, men are sometimes forced to uncover their bodies. Consider, for example, the differential treatment of male and female prisoners, most especially in the context of cross-gender supervision. Many countries require that prison guards are the same sex as the prisoners they are guarding. There are exceptions to this trend, and the United States is one notable case. Male guards are found in female prisons and female guards are found in male prisons. In some cases, guards who are not of the same sex as the prisoners are restricted from some functions within the prison in order to protect the prisoners from undue invasion of their bodily privacy by guards of the opposite sex. Often these measures do not grant complete protection.

Benatar, D. *The Second Sexism*. John Wiley & Sons, Inc., 2012. (p. 54).

33. This passage is primarily concerned with

    (A) equally valuing men's and women's right to privacy where the personal body is concerned.

    (B) exposing unfair treatment received by males at prisons.

    (C) detailing ways in which men are more disadvantaged when it comes to a lack of respect of bodily privacy.

    (D) explaining why women are often treated better in prisons than men are.

    (E) debasing women who do not value the higher respect they are given in society in regard to their personal body privacy.

34. The author mentions "burqas" in order to emphasize an area in which

    (A) males are more disadvantaged than females when it comes to bodily privacy in certain situations.

    (B) females are more disadvantaged than males when it comes to bodily privacy in certain situations.

    (C) males and females are equally disadvantaged when it comes to bodily privacy.

    (D) some segments of society are more negatively discriminated against when it comes to bodily privacy due to cultural biases.

    (E) religion places undue rigors on females in order to level the playing field for male discrimination.

GO ON TO NEXT PAGE

Questions 35–39 refer to the following passage.

People have surely been enjoying stories based on history since the first tales were told around fires in the night. Sometimes the stories are true, or at least as true as people can make them. Sometimes they are improved through creativity, adding elements that did not happen, or even could not happen. In our cultures, the oldest surviving stories were written down with huge doses of imagination. The first such story to survive was *The Epic of Gilgamesh*, which told of the founding king of Uruk in ancient Mesopotamia. King Gilgamesh not only interacted with gods and goddesses but, being partly divine, had superhuman strength himself. *The Iliad* and *The Odyssey*, the two ancient Greek epic poems traditionally attributed to Homer, centered around what was believed to have been a historical conflict in a very distant past: the Trojan War. The heroes of these epics, Achilles and Odysseus (or Ulysses, by his Latinized name), possessed respectively strength and intelligence within human capacity, although the narratives also included divine beings and dangerous monsters who wielded powers far greater than mere mortals. Today we call such stories "myths," even if they refer to events that may have happened and the characters in them might once have been living people. But for the listeners entertained by these stories, the tales held truth.

Pavlac, B. A. *Game of Thrones Versus History*. John Wiley & Sons, Inc., 2017. (p. 1).

35. The passage suggests which of the following?

(A) Myths are based solely on imagination and contain no truth.

(B) Myths are retellings of famous events from history.

(C) Myths are likely true, but have changed so much over time that no hint of truth actually remains in the stories.

(D) The only myths that can be categorized as containing some elements of truth are those from reputable sources, such as Odysseus or Achilles.

(E) Myths likely started as true stories or stories with some truth, but creativity has changed the tales over time so that no one really knows what is truth and what is imagination.

36. According to the passage, people are entertained by myths because

(A) they are a traditional form of storytelling.

(B) the stories make man look larger than life and the events take on a more heroic perspective.

(C) they are good to tell around a campfire because they have elements of excitement.

(D) they glorify man's achievement.

(E) they keep alive stories about our most famous heroes.

37. According to the passage, *The Epic of Gilgamesh* differs from *The Iliad* and *The Odyssey* in that *The Epic of Gilgamesh* was

(A) written earlier, and was therefore a purer form of myth.

(B) more historically accurate.

(C) meant to follow the traditional mythical genre more closely.

(D) not meant to be read as truth.

(E) written to contain more imaginative aspects with less reliance on historical accuracy.

38. The passage is primarily concerned with

(A) questioning the accuracy of new information when combined with old understandings about myths.

(B) providing an assessment of the veracity of certain myths.

(C) discussing the classification of mythical genres.

(D) evaluating the process modern literature enthusiasts use to distinguish myths from historical fiction.

(E) illustrating the difficulties faced when attempting to differentiate what is truth and what is fiction in ancient myths.

39. The author's allusion to "epic poems" references

(A) poems that were longer than other stories and, thus, were more likely to be true.

(B) works that are more impressive than those of any other ancient writer of that time period.

(C) stories that were written in a specific format of poetry.

(D) poems that are not known to have been definitively written by Homer, but are attributed to him.

(E) works that were much more outstanding in their literary scope than other works during that time, such as the tale of Gilgamesh.

Questions 40–42 refer to the following diagram.

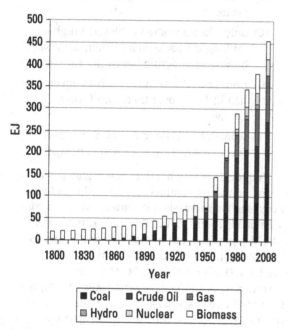

Bradshaw, 2014 / John Wiley & Sons

40. The diagram supports which of the following statements? Select *all* that apply.

(A) Biomass has remained at a relatively stable usage throughout the years.

(B) The usage of biomass varies according to the usage of other fuel forms.

(C) When other fuel forms were invented or came into more usage, biomass usage decreased.

41. The diagram supports which of the following statements? Select *all* that apply.

(A) The usage of alternative fuel sources has increased dramatically during recent times.

(B) The sale and usage of fossil fuels, such as coal and crude oil, have been negatively impacted by alternative fuel sources.

(C) Except for biomass, usage of all fuel types has increased more during the last 40–50 years than in the previous century.

42. During which year that is labeled in the diagram did nuclear energy see the greatest usage? Write your answer in the space provided.

_____

_____

Questions 43–48 refer to the following passages.

Passage 1

Decades of war in medieval Europe created a multitude of widows and many found themselves remarried, with or without their consent. Elizabeth Woodville, for instance, was the widow of a Lancastrian knight before becoming the wife of the Yorkist king, Edward IV. Roughly a decade later, Edward's brother Richard married Lady Anne Neville (1456–1485), who was previously married to the son of the Lancastrian king, Henry VI (r. 1422–1461; 1471). Unlike Elizabeth, Anne was from a prominent noble family, with a massive dowry and substantial landholdings in the north of England. Some chroniclers even hinted that Anne's money and family influence made it possible for Richard to claim the throne later.

Pavlac, B. A. *Game of Thrones Versus History.* John Wiley & Sons, Inc., 2017. (p. 21).

GO ON TO NEXT PAGE

A queen's position, while potentially powerful, was by no means invulnerable. Many kings found excuses to rid themselves of unwanted wives. Most infamous is Henry VIII of England (r. 1509–1547) with his six wives; but he was far from being the first. In 1483, just before he inherited the throne, Charles VIII of France (r. 1483–1498) was betrothed to Margaret of Austria (1480–1530), who was only three years old at the time. She came to the French court as a child and grew up there. In the autumn of 1491, however, Charles repudiated the betrothal and married instead Duchess Anne of Brittany (1477–1514), for blatantly political reasons.

Pavlac, B. A. *Game of Thrones Versus History.* John Wiley & Sons, Inc., 2017. (p. 26).

43. Which best describes the relationship between the two passages?

(A) Passage 2 qualifies the main argument in Passage 1.

(B) Passage 2 provides a counterargument to the claims made in Passage 1.

(C) Passages 2 offers an application of the theory that is presented in Passage 1.

(D) Passage 2 provides a solution to a problem described in Passage 1.

(E) Passage 2 emphasizes further the claim made in Passage 1 by providing additional examples.

44. Both passages are primarily concerned with

(A) methods of acquiring wealth and power used by medieval European women.

(B) objectives of medieval European women in acquiring wealthy and powerful husbands.

(C) the value placed on wealth and power during times of war.

(D) the effectiveness of the social structures in regard to wealth and position.

(E) the role of wealth in determining women's social status for medieval European women.

45. Passage 1 and Passage 2 agree that

(A) male attitudes about wealth were directly influenced by powerful women.

(B) female attitudes about marriage were directly influenced by the wealth of a potential mate.

(C) women's life situations were a consequence of male attitudes.

(D) men's life situations were a consequence of female attitudes.

(E) decision making in marriage during medieval times was greatly influenced by wealth and power.

46. The author of Passage 1 presents the claim that

(A) wealthy and powerful women could dictate their future courses, in regard to marriage.

(B) men only married to gain wealth or power.

(C) only when a woman achieved a high-ranking status, such as queen, could she be sure of directing her future course.

(D) even powerful women, such as queens, had little say over their own future courses.

(E) women had little to no say about their future courses, in regard to marriage.

A queen's position, while potentially powerful, was by no means invulnerable. Many kings found excuses to rid themselves of unwanted wives. Most infamous is Henry VIII of England (r. 1509–1547) with his six wives; but he was far from being the first. In 1483, just before he inherited the throne, Charles VIII of France (r. 1483–1498) was betrothed to Margaret of Austria (1480–1530), who was only three years old at the time. She came to the French court as a child and grew up there. In the autumn of 1491, however, Charles repudiated the betrothal and married instead Duchess Anne of Brittany (1477–1514), for blatantly political reasons.

47. In the underlined sentence of the preceding paragraph, the author does which of the following?

(A) introduces a new concept

(B) makes a concession

(C) introduces a digression

(D) anticipates an objection

(E) outlines a proposal

48. From Passage 2, the word "repudiated" most nearly means

(A) accepted

(B) reproved

(C) rescinded

(D) divorced

(E) acknowledged

Questions 49–51 refer to the following passage.

What a great idea! *Game of Thrones* versus history. Historians are storytellers, and the best historians, like the best storytellers, have ways of making their subject matter come to life. The challenge for the historian in the classroom is to find a hook or produce an example that will speak to a captive audience of students. It's particularly effective when a teacher can start from something everyone thinks they know to be true, and then proceed to show that it wasn't exactly true. Something like "people think Columbus believed the earth was flat, but really he knew it was round." In this sense, a negative example can be just as effective as a positive example.

Pavlac, B. A. *Game of Thrones Versus History.* John Wiley & Sons, Inc., 2017. (p. xiii).

49. The author's main purpose is to

(A) underscore history in a desire to incorporate more popular culture.

(B) explain differences in perception between traditional history teachers and nontraditional history teachers.

(C) defend a position taken by a portion of traditionalists.

(D) propose a creative approach for teaching history.

(E) admonish naysayers to accept a non-traditional approach to the teaching of history.

50. The example given primarily demonstrates

(A) an overload of irrelevant information an inexperienced teacher might use when introducing a new topic.

(B) ongoing cultural truisms that are being absorbed by historical teaching.

(C) interconnections between historical teachings and interdisciplinary content.

(D) connections between false facts and teaching opportunities.

(E) difficulties in continuing traditional history teaching methodologies.

51. It can be inferred from the passage that the author would most likely support which of the following teaching practices?

(A) examining Destiny's Child's *Independent Women* in close reading, taking notes on lyrics, costumes, dancing, and more

(B) comparing the lyrics in a Lady Gaga song to a Robert Frost poem

(C) parodying a famous scientific event in a student-produced drama

(D) rewriting the lyrics of a song from the perspective of a famous person

(E) having students create fictitious Facebook or Twitter accounts using actual facts from the life of a historical person

Questions 52–56 refer to the following passage.

One reason the story of patriarchal oppression has become so influential is that it has been disseminated in recent textbooks. The editor of a reader designed to illustrate *The Cultural Identity of Seventeenth-Century Woman*, for instance, states flatly that "Woman's place was within doors, her business domestic . . . Women of evident intelligence themselves accepted this divorce between the private (feminine) and public (masculine) spheres and, despite the recent precedents of Mary Queen of Scots, Mary Tudor and Elizabeth, they shared the age's "distaste . . . for the notion of women's involvement in politics." However, even the most sophisticated scholarship often includes similar claims.

For example, in what is likely to become a standard history of gender in early modern England, Anthony Fletcher writes, "It was conventional, as we have seen, to assume men and women had clearly defined gender roles indoors and out of doors . . . Femininity, as we have seen, was presented as no more than a set of negatives. The requirement of chastity was, as we have seen, the overriding measure of female gender. Woman not only had to be chaste but had to be seen to be chaste: silence, humility and modesty were the signifiers that she was so."

Callaghan, D. *A Feminist Companion to Shakespeare*. John Wiley & Sons, Ltd., 2016. (p. 60–1).

52. This passage is primarily concerned with which of the following?

(A) how women have been subjugated because of patriarchal oppression

(B) an explanation involving many reasons why patriarchal oppression is tolerated

(C) how some women rose above the oppressive influences of their day in order to achieve glory and honor

(D) the definition of conventional understandings regarding woman's place in the home

(E) a discussion of how the ideas of femininity have changed over time

53. The author mentions "the recent precedents" of Mary, Queen of Scots, and Mary Tudor and Elizabeth in order to give examples of

(A) powerful women who still could not escape patriarchal ideas of what the ideal female should be.

(B) trendsetters of powerful, yet feminine, women.

(C) women who became the historical standards of gender.

(D) models of women who were chaste, humble, silent, and modest.

(E) examples of matriarchal oppression.

54. Which of the following results of patriarchal oppression is NOT mentioned in the passage?

(A) a concern with domestic business

(B) a cultural identity focused on masculine approval

(C) a narrow focus on political matters to only include acceptable topics as deemed suitable

(D) an eschewing of evidence of intelligence

(E) a clearly defined, yet negative, gender role

55. Which of the following, if true, would most weaken the author's claims?

(A) Upper-class women were likely very highly educated and would learn to read and write, as well as speak multiple languages.

(B) During the 17th century, many women worked spinning cloth and were dyers, milliners, and embroiderers.

(C) A common job for women during this time period was to serve as a domestic servant.

(D) Women were often left as a sole beneficiary in a will so they could continue a husband's business when he died.

(E) Women during this time period were required to have extensive knowledge of medicine, and many became apothecaries and midwives.

56. It can be inferred from the passage that the author believes which of the following about male oppression?

(A) Male oppression had a proper time and place in history, but times are better now.

(B) Women still continue to suffer from patriarchal oppression.

(C) The oppression of the day only affected matters pertaining to domestic instances, and larger effects were short-lived.

(D) Such oppression permeated the history and culture of the time period.

(E) Women allowed the oppression and, had they been stronger, could have stood up for themselves.

STOP

DO NOT TURN THE PAGE UNTIL TOLD TO DO SO · DO NOT RETURN TO A PREVIOUS TEST

Part 2: Writing

TIME: 40 minutes for 40 selected-response questions

DIRECTIONS: Choose the best answer or answers to each question or statement. Mark the corresponding oval on the answer sheet.

DIRECTIONS: Each of the following questions consists of a sentence that contains four underlined portions. Read each sentence and decide whether any of the underlined parts contains a grammatical construction, a word use, an instance of incorrect or omitted punctuation, or capitalization that would be inappropriate in carefully written English. If so, select the underlined portion that must be revised to produce a correct sentence. If there are no errors in the sentence as written, select "No error." **No sentence has more than one error.**

1. While many praised the efforts of the protestors, several of the town's citizens, such as the mayor, felt they behaved coward when they blocked the city buses from exiting the compound and caused delays in city-wide transportation routes. No error.
   (A) town's citizens (B) mayor (C) behaved coward (D) city-wide transportation (E) No error.

2. However liberally minded Senator Scott was, she couldn't agree with the proposed legislation, rather, the bill's premise was sure to cause great furor that couldn't be supported by either side unbiasedly. No error.
   (A) liberally minded (B) legislation, (C) great furor (D) unbiasedly (E) No error.

3. Neither Oliver nor Emily believed they would receive the award even though countless hours went into the work and the unlimited budget allotted a plethora of resources not available to others. No error.
   (A) they would receive (B) even though (C) budget allotted (D) a plethora of resources (E) No error.

4. All of the students wanted to become a member of the ROTC after the school assembly emphasized patriotic duty, except for the drama club members who were immune to such tactics. No error.
   (A) a member (B) assembly emphasized (C) except for (D) who were (E) No error.

5. The Savannah College of Art and Design (SCAD), a private university with locations in Savannah and Atlanta, Georgia and China and France, affords fine arts degrees in both bachelor's and master's programs. No error.
   (A) (SCAD), (B) Georgia (C) France, (D) bachelor's and master's (E) No error.

6. After removing the defective wiring from the vintage lamp, Maude spent the better part of her evening fixing it so the addition could be added to the store's inventory first thing in the morning. No error.
   (A) After removing (B) defective wiring (C) vintage lamp (D) fixing it (E) No error.

7. The Philippines' location on the Pacific Ring of Fire makes it more prone to earthquakes, events that hardly encourage no increase in tourism, but do make it home to some of the world's greatest biodiversity. No error.
   (A) Philippines' (B) no increase (C) but do (D) world's (E) No error.

8. Alexander Hamilton is today considered to be a conservative nationalist and traditionalist economic supporter, but Hamilton has been known during his time as a radical and rebellious leader who argued strongly against the more conformist ideas of government. No error.
   (A) is today considered (B) to be a (C) has been known (D) who argued (E) No error.

GO ON TO NEXT PAGE

9. Although Sierra Leone has experienced

   <u>tremendously</u> upheavals and decimations
        A

   of parts of <u>its</u> infrastructure because of war
              B

   and an Ebola <u>outbreak</u>, a new parliamentary
                  C

   government has brought some stability to the

   <u>Western</u> African nation. <u>No error</u>.
     D   E

10. Both Juan and Mary <u>attended</u> the budget
                          A

    meeting where the new merger <u>was discussed</u>,
                                    B

    but neither Juan nor <u>her</u> could understand
                           C

    where the funds <u>were going to be allocated</u>
                        D

    from. <u>No error</u>.
            E

11. After <u>graduating</u> with her English degree,
             A

    Stephanie looked forward to a life full of

    choices, <u>including</u> <u>studying</u> law, teaching at
                B   C

    the local community college, and <u>she wanted</u>
                                         D

    to become a trial attorney. <u>No error</u>.
                                   E

12. During the Great Molasses Flood of <u>1919,</u>
                                          A

    thousands of people were forced <u>to flee</u>
                                        B

    Boston's North <u>End</u> when a large molasses
                      C

    storage tank <u>burst</u>, creating a wave of molas-
                    D

    ses that rushed through the streets, killing or

    injuring more than 170 people. <u>No error</u>.
                                      E

13. Although Susan <u>bore</u> a close <u>resemblance to</u>
                     A   B

    her brother John, the <u>dissimilarity between</u> her
                             C

    twin sister was <u>unnerving</u> and caused much
                       D

    confusion. <u>No error</u>.
                 E

14. <u>Mowing</u> the front lawn on the hot summer
      A

    day, the garter snake <u>sunning</u> <u>itself</u> on the dry
                            B   C

    patch of grass became alarmed and <u>slinked</u>
                                           D

    away to safety. <u>No error</u>.
                      E

15. Both <u>senators</u> were <u>adverse</u> to the proposals
           A   B

    <u>put forth</u> by their constituents, which delayed
      C

    the vote and eliminated the <u>possibility of</u> the
                                   D

    reform becoming permanent. <u>No error</u>.
                                  E

16. Because of Sri's high-scoring performance on

    the ACT and SAT, <u>particularly</u> on the verbal
                        A

    reasoning <u>portions</u>, he was <u>fortunate</u> to be
                 B   C

    able to choose <u>among</u> Princeton, Harvard, and
                      D

    Stanford. <u>No error</u>.
                E

17. Edgar Cayce, a Christian mystic <u>who answered</u>
                                       A

    prophetic questions while under a trance,

    <u>is known</u> during his lifetime for his psychic
      B

    abilities and <u>worked</u> for a time as a <u>traveling</u>
                    C   D

    stage hypnotist. <u>No error</u>.
                       E

18. Odysseus, also known by the Latin <u>Ulysses</u>,
                                         A

    was a legendary Greek king who wandered

    the world for ten years after the Trojan <u>War</u>
                                                B

    before returning <u>home, hence,</u> he has become
                        C   D

    a modern symbol for man's insatiable craving

    for new experiences and inability to commit to

    a cemented lifestyle. <u>No error</u>.
                            E

19. The island <u>state</u> of Tasmania, located across
                  A

    the Bass Strait from Australia and the

    <u>twenty-sixth</u> largest island in the world, <u>are</u>
      B   C

    the only place in the world where the Tasma-

    nian devil <u>can be found</u> in the wild. <u>No error</u>.
                 D   E

20. Ronald McDonald is a name now associated as much with fun and humor as with cheap food, an image that has grown bigger <u>than the symbol of the clown itself</u>.

   (A) than the symbol of the clown itself

   (B) than itself the symbol of the clown

   (C) than the symbol itself of the clown

   (D) than the symbol of the clown

   (E) than the symbol of the itself clown

21. Considered to be one of the greatest painters of all time, Leonardo Da Vinci, <u>who is considered the father of architecture, ichnology, and paleontology, likely also invented</u> the parachute, adding machine, and flying vehicles.

   (A) who is considered the father of architecture, ichnology, and paleontology, likely also invented

   (B) who is also considered the father of architecture, ichnology, and paleontology, he likely also invented

   (C) considered the father of architecture, ichnology, and paleontology, likely also inventing

   (D) having long been considered the father of architecture, ichnology, and paleontology, likely also to invent

   (E) was considered the father of architecture, ichnology, and paleontology, and likely also invented

22. Technology has finally invaded the home and can give homeowners a more convenient lifestyle with robotic vacuum cleaners, computerized personal assistance, <u>and the ability to secure and manage energy and electricity while away from home; all the while saving</u> homeowners money and giving them peace of mind.

   (A) and the ability to secure and manage energy and electricity while away from home; all the while saving

   (B) and the ability to secure and manage energy and electricity while away from home all the while saving

   (C) and the ability to secure and manage energy and electricity while away from home, all the while savings

   (D) and the ability to secure and manage energy and electricity while away from home, all the while saving

   (E) and securing and managing energy and electricity while away from home; all the while saved

23. Having received more Emmy Awards than any other primetime scripted TV series, <u>HBO's *Game of Thrones* has reached an international fan base and even been acclaimed</u> by the toughest critics for production, writing, and acting.

   (A) HBO's *Game of Thrones* has reached an international fan base and even been acclaimed

   (B) HBO's *Game of Thrones* has reached an international fan base because of acclaiming

   (C) HBO's *Game of Thrones*, which has reached in international fan base, having been acclaimed

   (D) HBO's *Game of Thrones*' reaching an international fan base to acclaim

   (E) HBO's *Game of Thrones* has reached an international fan base and has even been acclaimed

24. The International Ice Patrol tracks icebergs globally, a practice that allows the monitoring of their origins and other ocean processes.

   (A) The International Ice Patrol tracks icebergs globally, a practice that allows the monitoring of their origins and other ocean processes.

   (B) Icebergs being tracked globally by the International Ice Patrol is a practice that allows the monitoring of their origins and other ocean processes.

   (C) The International Ice Patrol can track icebergs globally, a practice that allows the monitoring of icebergs' origins and other ocean processes.

   (D) By tracking icebergs globally, the International Ice Patrol is granted allowance to monitor their origins and processes.

   (E) Tracking icebergs globally, the monitoring of their origins and other ocean processes by the International Ice Patrol is allowed.

25. Basil, commonly used in traditional Italian recipes, has a rich history of folklore and has been historically used to safeguard against scorpions and protecting against danger for those undertaking a journey.

   (A) protecting against danger for those undertaking

   (B) protecting against danger in those who undertake

   (C) to protect against danger for those undertaking

   (D) to protect against danger when they are undertaking

   (E) to protect against danger when they undertake

26. If visitors were to travel to the most eastern part of the western world, they would find themselves at Ilomantsi, Finland: a location sharing a 60-mile border with the Russian Republic of Karelia.

   (A) If visitors were to travel to the most eastern part of the western world, they would find themselves at Ilomantsi, Finland: a location sharing a 60-mile border with the Russian Republic of Karelia.

   (B) If visitors were to travel to the most eastern part of the western world, they would find themselves at Ilomantsi, Finland, a location sharing a 60-mile border with the Russian Republic of Karelia.

   (C) If visitors were to travel to the most eastern part of the western world, they would find themselves at a 60-mile border with the Russian Republic of Karelia, Ilomantsi, Finland.

   (D) When arriving at Ilomantsi, Finland, visitors would find they have traveled to the most eastern part of the western world, the 60-mile border of the Russian Republic of Karelia.

   (E) The 60-mile border of the Russian Republic of Karelia and Ilomantsi, Finland, is where visitors would find themselves if they were to travel to the eastern part of the western world.

27. Totem poles, monumental sculptures of Northwest Coast art, symbolized and commemorated cultural beliefs, some of which recounted familiar legends and others describing notable events.

   (A) some of which recounted

   (B) some of which had the ability to recount

   (C) and some of which recounted

   (D) some recounting

   (E) some of which recounting

28. Anglerfish, making up one of the world's most unusual species of fish, are known for the fleshy growth that hangs from their heads and acts as lure and including the luminescent lanterns located at the tips of their dorsal fins.

(A) and including

(B) as well as

(C) inclusive of

(D) and

(E) plus

29. Finishing her calculus homework containing more than 72 problems, a long and pleasurable night of relaxation in a tub with a good book was most on Amy's mind.

(A) a long and pleasurable night of relaxation in a tub with a good book was most on Amy's mind.

(B) Amy's mind was most on a long and pleasurable night of relaxation in a tub.

(C) Amy filled her mind with thoughts of a long and pleasurable night of relaxation in a tub with a good book.

(D) relaxation in a tub with a good book during a long and pleasurable night was most on Amy's mind.

(E) a long and pleasurable night of relaxation in a tub with a good book was foremost in the mind of Amy.

30. Gal Gadot, star of 2017's multi-million-dollar *Wonder Woman*, was training for months in the physical requirements of the film, including choreography with swords, kicks, jumping, and horseback riding.

(A) was training for months in the physical requirements

(B) was training for months for the physical requirements

(C) having been trained for months for the physical requirements

(D) had trained for months for the physical requirements

(E) has trained for the physical requirements for months

DIRECTIONS: The following passage is a draft of an essay. Some portions of the passage need to be strengthened through editing and revision. Read the passage and choose the best answers for the questions that follow. Some questions ask you to improve particular sentences or portions of sentences. In some cases, the indicated portion of the passage will be most effective as it is already expressed and thus will require no changes. In choosing answers, consider development, organization, word choice, style, and tone, and follow the requirements of standard written English. Remember, try to answer every question.

Fifty years ago, a port was a docking place for a seagoing vessel, while, today, a port is where a hand-held digital device is docked. It's still the same process, output and input, buying and selling. The only difference is the product. Goods are made cheaper, distributed quicker, and sold before the blink of an eye. Today, much of what a consumer purchases can't even be seen by the naked eye, much less loaded onto a vehicle. Globalization of resources used to refer to goods; now, that globalization refers to ideas and information.

True, all these "conveniences" do come with a price. With the explosion of technology and digital growth in the last few years, societies across the globe are having trouble keeping pace with the cybercriminals and the cyber-ethics that such growth brings. The American government originally used such technological advances to fight terrorism, but now finds it just as easy to use that same technology to, for all practical purposes, spy on its own citizens. It doesn't stop there, though, since they use that same technology and sell the data to companies who use the algorithms in an almost prompt data analysis that pushes product across the cyber desk. Businesses are both struggling to accept the demands and striving to fill in the holes. Gone are traditional offices and cubicles. More and more home offices are dotting the digital landscape with business deals sealed with Skype handshakes. This lowered cost of doing business benefits everyone involved, provided the virtual net doesn't entirely collapse.

GO ON TO NEXT PAGE

31. Which is the best version of the underlined portion of Sentence 1 (reproduced below)?

Fifty years ago, a port was a docking place for a seagoing vessel, <u>while</u>, today, a port is where a hand-held digital device is docked.

(A) No change.

(B) however

(C) for example

(D) consequently

(E) on the other hand

32. Which is the best version of the underlined portion of Sentences 3 and 4 (reproduced below)?

The only difference is the <u>product. Goods are made</u> cheaper, distributed quicker, and sold before the blink of an eye.

(A) No change.

(B) product. They make goods

(C) product, making the goods

(D) product; they made goods

(E) product; they made the goods

33. Where would the following sentence best be inserted?

The digital revolution is creating change in every part of society, from the foods that people eat to the patterns of daily communication.

(A) immediately after Sentence 3

(B) immediately after Sentence 4

(C) immediately after Sentence 6

(D) immediately after Sentence 7

(E) immediately before Sentence 9

34. What is the best way to deal with Sentence 9 (reproduced below)?

The American government originally used such technological advances to fight terrorism, but now finds it just as easy to use that same technology to, for all practical purposes, spy on its own citizens.

(A) No change.

(B) Move it to the end of the passage.

(C) Replace "The American government" with "Those who make policies for government."

(D) Replace "for all practical purposes" with "in effect."

(E) Replace "spy" with "snoop"

35. What is the best way to deal with Sentence 10 (reproduced below)?

It doesn't stop there, though, since they use that same technology and sell the data to companies who use the algorithms in an almost prompt data analysis that pushes product across the cyber desk.

(A) Replace "sell" with "offer."

(B) Replace "data" with "statistics."

(C) Replace "prompt" with "instantaneous."

(D) Move it to immediately after Sentence 12.

(E) Delete it from the passage.

36. In context, which of the following revisions of Sentence 14 (reproduced below) is most needed?

This lowered cost of doing business benefits everyone involved, provided the virtual net doesn't entirely collapse.

(A) Replace "This" with "This practice."

(B) Replace "benefits" with "profits."

(C) Replace "everyone involved" with "major shareholders."

(D) Move "entirely" to after "collapse."

(E) Replace "provided" with "so long as."

DIRECTIONS: The following selected-response questions are a test of your familiarity with basic research skills. For each question, choose the best answer. Remember, try to answer every question.

37. Davison, Scott. "Virtue and Violence: Can a Good Football Player Be a Good Person?" *The Philosophy of Popular Culture: Football and the Philosophy Going Deep.* Lexington, Kentucky: University Press of Kentucky, 2008. Print.

    In the preceding citation, the first reference to Kentucky indicates the

    (A) business address of the author.

    (B) scholarly affiliation of the publisher.

    (C) location of the football games being described in the article.

    (D) repository of the philosophical works referred to.

    (E) location of the publisher.

38. Which of the following is a primary source for an article on the life of Hillary Rodham Clinton?

    (A) A television documentary describing her time as the First Lady

    (B) A newspaper report documenting her rise from lawyer to Secretary of State

    (C) A book written by her husband, Bill Clinton

    (D) A script of a speech that she wrote and delivered to the UN while running for president

    (E) A memoir written by her bodyguard

39. A student wants to write an article on spring fashion lines. All of the following topics would narrow the focus of the subject EXCEPT

    (A) models showcasing the fashion on runways

    (B) the direction of a designer when choosing prints and fabrics

    (C) a discussion on the changes in style from winter to spring

    (D) an analysis of spring fashion trends and profitability

    (E) an analysis of recent cover pages of fashion magazines

40. Which of the following parts of a research paper contains a brief summary of the work at the beginning of the paper and is used to help the reader quickly ascertain the paper's purpose?

    (A) bibliography

    (B) abstract

    (C) outline

    (D) preface

    (E) table of contents

DO NOT TURN THE PAGE UNTIL TOLD TO DO SO **STOP** DO NOT RETURN TO A PREVIOUS TEST

Argumentative Essay

"Technology has become an inseparable part of our lives. People have become overly dependent on technology, and this dependence has created a negative influence."

Discuss the extent to which you agree or disagree with this point of view. Support your position with specific reasons and examples from your own experience, observations, or reading.

Source-Based Essay

TIME: 30 minutes

DIRECTIONS: Both of the following sources address the idea of animal rights. Read the two passages carefully and then write an essay in which you identify the most important concerns regarding the issue and why they are important. Your essay must draw on information from both of the sources. In addition, you may draw upon your own experience, observations, or reading. Be sure to cite the sources, whether you are paraphrasing or directly quoting.

When paraphrasing or quoting from the sources, cite each source by referring to the author's last name, the title of the source, or any other clear identifier.

Source 1

Adapted from: Singer, Peter. "All Animals are Equal." *Environmental Ethics.* Ed. Michael Boylan. Princeton, NJ: John Wiley & Sons, Inc. 2014. Print.

The life of every human being is sacred. Yet people who would say this about the infant do not object to the killing of nonhuman animals. How can they justify their different judgments? Adult chimpanzees, dogs, pigs, and members of many other species far surpass the brain-damaged infant in their ability to relate to others, act independently, be self-aware, and any other capacity that could reasonably be said to give value to life. With the most intensive care possible, some severely retarded infants can never achieve the intelligence level of a dog. Nor can we appeal to the concern of the infant's parents, since they themselves, in this imaginary example (and in some actual cases) do not want the infant kept alive. The only thing that distinguishes the infant from the animal, in the eyes of those who claim it has a "right to life," is that it is, biologically, a member of the species *Homo sapiens*, whereas chimpanzees, dogs, and pigs are not. But to use this difference as the basis for granting a right to life to the infant and not to the other animals is, of course, pure speciesism. It is exactly the kind of arbitrary difference that the most crude and overt kind of racist uses in attempting to justify racial discrimination.

Source 2

Adapted from: Regan, Tom. "The Radical Egalitarian Case for Animals Rights." *Environmental Ethics.* Ed. Michael Boylan. Princeton, NJ: John Wiley & Sons, Inc. 2014. Print.

What's wrong — what's fundamentally wrong — with the way animals are treated isn't the details that vary from case to case. It's the whole system. The forlornness of the veal calf is pathetic — heart wrenching; the pulsing pain of the chimp with electrodes planted deep in her brain is repulsive; the slow, torturous death of the raccoon caught in the leg hold trap, agonizing. But what is fundamentally wrong isn't the pain, isn't the suffering, isn't the deprivation. These compound what's wrong. Sometimes — often — they make it much worse. But they are not the fundamental wrong. The fundamental wrong is the system that allows us to view animals as our resources, here for us — to be eaten, or surgically manipulated, or put in our cross-hairs for sport or money. Once we accept this view of animals — as our resources — the rest is as predictable as it is regrettable. Why worry about their loneliness, their pain, their death? Since animals exist for us, here to benefit us in one way or another, what harms them really doesn't matter — or matters only if it starts to bother us, makes us feel a trifle uneasy when we eat our veal scampi, for example. So, yes, let us get veal calves out of solitary confinement, give them more space, a little straw, a few companions. But let us keep our veal scampi.

Inherent value, then, belongs equally to those who are the experiencing subjects of a life. Whether it belongs to others — to rocks and rivers, trees and glaciers, for example — we do not know. And may never know. But neither do we need to know, if we are to make the case for animal rights. We do not need to know how many people, for example, are eligible to vote in the next presidential election before we can know whether *I am*. Similarly, we do not need to know how many individuals have inherent value before we can know that some do. When it comes to the case for animal rights, then what we need to know is whether the animals who, in our culture are routinely eaten, hunted, and used in our laboratories, for example, are like us in being subjects of a life. And we do know this. We do know that many — literally, billions and billions — of these animals are subjects of a life in the sense explained and so have inherent value if we do. And since, in order to have the best theory of our duties to one another, we must recognize our equal inherent value, as individuals, reason — not sentiment, not emotion — reason compels us to recognize the equal inherent value of these animals. And, with this, their equal right to be treated with respect.

Part 3: Mathematics

TIME: 90 minutes for 56 questions

DIRECTIONS: Choose the best answer to each question. For multiple-choice questions, mark the corresponding oval on the answer sheet. Remember, try to answer every question.

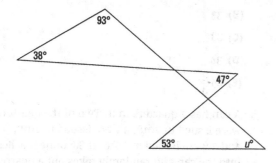

1. The above figure is composed of five segments that together form three triangles. What is the value of u in the figure?

    (A) 43

    (B) 49

    (C) 84

    (D) 96

    (E) 137

$$9.8 \quad 10.0 \quad 8.6 \quad 9.1 \quad 8.8$$

2. Joey received the above scores for events in a wingsuit flying acrobatics competition. He has one event remaining. What is the lowest score he can receive for the final event to have a mean score of at least 9.2?

    (A) 8.5

    (B) 8.9

    (C) 9.0

    (D) 9.3

    (E) 9.7

3. Which of the following is a factor of the numerator of the simplified form of the product of $\frac{8}{9}$ and $\frac{7}{2}$?

    (A) 4

    (B) 8

    (C) 12

    (D) 18

    (E) 21

$$4p - 2r = 5q - p$$

4. The above equation is a true statement. Which of the following is equal to the value of 3 times the variable r that is in the equation?

    (A) $15q + 15p$

    (B) $15q + \dfrac{p}{3}$

    (C) $\dfrac{-15q + 15p}{2}$

    (D) $\dfrac{-15p - 15q}{4}$

    (E) $\dfrac{15p - 15q}{4}$

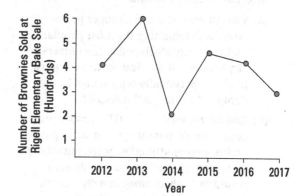

5. In which year represented in the above line graph did Rigell Elementary School have the biggest drop in brownies sold at their bake sale from the previous year?

    (A) 2013

    (B) 2014

    (C) 2015

    (D) 2016

    (E) 2017

GO ON TO NEXT PAGE

$$x + y + z = 40$$
$$x - y + z = 22$$

6. For the above system of equations, if the value of z is the cube of 3, which of the following is the value of xy?

(A) 9

(B) 16

(C) 27

(D) 36

(E) 81

7. James conducted a survey at a university to determine the most popular political party affiliation at the university. He conducted the entire survey at a meeting of the Campus Libertarians, a group of students who are members of the Libertarian Party. Which of the following statements about the survey is correct?

Select **all** such statements.

(A) The survey method is a proper procedure for determining the most popular political party affiliation at the university because all political parties are most likely proportionally represented at the Campus Libertarians' meetings.

(B) The survey method is NOT a proper procedure for determining the most popular political party affiliation at the university because only the Campus Republicans would be likely to work as a representative sample of the entire campus.

(C) The survey method is a proper procedure for determining the most popular political party affiliation at the university because all of the people surveyed would likely be students of the university.

(D) The survey method is NOT a proper procedure for determining the most popular political party affiliation at the university because the group surveyed is Libertarian and would work as a sample that only or mostly represents Libertarian Party affiliation.

(E) The survey method is NOT a proper procedure for determining the most popular political party affiliation at the university because political parties other than the Libertarian Party would not be likely to be represented by the sample.

8. Mike's Tennis Company sells tennis balls in containers that contain 3 balls each. If Gertrude needs 100 tennis balls from Mike's Tennis Company for a tournament at her sports club, how many containers does she need to order?

(A) 32

(B) 33

(C) $33\frac{1}{3}$

(D) 34

(E) $34\frac{2}{3}$

9. A can has 7 quarters in it. Two of the quarters were issued in 2018, 3 were issued in 2017, and 2 were issued in 2016. If Savonne reaches into the can and randomly takes out a quarter, what is the probability of her picking a quarter that was issued in 2018 or 2017?

(A) $\frac{6}{49}$

(B) $\frac{1}{7}$

(C) $\frac{3}{14}$

(D) $\frac{5}{7}$

(E) $\frac{6}{7}$

10. The diameter of a hydrogen atom is approximately 1.06×10^{-10} meters. What is that number in standard form?

(A) 0.000000000106

(B) 0.00000000106

(C) 1.06

(D) 10,600,000,000

(E) 106,000,000,000

$$3.5w - 12.5 = 1,905.5$$

11. If the value of w in the above equation is increased by 34.5 percent, which of the following correctly expresses the resulting value in scientific notation?

(A) 5.48×10^{-4}

(B) 7.3706×10^{2}

(C) $18,906 \times 10^{-2}$

(D) 5.48×10^{4}

(E) 737.06×10^{2}

12. On a map of Poseyville that is drawn to scale, one inch represents 2.4 miles. Gracyn drives from her house in Poseyville to a grocery store that is 7.8 miles away and in the same town. She then drives back to her house. If Gracyn uses a pen to trace only her driving on the map, how far does she move her pen?

(A) 3.25 inches

(B) 4.8 inches

(C) 6.5 inches

(D) 3.25 miles

(E) 6.5 miles

$$ab = b^3$$

13. With a and b having the same values they have in the above equation, which of the following is equal to $\dfrac{b^5}{a}$?

(A) b

(B) $3b$

(C) b^2

(D) b^3

(E) b^{5b}

14. Which of the following is closest to the mean tail length of house cats?

(A) 3 inches

(B) $\dfrac{1}{3}$ yard

(C) 64 inches

(D) $\dfrac{7}{5,280}$ mile

(E) 12 feet

15. A line has an x-intercept of -2 and a y-intercept of 8. What is the equation of the line in slope-intercept form?

(A) $y = 4x + 8$

(B) $y = -x + 8$

(C) $y - 8 = 4(x - 0)$

(D) $y = 8x - 1$

(E) $y - 1 = 4(x + 1)$

16. The sum of two consecutive even integers is 4 less than 3 times the lower integer. What is the higher integer?

(A) 4

(B) 6

(C) 8

(D) 14

(E) 22

17. What is the greatest common factor of the two following described values?

The least common multiple of 8 and 10

The greatest common factor of 84 and 72

Indicate your answer in the space provided.

18. All of the board members at a meeting are from New Jersey, Connecticut, or Mississippi. The name of each member is on one piece of paper in a hat, and the board director is going to randomly pick one piece of paper from the hat. If the probability that he will choose the name of a board member from Mississippi is $\dfrac{5}{8}$ and 15 of the board members are from Mississippi, how many board members are at the meeting?

(A) 16

(B) 24

(C) 30

(D) 48

(E) 64

19. What is the value of the following product?

$$\left(3.2854 \times 10^{15}\right)\left(9.407 \times 10^{-8}\right)$$

(A) 3.09057578×10^7

(B) 3.09057578×10^8

(C) 30.09057578×10^8

(D) 12.6924×10^9

(E) $3.09057578 \times 10^{23}$

GO ON TO NEXT PAGE

$$3.14 \quad \frac{22}{7} \quad \frac{43}{14} \quad 3.1415 \quad 3\frac{4}{21}$$

20. Which of the above numbers is fourth in order from greatest to least?

   (A) 3.14

   (B) $\frac{22}{7}$

   (C) $\frac{43}{14}$

   (D) 3.1415

   (E) $3\frac{4}{21}$

21. Trace made 12 gallons of tea in 2 hours. What is that rate in cups per minute?

   (A) 1.6 cups per minute

   (B) 2.2 cups per minute

   (C) 5.8 cups per minute

   (D) 30.2 cups per minute

   (E) 60.4 cups per minute

22. The expression $9v^2$ is multiplied by $-14vw^4$. Which of the following terms could be added to this product to get a sum that is one term with v and w in it?

   (A) $-126vw$

   (B) $17.4v^3w^3$

   (C) $3v^2w^4$

   (D) $85.2v^4w^3$

   (E) $-7.81v^3w^4$

$$(5)(-7)(2.3)(-17.4)(19)(-1)$$

23. By which of the following could the above value be multiplied to get a positive product?

   Indicate **all** such values.

   (A) -8.4

   (B) $(-1)^{997}$

   (C) 0

   (D) 2^{-1}

   (E) 15.04

24. Ben threw a flying disc 38 feet. Then he threw it 13 yards. After that, Ben threw the disc 478 inches. What is the total number of inches Ben threw the disc for the three throws?

   Indicate your answer in the space provided.

   ┌─────────────────────┐
   │   │
   └─────────────────────┘

High School	Number of Scholarships
McLeod	11
Scott	8
Spann	6
Casey	12
Bramlett	8

25. The previous table shows the numbers, for each of five local high schools, of seniors who received college scholarships in one school year. What is the standard deviation of the data, rounded to the nearest tenth?

   (A) 1

   (B) 1.8

   (C) 2.1

   (D) 2.2

   (E) 4.8

$$1, 3, 9, 27 \ldots$$

26. For the above sequence, by what number must the seventh term be multiplied to get the tenth term?

   (A) 3

   (B) 6

   (C) 9

   (D) 27

   (E) 54

12 12 12 12 12 12 12

27. For the previous set of data, which of the five following values is not equal to the other four?

(A) Mean

(B) Median

(C) Mode

(D) Range

(E) Highest number

Stem	Leaf
0	2 2 4 8
2	0 3 5 7
5	0 1 1 1 8
7	1 5 5
8	5 5

Key: 3|7 = 370

28. What is the mode of the data represented by the above stem-and-leaf plot?

(A) 5

(B) 51

(C) 85

(D) 510

(E) 750

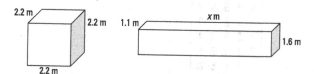

29. Both of the previous figures are right rectangular prisms, and they have the same volume. The side measures of the prisms are labeled. What is the value of x in the diagram?

(A) 6.05

(B) 6.821

(C) 7.23

(D) 8.1

(E) 8.34

30. Doris was adding sales figures for a department store. She made an error when she subtracted the price of a $143 dress instead of adding it. Doris cannot delete the mistake. Which of the following strategies can Doris use to fix the mistake and be on track to account for the next store item?

(A) Subtract $143 again

(B) Add $143

(C) Add $286

(D) Subtract $286

(E) Add $71.50

31. A number is multiplied by 3, and 7 is added to the product. The result is multiplied by 4. Which of the following is a correct set of steps for reversing the process in order to reach the original number?

(A) Divide the resulting number by 4, subtract 7 from the result, and divide the difference by 3.

(B) Divide the resulting number by 4, add 7 to the result, and divide the sum by 3.

(C) Multiply the resulting number by 4, subtract 7 from the result, and multiply the difference by 3.

(D) Divide the resulting number by 3, subtract 7 from the result, and divide the sum by 4.

(E) Divide the resulting number by 4, divide the quotient by 3, and subtract 7 from that quotient.

32. Which of the following questions is a statistics question?

(A) Have the Mets or Yankees won more World Series?

(B) How many 16-year-old girls have had braces?

(C) How much time do residents at a nursing home spend reading the newspaper each week?

(D) How long has Joe been a doctor?

(E) What percent of NFL quarterbacks have had knee injuries?

GO ON TO NEXT PAGE

33. Bethany was hired to sell tulips for a florist. The florist pays Bethany $8.25 per hour plus $1.45 for every bouquet of tulips Bethany sells. If Bethany works *h* hours and sells exactly *b* bouquets, which of the following expressions correctly represents the amount of money Bethany makes in that time?

 (A) $8.25h + $1.45b

 (B) $8.25h + $1.45h

 (C) $8.25bh + $1.45bh

 (D) $8.25h + $1.45bh

 (E) $8.25b + $1.45h

34. The value of *j* is between 10 and 20. The value of *k* is between 30 and 40. The value of $\frac{j}{k}$ must therefore be between what two numbers?

 (A) $\frac{1}{2}$ and $\frac{2}{3}$

 (B) $\frac{1}{4}$ and $\frac{2}{3}$

 (C) $\frac{1}{3}$ and $\frac{1}{2}$

 (D) $\frac{1}{4}$ and $\frac{1}{3}$

 (E) $\frac{1}{2}$ and $\frac{3}{4}$

35. The distance from the center of a circular merry-go-round to the edge is 7.3 feet. If the merry-go-round takes 4.87 seconds to complete a full rotation, which of the following speeds is closest to the rotation speed of the merry-go-round at its outer edge?

 (A) 9.42 feet/second

 (B) 9.43 feet/second

 (C) 9.51 feet/second

 (D) 9.82 feet/second

 (E) 10.75 feet/second

10 4 5 7 10

36. For the previous data set, what is the product of the median and the mode?

 (A) 17

 (B) 22

 (C) 40

 (D) 54

 (E) 70

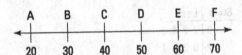

37. Matt profited $94.28 on Day 3 of selling candy at a stand. On Day 4, his profit level was at a 34.25 percent decrease from Day 3. Matt's prices include fractions of cents. Between which two points on the above number line is Matt's Day 4 profit level represented?

 (A) A and B

 (B) B and C

 (C) C and D

 (D) D and E

 (E) E and F

38. A team of 25 salespeople at a remote-control boat dealership sold 109 boats in one day. The number of boats sold by each salesperson is presented in the above table. Which histogram below correctly represents the data set?

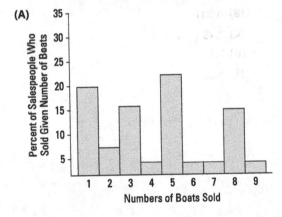

(B)

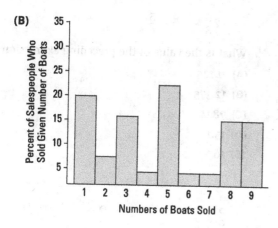

(C)

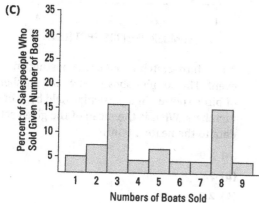

(D)

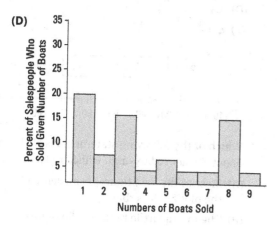

(E)

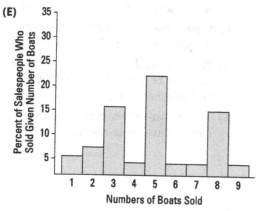

39. If $a = 3b$ and $b = \frac{1}{4}c$, which of the following is equal to $\frac{a}{2}$?

(A) $\frac{3c}{2}$

(B) $\frac{3c}{8}$

(C) $\frac{2c}{3}$

(D) $4c$

(E) $\frac{8c}{3}$

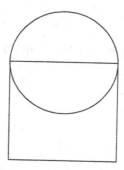

40. Mark exercises by walking the full distance of the edge of a square path once after work. One side of the square path goes over a circular pond, from one point on the edge of the pond to another, and runs directly over the center of the pond. The area of the pond is $14{,}981.76\pi$ m^2. How far does Mark walk to cover the entire square path?

(A) 122.4 m

(B) 244.8 m

(C) 979.2 m

(D) 1,012 m

(E) 1,489.6 m

41. Which of the following distances is the greatest?

(A) 5.873 kilometers

(B) 5,873 meters

(C) 587.3 centimeters

(D) 5,873 decameters

(E) 58,730 millimeters

GO ON TO NEXT PAGE

42. Robert has n nickels and d dimes in his piggy bank where he stores only nickels and dimes. The total amount of money he has in his piggy bank is $3.75. Which of the following expressions represents the number of dimes Robert has in his piggy bank?

(A) $75 - n$

(B) $\dfrac{375 + 5n}{n}$

(C) $\dfrac{n-2}{375}$

(D) $\dfrac{n-2}{75}$

(E) $\dfrac{75 - n}{2}$

43. Which of the following inequalities is equivalent to $3j - 7 > 21$?

(A) $j > \dfrac{28}{3}$

(B) $j > \dfrac{3}{28}$

(C) $j < \dfrac{28}{3}$

(D) $j > \dfrac{14}{3}$

(E) $j < \dfrac{3}{14}$

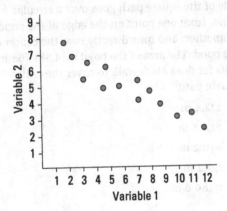

44. Which of the following statements correctly express the relationship between Variable 1 and Variable 2 in the above scatter plot?

Select **all** such statements.

(A) As Variable 1 increases, Variable 2 tends to increase.

(B) As Variable 2 increases, Variable 1 tends to increase.

(C) As Variable 1 increases, Variable 2 tends to decrease.

(D) As Variable 2 decreases, Variable 1 tends to increase.

(E) There is no correlation between the two variables.

$$-2\frac{5}{8} + 17.5 - \frac{15}{4}$$

45. What is the value of the preceding expression?

(A) 11.125

(B) 12.375

(C) 7824

(D) 15.1

(E) 16

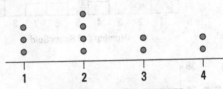

NUMBER OF BIRDS SPOTTED

46. A new bird-watching club was hosting an event. The dot plot above shows the number of birds spotted in a particular field by 11 of its members. What is the mean of the given set of data to the nearest tenth?

(A) 2.0

(B) 2.3

(C) 2.5

(D) 3.3

(E) 4.0

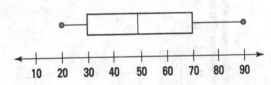

47. Which of the following statements is NOT true about the above box-and-whisker plot?

(A) Most of the data figures represented by the plot are less than 70.

(B) The interquartile range of the represented set of data is between 45 and 50.

(C) Most of the data figures represented by the plot are greater than 30.

(D) The mean of the represented set of data CANNOT be determined from the box-and-whisker plot alone.

(E) The median of the represented set of data is between 40 and 50.

$$x^2 + 10x + 21 = 0$$

48. What are the solutions to the preceding equation?

(A) {−7, −3}

(B) {1, 21}

(C) {2, −4}

(D) {3, 7}

(E) {−10, 21}

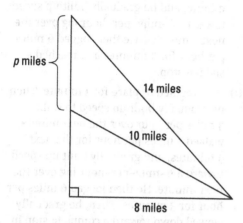

49. The above figure is a right triangle that contains a smaller right triangle. Some of the figure's segment measures are labeled. What is the value of *p*, rounded to the nearest hundredth?

Indicate your answer in the space provided.

50. Train A leaves a station at 9:15 a.m. at 160 miles per hour. Train B leaves the same station at 220 miles per hour at 11:30 a.m. that morning, in the opposite direction on the same track. If both trains maintain their speeds, at what time will they be 1,215 miles apart?

(A) 11:45 a.m.

(B) 12:15 p.m.

(C) 1:00 p.m.

(D) 1:45 p.m.

(E) 2:30 p.m.

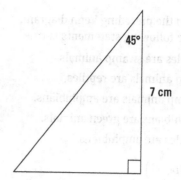

51. An acute angle of the above right triangle has a measure of 45°. The measure of a leg is 7 cm. What is the measure of the hypotenuse of the right triangle, rounded to the nearest tenth?

(A) 7.2 cm

(B) 9.9 cm

(C) 11.4 cm

(D) 14.1 cm

(E) 16.7 cm

52. Which of the following is a divisor of both 24 and 42?

Select **all** such numbers.

(A) 2

(B) 4

(C) 5

(D) 6

(E) 12

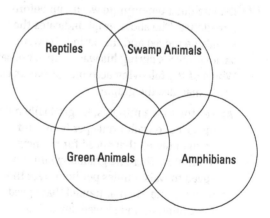

GO ON TO NEXT PAGE

53. According to the preceding Venn diagram, which of the following statements is true?

(A) No reptiles are swamp animals.

(B) No green animals are reptiles.

(C) No swamp animals are amphibians.

(D) No amphibians are green animals.

(E) No reptiles are amphibians.

$$4p^5qr\left(7pq^3r^7\right)^2$$

54. Which of the following is equal to the value of the above expression?

(A) $196p^7q^7r^{15}$

(B) $98p^7q^6r^{15}$

(C) $196p^7q^7r^{14}$

(D) $49p^7q^7r^{15}$

(E) $392p^5q^7r^{15}$

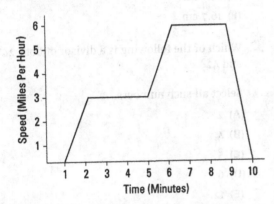

55. Dr. Fitz did a ten-minute warm-up before a road race. The above graph indicates the speeds he moved and the periods he went various speeds during his warm-up exercise. Which of the following accounts of events correctly matches the graph?

(A) For the first 3 minutes, he gradually built up speed to walk 1 mile per hour, and he maintained that speed for the next 3 minutes. Then, he gradually built up speed to walk 3 miles per hour over the next minute. He maintained that speed for 2 minutes and slowed down to a complete stop over the last minute.

(B) He stretched in place for the first minute. For the next minute, he gradually built up speed to walk 1 mile per hour, and he maintained that speed for the next 6 minutes. Then, he gradually slowed down to a complete stop over the last 2 minutes.

(C) He stretched in place for 1 minute. Then, he gradually built up speed to walk 1 mile per hour over the next 3 minutes. Next, he walked 3 miles per hour for the next minute, and he gradually built up speed toward a 6-mile-per-hour jog over the next 3 minutes. He then jogged 6 miles per hour for 3 minutes and reached a sudden stop.

(D) He stretched in place for 1 minute. Then, he gradually built up speed to walk 3 miles per hour over the next minute, walked 3 miles per hour for the next 3 minutes, and gradually built up speed toward a 6-mile-per-hour jog over the next minute. He then jogged 6 miles per hour for 3 minutes. Then, he gradually slowed down toward a complete stop in the last minute and stood in place at the 10-minute mark.

(E) In the first minute, he gradually built up speed to walk 3 miles per hour. He then walked 3 miles per hour for the next 3 minutes, and he gradually slowed down to 1 mile per hour over the next 6 minutes. In the next minute, he slowed down to a complete stop.

56. The following table displays the quantities of several types of units. According to the table, how many hiblems are in 8.9 zerberts?

Unit	Quantity
Wuzel	2.3 Zerberts
Nochel	7.4 Hiblems
Zerbert	4.8 Nochels

(A) 316.128

(B) 400

(C) 632.656

(D) 700

(E) 715.124

Chapter 15

Practice Exam 1: Answers and Explanations

Use the answers and explanations in this chapter to see how well you performed and to understand where you might have gone wrong on the answers you missed. Remember, the practice exam can help you determine where you need to focus your studies in preparation for the real Praxis Core. If you want to score your test quickly, flip to the end of the chapter, where the "Answer Key" gives only the letters of the correct answers.

TIP You can take this test online. Flip back to the Introduction for instructions on how to access this book's online test bank, where you can take more practice tests, review the answers and explanations, and get a personalized summary of your performance.

Part 1: Reading

1. **B. The modern use of the term *sports* focuses on traditional views solely focused on physical competition, while the author proposes that the study of *sport* can be a gauge to measure other aspects of particular cultures and time periods.** The author explains that the terms are different, in that *sports* is a traditional term referring to our current understanding of the topic with teams, players, and so on. *Sport*, however, is a term that encompasses viewing sport over time and can be used to better understand a certain civilization and time period in history.

   The correct answer is not Choice (A) because *sports*, as a term, can also refer to historical actions or events.

   The correct answer is not Choice (C). The point of the passage is that the author doesn't want the terms used interchangeably. In this context, he's stating that the terms mean different things.

   The correct answer is not Choice (D) because it's an oversimplification. The author is suggesting that *sport* might include other elements but doesn't necessarily state what those might be. In this paragraph, both terms still refer to some type of physical feat.

The correct answer is not Choice (E). The author doesn't suggest that one term is preferable or that one should be considered superlative in some way.

2. **A. In order to satisfy the public, Homer appealed with tales of epic heroic deeds.** The prompt asks for a supposed purpose for the writer Homer. The passage states that Homer's patrons "mandated that he applaud" heroes from a greater age of men. So, his purpose in writing was to appease his patrons.

   The correct answer is not Choice (B) because the prompt, and this part of the passage, isn't concerned with solving the "Homeric question."

   The correct answer is not Choice (C) because this choice attempts to solve the "Homeric question," which isn't the purpose of the prompt or the purpose of the passage. So, his purpose in writing was to appease his audience.

   The correct answers are not Choice (D) or (E). While both are true statements, they do not address the prompt. The prompt asks for the *purpose* of the writer Homer in writing such tales.

3. **D. thinking that involves an emphasis on an appreciation of nature and the common man.** Although the term "romanticism" can mean all of these things, here, "romanticism" is referring specifically to the thinking of seeing events with an appreciation of nature and the common man. Evidence is seen using the terms "bucolic" for natural settings and for "the people who gave us democracy."

   The correct answer is not Choice (A). Although the examples given are ones of a positive note, the tone stops short of idyllic.

   The correct answer is not Choice (B). Not all examples in the passage describe a rural life.

   The correct answer is not Choice (C). Although the term "romanticism" is often used this way, the passage does not suggest that the view is suddenly against previous views. Rather, the romantic view is the one that's traditional and long held.

   The correct answer is not Choice (E). This answer would best fit the word "haze," but not the term "romanticism."

4. **D. One myth of the cultural sports spectacle is that Greek sports have been wiser and better, while Roman sports have debased man's nature.** The author states the myth supposing that Greeks are somehow more positive than Romans without giving further examples to prove or disprove this.

   The correct answer is not Choice (A). The author does not suggest that Romans are more deserving of a positive viewpoint.

   The correct answer is not Choice (B). The author does not allude to any evidence that would support either side.

   The correct answer is not Choice (C). While man has historically cast one culture in a negative light, more evidence would be needed to prove this conclusion as true.

   The correct answer is not Choice (E). No evidence is given to prove that the myth against Romans is untrue.

5. **A. Hollywood has perpetrated a false image of gladiators that isn't supported by historical evidence.** The phrase "despite Hollywood" leads the reader to understand that this depiction of gladiators as being forced to perform to death as slaves is wrong. Rather, history shows that gladiators had many roles in society.

   The correct answer is not Choice (B). Gladiators weren't necessarily Spanish slaves. The word "gladiator" is from a Spanish root.

The correct answer is not Choice (C). The passage gives no details about general assumptions. The point of the text is that Hollywood has led to misunderstandings about history.

The correct answer is not Choice (D). According to the passage, gladiators have been both in history. Hollywood, though, has only portrayed them in one way.

The correct answer is not Choice (E). Hollywood actually supported the opposite — that gladiators were helpless slaves forced to perform.

6. **C. hydro.** Hydro has seen the steadiest use of energy consumption, which has varied little between the years 1800 and 2008.

The correct answers are not Choices (A), (B), (D), or (E) as all of these have seen sharp increases in certain years of consumption.

7. **B. Where future generations are born determines their per capita consumption rates.** The author is suggesting that, when forecasting energy demand, it matters greatly where those future generations are born because that determines to a large extent their per capita consumption rates.

The correct answer is not (A). The author gives factors for determining future energy demands.

The correct answers are not Choice (C) or (D). Although Americans do consume more now, the population growth will likely not keep up with developing nations, which makes this a false forecast. However, should that change, then the developing nations will not have the consumption rates in greater numbers. The rate varies due to the population. More people equals more energy consumption in the future.

The correct answer is not Choice (E). The author makes no direct causal effect between future consumption rates and standard of living.

8. **E. Although one might expect sexism to negatively affect women and girls, men and boys can also be targets of this kind of discrimination.** Although many expect to hear about gender discrimination against women and girls, men and boys also suffer and are victims.

The correct answers are not Choice (A). Although this is an assertion, this isn't necessarily a conclusion from the text.

The correct answers are not Choice (B) or (D) because no examples are given as to how sexism could be positive.

The correct answer is not Choice (C). Although this is also an assertion, it's not the best answer. The point the author is trying to make is that for men to be victims of this type of discrimination is unusual because it generally is believed to affect only females.

9. **A. In short, these and other studies suggest that boys tend to suffer more than girls as a result of divorce and of living with a single parent.** One can conclude that the author's final statement would be suggesting that the studies show similar information in regard to the suffering of boys post-divorce.

The correct answer is not Choice (B). After reading the snippets from the studies, the readers should not be surprised by such a conclusion.

The correct answer is not Choice (C) because the reader has no cause to question what the studies might have been lacking.

The correct answer is not Choice (D). The parents of children who suffer from the consequences of divorce aren't likely to feel better by a study that shows they are the cause of a child suffering because of these very actions.

The correct answer is not Choice (E). The author presents enough cohesive information and details to make a logical prediction about the continuation of the text.

10. **C. emphasize the danger of differentiating what is considered worthy, from a scholar's perspective, from an attitude of popular perspective.** The example given shows the danger in teaching only some of a subject or topic. If some knowledge is considered "good" and some "bad," then this *knowledge* will be acted upon and can be swayed by popular opinion.

The correct answer is not Choice (A). Faith and religion are used for the same purpose in this passage. These terms are not representing different concepts.

The correct answer is not Choice (B). The example given is one of using faith as knowledge, but doesn't explain *why* this happened so frequently in our past, only that it did often happen.

The correct answer is not Choice (D). The point is that knowledge shouldn't be considered on the basis of "good" or "bad." Knowledge should be shared in an unbiased way for its own sake.

The correct answer is not Choice (E). Here, hindsight clearly shows what was "bad" to teach since it resulted in deaths by unfounded witch hunts.

11. **E. A generalization is made followed by a specific example.** The author makes a claim and gives general examples. Then, she gives a specific example to more clearly illustrate the original point.

The correct answer is not Choice (A). No metaphor is given, although figurative language is used to liven up the topic.

The correct answer is not Choice (B). The author provides no objections to her claim.

The correct answer is not Choice (C). There are no comparisons or contrasts.

The correct answer is not Choice (D). The claim isn't "suspected." The author is quite clear on her viewpoints of the topic.

12. **C. Critical readings and writings by this group have not been treated with serious academic respect.** The author says such thinkers have been "scapegoats" and their thinking was little more than "pleasant fancy." Clearly, the author is suggesting no serious academic respect has been given to these views.

The correct answer is not Choice (A). The author is suggesting the opposite of this statement.

The correct answer is not Choice (B) because the author provides no "merit" for such treatment.

The correct answer is not Choice (D) because the author suggests no one has really taken the ideas seriously.

The correct answer is not Choice (E). The ideas have been dismissed, but a serious female academic Shakespeare expert was noted. Alas, her work was treated scornfully.

13. **D. strengthen.** Marriages during this time were often done for advantageous political purposes, meaning that such a marriage would strengthen relationships between the allegiances.

The correct answer is not Choice (A). While this is a synonym of "cement," it is not the best answer choice and does not quite fit the situation described.

The correct answers are not Choice (B) or Choice (C). Both words could be considered antonyms or near antonyms.

The correct answer is not Choice (E). Such a marriage might bring new life to political alliances that were stale, for example. However, the examples listed show the marriages provided a strength for these men and are the reasons they kept several wives.

14. **D. lend credence to the idea that Caesar cared more about Cleopatra's power than the idea of love.** Because Caesar was considered a "womanizer," he likely saw Cleopatra more as an advance to his own political goals and less as a traditional wife.

The correct answer is not Choice (A). Because he was understood to be a womanizer, this would be his normal moral code of character.

The correct answer is not Choice (B). No additional details in the passage support this idea.

The correct answer is not Choice (C). No other information indicates that accepted views of Caesar are incorrect.

The correct answer is not Choice (E). The passage states that there are fewer sources of descriptions of this marriage and more for Cleopatra's well-known love match, that of Antony.

15. **E. A controversial claim is presented, and then evidence and reasons are given to support one side of the controversy.** Trade deficits and energy usage is a controversial subject and one that can be argued with positive and negative points. Here, the author makes a direct claim and call to action and then gives reasons as to why this call to action should be followed.

The correct answer is not Choice (A). No unresolved question is stated.

The correct answers are not Choice (B) or Choice (D). A "movement" is not the best way to describe America's energy independence on other nations.

The correct answer is not Choice (C). Since the issue is ongoing, this isn't the best answer choice. Also, there is no one pivotal moment described.

16. **D. a desire to sell works to a specific audience.** The author states that any editor begins by thinking about what the audience wants. This segues into a discussion about book markets.

The correct answer is not Choice (A). While annotation has expanded in books, the appeal is not necessarily for a broader range. Rather, the appeal is for a specific audience — the undergraduate markets.

The correct answer is not Choice (B). The passage states this is a consideration when designing books, not that it has led to more annotations.

The correct answer is not Choice (C). Rather, more annotation has led to a cultivation of critical methodology and literary relevance.

The correct answer is not Choice (E). The passage gives no specific detail concerning how publishing has changed, only how annotation has changed.

17. **B. explain that evidence bears out the understood assumption that Ptolemy was a weak ruler.** The author first states that Ptolemy XII is understood to be a weak ruler because he was a prolific builder. The gateway at the Ptah temple bears this out because "it is small and would not have cost a great deal of money."

The correct answer is not Choice (A). According to the author, the prolific building projects mean the exact opposite.

The correct answer is not Choice (C). The point of the passage is that the author does not want the terms used interchangeably. In this context, she is stating that the terms mean different things.

The correct answers are not Choice (D) or Choice (E) because the information presented about the gateway supports the author's first statement rather than refuting it.

18. **C. sensationally touted.** Here, the word means that the relationship with China has been sensationally touted.

The correct answers are not Choice (A), Choice (D), or Choice (E). Although the word does have these multiple meanings, these nuances don't fit the context of the sentence.

The correct answer is not Choice (B) because the topic, the conversation concerning a trade deficit, is a substantial one. Again, the word nuance doesn't quite fit here.

19. **D. a decrease in traffic-related fatalities.** The passage states a decrease in the number of people killed in traffic accidents was the silver lining in the gas shortage, suggesting that the decrease in deaths could be attributed to this shortage.

The correct answer is not Choice (A). The author doesn't make this claim, necessarily. Choice (D) is the most obvious answer.

The correct answer is not Choice (B). The author doesn't suggest the lowered speed limits were a result of the gas shortage. A reader might assume this, but the direct correlation the author draws is the link between less gas and fewer deaths. Again, just not the best choice.

The correct answer is not Choice (C). No real information is given about the overall energy shortage, so there's no correlation between the two.

The correct answer is not Choice (E). Naturally, these two are linked. To make a direct correlation between them would have been a waste of time for an author.

20. **C. It was worn during his first fireside chat.** The only information given is that the sweater was worn during Carter's first fireside chat.

While all the other answer choices could be true as symbolic statements, the passage doesn't suggest any of these nor provide evidence for them. So, Choices (A), (B), (D), and (E) are incorrect.

21. **A. When assessing how much it costs to fight terrorism in the Persian Gulf, consideration has to be made for multifaceted effects.** The passage states that, although there have been many military fatalities, there have also been numerous other traumatic effects, such as the loss of life to journalists and innocent Iraqis, as well as the suffering of the families of those involved and a huge monetary cost.

The correct answer is not Choice (B). The author makes claims that are reasonable and don't need future evidence to support them.

The correct answer is not Choice (C). Although a number is given for military deaths, other data is not available here for comparison.

The correct answers are not Choice (D) or Choice (E). Both are opinion statements that aren't supported by evidence provided in the text.

22. **C. pointing out that the film *Olympia* gave credence to the Berlin Olympics through the propagandistic use of symbols featuring honor and glory.** The passage points out that the film *Olympia* is a propaganda film that features, and thus sanctions, the Berlin "Nazi" Olympics by comparing the sport to the "pure" Olympic Greek games.

The correct answer is not Choice (A). There are no direct or indirect warnings. The author is simply pointing out how this film helped to advance Nazi propaganda techniques.

The correct answer is not Choice (B). By stating the film is "propagandistic," the author is stating it was not inadvertent. Rather, it was purposeful. Choice (D) is wrong for this same reason. The two are linked because the subject of the film is the Berlin Olympics.

The correct answer is not Choice (E). The author does not purport the reader take any perspective, other than one of understanding how the film and Hitler are linked.

23. **B. while the film may have been made for nefarious reasons,** *Olympia* **has nevertheless changed cinematic history and inspired future sports films.** Although the film was one of propaganda, it still changed the way that future sports films and documentaries would be made because of its careful attention to detail and focus on physical glory and honor. The author explains that the film should be viewed not for the propaganda, but for the way it changed how sports films were made and produced.

The correct answer is not Choice (A). The passage does not state that Hitler designed the film. The film was the work of cinematographer Leni Riefenstahl.

The correct answer is not Choice (C). The author is not stating or suggesting ideas on how sports films should be made.

The correct answer is not Choice (D). The film is mentioned in connection with the Berlin Olympics because it's *about* the Berlin Olympics.

The correct answer is not Choice (E). The passage doesn't state where the film was unveiled.

24. **C. explaining that sport permeates modern society and, while that is primarily viewed in a positive light, there are also many negative effects.** The passage explains that sport is in every aspect of our culture and, although sport is generally viewed as a good thing, there are also some negative connotations. The author gives both positives (sports played at the YMCA and by schoolchildren) and negatives (the violence of sports and sport as a money-making business).

The correct answer is not Choice (A). Rather, more time is spent with negative examples than with positive examples.

The correct answer is not Choice (B). The tone is not one of refutation of a previous argument. The author is simply making a point.

The correct answer is not Choice (D). This is not simply a summary of facts. The author also has a point to make that might not occur to many or be viewed by the majority about the positive and negative aspects of sports in our culture.

The correct answer is not Choice (E). The author does not ask or encourage the reader, in this section of the text, to make that determination — whether one aspect outweighs other considerations.

25. **B. While sport is seen in mostly a positive light, the negative side of the argument encompasses both violence and commercialization.** In this passage, the author gives many examples as to how sports can be seen to have a negative effect regardless of the fact that many view it in a positive light.

The correct answer is not Choice (A) because the author gives many examples as to how sport has affected culture.

The correct answer is not Choice (C). Although the author says sports traditions tend to still be viewed positively, he doesn't propose this *should* be the case.

The correct answer is not Choice (D) because the author doesn't propose "culture" disagrees about sports. The author points out a potential disagreement about the influence of sports on modern society.

The correct answer is not Choice (E) because the author doesn't call on the reader to make a judgment or decision.

26. **B. The energy consumption of countries can be directly related to the wealth and income of the people who reside there.** The passage directly states the richest people in the world use more energy than those who have less wealth. So, the conclusion is that energy consumption can be directly related to the wealth and income of the people who inhabit that country.

The correct answer is not Choice (A). The information provided makes a clear case and provides no disagreement about the connection between energy consumption and economic development.

The correct answer is not Choice (C). The variations are actually used to make the point and do not cloud the issue.

The correct answer is not Choice (D). The author makes no distinctions regarding what would be "proper" or "improper" energy systems.

The correct answer is not Choice (E). The word "extravagantly" suggests the author is placing blame for the use of energy resources, and this isn't the case. The author is simply presenting the facts.

27. **A. often lack access to electricity and have to rely on biomass fuel options.** The author states that people in developing nations suffer from energy poverty, meaning they often don't have access to electricity, which causes them to rely on other forms of energy, such as biomass fuel options.

The correct answer is not Choice (B). This point seems to bring the reader to a Catch-22. Without the money, no development can begin, and with no development, no other energy options can be made available. However, the author's main point is that a lack of access to electricity is the main reason for energy poverty, not just a lack of development options.

The correct answer is not Choice (C). No information is provided about wealthier inhabitants of a country. The distinction is between the poorest and richest users the world over.

The correct answer is not Choice (D). The author doesn't suggest that the richest people have a monopoly on energy interests that isn't sharable. Rather, they have an easier time accessing better energy options because of their wealth.

The correct answer is not Choice (E). The author doesn't suggest that energy poverty is an option chosen because it is in keeping with cultural norms. Rather, no other options are available to the poorest.

28. **E. a lack of access to energy.** The author directly defines *energy poverty* as "the lack of access to energy services."

The correct answer is not Choice (A). No information is given about the interest of those who have no access to energy options.

The correct answer is not Choice (B). Although the energy-poor do also have a lack of resources, this isn't the definition given for "energy poverty."

The correct answers are not Choice (C) or Choice (D). Naturally, the poor don't have access to money, but this isn't the definition given for "energy poverty." Technically, a lack of money would simply be poverty.

29. **D. compare the huge discrepancies of energy consumption between the richest and poorest people in the world.** The author states that the richest billion people in the world use 25 times more energy than the poorest 2.5 billion. These statistics are given to point out the huge discrepancies of energy consumption between these two groups.

The correct answer is not Choice (A). Giving facts about the richest people wouldn't help to explain why the poorest people have so few energy options.

The correct answer is not Choice (B). No information is given about costs of energy development.

The correct answer is not Choice (C) because the author actually supports this idea.

The correct answer is not Choice (E) because the author supports the inference that those who were blessed being born in some areas of the world have better and richer lives than those who live in developing nations.

30. **D. How does not joining the military on a volunteer basis affect men?** The passage explains the many ways that men are affected when they don't voluntarily join the military. So, the question from Choice (D) could be answered by the passage. Effects given include shame, ostracism, and self-shame.

The correct answer is not Choice (A). The passage does refer to contemporary western times, but gives no other indications this is the most affected time and place by this issue. Therefore, this question can't be answered.

The correct answer is not Choice (B). The author states it's hard for those in contemporary western culture to understand but doesn't give reasons as to why. So, this question can't be answered.

The correct answer is not Choice (C). This question can't be answered because the passage doesn't differentiate between different types of men or give reasons as to why some do choose to join and others don't.

The correct answer is not Choice (E). No reason is given as to why women are treated differently with regard to this issue, so this question can't be answered.

31. **A. If men or boys choose not to join the military, there are clear effects from a societal and personal perspective.** Many effects are given about a male reluctance to join the military, including ostracism and shame. This sentence best sums up the entire passage.

The correct answer is not Choice (B) because only a small part of the passage is about how women are treated.

The correct answer is not Choice (C). This does not summarize information in the entire passage and may only be an inference a reader can draw.

The correct answer is not Choice (D) because this is a detail found in the text. It is not a summary of the entire passage.

The correct answer is not Choice (E) because no details are given about this and the passage is not mostly about the lack of military enlistees.

32. **E. to illustrate key differences in the treatment of women and men in regard to voluntary military service.** The author shows how men and women are treated in the same situation — a reluctance to voluntarily join the military. The difference in the treatment received illustrates key differences between men and women and the repercussions for such a decision.

The correct answer is not Choice (A) because women are treated much differently. According to the author, they aren't shown any bias for making the same decision.

The correct answer is not Choice (B) because the author does not suggest women are held in higher esteem, only that the repercussions for the decision are not as severe.

The correct answer is not Choice (C). No reasons are given, other than gender, for why men are treated differently.

The correct answer is not Choice (D) because the author doesn't address this other than to say it exists.

33. **C. detailing ways in which men are more disadvantaged when it comes to a lack of respect of bodily privacy.** The passage details the ways that men are actually more disadvantaged than women when it comes to a lack of respect for bodily privacy, such as differential treatment in prisons.

The correct answer is not Choice (A). The author takes pains to point out the differences between gender treatment and doesn't necessarily take pains to say each should be valued equally.

The correct answers are not Choice (B) or Choice (D). The example in the prisons is given to make a point. The passage isn't mainly concerned with how men or women are treated as prisoners.

The correct answer is not Choice (E). The author is not suggesting that women should be treated worse or that they don't enjoy their "better" treatment. The point is that men also suffer from this issue, although many may not realize it.

34. **B. females are more disadvantaged than males when it comes to bodily privacy in certain situations.** In this example, the author specifically chooses a female clothing item to illustrate that females are more negatively influenced when it comes to issues of body privacy.

The correct answer is not Choice (A) because the burqa is said to be worn by *women* in a way that shows a greater disadvantage for that gender in parts of the world where it is worn. An example that shows men are also negatively influenced comes later with the prison details.

The correct answer is not Choice (C). Although the author does give examples for both, the burqa is attributed to the female gender example.

The correct answer is not Choice (D) because the author doesn't suggest the issue is a cultural problem directed at only some segments of society. The issue is one of gender.

The correct answer is not Choice (E) because the author doesn't make any statements concerning religion. Again, the issue is one of gender.

35. **E. Myths likely started as true stories or stories with some truth, but creativity has changed the tales over time so that no one really knows what is truth and what is imagination.** Although myths are enjoyable, many of the first stories were also based in truth, at least in part. Although some aspects are fantastical, other tales refer to events that actually happened in history.

The correct answer is not Choice (A). Some notes are made suggesting that myths are likely based on some truths.

The correct answer is not Choice (B). Myths include imaginative and creative aspects and can't be simple retellings.

The correct answer is not Choice (C). Although it's hard to find elements of the truth, the examples given show that some elements of truth may be traced.

The correct answer is not Choice (D). The author doesn't give these two authors any more credibility than other unnamed authors.

36. **B. the stories make man look larger than life and the events take on a more heroic perspective.** The author discusses how creative elements have been added that blend the divine and dangerous with human abilities and celebrate historic achievements of our past.

The correct answer is not Choice (A). Although myths are old and traditional forms of storytelling, the author gives many more reasons for why they have lasted so long.

The correct answer is not Choice (C). Myths most likely started as tales around campfires but are now shared in other situations.

The correct answer is not Choice (D). The author infers that man's achievements have been elevated, but also takes pains to point out elements that are obviously unrealistic. So, this is not the best answer choice.

The correct answer is not Choice (E) because it's unclear whether these "heroes" were real, actual individuals.

37. **E. written to contain more imaginative aspects with less reliance on historical accuracy.** *The Epic of Gilgamesh* centered on divine aspects of gods and goddesses, but the other two focused on an actual historical event.

The correct answer is not Choice (A). *The Epic of Gilgamesh* is older because it's the oldest surviving myth, but no claim is made that this makes it a purer form of myth.

The correct answer is not Choice (B). *The Epic of Gilgamesh* is less historically accurate because it contains divine, and therefore, imaginative aspects that aren't real.

The correct answer is not Choice (C). The author suggests all are examples of traditional myths, even though they are different.

The correct answer is not Choice (D). It's unclear whether early writers of myths wanted their tales to be remembered as truth or as stories.

38. **E. illustrating the difficulties faced when attempting to differentiate what is truth and what is fiction in ancient myths.** The passage mostly discusses the difficulties modern people have when reading myths and determining what's true and what's made up.

The correct answer is not Choice (A) because no new information or details are present. The author is relying on the understanding that modern man and ancient man have a commonality in that both suppose some aspects of those myths are true.

The correct answer is not Choice (B). No assessment is detailed as being able to distinguish truth from fiction.

The correct answer is not Choice (C) because the only literary classification listed is that of "myth."

The correct answer is not Choice (D) because no process is detailed, nor is there information on who ultimately makes the determination that a story should or should not be a myth.

39. **C. stories that were written in a specific format of poetry.** An *epic poem* is a long and serious narrative poem that features a hero, such as Odysseus.

The correct answer is not Choice (A). Just because the poems are longer doesn't mean they are more likely to be true.

The correct answers are not Choice (B) or Choice (E). The author only lists the Homeric poems as examples, not the most impressive examples. *The Epic of Gilgamesh* is also listed, and neither is suggested as being "better" than the other.

The correct answer is not Choice (D). The author previously states this information, but it's not a reference to or understanding of the term "epic poem."

40. **A. Biomass has remained at a relatively stable usage throughout the years.** Biomass fuel usage has remained relatively stable from 1800 to 2008.

The correct answer is not Choice (B). The usage of biomass hasn't changed greatly and appears to have no connections to other fuel forms used.

The correct answer is not Choice (C). The introduction or invention of other fuel forms doesn't seem to have affected biomass fuel use.

41. **A and C. (A) The introduction of alternative fuel sources has increased dramatically during recent times. (C) Except for biomass, usage of all fuel types has increased more during the last 40–50 years than in the previous century.** Both statements are simultaneously true. Using information from the chart, the reader can see that *alternative fuel* sources have increased dramatically during recent times. Although the chart traces back more than 200 years, usage of *all fuel types except biomass* is seen as increasing since approximately 1970. The previous century, the 1800s, saw little or no increase in other forms of energy usage.

The correct answer is not Choice (B). Because biomass fuels have remained steady, there has been no negative impact on other usage types, at least according to this chart.

42. **2008.** According to the chart, this category shows the largest usage of nuclear energy. There is no nuclear energy usage shown before 1980, and all other years indicate less usage than the year 2008.

43. **B. Passage 2 provides a counterargument to the claims made in Passage 1.** Passage 1 suggests that women from important families and wealthy positions were powerful, but Passage 2 counters that claim by providing examples of wealthy and important women who were swept aside by their respective husbands.

The correct answer is not Choice (A). The examples given are about two different claims.

The correct answer is not Choice (C). Passage 2 doesn't support the theory from Passage 1.

The correct answer is not Choice (D). There's no problem or solution in this text.

The correct answer is not Choice (E) because the examples are for two different suppositions.

44. **E. the role of wealth in determining women's social status for medieval European women.** Both passages discuss the role that wealth and power played when determining the social status of European women during medieval times.

The correct answer is not Choice (A). Only Passage 1 alluded to how some women attained wealth and power — through widowhood.

The correct answer is not Choice (B). Neither passage suggests that the objective of women during this time period was to acquire wealth and power.

The correct answer is not Choice (C) because the selection only refers to war as a way to explain how war caused many women to become widows.

The correct answer is not Choice (D). Neither passage discusses how effective wealth and power were, so much as it discusses the causes and then subsequent effects of it.

45. **C. women's life situations were a consequence of male attitudes.** Both passages give examples of how male attitudes about wealth and power directly influenced the lives of individual women, both positively and negatively.

The correct answer is not Choice (A). Neither passage suggests that women had any influence on men during this time period, other than as objects of wealth and power.

The correct answer is not Choice (B). The feelings of females were not considered important in the discussion in either passage.

The correct answer is not Choice (D). Men were not held to a consequence in either passage. They maintained control in both examples.

The correct answer is not Choice (E). Although this would apply to men, the same could not be said of women. So, this statement isn't the best answer.

46. **E. women had little to no say about their future courses, in regard to marriage.** The passage says that, although many women might have been left wealthy widows, they were often remarried without their own consent. So, they had little to no say about their future circumstances.

The correct answer is not Choice (A) because the author states that women were often remarried without their own consent.

The correct answer is not Choice (B) because the author gives no suggestion that men married *only* for wealth and power.

The correct answer is not Choice (C). Passage 1 does not give this example.

The correct answer is not Choice (D) because this is the premise of Passage 2.

47. **A. introduces a new concept.** In Passage 2, a new concept is introduced, the concept of a potentially powerful woman. Although the treatment given her is the same, this idea is different than in Passage 1, where women were forced to rely on men for attainment of wealth. Here, the queen could have her own power and wealth independent of a husband, but often still suffered the same consequence.

The correct answer is not Choice (B). No concessions are made that showed the original theory didn't hold up.

The correct answer is not Choice (C). There are no digressions from topic.

The correct answer is not Choice (D). The highlighted example doesn't anticipate an objection. It introduces, rather, a differing viewpoint on the same topic.

The correct answer is not Choice (E). There's no proposal of a new social hierarchy, for example.

48. **C. rescinded.** *Rescind* means to agree to something, then to take back or break the agreement. Here, Charles VIII had agreed to marry Margaret of Austria, but then changed his mind and broke the agreement.

The correct answer is not Choice (A). This is nearly an antonym of the word "repudiated."

The correct answer is not Choice (B). *Reprove* means to reprimand or rebuke someone. It's not the best choice here.

The correct answer is not Choice (D). By breaking the betrothal agreement, Charles VIII didn't actually marry Margaret of Austria and didn't then divorce her.

The correct answer is not Choice (E). "Acknowledged" is not a synonym or antonym of the word "repudiated." This word choice just doesn't make sense in the sentence.

49. **D. propose a creative approach for teaching history.** This passage attempts to challenge teachers to find something that will appeal to a modern student audience, such as the TV show or book series *Game of Thrones.*

The correct answer is not Choice (A). The purpose of the passage is a suggestion that history is better learned via new methods, not to underscore the subject completely.

The correct answer is not Choice (B). No differences are given. The purpose of the passage is simply to suggest a new idea.

The correct answer is not Choice (C). The passage is suggesting something not necessarily traditional, so it isn't a defense of traditional teaching methods.

The correct answer is not Choice (E). No admonishments are given, nor is there any indication that anyone would be opposed to such an idea.

50. **D. connections between false facts and teaching opportunities.** Although *Game of Thrones* might not stick to a strictly historically accurate script, rethinking false facts can actually provide opportunities for more knowledge. In effect, teaching how something isn't true can also result in positive gains in learning the subject.

The correct answer is not Choice (A). The example given is one that is shown as important to understand from a pedagogical perspective and isn't being attributed to a rookie teaching mistake.

The correct answer is not Choice (B). This isn't a modern cultural truism. This is an ancient cultural truism.

The correct answer is not Choice (C). The example is still within the discipline of history.

The correct answer is not Choice (E) because no modern beginning teacher would teach a "flat Earth" theory.

51. **C. parodying a famous scientific event in a student-produced drama.** One point of the passage is that history can be learned from the perspective of differentiating between truth and untruths. Being able to parody a famous scientific event means a student would have the critical thinking skills necessary to distinguish between truth and parody.

The correct answers are not Choice (A), Choice (B), or Choice (E). These choices simply use some aspect of pop culture to learn more about a topic. They don't require a student to correct any misunderstandings about a subject.

The correct answer is not Choice (D). Assuming a point of view would give a different perspective of a subject but wouldn't require the higher-order thinking skills referenced in the passage.

52. **A. how women have been subjugated because of patriarchal oppression.** Both paragraphs explain patriarchal oppression in terms of thinking in past times.

The correct answer is not Choice (B). No explanation is given as to why the oppression has been tolerated.

The correct answer is not Choice (C). No part of the passage exemplifies women who achieved glory and honor by rising above patriarchal oppression.

The correct answer is not Choice (D). An explanation is given of conventional thinking, but no definition.

The correct answer is not Choice (E). Although ideas from the past on femininity are discussed, no explanation is given as to how these ideas changed over time. The reader has to rely on their own understanding of the subject in order to understand this change.

53. **A. powerful women who still could not escape patriarchal ideas of what the ideal female should be.** All three women are mentioned to show that women were expected to conform to ideas regarding behavior and thought. Politics was outside the range of acceptable thinking for women of the time, even the queens and powerful women of the day.

The correct answer is not Choice (B) because the women aren't mentioned as having set new trends in ways of thinking.

The correct answer is not Choice (C) because it doesn't exactly make sense. A historical standard of women? *History* doesn't have a standard for how people should behave.

The correct answer is not Choice (D) because none of these women were models of these qualities. In fact, most broke the mold for being outspoken and forward-thinking.

The correct answer is not Choice (E) because no examples are given of how women subjugated others, only how women were oppressed by a male-controlled society.

54. **C. a narrow focus on political matters to only include acceptable topics as deemed suitable.** The author states that all matters of politics were seen as distasteful and better left to men.

The correct answer is not Choice (A). Women's prime purpose was considered to be with *only* domestic business and is clearly mentioned.

The correct answer is not Choice (B). The entire passage suggests all ideas of femininity had to be approved of by the masculine ideas of the time.

The correct answer is not Choice (D). The passage explains that any obvious sign of womanly intelligence could be evidenced "indoors" but shouldn't be seen by the larger, general public.

The correct answer is not Choice (E). The passage explains that the clearly defined role of femininity was mostly negative in tone and effect.

55. **A. Upper-class women were likely very highly educated and would learn to read and write, as well as speak multiple languages.** This true fact would not be used to show how women were kept under the thumbs of male oppression because this would show that women were capable of intelligence and independent thought not centered around running a household.

The correct answer is not Choice (B) because all these examples are centered around domestic business.

The correct answer is not Choice (C) as this certainly shows a purpose of domestic business.

The correct answer is not Choice (D) because this example also shows a woman's circumstances relying on male decision-making.

The correct answer is not Choice (E). Taking care of others still fits in the traditional and acceptable "female" pursuits of the time.

56. **D. Such oppression permeated the history and culture of the time period.** The author notes that the thinking of the time influenced politics, as well as books written during and even after the time period.

The correct answer is not Choice (A) or Choice (B). No comparison is made of femininity then and now.

The correct answers are not Choice (C). The opposite is true. Matters of politics were certainly influenced, as noted by the examples and how they were viewed with distaste.

The correct answer is not Choice (E). The author doesn't make or suggest such a claim.

Part 2: Writing

1. **C. behaved coward.**

   Although "coward" could perhaps be used to label each of the individuals in the scenario, it isn't an adverb. Rather, it's a noun. To modify the verb "behave," you have to use an adverb and not a noun. You could also use "coward" as a noun instead of an adverb to create a correct sentence. To be correct, the sentence might have read, ". . . felt every protestor behaved like a coward. . ."

   The right answer is not Choice (A). This is the correct way to show possession of the citizens who belonged to the town.

The right answer is not Choice (B). "Mayor" doesn't need to be capitalized. Although this is a title, it's being used more generally here, such as with the word "the" in front of it. Had there been a name after "mayor," it would have been capitalized.

The right answer is not Choice (D). Here, the hyphen joins two words that serve as a single adjective before the noun "transportation."

The right answer is not Choice (E) because there is, in fact, an error in the sentence.

2. B. legislation,

Because two independent clauses are given, a semicolon is needed after "legislation" rather than a comma. The sentence should read, "However liberally minded Senator Scott was, she couldn't agree with the proposed legislation; rather, the bill's premise was sure to cause great furor that couldn't be supported by either side unbiasedly."

The right answer is not Choice (A). "Liberally minded" is an adverb-adjective combination. The adjective "minded" modifies the noun "Senator Scott," and the adverb "liberally" modifies "minded." "Liberally minded" is not a compound adjective, so no hyphen is required.

The right answer is not Choice (C). This is the correct way to show the positive of "furor."

The right answer is not Choice (D). This is an adverb that modifies "supported."

The right answer is not Choice (E) because there is, in fact, an error in the sentence.

3. A. they would receive

Because the subject is single ("Neither"), the pronoun should also be singular. "They" is a plural pronoun and is not correct.

The right answer is not Choice (B). "Even though" is a conjunction and is used correctly here.

The right answer is not Choice (C). This is a correct subject-verb agreement.

The right answer is not Choice (D). The word "plethora" should be used with "of" to indicate what there is too much, or an abundance, of.

The right answer is not Choice (E) because there is, in fact, an error in the sentence.

4. A. a member

Because the description applies to multiple students ("all of the students"), there should be multiple members who wanted to join the ROTC. However, "a member" indicates only one member, which is incorrect.

The right answer is not Choice (B). The assembly could have emphasized patriotic duty, and this is represented in a correct way, grammatically speaking.

The right answer is not Choice (C). The preposition "except for" is used correctly here, not including the drama club members.

The right answer is not Choice (D). The subjective pronoun "who" is used correctly as the subject of the verb "were."

The right answer is not Choice (E) because there is, in fact, an error in the sentence.

5. B. Georgia

"Georgia" should have a comma after it because a comma is required after the state name. So that part of the sentence should read this way, ". . . Savannah and Atlanta, Georgia, . . ."

The correct answer is not Choice (A). An acronym can be placed in parentheses after the word or phrase it represents.

The correct answer is not Choice (C). A comma is necessary for closing the appositive phrase because it's preceded by a comma.

The correct answer is not Choice (D). You only need to capitalize "bachelor" and "master" when giving an official name of a degree, not the general degree.

The right answer is not Choice (E) because there is, in fact, an error in the sentence.

6. **D. fixing it.**

This is a vague pronoun reference. What, exactly, did Maude fix — the wiring or the lamp? The pronoun doesn't have a clear antecedent and is considered faulty.

The correct answer is not Choice (A). This is the beginning of an introductory prepositional phrase, in which the object is a gerund phrase, and it's correct.

The correct answer is not Choice (B). Although the wiring might be defective, this part of the sentence is correct and works.

The correct answer is not Choice (C). "Vintage" can correctly modify the "lamp."

The right answer is not Choice (E) because there is, in fact, an error in the sentence.

7. **B. no increase**

This sentence falls into the double negative category. When two or more negatives are used in regard to the same word, the meaning can be unclear, and two negatives used together cancel each other out to make a positive. Because this sentence has both "hardly" and "no," one of them must be eliminated for clarity.

The right answer is not Choice (A). Because "Philippines" ends with an "s" and is a proper noun, possession can be shown with just an apostrophe at the end.

The right answer is not Choice (C). There is no error as the verb "do" agrees with the subject.

The right answer is not Choice (D). This is a correct way to show possession of "world."

The right answer is not Choice (E) because there is, in fact, an error in the sentence.

8. **C. has been known**

Here, the tense doesn't agree. During his time, Alexander *had* been known as a radical and rebellious leader.

The right answer is not Choice (A) or Choice (B). Both tenses agree with their subject.

The right answer is not Choice (D). Again, the wording here agrees in number and tense.

The right answer is not Choice (E) because there is, in fact, an error in the sentence.

9. **A. tremendously**

This is a misuse of an adjective. The word "tremendously" is being used here as an adverb, but the adjective form is needed to modify "upheavals."

The right answer is not Choice (B). This is the correct word usage.

The right answer is not Choice (C). The word is a compound noun that's written as a single word without a hyphen.

The right answer is not Choice (D). Western Africa is a subregion of Africa that has defined inclusion of certain countries and is a proper noun.

The right answer is not Choice (E) because there is, in fact, an error in the sentence.

10. C. her

This sentence has a pronoun case agreement problem. Here, the pronoun should be the subjective form for Mary, not the objective form. So, this sentence part should read, ". . . neither Juan nor she . . ."

The right answers are not Choice (A), Choice (B), or Choice (D) because all are correct verb tenses.

The right answer is not Choice (E) because there is, in fact, an error in the sentence.

11. D. she wanted

The sentence is incorrect because it does not have parallel structure. Because the other forms include "–ing," this verb should, as well. So, this part of the sentence should read, ". . . and wanting to become . . ."

The right answers are not Choice (A), Choice (B), or Choice (C). All these forms are parallel and are error free.

The right answer is not Choice (E) because there is, in fact, an error in the sentence.

12. E. No error.

There are no errors in the sentence in terms of either word choice or punctuation.

The right answer is not Choice (A). Because the sentence begins with an introductory prepositional phrase that has more than four words, a comma is appropriate here.

The right answer is not Choice (B). The infinitive verb is used appropriately here.

The right answer is not Choice (C). Because the word "North" is capitalized, a reader should understand that this likely refers to a specific part of Boston. So, both words form a proper noun and should be capitalized.

The right answer is not Choice (D) because this is the correct past tense of the verb "burst."

13. C. dissimilarity between

The word "dissimilarity," because it shows a comparison, should either have a "to" after it or should have another reference in the sentence, such as ". . . the dissimilarity between her twin sister and her was unnerving."

The right answer is not Choice (A). This is the correct tense for the verb form "to bear."

The right answer is not Choice (B). The word "resemblance," like the word "dissimilarity," needs a "to" here.

The right answer is not Choice (D). This is an appropriate word choice and usage.

The right answer is not Choice (E) because there is, in fact, an error in the sentence.

14. A. Mowing

This is an example of a dangling modifier. It's unclear who was mowing the front lawn. However, the way the sentence is written, it appears as if the *snake was mowing* the lawn and sunning itself. Clearly, this isn't correct.

The right answer is not Choice (B). This modifier identifies which snake became alarmed — the one sunning itself.

The right answer is not Choice (C). This reflexive pronoun is referring back to the snake and is appropriate.

The right answer is not Choice (D). This past tense form of the verb "slink" is correct usage.

The right answer is not Choice (E) because there is, in fact, an error in the sentence.

15. B. adverse

This is an incorrect use of the word "adverse" because, although it does mean "unfavorable or opposed," it's usually applied to a *condition*, *situation*, or *event*. Instead, the word "averse" is needed here, which also means "opposed to" but applies to a *person*. The two words are commonly confused with one another.

The right answer is not Choice (A). This word doesn't need to be capitalized because it's a general use of the term and not used as a proper noun with the names of the senators.

The right answer is not Choice (C). The idiom "put forth" is used correctly here.

The right answer is not Choice (D). The preposition "of" goes with the word choice "possibility."

The right answer is not Choice (E) because there is, in fact, an error in the sentence.

16. D. among

The word "between" should be used instead. When referring to distinct and individual items, "between" is used; "among" is used to refer to general things. Because specific colleges are named, this is a mistake.

The right answer is not Choice (A). This adverb is used correctly.

The right answer is not Choice (B). The number refers to both the ACT and SAT verbal reasoning portions.

The right answer is not Choice (C). This is a correct use of the adjective "fortunate."

The right answer is not Choice (E) because there is, in fact, an error in the sentence.

17. B. is known

This part of the sentence has an inappropriate verb tense shift. Because the statement uses other verbs and situations in the past, this part of the sentence can't be in the present.

The right answer is not Choice (A). This is a correct use of the subjective pronoun "who."

The right answer is not Choice (C). Again, all tenses should be in the past.

The right answer is not Choice (D). Here, the word "traveling" is an adjective and modifies the word "hypnotist."

The right answer is not Choice (E) because there is, in fact, an error in the sentence.

18. C. home,

This involves a comma splice and is a run-on sentence. The two sentences should be joined here either by a semicolon or by a period and new sentence.

The right answer is not Choice (A). Although the two names are used interchangeably, putting the Latin form in italics isn't incorrect.

The right answer is not Choice (B). "War" does need to be capitalized because it is referring to a specific war and is a proper noun.

The right answer is not Choice (D). "Hence" typically begins a sentence. It is an appropriate usage here and is often followed by a comma.

The right answer is not Choice (E) because there is, in fact, an error in the sentence.

19. C. are

This is a subject-verb agreement problem. The subject ("state") is singular and should have a singular verb ("is").

The right answer is not Choice (A). The word "state" is used here as a general term, not as a proper noun.

The right answer is not Choice (B). Any compound-word from twenty-one through ninety-nine is hyphenated when written out.

The right answer is not Choice (D). This part of the sentence contains no usage error.

The right answer is not Choice (E) because there is, in fact, an error in the sentence.

20. A. than the symbol of the clown itself

Here, "itself" is correctly used as an intensive reflexive pronoun that serves to emphasize its antecedent, clown.

The right answer is not Choice (B). An intensive pronoun appears after the noun that it's emphasizing, which is "clown" in this example.

The right answer is not Choice (C). "Symbol" isn't the word that "itself" is referring to.

The right answer is not Choice (D). Intensive pronouns are used to draw attention to a word or phrase. So, although intensive pronouns aren't essential to the basic meaning of a sentence, leaving it out here changes the tone of the statement or the author's purpose, which was to draw attention to the relationship between the two words.

The right answer is not Choice (E) because this doesn't sound right. The pronoun occurs after the noun or pronoun it refers to, not before.

21. A. who is considered the father of architecture, ichnology, and paleontology, likely also invented

This clause must be separated by commas. The sentence itself is correct for subject-verb agreement in terms of tense.

The right answer is not Choice (B). "Leonardo Da Vinci" is the subject. Adding an additional pronoun is incorrect.

The right answer is not Choice (C). This choice involves improper verb form. A helping verb, such as "was," would be necessary to make the main verb of the sentence complete. Otherwise, "inventing" in this case would be a participle.

The right answer is not Choice (D). This choice also uses improper verb form. "To invent" has a *verb form* (a word that can be used as a verb in other contexts) in it, but it's an infinitive.

The right answer is not Choice (E). Removing the "who" from the phrase creates a verb phrase. A verb would not be separated from the subject by a comma.

22. D. and the ability to secure and manage energy and electricity while away from home, all the while saving

The word "home" should be followed by a comma instead of a semicolon because what follows the semicolon isn't an independent clause.

The right answer is not Choice (A). A semicolon should only be used to separate independent clauses. Semicolons can be used to separate independent clauses, but not to separate participial phrases from previous parts of sentences.

The right answer is not Choice (B). A comma needs to be used to set off the afterthought.

The right answer is not Choice (C). Adding an "s" to the end of "saving" changes it from a verb to a noun and doesn't make any sense.

The right answer is not Choice (E). The participle "saved" is improper in this context, and a semicolon shouldn't be used because what follows isn't an independent clause.

23. **E. HBO's *Game of Thrones* has reached an international fan base and has even been acclaimed**

The original sentence is simply missing the present perfect "has" in the second verb, which should be the compound verb "has been."

The right answer is not Choice (A) because of the missing word. Leaving it out creates an unbalanced and incorrect sentence.

The right answer is not Choice (B). This change creates a meaning change. There's no indication that an international fan base is *because of* the acclaim by critics.

The right answer is not Choice (C). This change causes the first verb to become part of a subordinate clause and the second verb to become a participle, creating a situation in which the independent clause has no verb. In other words, the result is a sentence with no main verb.

The right answer is not Choice (D). This change also changes the main verbs into other parts of speech (participle and infinitive) and creates a sentence that has no main verb. Furthermore, the change suggests that the critics' acclaim is due to the international fan base.

24. **A. The International Ice Patrol tracks icebergs globally, a practice that allows the monitoring of their origins and other ocean processes.**

The sentence is correct. The focus is on the pronoun "their" and what it refers to. This choice makes it clear that the icebergs are being monitored.

The right answer is not Choice (B). Here, it seems as if the International Ice Patrol is being monitored because "their" is referring to that organization instead of the icebergs.

The right answer is not Choice (C). Clearly a pronoun is needed to avoid word repetition.

The right answer is not Choice (D). The change makes it seem as if the International Ice Patrol has somehow gotten permission to do this task.

The right answer is not Choice (E). The change suggests that monitoring is a thing that tracks icebergs instead of being an activity.

25. **C. to protect against danger for those undertaking**

This sentence suffers from an error in parallel structure. Because "to safeguard" was used, the same structure needs to be after the conjunction. So, it would be "to protect."

The right answers are not Choice (A) or Choice (B). Neither choice corrects the incorrect parallel structure problem.

The right answers are not Choice (D) or Choice (E). Although the parallel structure has been corrected here, there's no reference for the pronoun "they."

26. **B. If visitors were to travel to the most eastern part of the western world, they would find themselves at Ilomantsi, Finland, a location sharing a 60-mile border with the Russian Republic of Karelia.**

This is the clearest, most correct, and most succinct of the choices.

The right answer is not Choice (A). This answer incorrectly uses a colon to separate the last phrase from the rest of the sentence.

The right answer is not Choice (C). Although most of the information is correct, the exact location isn't the border. This section puts most of the emphasis on the border, rather than Ilomantsi.

The right answer is not Choice (D). Again, the emphasis is on the border, not the exact location. This nuance affects the meaning.

The right answer is not Choice (E) because this isn't correct. Again, the location for the easternmost part of the western world isn't the border, but Ilomantsi, Finland.

27. **D. some recounting**

Of all the choices, this one best corrects the structure of the sentence so that the conjunction joins parallel structures.

The right answer is not Choice (A). The conjunction "and" doesn't join parallel structures.

The right answer is not Choice (B). A wooden pole doesn't have the *ability* to recount legends. This is just a poor word choice.

The right answer is not Choice (C). The word "and" isn't needed and doesn't join two events or things. Also, the structure is not parallel.

The right answer is not Choice (E) because, again, the conjunction doesn't join parallel structures.

28. **B. as well as**

"As well as" connects the two unique physical features of these fish — the growths that hang from their heads and the lanterns located on their fins.

The right answers are not (A) or Choice (C). The way they're written makes it seem as if the growths include the lanterns, which isn't correct.

The right answers are not Choice (D) or (E). The wording of both suggests that the fleshy growths act as the luminescent lanterns.

29. **C. Amy filled her mind with thoughts of a long and pleasurable night of relaxation in a tub with a good book.**

Because the pronoun "her" has been used, it must refer to Amy, not Amy's mind. So, this is the best choice.

The right answers are not Choice (A), Choice (B), or Choice (D). Who's finishing her calculus? Amy's mind? The pronoun references are unclear in these choices.

The right answer is not Choice (E). Although grammatically correct, it's long and awkward.

30. **D. had trained for months for the physical requirements**

She was training *for* the physical requirements. Also, the tense needs to be past participle because the event had already occurred before the filming of the movie.

The right answer is not Choice (A). The tense is wrong in this choice, and she wasn't trained *in* the requirements. This is just an odd word choice.

The right answer is not Choice (B). Again, the tense is wrong.

The right answer is not Choice (C). This change replaces the verb with a participle, causing the sentence not to have a verb.

The right answer is not Choice (E) because, again, the tense is wrong.

31. **A. No change.**

The word "while" is an appropriate choice to show the transition of such changes over time. Also, it's the only choice that's a coordinating conjunction, which is needed between the independent clauses.

The right answer is not Choice (B). This word choice means "but" and doesn't make the most sense here. Also, this word generally separates independent clauses, like with a semi-colon, or introduces a new thought in a separate sentence.

The right answer is not Choice (C). The information about today's society is not an example from fifty years ago. These are two different things.

The right answer is not Choice (D). This word choice means "so" or "therefore." The relationship between these two ideas is not one of cause and effect, but change over time.

The right answer is not Choice (E). This idiom shows two opposite ways of thinking about something. The ideas here aren't opposite ways of thinking, but changes over time.

32. **A. No change.**

Although the ideas are conjoined, these two can exist as separate and independent sentences. Of all the answer choices, this one is the best and most correct.

The right answer is not Choice (B). It's unclear who "they" are.

The right answer is not Choice (C). In this choice, it seems as if the product is making the goods.

The right answer is not Choice (D). Again, "they" has no reference, and the tense is wrong.

The right answer is not Choice (E) because there's a difference between goods and *the* goods. In this example, no specific goods are mentioned, so the article isn't needed.

33. **C. immediately after Sentence 6**

This placement makes the most sense. The previous sentence refers to goods, ideas, and information, and this sentence gives examples of both goods (food) and ideas and information (patterns of daily communication).

The right answer is not Choice (A). Sentences 3 and 4 are connected by topic, so this choice wouldn't make sense.

The right answer is not Choice (B). Sentence 4 refers to goods, and this sentence is about a different topic.

The right answer is not Choice (D). Sentence 7 talks about the price of such technology, and this sentence wouldn't elaborate on that idea.

The right answer is not Choice (E). Sentence 9 is a completely new topic, and this sentence wouldn't further that thought in any way.

34. **D. Replace "for all practical purposes" with "in effect."**

The words "in effect" mean this is one resulting effect of such actions.

The right answer is not Choice (A). It isn't actually practical for the government to spy on its citizens, so Choice (D) makes the most sense.

The right answer is not Choice (B). The sentence is connected to the one before it with a similar idea.

The right answer is not Choice (C). Here, the government is seen as the entity, not necessarily the people who make up the government. For example, lawmakers are not responsible for this effect of technology.

The right answer is not Choice (E). "Snoop" is a gentler version of the same idea, but the stronger "spy" is called for here.

35. **c. Replace "prompt" with "instantaneous."**

Something can't be *almost* prompt. It can, however, be almost instantaneous. This change makes the most sense with the topic.

The right answer is not Choice (A). The intent is that the information is being actually sold, not simply offered as a service.

The right answer is not Choice (B). The data includes more than just statistics.

The right answer is not Choice (D). The pronoun "it" directly refers to the idea presented in the previous sentence.

The right answer is not Choice (E). This sentence is needed because it further elaborates a point made.

36. **e. Replace "provided" with "so long as."**

Although the two can be used interchangeably, "provided" doesn't make as much sense as "so long as." This would be the best change to make.

The right answer is not Choice (A). The change would add an additional subject and make the sentence confusing and incorrect.

The right answer is not Choice (B). This revision would change the nuance of the sentence from something that's simply advantageous to something that has a monetary value.

The right answer is not Choice (C). "Everyone" doesn't just refer to the major shareholders; it would literally benefit every person involved. Besides, who would the major shareholders be?

The right answer is not Choice (D). This isn't a needed change and wouldn't drastically improve the sentence.

37. **e. location of the publisher.**

The publisher is located in Lexington, Kentucky.

The right answer is not Choice (A). The business address of the author isn't given in a citation.

The right answer is not Choice (B). The scholarly affiliation, or name of the publisher, is the second reference to Kentucky, the University Press of Kentucky.

The right answer is not Choice (C). There's no indication that specific games are being discussed as being more philosophical than others.

The right answer is not Choice (D). The book itself is the collected philosophies of this topic.

38. **d. A script of a speech that she wrote and delivered to the UN while running for president.**

A primary source is a first-person account written by the person who participated in and witnessed events. A text written by the person about their experiences is the only example that's correct here.

The right answers are not Choice (A) or Choice (B). Both choices are researched and referenced, meaning the information comes from another source.

The right answers are not Choice (C) or Choice (E). These two choices may give information that's more original, but they're still considered secondhand sources. In this example, only the words of Hillary Rodham Clinton are considered firsthand.

39. A. models showcasing the fashion on runways

This topic is somewhat related in that both are about fashion. However, this topic doesn't narrow the article focus.

The right answers are not Choice (B), Choice (C), Choice (D), or Choice (E). All of these are on topic and would narrow the focus of the article.

40. B. abstract

Abstracts appear at the beginning of a text and are used to help the reader quickly see the main points and purposes of the text.

The right answer is not Choice (A). A *bibliography* is a list of works referred to in a scholarly work. Bibliographies are usually printed as an appendix, at the end.

The right answer is not Choice (C). An *outline* is a general description of the plan of a work. It is usually not seen or printed with a text, but is used by a writer when organizing and completing the text.

The right answer is not Choice (D). A preface is found in a book, not a research paper. However, it does appear at the beginning and often gives the subject, scope, or aim of the work.

The right answer is not Choice (E). Although appearing at the beginning of a work, the table of contents doesn't provide a summary. It simply shows the organization of the work.

Argumentative essay

Take a look at the following essay written in response to Question 41 in Chapter 14. To score your own essay, flip back to Chapter 11, where you can find a checklist to help you evaluate your own writing.

It is hard to imagine a day without technology to accomplish even the simplest of things. An evening without power after a storm is the closest most of us get and those long hours with no quick access to electricity make the <u>Little House on the Prairie</u> book series seem more like a work of horror than historical fiction. Asking a young person to imagine a day without their cell phone would probably reveal it would be impossible to go an <u>hour</u> without those important connections to a cyber world. Have we, though, as a technologically-savvy generation become too dependent on technology? Yes, our generation *is* too dependent on technology and the negative aspects of the isolation caused by technology should be a cause for serious alarm.

Many would say that the word "dependence" is not nearly critical enough, that this generation has passed dependency and has, instead, become addicted to technology. Much research has been done to show that overuse of the Internet and overuse of technology leads to addiction. Those who overuse the Internet have the classic symptoms of compulsive behavior that is similar to gambling addiction and compulsive shopping. People who become preoccupied with the Internet and are unable to control their usage should be labeled "addicted," in the same way that people who are preoccupied with alcohol or drugs are labeled as addicts. Such addiction ruins lives and marriages, from the grandmother who spends her retirement savings by shopping online to the lonely teenager who visits online porn sites and resists interacting with the "real," outside world. This isolationism is translating into youth who never go on a date and only communicate with virtual mates online. MTV's Catfish, a reality show that brings together couples who have interacted, often disastrously, solely through technology, is this generation's Dating Game.

The rise of such "real-time" technologies, like Internet relay chat, live chat, and multi-user domains in virtual worlds are creating a generation of people who struggle to interact in social situation when confronted with a live person. This new technology will likely cause rising incidents of a new population, youth, who would regularly choose to use this technology and completely avoid interaction making interviewing for jobs, establishing stable relationships, and even simple friendships next to impossible.

Many would argue that technology is necessary for business and this argument is overgeneralizes American technological success. While technology can certainly improve work results, an overreliance on that technology can also result in technology addiction. The overreliance of something as simple as mobile email use can cause feelings of perceived work overload and increased examples of work-family conflict. The reliance of having email always handily available does not actually increase work performance; rather, it can decrease performance because of feelings of inadequacy. Checking emails and social media constantly throughout the day to see what "hit" can leave users feeling a disconnection from the world while amid a family or social gathering. Clearly, technology has skewed our vision of what the term "communication" means, a back and forth dialogue between people. Instead, technology has created a generation of introverts who only seek ideas and information and never hone the practice of imparting or conveying messages.

Today, we are dependent on technology for every aspect of our lives, from the way we get our news to way we pay our bills. The first thing most people reach for in the morning is the phone, either to silence an alarm or to fast-check what event might have happened during the hours allotted to sleeping. Breakfast is cooked with a microwave, the laptop is packed for a busy workday, and cars or buses with computerized chips drive us to a location where we once again engage in a virtual world. This discussion might be better argued with, "Can we even live without technology?" What part of you day is isolated from any type of technology? Realistically, perhaps only sleeping on a mattress in a darkened room is the only thing that remains.

While computers and technology are staples of the modern world, a balance must be reached between what is needed to enhance life and what becomes life-draining as far as time as resources go. The distinction between use and addiction is one that can be debated, but there is no doubt technology has taken over our lives.

Using the checklist in Chapter 11, here's why this essay would receive a score of 6:

>> **Introduction:** The introduction captures the reader's attention in two ways. First, it forms a connection with the reader. By asking you, the reader, to imagine a day without technology, a connection is made between the reader and the writer. For most of us, going without technology for even one day is impossible to think about . . . and yet, we also know this isn't necessarily a good thing. This connection with the reader is persuasive because the writer has already capitalized on common ground. Another attention getter is the reference to Little House on the Prairie. Because it was a popular book and TV show, the humorous point about it being a "work of horror" because of the lack of technology is appealing and starts the argument out in a way that doesn't alienate the reader.

There are grammatical and syntactical errors. So, although the essay isn't perfect, it doesn't have to be. The checklist doesn't require perfection, only a high degree of competence. Here, the writer's position is clear and well organized. There are strong supporting details and excellent use of grammar with a particular purpose in mind — appealing to an audience that relies on technology.

Source-based essay

Take a look at the following essay written in response to Question 42 in Chapter 14. To score your own essay, flip back to Chapter 11 and use the checklist to help you evaluate your own writing.

Both passages address the topic of animal rights with a consideration of what it means to have a "right." By human standards, most Americans probably would first call to mind constitutional rights — the right to life, liberty, and the pursuit of happiness given by our forefathers in the Declaration of Independence. These "rights," though, were lawfully and rationally designed for the purposes of government. Certainly the U.S. is not alone as all countries have laws that propose much the same thing. These rights were granted to humans by other humans, and the government has the duty to protect those rights. So, then, a right is anything that is morally good and justified as being worthy. A look at any major religion or culture across the globe from the beginnings of time will show that such rights are not new concepts, but are considered basics. The protection and reverence for life is a basic rule that humans, and animals, hold sacred.

"Animals hold life sacred?" you may be skeptically asking. The well-known phrase "protecting young like a mother bear" settles that question, but there are other instances of this sanctity of life in the animal kingdom. Mothers who wail and yearn for missing or dead young, colonies who spend lifetimes protecting one another, paired mates raising a family, and chimpanzees and elephants who bury their dead — all these are instances of the value of life placed on different species and are not just human concepts. A counterargument might point out the obvious kill-or-be-killed disposition found among species, both in the wild with lions and bears and in every backyard with mice and cats. However, the same could be said of man with his countless wars. Protecting the valued lives of ones held closest or for survival is not casting off the value of life, but another example of the extreme reverence placed upon it.

Singer insists that accepting this viewpoint of animals, only regarding the relationship they have with humans, is flawed thinking, and he likens it to the rationalization a racist brings to those acts and thoughts — the idea that some other thing can only be valued in comparison to me (Singer 2014). If we only look at an animal regarding how it will enhance or improve our own quality of life, we diminish that which we all hold sacred — the value of life itself. For at what point does any one human life weigh more than another? The judgment should not be on which life is more valuable. All lives, according to Singer, should be afforded that honor.

Regan also points out that the way we view animals, as an entity completely separate from ourselves, is inherently wrong. The assumption that animals are here for our own pleasure and enjoyment, as "resources," is a fundamental flaw in our reasoning (Regan 2014). Humans misunderstand the purpose for animals as a core concept because we can only understand the value in other things in relation to the value it brings to us. Once we start to view animals as something separate from our own "self aware[ness]," then we can better understand that an animal has its own separate value and a right to life (Regan 2014). Animals exist not to bring us pleasure, but for their own sake.

Regan uses the term "inherent" to qualify the value of life — both human and animal. This term insists that the value of life, then, is something that is essential to life itself (Regan 2014). This "inherent" quality emphasizes that the understanding of life value is one that is inborn in all life forms; it is an essential and natural instinct and one that has not been learned by humans over time through discourse and discussion. The conclusion, then, is that humans do not decide the value of life and therefore should not be taking life from animals.

Of course, the larger concept is what to do about such gleanings? Should man no longer have pets? Should we all become a vegetarian or fruitarian, eating only what nature can produce? Would the next discussion be directed to the nuances of a vegan or vegetarian lifestyle? Neither author proposes what to do after accepting the proposed viewpoint, and perhaps that acceptance is enough. To understand that animals should not be cruelly abused or used for sport might just be enough of a starting point for animal activism. Both passages promote the basic premise for animal rights — an understanding that all animals, human and other, are entitled to possession of their lives and that these interests should be affording respect and consideration.

Using the checklist in Chapter 11, here's why this essay would receive a score of 6:

>> **Introduction:** The introduction states the thesis right away and finds the common ground between the two readings. Comparing the ideas in the reading is crucial to this type of essay. Logical arguments will always win out over a great opening statement, a catchy title, or engaging lead. You can never go wrong presenting your case up front with a clear thesis. Right away, the reader can anticipate the rest of the essay.

>> **The middle paragraphs:** These paragraphs stick to the topic and support the thesis. It's important to give strong and specific evidence to support your points. Here, the writer gives strong examples from both readings with exact quotes that clearly connect to the thesis. And they're correctly cited.

>> **Conclusion:** All well-written essays should end with some kind of call to action, and this one is no different. Although the reader isn't encouraged to become a vegetarian overnight, the essay has given the reader something to think about.

Again, this essay isn't perfect. However, a high degree of competence is displayed, with evidence of a presentation of a thesis, discussion of the argument, and then conclusion of the main points. Using strong and specific language with sentence variety is always the key to moving your essay up the checklist.

Part 3: Mathematics

1. A. 43

Two interior angle measures are given for the top triangle, and that's enough information for you to find the third angle measure. The sum of the interior angle measures of every triangle is 180°. You can add the two given angle measures and subtract their sum from 180° to get the third angle measure.

$$180 - (38 + 93) = 180 - 131$$
$$= 49$$

Because that angle measure is 49°, the upper-left angle of the second triangle down is also 49° because those are vertical angles, and vertical angles are always congruent. You can find the number of degrees in the third angle by subtracting the sum of 49 and 47 from 180.

$$180 - (49 + 47) = 180 - 96$$
$$= 84$$

Because that angle is 84°, the top angle of the bottom triangle is also 84° because those are vertical angles. The sum of 84° and 53° is 137° You can subtract 137 from 180 to find the number of degrees in the third angle, and that is the value of u.

$$180 - 137 = 43$$

The measure of the bottom-right angle of the bottom triangle is 43°, so the value of u is 43.

2. B. 8.9

You can use a variable, such as x, to represent the minimum score and write an equation with it. The mean of a set of data is the ratio of the sum of the numbers to the number of numbers. You can write an equation in which that ratio is set equal to the minimum mean score of 9.2, and solve for the variable.

$$\frac{9.8 + 10 + 8.6 + 9.1 + 8.8 + x}{6} = 9.2$$
$$\left(\frac{9.8 + 10 + 8.6 + 9.1 + 8.8 + x}{6}\right)(6) = 9.2(6)$$
$$9.8 + 10 + 8.6 + 9.1 + 8.8 + x = 55.2$$
$$46.3 + x = 55.2$$
$$46.3 + x - 46.3 = 55.2 - 46.3$$
$$x = 8.9$$

A score of 8.9 for the final event would cause Joey's mean score to be 9.2, and anything above 8.9 for the final event would give Joey a mean score that's higher than 9.2. Therefore, 8.9 is the lowest score Joey can receive for the final event to get a mean score of at least 9.2 for the overall competition.

3. A. 4

First, multiply the two fractions by putting the product of the numerators over the product of the denominators.

$$\frac{8}{9} \times \frac{7}{2} = \frac{8 \times 7}{9 \times 2}$$
$$= \frac{56}{18}$$

Then, simplify the result by dividing the numerator and denominator by their greatest common factor.

$$\frac{56}{18} = \frac{56 \div 2}{18 \div 2}$$
$$= \frac{28}{9}$$

The numerator in the simplified form of the product of $\frac{8}{9}$ and $\frac{7}{2}$ is 28. To find the factors of 28, write its prime factorization, which is an expression of 28 as the product of all prime numbers.

$$28 = 14 \times 2$$
$$= 7 \times 2 \times 2$$

The factors of 28 include only those prime numbers and all of the products of combinations of them, and also 1. The only choice that is such a number is Choice (A). It is the product of 2×2.

4. **C.** $\dfrac{-15q + 15p}{2}$

The problem does not give enough information for the numerical value of r to be determined, but you can find the value of r in terms of the other variables by getting r by itself on one side of the equation.

$$4p - 2r - 4p = 5q - p - 4p$$
$$-2r = 5q - 5p$$
$$\frac{-2r}{-2} = \frac{5q - 5p}{-2}$$
$$r = \frac{-5q + 5p}{2}$$

You can multiply that rational expression, which represents the value of r, by 3 to find the value of $3r$.

$$r = \frac{-5q + 5p}{2}$$
$$3(r) = 3\left(\frac{-5q + 5p}{2}\right)$$
$$3r = \frac{-15q + 15p}{2}$$

5. **B. 2014**

The line graph drops from 2013 to 2014, and the drop is approximately 400. The only other decreases are from 2015 to 2016 and from 2016 to 2017, and both drops are clearly well under 400. The changes from 2012 to 2013 and from 2014 to 2015 are increases.

6. **D. 36**

This system has three variables but only two equations. However, the value of z is given, so you can substitute the value of z in for z in both equations and get a system of two equations with two variables. That is enough information for you to solve the system. The cube of 3 is 27, so the value of z is 27.

$$x + y + z = 40$$
$$x - y + z = 22$$

$$x + y + 27 = 40$$
$$x - y + 27 = 22$$

Next, subtract 27 from both sides so each equation will have only one constant. That can be done later, but the path to solution might be clearer if you do it at this point.

$$x + y + 27 = 40$$
$$x - y + 27 = 22$$

$$x + y + 27 - 27 = 40 - 27$$
$$x - y + 27 - 27 = 22 - 27$$

$$x + y = 13$$
$$x - y = -5$$

Because the coefficients of y are opposites, you can add the two equations to get rid of y. That will result in an equation with one variable. An equation with one variable can be solved, if the equation has a solution.

$$x + y = 13$$
$$x - y = -5$$

$$2x \quad = 8$$

$$\frac{2x}{2} = \frac{8}{2}$$
$$x = 4$$

Because x has a value of 4, you can substitute 4 in for x in any equation used so far and have an equation with one variable. Then you can solve the equation for y because the equation will have only one variable.

$$x + y = 13$$
$$4 + y = 13$$
$$4 + y - 4 = 13 - 4$$
$$y = 9$$

The value of x is 4, and the value of y is 9. The product of 4 and 9 is 36, so the value of xy is 36.

7. **D and E. (D) The survey method is NOT a proper procedure for determining the most popular political party affiliation at the university because the group surveyed is Libertarian and would work as a sample that only or mostly represents Libertarian Party affiliation. (E) The survey method is NOT a proper procedure for determining the most popular political party affiliation at the university because political parties other than the Libertarian Party would not be likely to be represented by the sample.**

For a sample to represent a larger group properly, it can't be a biased sample. In other words, it has to have reasonably close to accurate portions of the different categories that are represented in the data that's collected. The members of the Campus Libertarians are all or nearly all members of the Libertarian Party, so the portions of other political party members at the university would not be correctly represented. Therefore, the survey method described in regard to this question is not proper because the sample is not accurately representative. That makes Choices (D) and (E) correct. Those choices make basically the same point from different angles.

The reasoning described here also makes Choices (A) and (C) incorrect. Both of those choices say that the procedure is proper, which it isn't. By the reasoning explained here, the rest of the statements for Choices (A) and (C) are also false.

Choice (B) is false because it says that the Campus Republicans would be representative of the entire campus. That is false. No campus group representing a political party is politically representative of the entire campus.

8. **D. 34**

The first step is to divide 100 by 3 to get an initial picture of how many sets of three balls are needed.

$$100 \div 3 = \frac{100}{3}$$
$$= 33\frac{1}{3}$$

That is precisely how many sets of 3 balls are in 100 balls. However, an extra issue is involved in this scenario. The situation is not described as having any sets of tennis balls other than those that contain 3 tennis balls. There is no mention of containers with 1 ball each. Because of that, an entire container of three balls is necessary beyond the first 33 containers. That will make a total of 102 balls, but it is the only way to cover 100 balls. That means 34 containers are necessary.

9. **D. $\frac{5}{7}$**

The probability of an event is the ratio of the number of qualifying outcomes to the number of possible outcomes. Two 2018 coins and 3 coins from 2017 are in the can. That covers 5 outcomes that would qualify as what is described. Five of the possible outcomes qualify as picking a 2018 or 2017 coin. The number of possible outcomes is 7 because there are 7 coins in the can. Therefore, the ratio of the number of qualifying outcomes to the number of possible outcomes is $\frac{5}{7}$.

10. **A. 0.000000000106**

To convert a number from scientific notation to standard form, move the decimal point the number of spaces that is equal to the 10's exponent. If the exponent is positive, move the decimal point to the right. Move it to the left if the exponent is negative. In this case, the exponent is –10, so move the decimal point 10 spaces to the left. Keep in mind that 10 with a negative exponent is a number less than 1, so multiplying a positive number by it will result in a smaller number.

11. **B. 7.3706×10^2**

First, determine the value of w by getting w by itself on one side of the equation.

$$3.5w - 12.5 = 1,905.5$$
$$3.5w - 12.5 + 12.5 = 1,905.5 + 12.5$$
$$3.5w = 1,918$$
$$\frac{3.5w}{3.5} = \frac{1,918}{3.5}$$
$$w = 548$$

Next, find 34.5 percent of 548. You can put 34.5 percent in decimal form and multiply it by 548. To put 34.5 percent in decimal form, drop the percent symbol (%) in 34.5% and compensate for that by moving the decimal point two places to the left.

$$34.5\% \times 548 = 0.345 \times 548$$
$$= 189.06$$

Next, add 189.06 to 548 to find the result of increasing 548 by 34.5 percent.

$$548 + 189.06 = 737.06$$

That's the number you need to express in scientific notation. To do so, move the decimal point to where only one digit is before it. That's two places to the left. To compensate for moving the decimal point two places to the left and thereby getting a smaller number, multiply the result by 10 with an exponent of 2.

$$737.06 = 7.3706 \times 10^2$$

12. C. 6.5 inches

First, determine Gracyn's actual driving distance. She drove 7.8 miles to a store and drove the same distance on the way home. The total distance is therefore 2×7.8 miles, which is 15.6 miles. Because one inch on the map represents 2.4 real-world miles, you can divide 15.6 by 2.4 to determine the number of inches covered on the map.

You could also set up a proportion and solve for the unknown. You can use a variable to represent the number of inches of map covered. The proportion should contain two fractions set equal to each other, with each fraction representing inches to miles or miles to inches. Either type of ratio will work, but both ratios must have the same format.

$$\frac{1}{2.4} = \frac{x}{15.6}$$
$$2.4 \cdot x = 1 \cdot 15.6$$
$$2.4x = 15.6$$
$$\frac{2.4x}{2.4} = \frac{15.6}{2.4}$$
$$x = 6.5$$

Gracyn moves her pen 6.5 inches.

13. D. b^3

All of the choices are in terms of b, so solve for a in terms of b so that you can substitute the value in for a in the rational expression in the question.

$$ab = b^3$$
$$\frac{ab}{b} = \frac{b^3}{b}$$
$$a = b^{3-1}$$
$$a = b^2$$

Because $a = b^2$, you can put b^2 in for a in $\frac{b^5}{a}$.

$$\frac{b^5}{a} = \frac{b^5}{b^2}$$
$$= b^{5-2}$$
$$= b^3$$

14. B. $\frac{1}{3}$ yard

This question requires number sense. Specifically, it calls for ballpark knowledge of the measurements of common objects. The mean of a set of numbers is the set's average. The average tail length of house cats is 1 foot. You're not required to know facts like that, but you are required to have enough knowledge of common objects and measurement principles to approximate average measures of common objects and identify what measurements are far from them. The choices other than Choice (B) are nowhere near one foot. They are all outrageous. A foot is $\frac{1}{3}$ of a yard, so the correct answer is Choice (B). Choice (A) is a quarter of a foot. Choice (C) is equal to 5 feet and 4 inches. Choice (D) is 7 feet.

15. A. $y = 4x + 8$

You can write the equation of any line if you have two pieces of information: a point and the slope. Plugging both into the point-slope formula will result in an equation in point-slope form that can be converted to slope-intercept form. However, sometimes there is a shortcut. If you know the slope and the y-intercept of a line, you can use the slope-intercept formula and immediately get an equation in slope-intercept form. With the information given for this problem, you can figure out the slope, and the y-intercept is given. Because the x-intercept of a line is the x-coordinate of the point where the line intersects the x-axis and every point on the x-axis has a y-coordinate of 0, the line intersects the x-axis at $(-2, 0)$. The x-coordinate of every point on the y-axis is 0, and the y-intercept of the line in question here is 8, so the line passes through $(0, 8)$. You can plug those two points into the slope formula and determine the slope of the line.

$$m = \frac{y_2 - y_1}{x_2 - x_1}$$
$$= \frac{8 - 0}{0 - (-2)}$$
$$= \frac{8}{2}$$
$$= 4$$

The slope of the line is 4. The question provided the fact that the y-intercept is 8. You can plug those numbers into the slope-intercept formula, in which m represents the slope and b represents the y-intercept.

$$y = mx + b$$
$$y = 4x + 8$$

16. C. 8

The first sentence describes an equation. You need to translate the equation from English to math language. You can use a variable to represent the lower integer, and another algebraic expression involving that variable to represent the higher integer. Because consecutive even integers are always 2 apart, you can call the lower integer x and the higher integer $x + 2$. After you write the equation, you can solve it.

$$x + x + 2 = 3x - 4$$
$$2x + 2 = 3x - 4$$
$$2x + 2 - 2x = 3x - 4 - 2x$$
$$2 = x - 4$$
$$2 + 4 = x - 4 + 4$$
$$6 = x$$
$$x = 6$$

Since the value of x is 6, the lower integer is 6. The higher integer is 2 more than that, so it is 8.

17. 4

First, determine the least common multiple of 8 and 10 and the greatest common factor of 84 and 72. To find the least common multiple of 8 and 10, you can write the first few or so multiples of 8 and 10 and find the lowest number that's a multiple of both. Once you find the lowest multiple of 10 that is also a multiple of 8, you can stop writing the multiples of 10 because that is the least common multiple.

Multiples of 8: 8, 16, 24, 32, 40, 48, 56, 64

Multiples of 10: 10, 20, 30, 40

You can stop at 40 for multiples of 10 since 40 is also a multiple of 8. The least common multiple of 8 and 10 is 40.

Now, find the greatest common factor of 84 and 72 by listing all the factors of both. You can use the prime factorization of each to find their factors. Every factor of a whole number is the product of a combination of multiplying prime factors, except 1 is also a factor of every whole number.

Factors of 84: 1, 2, 3, 4, 6, 7, 12, 14, 21, 28, 42, 84

Factors of 72: 1, 2, 3, 4, 6, 8, 9, 12, 18, 24, 36, 72

The greatest number that's a factor of both 84 and 72 is 12, so the greatest common factor of 84 and 72 is 12.

Thus, what you are looking for in this situation is the greatest common factor of 40 and 12. You can write the factors of each number and look for the greatest factor they have in common.

Factors of 40: 1, 2, 4, 5, 8, 10, 20, 40

Factors of 12: 1, 2, 3, 4, 6, 12

The greatest number that is a factor of 40 and 12 is 4, so 4 is the greatest common factor of 40 and 12.

Note: There are other methods you can use to find least common multiples and greatest common factors. A quicker method for finding the greatest common factor of two numbers is to write the prime factorization of both and line up all instances of prime factors. You can multiply every instance of a number that is a common prime factor. The product will be the greatest common factor of the two numbers in question.

$$84 = 2 \cdot 2 \cdot 3 \cdot 7$$
$$72 = 2 \cdot 2 \cdot 2 \cdot 3 \cdot 3$$

You can see that there are two matchings of 2 and one matching of 3. Therefore, the greatest common factor of 84 and 72 is $2 \cdot 2 \cdot 3$, or 12.

18. B. 24

The probability of an event is the ratio of the number of favorable, or qualifying, outcomes to the number of possible outcomes. The probability that the name of a person from Mississippi will be drawn from the hat is a ratio of 15 to the number of people at the board meeting, the number which is the answer to the question. That ratio is equal to $\frac{5}{8}$. You can set the two ratios equal to each other in an equation. Because the number of people at the board meeting is unknown, you can use a variable to represent it. Then you can solve the equation, which is a proportion because it involves a ratio set equal to a ratio. When a proportion is true, the cross products of it are equal.

$$\frac{15}{x} = \frac{5}{8}$$
$$5x = 15(8)$$
$$5x = 120$$
$$\frac{5x}{5} = \frac{120}{5}$$
$$x = 24$$

The number of people at the board meeting is 24.

19. B. 3.09057578×10^8

You could put both scientific notation expressions in standard form, multiply them, and convert the product into scientific notation to get an idea of the answer (the question doesn't specify that the answer has to be in scientific notation), but there's a much easier way. You can multiply 3.2854 by 9.407 and set the product times 10 with an exponent. You can determine that exponent by adding the exponents of the two 10's.

$$(3.2854 \times 10^{15})(9.407 \times 10^{-8}) = 3.2854 \times 10^{15} \times 9.407 \times 10^{-8}$$
$$= 3.2854 \times 9.407 \times 10^{15} \times 10^{-8}$$
$$= 30.9057578 \times 10^{15+(-8)}$$
$$= 30.9057578 \times 10^7$$

That expression form isn't one of the choices, but if you put it in scientific notation, you get one of the choices. To put the expression in scientific notation, move the decimal point one space to the left so that only one digit is before it. To compensate for making the value $\frac{1}{10}$ of what it was by doing that, multiply by 10 by making the 10's exponent 1 higher.

$$30.9057578 \times 10^7 = 3.09057578 \times 10^8$$

That is Choice (B). None of the other choices are equal to it.

20. A. 3.14

When the order of a group of numbers is not clear, convert the numbers to the same form, such as fraction or decimal. In this case, decimal is probably the best form because using the necessary common denominator would be extremely tedious. You can convert a fraction to a decimal by dividing the numerator by the denominator. In decimal form, it's best to give the numbers the same number of digits after the decimal so that they can be most easily compared. However, you should not round up the last digit. You can put dots after it to indicate that the digits continue for numbers in which they do.

$$3.14 \rightarrow 3.1400$$
$$\frac{22}{7} \rightarrow 3.1428\ldots$$
$$\frac{43}{14} \rightarrow 3.0714\ldots$$
$$3.1415 \rightarrow 3.1415$$
$$3\frac{4}{21} \rightarrow 3.1904\ldots$$

These are those numbers in decimal form, from greatest to least:

$$3.1904\ldots, 3.1428\ldots, 3.1415, 3.1400, 3.0714\ldots$$

Therefore, the correct order of the number forms in the question, from greatest to least, is this:

$$3\frac{4}{21}, \frac{22}{7}, 3.1415, 3.14, \frac{43}{14}$$

The fourth number in that order is 3.14.

21. **A. 1.6 cups per minute**

You can write the given rate as a ratio and then convert it by writing the numerator in terms of cups and the denominator in terms of minutes, and then dividing. One gallon is equal to 16 cups, and 1 hour is equal to 60 minutes.

$$\frac{12 \text{ gallons}}{2 \text{ hours}} = \frac{12(16 \text{ cups})}{2(60 \text{ minutes})}$$
$$= \frac{192 \text{ cups}}{120 \text{ minutes}}$$
$$= \frac{1.6 \text{ cups}}{1 \text{ minute}}$$
$$= 1.6 \text{ cups/minute}$$

22. **E. $-7.81v^3w^4$**

First, multiply $9v^2$ by $-14vw^4$. To multiply terms with variables, multiply the coefficients and then multiply the variables. For any variable that's in both terms, write the variable with an exponent that's the sum of its exponents in the multiplied terms.

$$9v^2\left(-14vw^4\right) = 9(-14)v^{2+1}w^4$$
$$= -126v^3w^4$$

Like terms have either no variable or all the same variables, and every variable has the same exponent in each case. All such terms are like terms, no matter what their coefficients are. Thus, any term that's a like term to $-126v^3w^4$ contains v^3w^4 and no other variables. The only way two terms can be combined into one term is if they are like terms. The only choice with the variable and exponent combination v^3w^4 is Choice (E).

23. **A. −8.4 and B. (−1)⁹⁹⁷**

What's most relevant about the product of the factors in the question is that the product is negative. If 0 is not a factor, the product of factors in which an odd number of factors are negative is a negative product. If an even number of factors are multiplied and 0 is not a factor, the product is positive. In $(5)(-7)(2.3)(-17.4)(19)(-1)$, zero is not a factor, and 3 of the numbers are negative. Because 3 is an odd number, the product is negative. For a negative number to be multiplied by a number to get a positive product, the second number must also be negative. A negative number times a negative number is a positive number in all cases, and a negative number times a positive number is a negative number in all cases. That means any correct answer to this problem must be a negative real number, and that's the only requirement. Choice (A) is a negative number, so it qualifies as a correct answer. Choice (B) is also negative and therefore a correct answer. It's a negative number with an odd exponent. The odd exponent indicates that −1 is multiplied as a factor 997 times, an odd number of times. That makes the value negative.

24. **1,402**

Because the question asks for a number of inches, convert the first two distances to numbers of inches.

$$38 \text{ feet} = 38(12 \text{ inches})$$
$$= 456 \text{ inches}$$
$$13 \text{ yards} = 13(3 \text{ feet})$$
$$= 13(3)(12 \text{ inches})$$
$$= 468 \text{ inches}$$

The last distance was 478 inches.

The total distance is the sum of the three separate distances. You can use your calculator to add the three numbers of inches.

$$456 + 468 + 478 = 1,402$$

Ben threw the flying disc a total distance of 1,402 inches.

25. **D. 2.2**

The standard deviation of a set of data is the square root of the mean of the squares of the distances from the mean of the set of data. That's a lot to deal with at the same time, so we can break it down into steps. First, find the mean of the set of data.

$$\frac{11 + 8 + 6 + 12 + 8}{5} = \frac{45}{5}$$
$$= 9$$

Now, find the distances between each data item and the mean, 9. You can do that by subtracting each number from 9. Whether a distance is positive or negative doesn't matter because all of them are going to be squared.

$$9 - 11 = -2$$
$$9 - 8 = 1$$
$$9 - 6 = 3$$
$$9 - 12 = -3$$
$$9 - 8 = 1$$

Next, find the mean of the squares of those differences.

$$(-2)^2 + 1^2 + 3^2 + (-3)^2 + 1^2 = 4 + 1 + 9 + +9 + 1$$
$$= 24$$

$$\frac{24}{5} = 4.8$$

The variance of the data set is 4.8. The standard deviation is the square root of the variance.

$$\sqrt{4.8} = 2.19089023\ldots$$

That number rounded to the nearest tenth is 2.2. Choice (E) is the variance of the data set. Remember that you have to find the square root of the variance to determine the standard deviation.

26. D. 27

The sequence is geometric because each term is multiplied by 3 to get the next term. You could determine what the seventh and tenth terms are and then divide the tenth term by the seventh term to get the correct answer to the problem.

The seventh term is 729, and the tenth term is 19,683.

$$\frac{19,683}{729} = 27$$

There's another way to solve this problem: Because every term is multiplied by 3 to get the next term, the seventh term must be multiplied by 3 to get the eighth term, which must be multiplied by 3 to get the ninth term, which has to be multiplied by 3 to get the tenth term. That means the seventh term is multiplied by $3 \times 3 \times 3$ to get the tenth term. The seventh term is multiplied by 3 with an exponent that's the number of places from seventh to tenth. Thus, the seventh term must be multiplied by 3^3 to reach a product that is the tenth term. Since 3^3 is 27, the correct answer is 27.

27. D. Range

The range is 0 because 12 is the highest and lowest number in the data set, and 12 minus itself is 0. The value of all of the other four choices is 12. Choice (A) is 12 because adding 12 a number of times and dividing the result by that number results in 12. The average number in the set is 12 because it's the only number in the set. Choice (B) is 12 because 12 is the middle number when the numbers are in order (which they automatically are, no matter how they are arranged). Even with an even number of data items that are all 12, the mean of the two middle items would be 12. Choice (C) is 12 because 12 is the only number in the set and therefore the number that appears the most. Choice (E) is 12 because 12 is the only number in the set and is therefore the highest.

28. D. 510

For the stem-and-leaf plot, the numbers on the left are the stems, and they represent hundreds. The numbers on the right are leaves, and they represent tens. That's indicated by the key at the bottom. The mode of a set of data is the number that's in the data in the greatest number of instances. It's the number that appears the most. Because no stem is ever repeated in a proper stem-and-leaf plot, you can look at just the leaves and find the number that appears the most on one level of the plot. For the stem-and-leaf plot in question here, that number is 1. It appears three times next to the stem of 5. That means 510 is the number that appears the most and is therefore the mode of the set of data.

29. A. 6.05

The volume of a right rectangular prism is equal to its base area times its height. Because any face of a right rectangular prism can be considered a base and the accompanying height will be the remaining side measure, the volume of a right rectangular prism is the product of its length, width, and height, and it's irrelevant which sides are considered which. Their product will be the same regardless. The volume of the prism on the left, which is a cube, is $2.2 \times 2.2 \times 2.2$ m^3, or 10.648 m^3. If you multiply the two known side measures of the prism on the right, you get 1.76 m^2. If you multiply that by x m, you get a product of 10.648 m^3 because that prism has the same volume as the other one. The issue is therefore by what 1.76 must be multiplied to get 10.648.

$$1.76x = 10.648$$
$$\frac{1.76x}{1.76} = \frac{10.648}{1.76}$$
$$x = 6.05$$

The previously unknown side measure is 6.05 m, so the value of x is 6.05.

30. **C. Add $286**

Because Doris made the mistake of subtracting the price of the dress rather than adding it, she needs to add the price of the dress just to be where she was before the mistake. Then, she needs to add the price of the dress for the purpose of accounting for it. That means she must add $143 twice to fix the mistake and be back on track. That makes a total of $286 she must add to fix the mistake.

31. **A. Divide the resulting number by 4, subtract 7 from the result, and divide the difference by 3.**

In order to reverse the operation process, you need to do the opposite operation for every step, starting with the last and ending with the first. The last step of the described process was multiplying by 4. In order to undo that step, you must divide by 4. Then you will need to reverse adding 7 by subtracting 7. To undo multiplying the original number by 3, you need to divide by 3. At that point, you've reached the original number.

32. **C. How much time do residents at a nursing home spend reading the newspaper each week?**

To answer Choice (C), one would have to record how much time residents spend reading the newspaper. Some days and weeks would have different amounts.

Statistics is the area of math that deals with presentation and analysis of numerical data. Statistical questions are answered by collecting data with variability.

The answer is not Choice (A) because it's a matter of totaling wins and comparing; there's not much variation in the data. Choice (B) is simply yes or no, depending on the sample group of 16-year-old girls. Choice (D) simply requires giving a total number of years, and Choice (E) again only asks for a part of the total and isn't considered statistical.

33. **A. $8.25h + $1.45b**

Because Bethany makes $8.25 per hour just for working, she makes $8.25 times the number of hours she works, just for working. The figure that represents that part of her pay is $8.25h. In addition to that, she gets $1.45 for every bouquet she sells. She sells b bouquets, so the part of her pay that comes from successfully selling bouquets of tulips is $1.45 times the number of bouquets she sells. The term which represents that part of her pay is thus $1.45b. Therefore, Bethany's total pay for selling b bouquets for h hours is $8.25h + $1.45b.

34. **B. $\frac{1}{4}$ and $\frac{2}{3}$**

The lower limit of what the ratio can be is the low limit of j divided by the high limit of k. That is $\frac{10}{40}$, or $\frac{1}{4}$. The upper limit of what the ratio can be is the high limit of j over the low limit of k. That is $\frac{20}{30}$, or $\frac{2}{3}$. Therefore, $\frac{j}{k}$ must be above $\frac{1}{4}$ and below $\frac{2}{3}$. It cannot possibly be anything outside of that range.

35. **A. 9.42 feet/second**

To determine the speed of the merry-go-round's outer edge, you need to figure out the distance traveled by a point on the outer edge in one rotation. That distance is the same as the circumference of the merry-go-round. The formula for the circumference of a circle is $C = 2\pi r$. In this case, $2\pi r$ is $2\pi(7.3)$. Because the answer choices don't have π in them, you need to round π. That requires knowing its approximate value. It's an irrational number, so you can't calculate with its exact value unless you use a calculator with a π key, which the current Praxis Core calculator doesn't have. If you round π to four decimal places, it's

3.1416. You can use that rounded number — and in many cases, you can use 3.14, depending how close to the exact answer the choices require you to get. For the sake of this calculation, we used 3.1416.

$$2(3.1416)(7.3) = 45.86736$$

That's the approximate number of feet in the circumference of the merry-go-round. That number of feet divided by 4.87 seconds is the approximate number of feet per second the outer edge of the merry-go-round travels.

$$\frac{45.86736 \text{ feet}}{4.87 \text{ seconds}} = 9.418349076\dots \text{ feet/second}$$

The choice that's closest to that rounded speed is Choice (A).

36. **E. 70**

To find the median, put the numbers in order and then determine the middle number.

4 5 7 10 10

The middle number is 7, so it's the median. (If there were two middle numbers, you'd find the mean of them to get the median.) The mode is the number that appears the most, so it's 10. The product of 7 and 10 is 70.

$$7 \times 10 = 70$$

37. **E. E and F**

There was a 34.25 percent decrease from Day 3 to Day 4, so the profit level went from $94.28 to a number 34.25 percent less than itself. You can find 34.25 percent of $94.28 by converting 34.25 percent to a decimal, multiplying the result by $94.28, and subtracting that product from $94.28. The calculator for the Praxis Core exam math test follows the order of operations, so you can perform the entire calculation at the same time.

$$94.28 - 0.3425(94.28) = 61.9891$$

Matt's profit level on Day 4 was $61.9891. That number is between 60 and 70, so it's represented on the number line between points E and F.

38. **A.**

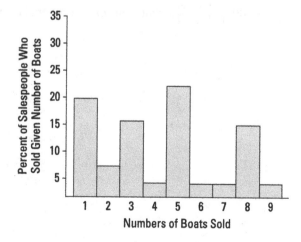

The bars of the histogram represent the percents of salespeople who sold each given number of boats. Because the histogram represents the sale numbers of 25 salespeople, each sale number is a portion of 25. For example, the number of salespeople who sold 3 boats is 4, so 3 appears in the table 4 times. That means 4 of the 25 salespeople sold that many boats. You can find the percent of salespeople who sold that many boats by dividing 4 by 25, moving the decimal point of the result two places to the right, and putting a percent sign (%) after the resulting number. An easier way is to simply multiply the number of salespeople for a given sale number by 4 because 25 times 4 is 100.

$$\frac{4}{25} = \frac{x}{100}$$
$$\frac{4(4)}{25(4)} = \frac{16}{100}$$

In other words, you can take any number of occurrences of a sale number (number of salespeople who sold that many) in the table and multiply it by 4 to get the percent of salespeople who achieved the sale number. You could also cross multiply and solve for x. This table illustrates the results.

Number of Boats Sold	Number of Salespeople	Percent of Salespeople
1	5	20
2	2	8
3	4	16
4	1	4
5	6	24
6	1	4
7	1	4
8	4	16
9	1	4

The only histogram that correctly represents those results is Choice (A).

39. B. $\frac{3c}{8}$

Because $a = 3b$ and $b = \frac{1}{4}c$, $a = 3\left(\frac{1}{4}c\right)$, or $\frac{3c}{4}$. That value of that rational expression over 2 can be calculated.

$$\frac{\frac{3c}{4}}{2} = \frac{3c}{4} \div 2$$
$$= \frac{3c}{4} \times \frac{1}{2}$$
$$= \frac{3c}{8}$$

40. **C. 979.2 m**

The area of the circular pond is $14{,}981.76\pi$ m^2. The formula for the area of a circle is $A = \pi r^2$. You can use that formula to find the radius of the circular pond by filling in the known values and solving for r.

$$A = \pi r^2$$
$$14{,}981.76\pi = \pi r^2$$
$$\frac{14{,}981.76\pi}{\pi} = \frac{\pi r^2}{\pi}$$
$$14{,}981.76 = r^2$$
$$\sqrt{14{,}981.76} = \sqrt{r^2}$$
$$122.4 = r$$
$$r = 122.4$$

The radius of the pond, rounded to the nearest tenth, is 122.4 m. The diameter of a circle is twice its radius, so the diameter of the pond is $122.4(2)$ m, or 244.8 m. The diameter of the pond is also the measure of one side of the square path. The perimeter of a square is 4 times the measure of one of its sides, so the square path is $244.8(4)$ m, or 979.2 m.

41. **D. 5,873 decameters**

You can see the answer to the question if you convert all of the measurements into numbers of the same unit, the easiest of which is meters because the other units are based on meters. To convert each measurement into meters, move the decimal point a number of places that's equal to the number of places the prefix is away from "main unit" ("1") on the Metric System Prefixes chart (in the section "Reasoning with Quantities" in Chapter 4), which (for Praxis Core purposes) has "milli" at the top and "kilo" at the bottom. Both of those prefixes are 3 spaces from "main unit," which is just "meters" in this case. You also need to consider which direction to move the decimal. There are fewer kilometers and decameters than centimeters and millimeters in any distance. Smaller units require greater numbers for equal distances. If you're converting from a greater prefix to a lesser prefix, the number must get bigger and vice versa. If the number must be bigger, move the decimal to the right. If the number has to be smaller, move the decimal to the left.

You can also think of the conversion process in terms of what you need to multiply or divide a number by to change to a different metric prefix. If you multiply or divide by 10, move the decimal one place. If you multiply or divide by 100, move the decimal two places, and so forth.

$$5.873 \text{ kilometers} = 5{,}873 \text{ meters}$$
$$5{,}873 \text{ meters} = 5{,}873 \text{ meters}$$
$$587.3 \text{ centimeters} = 5.873 \text{ meters}$$
$$5{,}873 \text{ decameters} = 58{,}730 \text{ meters}$$
$$58{,}730 \text{ millimeters} = 58.73 \text{ meters}$$

There are 10 meters in 1 decameter, so any number of decameters has 10 times the number of meters. That means a distance of 5,873 decameters is 58,730 meters. Multiplying by 10 is the same as moving the decimal one place to the right. Also, "deca" and "main unit" are 1 place apart on the Metric Prefixes chart, so the decimal point needs to move 1 place. It needs to move to the right because the number has to get bigger because there are more meters than decameters in a distance. The distance of 5,873 decameters is 58,730 meters, so it's the greatest distance of the choices.

42. E. $\dfrac{75-n}{2}$

Robert has 5 cents for every nickel and 10 cents for every dime he has in his piggy bank. Because the total amount of money he has in his piggy bank for only nickels and dimes is $3.75, which is 375 cents, what he has in the piggy bank can be represented by the equation $5n + 10d = 375$. With that equation, you can solve for d to represent the number of dimes in the piggy bank.

$$5n + 10d = 375$$
$$5n + 10d - 5n = 375 - 5n$$
$$10d = 375 - 5n$$
$$\frac{10d}{10} = \frac{375 - 5n}{10}$$
$$d = \frac{375 - 5n}{10}$$
$$d = \frac{75 - n}{2}$$

43. A. $j > \dfrac{28}{3}$

The answer choices are in the forms of solutions to inequalities. To determine the correct answer choice, solve the original inequality.

$$3j - 7 > 21$$
$$3j - 7 + 7 > 21 + 7$$
$$3j > 28$$
$$\frac{3j}{3} > \frac{28}{3}$$
$$j > \frac{28}{3}$$

44. C and D. (C) As Variable 1 increases, Variable 2 tends to decrease. (D) As Variable 2 decreases, Variable 1 tends to increase.

You can follow the numbers for Variable 1 in increasing order and see that the numbers for Variable 2 get lower over long enough stretches. However, Variable 2 doesn't decrease in every instance of a Variable 1 increase. Variable 2 merely tends to decrease as Variable 1 increases because it can take certain amounts of distance along the Variable 1 numbers to reach a decrease in Variable 2. Over long enough stretches, Variable 2 does decrease with increases in Variable 1.

You can see that more clearly if you draw a line of best fit through the data points. A line of best fit is a line that exists inside the group of data points. Such a line in this case would go down from left to right, and it would thus indicate that as Variable 1 increases, Variable 2 tends to decrease.

45. A. 11.125

You can convert all of the terms to improper fractions or decimals and then combine them, but you can also just use your calculator. The Praxis Core calculator follows the order of operations. Keep in mind that a fraction represents division of the numerator by the denominator. Also, it's important to remember that a negative mixed number is not the sum of a negative whole number and a positive fraction. It's the negative of the sum of a whole number and a fraction.

$$-2\frac{5}{8} + 17.5 - \frac{15}{4}$$

$$-2\frac{5}{8}+17.5-\frac{15}{4}=-(2+5\div8)+17.5-15\div4$$
$$=11.125$$

46. B. 2.3

The dot plot shows that 3 people saw 1 bird, 4 people saw 2 birds, 2 people saw 3 birds, and 2 people saw 4 birds. This represents the data as

1, 1, 1, 2, 2, 2, 2, 3, 3, 4, 4.

To find the mean of this information, simply add and divide by the number of people.

$$\frac{25}{11}=2.27\overline{27}\approx2.3$$

47. B. The interquartile range of the represented set of data is between 45 and 50.

The interquartile range is the distance from the first quartile to the third quartile. Those quartiles are marked by the edges of the box, and they're 30 and 70. The interquartile range is therefore 40 because $70-30=40$. Because 40 isn't between 45 and 50, Choice (B) is a false statement, so it's the correct answer.

The idea that Choice (B) is a true statement can result from thinking the mark inside the box is the interquartile range. That mark represents the median, which is approximately 49. Choice (E) is therefore a true statement. Choice (A) is true because the third quartile is 70 and most of the data in a set is less than the third quartile in all cases. Most of the data in any set is greater than the first quartile, so Choice (C) is true. Choice (D) is true because box-and-whisker plots display the beginnings and ends of sections of data but don't display means or even enough information to determine them.

48. A. {−7, −3}

The equation is a quadratic equation, and it is in quadratic form. Because you can factor the quadratic expression, you should factor it and use the factors to solve the equation. You can use reverse FOIL to factor the quadratic expression.

$$x^2+10x+21=0$$
$$(x+7)(x+3)=0$$

It's impossible to multiply and get 0 without multiplying by 0. That means either $x+7$ or $x+3$ has to be 0. You can use both possibilities to find the solutions to the equation.

$$x+7=0$$
$$x+7-7=0-7$$
$$x=-7$$

$$x+3=0$$
$$x+3-3=0-3$$
$$x=-3$$

Both −7 and −3 make the equation true, so they are its solutions. There are various ways solutions to an equation can be presented together. A very common one is to put them in braces, which are these symbols: { }. The other representations tend to be clearer to those unfamiliar with them. They're in forms such as "−3 and −7" and "$x=-3, x=-7$." The correct answer to the problem here is {−7, −3}.

49. 5.49

The diagram shows the measures of the leg that the two triangles have in common and the hypotenuses of the two triangles. The measure of the other leg of the smaller triangle isn't known, and neither is the other leg of the larger triangle. The value of p is the positive difference of the two missing leg measures. You can use the Pythagorean theorem to find both leg measures, and then you can find their difference to determine the value of p. You can use variables to represent the two unknown leg measures.

$$8^2 + x^2 = 10^2$$
$$64 + x^2 = 100$$
$$64 + x^2 - 64 = 100 - 64$$
$$x^2 = 36$$
$$x = 6$$

$$8^2 + y^2 = 14^2$$
$$64 + y^2 = 196$$
$$64 + y^2 - 64 = 196 - 64$$
$$y^2 = 132$$
$$y = 11.4891\ldots$$

The difference of $11.4891\ldots - 6$ is the value of p. The value of p is therefore $5.4891\ldots$ That number rounded to the nearest hundredth is 5.49.

50. D. 1:45 p.m.

The best way to approach this starts with determining how far apart the trains are at the moment the second train leaves the station. The second train leaves 2 hours and 15 minutes after the first one. That is $2\frac{1}{4}$ hours later. Because Train A, the first train to leave the station, is traveling 160 miles per hour, the distance it has traveled at 11:30 a.m. is $160 \times 2\frac{1}{4}$ miles. You can determine that distance by converting $2\frac{1}{4}$ to decimal form and multiplying 160 by it.

$$160 \times 2\frac{1}{4} = 160 \times 2.25$$
$$= 360$$

At 11:30 a.m., Train A has already traveled 360 miles. The question asks what time the trains will be 1,215 miles apart. The trains have another $1{,}215 - 360$ miles, or 855 miles to travel apart to reach that point. If you determine how long it will take for the trains to be another 855 miles apart, you can add that amount of time to 11:30 a.m. to find the answer to the question. From 11:30 a.m. onward, the trains will be traveling the same amount of time to reach 1,215 miles apart from each other. That amount of time is unknown, and you can use a variable to represent it. One speed times that amount of time plus the other speed times that amount of time equals 855.

$$160x + 220x = 855$$
$$380x = 855$$
$$\frac{380x}{380} = \frac{855}{380}$$
$$x = 2.25$$

When the trains are 1,215 miles apart, the time will be 2.25 hours after 11:30 a.m. You can convert 2.25 hours to 2 hours plus 0.25×60 minutes. That's 2 hours and 15 minutes. The time of day that's 2 hours and 15 minutes after 11:30 a.m. is 1:45 p.m.

51. B. 9.9 cm

Because one acute angle of the right triangle is 45 degrees, the other acute angle is also 45 degrees.

$$180 - (90 + 45) = 180 - 135$$
$$= 45$$

Because the two acute angles are congruent, the sides opposite them are congruent. That means the other leg measure is also 7 cm. You can use the 45-45-90 triangle rule (which says that the hypotenuse measure equals a leg measure multiplied by $\sqrt{2}$) to determine that the measure of the hypotenuse is $7\sqrt{2}$, which rounded to the nearest tenth is 9.9. You can also use the Pythagorean theorem to find the measure of the hypotenuse.

$$a^2 + b^2 = c^2$$
$$7^2 + 7^2 = c^2$$
$$49 + 49 = c^2$$
$$98 = c^2$$
$$c^2 = 98$$
$$\sqrt{c^2} = \sqrt{98}$$
$$c \approx 9.9$$

52. A and D. (A) 2. (D) 6.

A *divisor*, as the term is used in the context here, is the same as a factor. The question asks which choices are factors of 24 and 42. You can find the answer by writing all of the factors of 24 and 42 and seeing which ones they have in common. You can find the factors of a whole number by determining its prime factorization and then multiplying every possible combination of prime factors. Also, 1 is a factor of every whole number.

$$24 = 2 \times 2 \times 2 \times 3$$
$$42 = 2 \times 3 \times 7$$

Factors of 24: 1, 2, 3, 4, 6, 8, 12, 24

Factors of 42: 1, 2, 3, 6, 7, 14, 21, 42

The factors (divisors) that 24 and 42 have in common are 1, 2, 3, and 6. Because of those four numbers, only 2 and 6 are choices, they're the correct answers.

53. E. No reptiles are amphibians.

Every circle in the diagram overlaps every other circle, except the circles for reptiles and amphibians, which don't overlap each other. The absence of the overlap indicates that no animal in the world is both a reptile and an amphibian. The other choices are shown to be false by circle overlaps that exist in the Venn diagram.

54. **A.** $196p^7q^7r^{15}$

To determine the value, first raise what's in parentheses to the second power. To raise a power to a power, multiply the exponents. Then, multiply the result by what's before the parentheses. You can start by multiplying the coefficients. When multiplying a variable that has an exponent by the same variable that has an exponent, add the exponents.

$$4p^5qr\left(7pq^3r^7\right)^2 = 4p^5qr\left(7^2p^2q^{3\cdot2}r^{7\cdot2}\right)$$
$$= 4p^5qr\left(49p^2q^6r^{14}\right)$$
$$= 4\cdot49p^{5+2}q^{1+6}r^{1+14}$$
$$= 196p^7q^7r^{15}$$

55. **D.** **He stretched in place for 1 minute. Then, he gradually built up speed to walk 3 miles per hour over the next minute, walked 3 miles per hour for the next 3 minutes, and gradually built up speed toward a 6-mile-per-hour jog over the next minute. He then jogged 6 miles per hour for 3 minutes. Then, he gradually slowed down toward a complete stop in the last minute and stood in place at the 10-minute mark.**

The graph indicates time horizontally and speed vertically. It indicates that Dr. Fitz had no speed for the first minute of the warm-up, so he could have been stretching in place during that time. Over the next minute, he increased his speed to what corresponds to 3 vertically, so he increased his speed to 3 miles per hour. He maintained that speed until the 5-minute mark. That's why the graph is horizontal until it reaches 5 minutes. The graph then moves up toward a speed of 6 miles per hour until the 6-minute mark, after which Dr. Fitz maintains 6 miles per hour until the 9-minute mark (3 minutes later). Maintaining that speed is what makes the graph horizontal for that interval. Over the next minute, the speed is reduced until it reaches 0 at 10 minutes.

56. **A.** **316.128**

The table shows that there are 7.4 hiblems in 1 nochel and 4.8 nochels in one zerbert. That means there are 7.4×4.8 hiblems in 1 zerbert. There are 8.9 times that many hiblems in 8.9 zerberts, so the number of hiblems in 8.9 zerberts is $7.4 \times 4.8 \times 8.9$. The product of that multiplication is 316.128. There are thus 316.128 hiblems in 8.9 zerberts.

Answer Key

Part 1: Reading

1.	B	15.	E	29.	D	43.	B
2.	A	16.	D	30.	D	44.	E
3.	D	17.	B	31.	A	45.	C
4.	D	18.	C	32.	E	46.	E
5.	A	19.	D	33.	C	47.	A
6.	C	20.	C	34.	B	48.	C
7.	B	21.	A	35.	E	49.	D
8.	E	22.	C	36.	B	50.	D
9.	A	23.	B	37.	E	51.	C
10.	C	24.	C	38.	E	52.	A
11.	E	25.	B	39.	C	53.	A
12.	C	26.	B	40.	A	54.	C
13.	D	27.	A	41.	A, C	55.	A
14.	D	28.	E	42.	2008	56.	D

Part 2: Writing

1.	C	11.	D	21.	A	31.	A
2.	B	12.	E	22.	D	32.	A
3.	A	13.	C	23.	E	33.	C
4.	A	14.	A	24.	A	34.	D
5.	B	15.	B	25.	C	35.	C
6.	D	16.	D	26.	B	36.	E
7.	B	17.	B	27.	D	37.	E
8.	C	18.	C	28.	B	38.	D
9.	A	19.	C	29.	C	39.	A
10.	C	20.	A	30.	D	40.	B

Part 3: Mathematics

1.	A	15.	A	29.	A	43.	A
2.	B	16.	C	30.	C	44.	C, D
3.	A	17.	4	31.	A	45.	A
4.	C	18.	B	32.	C	46.	B
5.	B	19.	B	33.	A	47.	B
6.	D	20.	A	34.	B	48.	A
7.	D, E	21.	A	35.	A	49.	5.49
8.	D	22.	E	36.	E	50.	D
9.	D	23.	A, B	37.	E	51.	B
10.	A	24.	1,402	38.	A	52.	A, D
11.	B	25.	D	39.	B	53.	E
12.	C	26.	D	40.	C	54.	A
13.	D	27.	D	41.	D	55.	D
14.	B	28.	D	42.	E	56.	A

Chapter **16**

Practice Exam 2

I f you didn't get the starring role in "Acing the Praxis Core" when you took the practice exam in Chapter 14, you have a second chance here. Refocus, reexamine, review, and reassess the areas where you didn't score so well:

» Refocus by redefining your goal — to ace the Praxis Core.

» Reexamine the questions you missed on the first practice exam.

» Review concepts that you weren't clear on during the first practice test.

» Reassess — prepare to take the next practice test.

You must remember that this is a timed test. De-gadgetizing (setting aside your cellphone, the TV remote, and other such gadgets) is still a must — although you can use a calculator when you reach the math practice test. Make sure you're aware of the amount of time allowed for each section so that you don't spend too much time on one question. Don't leave any answers blank. Stay focused on your goal — to ace the Praxis Core.

TIP

This practice test is available online. (See the Introduction for instructions on how to access this book's online test bank.) After you answer the questions, you can review a summary of your performance on this test and any other tests you've taken. (We've included four unique tests online that aren't printed in the pages of this book.) This summary provides you with a snapshot of your strengths and weaknesses so that you know where you need to spend more time studying.

Answer Sheet for Practice Exam 2

Reading

1. Ⓐ Ⓑ Ⓒ Ⓓ Ⓔ
2. Ⓐ Ⓑ Ⓒ Ⓓ Ⓔ
3. Ⓐ Ⓑ Ⓒ Ⓓ Ⓔ
4. Ⓐ Ⓑ Ⓒ Ⓓ Ⓔ
5. Ⓐ Ⓑ Ⓒ Ⓓ Ⓔ
6. Ⓐ Ⓑ Ⓒ Ⓓ Ⓔ
7. Ⓐ Ⓑ Ⓒ Ⓓ Ⓔ
8. Ⓐ Ⓑ Ⓒ Ⓓ Ⓔ
9. Ⓐ Ⓑ Ⓒ Ⓓ Ⓔ
10. Ⓐ Ⓑ Ⓒ Ⓓ Ⓔ
11. Ⓐ Ⓑ Ⓒ Ⓓ Ⓔ
12. Ⓐ Ⓑ Ⓒ Ⓓ Ⓔ
13. Ⓐ Ⓑ Ⓒ Ⓓ Ⓔ
14. Ⓐ Ⓑ Ⓒ Ⓓ Ⓔ
15. Ⓐ Ⓑ Ⓒ Ⓓ Ⓔ
16. Ⓐ Ⓑ Ⓒ Ⓓ Ⓔ
17. Ⓐ Ⓑ Ⓒ Ⓓ Ⓔ
18. Ⓐ Ⓑ Ⓒ Ⓓ Ⓔ
19. Ⓐ Ⓑ Ⓒ Ⓓ Ⓔ
20. Ⓐ Ⓑ Ⓒ Ⓓ Ⓔ
21. Ⓐ Ⓑ Ⓒ Ⓓ Ⓔ
22. Ⓐ Ⓑ Ⓒ Ⓓ Ⓔ
23. Ⓐ Ⓑ Ⓒ Ⓓ Ⓔ
24. Ⓐ Ⓑ Ⓒ Ⓓ Ⓔ
25. Ⓐ Ⓑ Ⓒ Ⓓ Ⓔ
26. Ⓐ Ⓑ Ⓒ Ⓓ Ⓔ
27. Ⓐ Ⓑ Ⓒ Ⓓ Ⓔ
28. Ⓐ Ⓑ Ⓒ Ⓓ Ⓔ
29. Ⓐ Ⓑ Ⓒ Ⓓ Ⓔ
30. Ⓐ Ⓑ Ⓒ Ⓓ Ⓔ
31. Ⓐ Ⓑ Ⓒ Ⓓ Ⓔ
32. Ⓐ Ⓑ Ⓒ Ⓓ Ⓔ
33. Ⓐ Ⓑ Ⓒ Ⓓ Ⓔ
34. Ⓐ Ⓑ Ⓒ Ⓓ Ⓔ
35. Ⓐ Ⓑ Ⓒ Ⓓ Ⓔ
36. Ⓐ Ⓑ Ⓒ Ⓓ Ⓔ
37. Ⓐ Ⓑ Ⓒ Ⓓ Ⓔ
38. Ⓐ Ⓑ Ⓒ Ⓓ Ⓔ
39. Ⓐ Ⓑ Ⓒ Ⓓ Ⓔ
40. Ⓐ Ⓑ Ⓒ Ⓓ Ⓔ
41. Ⓐ Ⓑ Ⓒ Ⓓ Ⓔ
42. Ⓐ Ⓑ Ⓒ Ⓓ Ⓔ
43. Ⓐ Ⓑ Ⓒ Ⓓ Ⓔ
44. Ⓐ Ⓑ Ⓒ Ⓓ Ⓔ
45. Ⓐ Ⓑ Ⓒ Ⓓ Ⓔ
46. Ⓐ Ⓑ Ⓒ Ⓓ Ⓔ
47. _____
48. Ⓐ Ⓑ Ⓒ Ⓓ Ⓔ
49. Ⓐ Ⓑ Ⓒ Ⓓ Ⓔ
50. Ⓐ Ⓑ Ⓒ Ⓓ Ⓔ
51. Ⓐ Ⓑ Ⓒ Ⓓ Ⓔ
52. Ⓐ Ⓑ Ⓒ Ⓓ Ⓔ
53. Ⓐ Ⓑ Ⓒ Ⓓ Ⓔ
54. Ⓐ Ⓑ Ⓒ Ⓓ Ⓔ
55. Ⓐ Ⓑ Ⓒ Ⓓ Ⓔ
56. Ⓐ Ⓑ Ⓒ Ⓓ Ⓔ

Writing

1. Ⓐ Ⓑ Ⓒ Ⓓ Ⓔ
2. Ⓐ Ⓑ Ⓒ Ⓓ Ⓔ
3. Ⓐ Ⓑ Ⓒ Ⓓ Ⓔ
4. Ⓐ Ⓑ Ⓒ Ⓓ Ⓔ
5. Ⓐ Ⓑ Ⓒ Ⓓ Ⓔ
6. Ⓐ Ⓑ Ⓒ Ⓓ Ⓔ
7. Ⓐ Ⓑ Ⓒ Ⓓ Ⓔ
8. Ⓐ Ⓑ Ⓒ Ⓓ Ⓔ
9. Ⓐ Ⓑ Ⓒ Ⓓ Ⓔ
10. Ⓐ Ⓑ Ⓒ Ⓓ Ⓔ
11. Ⓐ Ⓑ Ⓒ Ⓓ Ⓔ
12. Ⓐ Ⓑ Ⓒ Ⓓ Ⓔ
13. Ⓐ Ⓑ Ⓒ Ⓓ Ⓔ
14. Ⓐ Ⓑ Ⓒ Ⓓ Ⓔ
15. Ⓐ Ⓑ Ⓒ Ⓓ Ⓔ
16. Ⓐ Ⓑ Ⓒ Ⓓ Ⓔ
17. Ⓐ Ⓑ Ⓒ Ⓓ Ⓔ
18. Ⓐ Ⓑ Ⓒ Ⓓ Ⓔ
19. Ⓐ Ⓑ Ⓒ Ⓓ Ⓔ
20. Ⓐ Ⓑ Ⓒ Ⓓ Ⓔ
21. Ⓐ Ⓑ Ⓒ Ⓓ Ⓔ
22. Ⓐ Ⓑ Ⓒ Ⓓ Ⓔ
23. Ⓐ Ⓑ Ⓒ Ⓓ Ⓔ
24. Ⓐ Ⓑ Ⓒ Ⓓ Ⓔ
25. Ⓐ Ⓑ Ⓒ Ⓓ Ⓔ
26. Ⓐ Ⓑ Ⓒ Ⓓ Ⓔ
27. Ⓐ Ⓑ Ⓒ Ⓓ Ⓔ
28. Ⓐ Ⓑ Ⓒ Ⓓ Ⓔ
29. Ⓐ Ⓑ Ⓒ Ⓓ Ⓔ
30. Ⓐ Ⓑ Ⓒ Ⓓ Ⓔ
31. Ⓐ Ⓑ Ⓒ Ⓓ Ⓔ
32. Ⓐ Ⓑ Ⓒ Ⓓ Ⓔ
33. Ⓐ Ⓑ Ⓒ Ⓓ Ⓔ
34. Ⓐ Ⓑ Ⓒ Ⓓ Ⓔ
35. Ⓐ Ⓑ Ⓒ Ⓓ Ⓔ
36. Ⓐ Ⓑ Ⓒ Ⓓ Ⓔ
37. Ⓐ Ⓑ Ⓒ Ⓓ Ⓔ
38. Ⓐ Ⓑ Ⓒ Ⓓ Ⓔ
39. Ⓐ Ⓑ Ⓒ Ⓓ Ⓔ
40. Ⓐ Ⓑ Ⓒ Ⓓ Ⓔ

Math

1. Ⓐ Ⓑ Ⓒ Ⓓ Ⓔ
2. Ⓐ Ⓑ Ⓒ Ⓓ Ⓔ
3. Ⓐ Ⓑ Ⓒ Ⓓ Ⓔ
4. Ⓐ Ⓑ Ⓒ Ⓓ Ⓔ
5. Ⓐ Ⓑ Ⓒ Ⓓ Ⓔ
6. Ⓐ Ⓑ Ⓒ Ⓓ Ⓔ
7. Ⓐ Ⓑ Ⓒ Ⓓ Ⓔ
8. Ⓐ Ⓑ Ⓒ Ⓓ Ⓔ
9. Ⓐ Ⓑ Ⓒ Ⓓ Ⓔ
10. Ⓐ Ⓑ Ⓒ Ⓓ Ⓔ
11. Ⓐ Ⓑ Ⓒ Ⓓ Ⓔ
12. Ⓐ Ⓑ Ⓒ Ⓓ Ⓔ
13. Ⓐ Ⓑ Ⓒ Ⓓ Ⓔ
14. Ⓐ Ⓑ Ⓒ Ⓓ Ⓔ
15. Ⓐ Ⓑ Ⓒ Ⓓ Ⓔ
16. Ⓐ Ⓑ Ⓒ Ⓓ Ⓔ
17. Ⓐ Ⓑ Ⓒ Ⓓ Ⓔ
18. Ⓐ Ⓑ Ⓒ Ⓓ Ⓔ
19. Ⓐ Ⓑ Ⓒ Ⓓ Ⓔ
20. Ⓐ Ⓑ Ⓒ Ⓓ Ⓔ
21. Ⓐ Ⓑ Ⓒ Ⓓ Ⓔ
22. Ⓐ Ⓑ Ⓒ Ⓓ Ⓔ
23. Ⓐ Ⓑ Ⓒ Ⓓ Ⓔ
24. Ⓐ Ⓑ Ⓒ Ⓓ Ⓔ
25. Ⓐ Ⓑ Ⓒ Ⓓ Ⓔ
26. Ⓐ Ⓑ Ⓒ Ⓓ Ⓔ
27. Ⓐ Ⓑ Ⓒ Ⓓ Ⓔ
28. Ⓐ Ⓑ Ⓒ Ⓓ Ⓔ
29. Ⓐ Ⓑ Ⓒ Ⓓ Ⓔ
30. Ⓐ Ⓑ Ⓒ Ⓓ Ⓔ
31. Ⓐ Ⓑ Ⓒ Ⓓ Ⓔ
32. Ⓐ Ⓑ Ⓒ Ⓓ Ⓔ
33. _____
34. Ⓐ Ⓑ Ⓒ Ⓓ Ⓔ
35. Ⓐ Ⓑ Ⓒ Ⓓ Ⓔ
36. Ⓐ Ⓑ Ⓒ Ⓓ Ⓔ
37. Ⓐ Ⓑ Ⓒ Ⓓ Ⓔ
38. Ⓐ Ⓑ Ⓒ Ⓓ Ⓔ
39. Ⓐ Ⓑ Ⓒ Ⓓ Ⓔ
40. Ⓐ Ⓑ Ⓒ Ⓓ Ⓔ
41. Ⓐ Ⓑ Ⓒ Ⓓ Ⓔ
42. Ⓐ Ⓑ Ⓒ Ⓓ Ⓔ
43. Ⓐ Ⓑ Ⓒ Ⓓ Ⓔ
44. Ⓐ Ⓑ Ⓒ Ⓓ Ⓔ
45. Ⓐ Ⓑ Ⓒ Ⓓ Ⓔ
46. Ⓐ Ⓑ Ⓒ Ⓓ Ⓔ
47. Ⓐ Ⓑ Ⓒ Ⓓ Ⓔ
48. Ⓐ Ⓑ Ⓒ Ⓓ Ⓔ
49. Ⓐ Ⓑ Ⓒ Ⓓ Ⓔ
50. Ⓐ Ⓑ Ⓒ Ⓓ Ⓔ
51. Ⓐ Ⓑ Ⓒ Ⓓ Ⓔ
52. Ⓐ Ⓑ Ⓒ Ⓓ Ⓔ
53. Ⓐ Ⓑ Ⓒ Ⓓ Ⓔ
54. Ⓐ Ⓑ Ⓒ Ⓓ Ⓔ
55. Ⓐ Ⓑ Ⓒ Ⓓ Ⓔ
56. Ⓐ Ⓑ Ⓒ Ⓓ Ⓔ

Part 1: Reading

TIME: 85 minutes for 56 questions

DIRECTIONS: Each statement or passage in this test is followed by a selected-response question or questions based on its content. After reading a statement or passage, choose the best answer or answers to each question from among the choices given. Answer all questions following a statement or passage on the basis of what is *stated* or *implied* in that statement or passage; you are not expected to have any previous knowledge of the topics presented in the statements and passages. Remember, try to answer every question.

People often comment on the irony of the fact that Alfred Nobel, the man who endowed the famous Nobel Prizes, spent his life inventing military explosives (including dynamite). Fewer people, however, know how directly related Nobel's two legacies actually are: When a French newspaper believed him dead and mistakenly printed his obituary in 1888, Nobel was horrified to see himself referred to as "the merchant of death." In an effort to make amends for the harm his inventions had caused, he changed his will, leaving nearly his entire estate to endow the famous prizes in Peace, Literature, and various natural sciences that now bear his name.

1. According to the passage, Alfred Nobel endowed the Nobel Prizes in an effort to

    (A) make more money.

    (B) prolong his life.

    (C) conceal other things he had done.

    (D) ensure that his name would live forever.

    (E) change his legacy.

It's certainly an exciting time for killer whales, or at least for the marine biologists who study them. Only in the last couple of decades has genetic testing revealed killer whales to be a large species of dolphin, much more closely related to those cute fellows than to the larger whales. We've also learned that at least three, and possibly as many as six, subspecies of killer whales diverged from one another around two million years ago, and all have distinct markings, diets, and systems of communication. Even the name *killer whale* is falling out of fashion; most scientists now prefer to use the term *orca*.

2. The primary purpose of the passage is to

    (A) explain how killer whale subspecies diverged from one another.

    (B) explore the ways in which scientists and the general public see killer whales differently.

    (C) report on new and exciting discoveries about killer whales.

    (D) argue that people should use the term *orca* instead of *killer whale*.

    (E) humorously humanize killer whales for an audience of schoolchildren.

The archaeological excavation of Göbekli Tepe in southeastern Turkey in the 1990s revolutionized our knowledge about early human civilization. The site's stone pillars are not only larger and heavier than those at the more famous Stonehenge in England but also have meticulous artworks carved into them that are clearly the work of specialist craftsmen. The place was obviously labored over in a highly organized fashion for many years, beginning around 10,000 BCE, and yet it contains no residences or any evidence of permanent human habitation; humans had not yet invented agriculture and were still nomadic, so Göbekli Tepe must have been a place of worship to which people returned at important times of the year. This is the first confirmation that early humans built elaborate structures for their gods before they even built permanent homes for themselves.

GO ON TO NEXT PAGE

3. According to the passage, the theory that Göbekli Tepe was a religious site rests primarily on

(A) the fact that it is so large.

(B) the elaborate nature of its artwork.

(C) evidence that nobody actually lived there.

(D) the close resemblance it bears to Stonehenge.

(E) its role in the invention of agriculture.

Questions 4 through 6 are based on the following passage.

Often named as one of the greatest female sculptors of all time, Malvina Hoffman was born in New York City in 1887. Early in her career, she studied under the famous Auguste Rodin, as well as with Gutzon Borglum, the Danish-American who would go on to create Mount Rushmore. Hoffman's crowning achievement was a series of bronze sculptures, commissioned by the Field Museum of Natural History in Chicago, exploring physical and cultural differences among humans. She traveled extensively in order to study her subjects in life and eventually produced 105 spectacularly detailed and lifelike pieces depicting people from all over the world. Hoffman's sculptures were a centerpiece of the 1933 Chicago World's Fair, and an entire hall at the Field Museum was dedicated to their subsequent display. By the 1960s, however, the notion of physical differences among various types of humans had become a touchy subject; some argued that Hoffman's work was racist. Three years after her death in 1966, the Field Museum moved most of Hoffman's work into basement storage. A few pieces remain displayed without fanfare in select corners of the museum, but the vast majority of the masterpiece collection of this pioneering female artistic genius has not been seen in nearly 50 years.

4. The primary purpose of the passage is to

(A) offer a professional and personal biography of Malvina Hoffman.

(B) argue that it was wrong of the Field Museum to move Hoffman's work into storage.

(C) explain why some people were offended by Hoffman's sculptures.

(D) inform readers about Hoffman and the controversy surrounding her work.

(E) raise questions about why there aren't more famous female sculptors.

5. The author most probably uses the word *pioneering* in the final sentence to mean

(A) trailblazing.

(B) controversial.

(C) rebellious.

(D) perceptive.

(E) hardworking.

6. The paradox raised by the passage concerns the need to balance

(A) the cultural values of the past with those of the future.

(B) multicultural sensitivity with celebration of the achievements of women.

(C) scientific approaches to deep questions with artistic approaches to them.

(D) intentionalist artistic criticism with interpretive artistic criticism.

(E) the mission of a museum with the values of the public.

Questions 7 through 11 are based on the following passage.

Everyone knows that the Renaissance was an explosion of artistic brilliance and scientific advancement in the Europe of the 15th and 16th centuries and that it was especially welcome after the preceding centuries of ignorance and violent political oppression now referred to as the Dark Ages. But why did the Renaissance happen when it did? For that matter, why did it happen at all? Believe it or not, this European golden age we call the Renaissance may simply be the term we've given to the direct aftereffects of Europe's worst nightmare: the Black Plague.

Line

(05)

(10)

Originating in the plains of central Asia, the
Black Death hit Europe in 1347, when merchant
(15) ships laden with Asian goods landed in southern
Italy, unwittingly bringing along the rats whose
fleas carried the deadly plague bacteria. By the end
of the century, more than 50 percent of Europe's
total population had died. This time must have
(20) been indescribably horrific to live through, but
those who did were changed by the experience:
Desperation to stop the devastation had gotten
people thinking seriously about science and
medicine, and daily confrontation with so much
(25) death focused their hearts and minds on the
human experience and the things that made life
worth living. Perhaps most importantly, the Black
Death meant the collapse of the feudal system. The
masses of commoners who had been bound to work
(30) the lands of their lords as serfs had been too badly
annihilated for the arrangement to remain feasible.
The survivors were allowed to buy their freedom
and go into business for themselves as skilled
tradesmen, leading to the emergence of a middle
(35) class and the birth of our modern free-market
economic system. In a multitude of ways, human
life was suddenly more valuable than ever before.

7. Which of the following best describes the purpose and organization of the passage?

(A) It examines a familiar concept from an
unorthodox viewpoint.

(B) It challenges a traditional explanation
via a conspiracy theory.

(C) It walks a fine line between the two sides
of a controversy.

(D) It compares and contrasts the art of two
different periods.

(E) It scientifically analyzes the origins of an
epidemic.

8. When the author says in Line 25 that the Black
Death "focused their hearts and minds on
the human experience," he is likely alluding
to which phenomenon mentioned in the first
paragraph?

(A) "artistic brilliance"

(B) "scientific advancement"

(C) "violent political oppression"

(D) "this European golden age"

(E) "Europe's worst nightmare"

9. As used in Line 31, "feasible" most nearly
means

(A) lucrative.

(B) legal.

(C) ethical.

(D) comprehensible.

(E) coherent.

10. According to the passage, which of the following was indicated as a reason for the collapse
of the feudal economic system of the Middle
Ages?

(A) New philosophies led people in power to
consider issues of social justice.

(B) Scientific discoveries led to a wider range
of job options for the middle class.

(C) Laborers became so scarce that they
were in a better bargaining position.

(D) Trade between Asia and the Mediterranean led to increased mechanization.

(E) The Black Death prompted feudal lords
to flee their castles and abandon their
lands.

11. When the author suggests that the Renaissance "may simply be the term we've given
to the aftereffects of" the Black Plague, he is
suggesting that which of the following is true?

(A) The Renaissance did not actually happen.

(B) The Renaissance was the inevitable
result of the vastly reduced population.

(C) The Renaissance actually started in central Asia.

(D) The Renaissance is a modern concept we
have projected onto the wrong historical
period.

(E) "The Renaissance" is a dishonest euphe-
mism for a much darker idea.

GO ON TO NEXT PAGE

Perhaps no term that has entered mainstream discourse via the language of philosophy is more misunderstood than *nihilism*. The word conjures up images of melancholy iconoclasts dressed in black, and it is doubtlessly largely for that reason that it has become something of a byword among rebellious youngsters. Even more serious and educated people frequently seem to believe that nihilism is a philosophy built around the idea that life is meaningless and that there is therefore no such thing as morality. But in actuality, *nihilism* doesn't mean that and isn't even a term for a school of philosophy at all. All the philosophers who have used the term *nihilism* — even Friedrich Nietzsche, with whom it is most closely associated — have not espoused it themselves, but rather used it pejoratively to describe other philosophies with which they disagreed. Used properly, *nihilistic* is an insult for a philosophical viewpoint that (in the speaker's opinion) sucks all the significance out of life due to some massive flaw or contradiction. Though certain philosophers such as Nietzsche and Kierkegaard claimed that they welcomed nihilism, they did so because they saw nihilism not as an end in itself but rather as a necessary step on the path toward creating greater significance.

12. In his passage, the author's intention was presumably to

    (A) espouse a particular philosophy.

    (B) correct a widespread misconception.

    (C) take sides in a philosophical debate.

    (D) suggest a new take on an old idea.

    (E) defend an unpopular viewpoint.

13. According to the passage, *nihilism* is a term that

    (A) is not used by any actual philosophers.

    (B) is used by different philosophers to mean different things.

    (C) philosophers use to describe others' work rather than their own.

    (D) was only popular among philosophers during one specific period.

    (E) young people often deliberately misuse.

14. The tone of the passage can best be described as

    (A) sardonic.

    (B) condescending.

    (C) jovial.

    (D) dispassionate.

    (E) apprehensive.

ASMR, or *Autonomous Sensory Meridian Response*, is a pleasant, trancelike state that some people claim to experience as a result of exposure to auditory *triggers* such as the sounds of whispering, nail tapping, paper crinkling, or gum chewing. In the last year or so, hundreds of ASMR videos designed to help viewers fall asleep or reduce stress have popped up on YouTube; some of the more prolific and creative *ASMRtists* have become minor Internet celebrities. Professional psychologists have largely declined to comment on whether there is a scientific basis for the effects that ASMR enthusiasts, known as *tingleheads*, are purported to experience, but by the standards of pop psychology, the ASMR movement is one of the most coherent and fast-growing we've seen in years.

15. Certain terms in the passage are placed in italics because they are examples of

    (A) irony.

    (B) emphasis.

    (C) proper nouns.

    (D) misused terms.

    (E) jargon.

The tiny dunnart of Australia is casually referred to as a "marsupial mouse," but of course, it isn't really a mouse at all. As a marsupial, it is necessarily more closely related to all other marsupials — to the kangaroo, for example, or to the koala or Tasmanian devil — than it is to any non-marsupial mammal, such as a mouse. So why does it look exactly like a mouse? Because of a process called *convergent evolution*. The fact is that there are good reasons for animals to have the forms that they have. A mammal that is the size of a mouse and fulfills a mouselike niche will likely also have a stocky body, big ears, a longish snout, and so forth. In other words, it will end up looking like a mouse even though it isn't one.

16. The purpose of the passage is to

   (A) explain the differences between marsupials and non-marsupials.

   (B) define what does or doesn't count as a mouse.

   (C) use a specific animal as an example to explain a particular term.

   (D) excoriate people who use a certain scientific term incorrectly.

   (E) pinpoint why the dunnart is so important to evolutionary theory.

As far as the public is concerned, 1941's *Chaplinksy v. New Hampshire* might well be the most misunderstood Supreme Court case of all time. While it's true that *Chaplinksy* established the famous "fighting words" doctrine, it's also true that this doctrine doesn't mean what many people appear to think it means. The decision is often taken to mean that a citizen has the right to physically assault another citizen who gravely insults him, but anyone who tries to use that defense in court will be in for a rude awakening. All the Supreme Court actually did in that decision was uphold the right of a police officer to arrest a citizen who had verbally abused him, in accordance with a New Hampshire state law that the defendant subsequently tried to argue was unconstitutional. Ironically, in light of the fact that *Chaplinksy* has come to be known as "the 'fighting words' decision," no fight actually took place, and no one has ever successfully used *Chaplinsky* as a defense for a violent response to an insult.

17. The author suggests which of the following about *Chaplinsky v. New Hampshire*?

   (A) No one is sure what the decision actually means.

   (B) It has been rendered inconsequential by subsequent Supreme Court decisions.

   (C) It does not in fact provide a legal excuse for violence.

   (D) The state law it upheld was probably unconstitutional.

   (E) None of the above.

Questions 18 through 20 are based on the following passage.

He is arguably the most famous and influential fictional character ever created, so it usually surprises people to learn that the world's greatest detective, the peerless Sherlock Holmes, was essentially a rip-off. Years before Arthur Conan (05) Doyle published the first Sherlock Holmes adventure in 1887, the American master of horror, Edgar Allan Poe, published a trilogy of short stories featuring his own detective character, Auguste Dupin. Debuting in 1841's "The Murders in the Rue (10) Morgue," Dupin shares many similarities with the later and far more famous Holmes beyond the simple fact that he is a master amateur sleuth whom the police consult when they are baffled: He smokes a pipe, he lives with a best friend who (15) narrates his adventures, and he has a tendency to go on at length about logic in a condescending and socially oblivious manner. Doyle himself always admitted the obvious influence and gave Poe credit for inventing the detective genre, but the question (20) remains: Why did Sherlock Holmes immediately become a popular literary phenomenon, when a nearly identical character who debuted nearly half a century earlier did not? Perhaps Poe and his Dupin were simply ahead of their time. (25)

18. The primary purpose of the passage is to

   (A) accuse Arthur Conan Doyle of plagiarism.

   (B) argue that Poe's detective stories were better than Doyle's.

   (C) explain that a very famous character was heavily based on a lesser-known one.

   (D) cast doubt on the traditional explanation of who invented the detective story.

   (E) clear up confusion about the differences between Sherlock Holmes and Auguste Dupin.

19. In the concluding sentence of the passage, the author is using

   (A) conjecture.

   (B) foreshadowing.

   (C) synecdoche.

   (D) allusion.

   (E) poetic license.

GO ON TO NEXT PAGE

20. By the phrase "socially oblivious" in Line 18, the author most nearly means

(A) newfangled.

(B) gauche.

(C) egomaniacal.

(D) iconoclastic.

(E) smarmy.

Questions 21 through 24 are based on the following passage.

Line
    The current rule of thumb in English departments of American colleges when it comes to the teaching of "freshman comp" — the introductory writing courses that virtually all incoming students
(05) are required to take — is that instructors are supposed to grade and correct student work based on the students' writing alone, without attempting to change or influence the students' opinions. This is a polite notion, and for that reason it is popular
(10) with administrators, whose primary motivation is to avoid controversy. But there are more than a few problems with this nice-sounding idea. The first is that, in practice, it's impossible, rather like the paradox from the climax of Shakespeare's *The*
(15) *Merchant of Venice*, where Shylock is challenged by the disguised Portia to take a pound of flesh without spilling a drop of blood. If a student's opinion, or any of the supposed facts cited in support of it, is objectively false, then how can the
(20) organization of the argument be analyzed as a discrete aspect of the paper?

    More importantly and more dangerously, such a yardstick carries the implication that *everything* is simply a matter of opinion, which of course is not
(25) true. Although it might well lead to more tension in the classroom and more hurt feelings on the parts of some students, the inescapable fact is that there are simply better reasons to believe some things than there are to believe other things. If
(30) politeness dictates that this fact cannot be acknowledged, even at the college level, then the students are being taught far less than they could or should be, and the function of the professor is demoted to that of a simple proofreader.

21. The author's attitude toward the "rule of thumb" mentioned in the first paragraph and analyzed throughout the passage as a whole can best be described as one of

(A) intellectual disdain.

(B) shocked cynicism.

(C) melancholy regret.

(D) paranoid alarm.

(E) droll dismissiveness.

22. In Line 21, "a discrete aspect of the paper" refers to an element of the paper that is

(A) comprehensible.

(B) scientifically expressible.

(C) well done.

(D) vague or confusing.

(E) self-contained.

23. In the passage, the author suggests that the standard under discussion was put in place at the behest of

(A) lazy teachers.

(B) offended students.

(C) naïve administrators.

(D) poorly trained scientists.

(E) angry parents.

24. Based on the passage, the author would most likely suggest that college composition instructors should

(A) deliberately offend students as a test of their argumentative skills.

(B) draw the line at respecting opinions that are demonstrably untrue.

(C) be free to teach their own personal opinions without administrative interference.

(D) place more emphasis on grammar, mechanics, and eloquence than on logic.

(E) find excuses to flunk students whose general knowledge is woefully insufficient.

Questions 25 through 27 are based on the following passage.

It's the most famous series of words ever composed in the English language. Everyone has heard of it, and most people even know a little bit of it by heart, regardless of whether they ever made a deliberate effort to commit it to memory. And virtually everyone, including many English teachers and a fair number of the actors who have delivered it on stage, is dead wrong about what it means. The plain fact is that Hamlet's "To be or not to be" soliloquy is *not* about whether to commit suicide. Hamlet already flatly ruled out suicide on ethical grounds in his first soliloquy back in Act 1. The immortal showstopper from Act 3 is about something much more complex and much more deeply related to the grander themes of the play than that. When the melancholy prince asks "Whether 'tis nobler in the mind to suffer/The slings and arrow of outrageous fortune/Or to take arms against a sea of troubles," he is not simply debating whether to cash in his chips, but instead pondering an eternal paradox of morality: Should a good person "turn the other cheek" in the face of evil, as scripture advises? Or should he attempt to make the world a better place by actively combating the wicked, running the risk not only of dying in the process, but — even more troublingly — of becoming just as bad as the people he seeks to oppose?

25. The author's argument is that the "To be or not to be" soliloquy is actually about

(A) whether it is better to go on living or to die.

(B) whether there is really a God.

(C) whether to retreat from the world or try to improve it.

(D) whether it is wiser to fight evil openly or to use subterfuge.

(E) something so complex that it is nearly impossible to grasp.

26. According to the passage, Hamlet's viewpoint on suicide is that it's

(A) preferable to unethical action.

(B) an eternal paradox of morality.

(C) attractive but frightening.

(D) inevitable.

(E) unacceptable.

27. The passage is primarily concerned with the author's goal of

(A) taking an ethical stand.

(B) simplifying a complex issue.

(C) issuing a warning about the future.

(D) correcting a misreading.

(E) apologizing for a mistake.

Founded in 1994 by philosophers Peter Singer and Paola Cavalieri, the Great Ape Project is an international organization that lobbies for a United Nations Declaration of the Rights of Great Apes. These proposed rights would include not only life but also liberty, meaning that great apes could no longer be experimented upon or even kept in zoos. The reasoning goes that, because great apes are intelligent enough to understand their status as captives in a zoo, keeping them in one is morally equivalent to imprisoning a human who has committed no crime.

28. The passage provides information for answering most fully which of the following questions?

(A) Why should great apes have rights similar to human rights?

(B) What is the difference between a great ape and a monkey?

(C) Who are the most famous supporters of the Great Ape Project?

(D) Are more great apes used in scientific research or zoo exhibitions?

(E) How is intelligence in great apes measured?

The words "rabbit" and "hare" are often used interchangeably (especially in the titles of Bugs Bunny cartoons), but the two animals are quite different. Hares live and bear their young in nests, not in underground burrows like rabbits do, and those young are born already furred and able to see, as opposed to blind and hairless like newborn rabbits. Unlike rabbits, who live in groups, hares are loners. A hare has 48 chromosomes to the rabbit's 44, and its jointed skull is unique among mammals. Hares and rabbits really aren't that difficult to tell apart if you know what to look for, although it doesn't help that the animal known as a jackrabbit is actually a hare, and that the pet breed called a Belgian hare is really a rabbit.

GO ON TO NEXT PAGE ►

29. According to the passage, which of the following is true of hares?

(A) They are the only animal with a jointed skull.

(B) They have fewer chromosomes than do rabbits.

(C) They are born blind and hairless.

(D) They do not make use of underground burrows.

(E) They live in groups.

Questions 30 through 32 are based on the following passage.

Line   Are time machines and time travel possible? Many physicists, including the great Stephen Hawking, now say yes. But before you get too excited, understand that there is a lot of fine print.
(05) Firstly, virtually all authorities on the subject agree that time travel to the past is an impossibility. Traveling backward in time would open the door to all sorts of insoluble conundrums, like the famous Grandfather Paradox ("What if you went back in
(10) time and killed your own grandfather, thereby preventing yourself from ever existing in the first place?"). As Hawking succinctly explains, when it comes to physics, things that would create para- doxes tend not to happen — not directly because
(15) they would create the paradoxes, but because they must be impossible for some other reason. Time travel to the future, however, is eminently pos- sible, even if the process is less exciting than in the movies. All you'd have to do is move really fast.

(20)   As Einstein discovered, time slows down for moving objects as they approach the speed of light. A traveler in a spaceship moving at half the speed of light would only experience the passing of one day for every two days that passed on Earth. Get up
(25) to 99 percent of the speed of light, and a year would pass on Earth for every day on the ship. So if you want to travel through time, all you have to do is build a spaceship that can go really fast and then hang around in space for a while, going really fast.
(30) When you come back to Earth, you will have traveled into the future, simply because less time will have passed for you than for everyone else. A "time machine," then, is just anything that can move fast enough to function as one.

30. Which of the following, if true, would resolve an objection made in the passage?

(A) It's possible to exceed the speed of light.

(B) It's not possible to exceed the speed of light.

(C) Matter can be sent into the past, but not living beings.

(D) The past exists currently, but in another dimension.

(E) Time as it passes on Earth is not the most accurate definition of "time."

31. The author uses the phrase "fine print" in Line 4 to most nearly mean

(A) complicated explanations.

(B) exceptions and qualifications.

(C) dangerous possibilities.

(D) missing information.

(E) unexpected tricks.

32. The passage indicates which of the following about time travel to the future?

(A) We have achieved it already without realizing that we had.

(B) It would automatically resolve whatever paradoxes it creates.

(C) It's an illusion, but an extraordinarily convincing one.

(D) It's a natural consequence of the rela- tionship between speed and time.

(E) Technically, everything constitutes time travel to the future.

Questions 33 through 38 are based on the following passages.

Passage 1

Line   The theory that the Cretaceous-Paleogene Event — the mass extinction 65 million years ago that is most famous for having killed the dino- saurs, although many other species disappeared as well — was caused by an asteroid impact is now so (05) widely accepted that it can be hard to believe the idea was little more than a rogue hypothesis until fairly recently. Although paleontologists had previ- ously realized that the extinction would be com- patible with an asteroid impact, there was no hard (10)

evidence for one until 1980, when Luis Alvarez and his team discovered that the geologic record contains massive levels of iridium, an element rare on Earth but plentiful in asteroids, at the Creta-
(15) ceous-Paleogene Boundary. The fact that the actual location of the impact was the Chicxulub Crater in Mexico's Yucatan Peninsula wasn't established until 1990.

Passage 2

Line Increasing numbers of paleontologists are leaning toward the idea that the scientific commu-nity was too hasty in ascribing the extinction of the dinosaurs solely to an asteroid impact. After all,
(05) doing so involves writing off the idea that any role in the mass dying was played by the Deccan Traps, a nearly 200,000-square-mile grouping of volcanic flood basalts in what is now India. We know that they formed between 60 and 68 million years ago,
(10) releasing huge amounts of lava and toxic gases in the process. No one is denying that the Chicxulub asteroid impact did in fact occur, and that it almost certainly played a substantial role in the extinc-tion, but there is also no good reason to insist that
(15) the Cretaceous-Paleogene Event had only a single cause.

33. Which best describes the relationship between Passage 1 and Passage 2?

(A) Passage 1 and Passage 2 present two mutually exclusive scientific theories.

(B) Passage 1 and Passage 2 examine the same theory from two different angles.

(C) Passage 2 presents a new theory that has replaced the theory in Passage 1.

(D) Passage 1 explains the origin of a theory that Passage 2 then modifies.

(E) Passage 1 presents raw data, and Passage 2 forms a theory based on those data.

34. As used in Passage 2, Line 5, the phrase "writ-ing off" most nearly means

(A) ignoring.

(B) misrepresenting.

(C) obscuring.

(D) exaggerating.

(E) plagiarizing.

35. How do the two authors differ in their view-points concerning the Chicxulub asteroid?

(A) One author believes it killed the dino-saurs, and the other does not.

(B) Both authors agree that it killed the dinosaurs, but they disagree about when it hit Earth.

(C) One author believes it killed the dino-saurs, and the other believes it was one of multiple causes.

(D) Both authors believe it killed the dino-saurs, but they disagree about its chemi-cal composition.

(E) Both authors agree that it's a plausible extinction theory, but neither is 100 per-cent sure it's correct.

36. Which of the following is an accurate state-ment about a difference between the two passages?

(A) Passage 1 bases its argument on chemis-try, and Passage 2 bases its argument on physics.

(B) Passage 1 argues that dinosaurs lived in North America, and Passage 2 argues that they lived in Asia.

(C) Passage 1 is written for a scientific audience, and Passage 2 is written for a general audience.

(D) Passage 1 analyzes an older theory, whereas Passage 2 suggests an original one.

(E) Passage 1 explains the history of its theory, whereas Passage 2 does not.

37. The attitude of the author of Passage 2 toward the content of Passage 1 is that it's

(A) false.

(B) limited.

(C) outdated.

(D) self-contradictory.

(E) elitist.

GO ON TO NEXT PAGE

38. Both passages are primarily concerned with determining

(A) when dinosaurs lived.

(B) whether all dinosaurs went extinct at the same time.

(C) whether an asteroid struck Earth 65 million years ago.

(D) the causes of an agreed-upon event.

(E) the reasons for the popularity of a particular theory.

Ask any schoolchild (or virtually any adult) to draw a picture of a medieval knight, and the odds are that you'll wind up with a depiction of someone encased from head to foot in a suit of armor. This is one of the most widespread misconceptions about history. The iconic "suit of armor" that we now associate so closely with the period actually didn't develop until the tail end of the Middle Ages, and it didn't become common on the battlefield until well into what we now call the Renaissance. European warriors of the true Medieval period, even the wealthier and more aristocratic ones such as knights, would have worn scattered pieces of plate armor over chain-mail suits, but not "suits of armor" as we now picture them.

39. The passage relies on drawing a sharp distinction between

(A) what children know and what adults know.

(B) armor and everyday clothing.

(C) the Medieval Period and the Renaissance.

(D) European warriors and non-European warriors.

(E) wealthy warriors and less wealthy warriors.

People often prickle at evolutionary or instinctual explanations for human behavior based on the idea that it's been a long time since humans lived in a state of nature. But this depends upon a rather sizeable misapplication of the phrase "a long time." When people speak of "human civilization" — meaning the existence of permanent settlements, agriculture, some rudimentary form of government — they're talking about things

that only appeared about 10,000 years ago. Conversely, the first humans — members of the genus *Homo* — reared their heads just over two million years ago. Humans were evolving for a heck of a long time before they were "civilized."

40. The primary implication made by the passage is that

(A) human civilization arose much later than most people believe.

(B) the development of agriculture and government marked a sharp turn in human genetics.

(C) civilization hasn't existed long enough to substantially alter human instinct.

(D) human evolution stopped when humans organized the first civilizations.

(E) experts disagree about the timescale of human evolution.

The title of "the southernmost city in the world" is valuable bait when it comes to attracting tourists, but the question of which burg — and, accordingly, which nation — can boast it is not such an easy matter to settle. It all comes down to the fact that there is no hard-and-fast definition of what counts as a "city." Ushuaia, the southernmost city in Argentina, has a population of 64,000. Just across the Beagle Channel, however, lies Chile's Puerto Williams. The latter is farther south, but it has a population of only about 3,000. Does that make it populous enough to count as a city? Unsurprisingly, Chile says yes, and Argentina says no.

41. The author's primary purpose in writing the passage was most likely to call attention to the fact that

(A) geography is a more complex matter than people realize.

(B) apparently straightforward questions can be muddled by vague definitions.

(C) nations will argue over silly things when money is at stake.

(D) Chile's claim to the southernmost city is better than Argentina's.

(E) Argentina's claim to the southernmost city is better than Chile's.

You don't hear the name of William Tyndale every day, but if you speak English, he probably had a greater influence on the words that come out of your mouth than anyone besides William Shakespeare. An English Protestant reformer of the early 1500s, Tyndale was the first since the invention of the printing press to translate the Bible into English (John Wycliffe's handwritten translations of the 1300s were quickly banned and easily destroyed by authorities because the process of producing them was so laborious). Translating the Bible was an act punishable by death, as the ability of the common man to read scripture in his own language would weaken the power of the Church, so Tyndale had to do his work in hiding on continental Europe.

He was captured in 1535 and executed the following year, but ironically, Tyndale's Bible became the standard in England soon afterward, when Henry VIII broke with Rome. The more famous King James Bible of 1611, finalized by a committee of scholars, is largely just a revision of Tyndale's single-handed work, which established the tone and conventions of literary Early Modern English. As the formulator of such famous idioms as "eat, drink, and be merry," "fight the good fight," and "salt of the earth," Tyndale is surpassed in the coining of English expressions only by Shakespeare, who developed his own ear for literary English by reading Tyndale's Bible as a schoolboy.

42. Which of the following best describes the relationship between the two paragraphs of the passage?

(A) The first paragraph concentrates on the history of English-language Bibles in general, and the second concentrates specifically on William Tyndale's translation.

(B) The first paragraph mainly presents details of William Tyndale's life, and the second deals more closely with his influence.

(C) The first paragraph explains the influence of William Tyndale's Bible, and the

second concentrates on the influence of the King James Version.

(D) The first paragraph deals with William Shakespeare's influence on the English language, and the second with William Tyndale's influence on Shakespeare.

(E) The first paragraph discusses English translations of the Bible made before the invention of the printing press, and the second discusses those translations done after its invention.

43. The passage repeatedly invokes the name of William Shakespeare primarily in order to

(A) use him as the standard by which influence on the English language is measured.

(B) argue that the greatest influence on Shakespeare himself was William Tyndale.

(C) set up a comparison between the language of Tyndale's Bible and Shakespeare's plays.

(D) distinguish idioms coined by Tyndale from those coined by Shakespeare.

(E) compare the political constraints on Shakespeare's work to those on Tyndale's.

44. The author would most likely agree with which of the following statements?

(A) The plays of William Shakespeare were more influenced by religion than many realize.

(B) William Tyndale's translation of the Bible was politically superior to later translations.

(C) William Tyndale should be given more credit for Henry VIII's break with Rome.

(D) Translations done by individuals are generally superior to those done by committees.

(E) The character of modern literary English was largely established in the 16th century.

GO ON TO NEXT PAGE

45. The passage brings up John Wycliffe as an example of someone

(A) whose work had a considerable degree of influence on William Tyndale's.

(B) whose politics were more extreme than Tyndale's, but whose talent was equal.

(C) who attempted a similar project to Tyndale's but was thwarted.

(D) whose influence on the English language is harder to measure than Tyndale's.

(E) who was more earnestly religious but less talented than Tyndale.

46. The metaphoric use of the phrase "ear for" in the final sentence is roughly synonymous with

(A) appreciation of.

(B) interest in.

(C) consumption by.

(D) knack for.

(E) recognition of.

Questions 47 through 49 are based on the following chart.

Following is a chart showing the change in Oregon's wolf populations between 2009 and 2012.

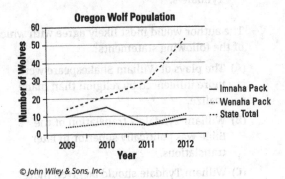

© John Wiley & Sons, Inc.

47. In which year was there the greatest disparity between the populations of the Imnaha and Wenaha wolf packs? Write your answer in the space provided.

_____

48. Besides the Imnaha and Wenaha packs, when were there apparently other wolf packs in the state of Oregon?

Select **all** that apply.

(A) 2009

(B) 2010

(C) 2011

(D) 2012

49. The year in which the wolves of the Imnaha pack comprised the greatest percentage of the total number of wolves in the state of Oregon was

(A) 2009.

(B) 2010.

(C) 2011.

(D) 2012.

(E) The graph does not reveal this information.

Questions 50 through 53 are based on the following passage.

What, if anything, is the actual difference between a *psychopath* and a *sociopath*? The average person's confusion on this point is forgivable, because the fact is that psychologists and neurologists themselves disagree: Some consider the terms (05) interchangeable, others favor dispensing with both in favor of the more modern diagnosis of *antisocial personality disorder* (which fits in more neatly with the spectrum of other personality disorders), and even the professionals who favor the contin- (10) ued and distinct use of both terms cannot form an agreement about what the difference is. Adding to the confusion is the fact that psychopaths and/or sociopaths are notably hard to study. For obvious reasons, an individual being screened for psy- (15) chopathy is likely to lie, so only a highly skilled professional can make such a diagnosis concerning a living person. Diagnosing psychopathy and/or sociopathy postmortem is comparatively simpler, as there is agreement that the conditions involve (20) observable differences in brain structure, but an autopsy cannot reveal whether such differences were present at birth or acquired. Nor can it say very much about the individual's subjective experience of the condition, and most agree the (25)

Line

difference between psychopathy and sociopathy probably lies in this subjective experience. At the moment, the viewpoint that a psychopath has (30) *no* sense of morality, whereas a sociopath has a *twisted* one, is gaining traction. In other words, although both psychopaths and sociopaths have highly reduced capacities for empathy, a psychopath does not know or care whether his or her ac- (35) tions are right or wrong; a sociopath, meanwhile, believes his or her actions to be right but has a definition of "right" that the average person would find horrifying.

50. You can infer from the passage that the majority of psychological and neurological professionals agree about which of the following statements?

   (A) Both psychopathy and sociopathy are observable via brain autopsy.

   (B) Both psychopathy and sociopathy are synonymous with antisocial personality disorder.

   (C) Psychopathy and sociopathy are two different things.

   (D) Neither psychopaths nor sociopaths know the difference between right and wrong.

   (E) Neither psychopathy nor sociopathy is detectable via psychological examination.

51. The author's argument developed in the passage most likely results from the desire to

   (A) criticize the psychological community.

   (B) voice a personal opinion about psychopaths.

   (C) diagnose a particular person as either a psychopath or a sociopath.

   (D) warn professionals about means used by psychopaths to evade detection.

   (E) clear up confusion on the parts of general readers.

52. As used in Line 3, *forgivable* most nearly means

   (A) morally excusable.

   (B) initially confusing.

   (C) logically expectable.

   (D) disturbingly amusing.

   (E) only mildly annoying.

53. The closing sentences suggest that sociopaths have a definition of right and wrong that is

   (A) ineffable.

   (B) idiosyncratic.

   (C) inextricable.

   (D) remunerative.

   (E) eleemosynary.

The poetry of William Butler Yeats, who in 1923 became the first Irishman to receive the Nobel Prize for Literature, went through so many distinct phases during his long career that to read him is almost to read several different poets. The mystical and deliberately archaic-sounding verse of his early books borders on psychedelic; the strident political poems he produced at the time of World War I are awe-inspiring in their scope and confidence; and the lonely reflections on old age he published in his last years are as different from the first two phases as they are from each other.

54. The passage suggests that the poetry of William Butler Yeats can accurately be described as

   (A) exclusionary.

   (B) impudent.

   (C) indeterminate.

   (D) multifaceted.

   (E) lugubrious.

Popular tradition holds that celebrities die in groups, but all superstition aside, the truth is that sometimes one famous individual is too lightly mourned solely because of having passed away in too close proximity to another celebrity. Perhaps no great American ever received a more insufficient send-off than show-business legend Groucho Marx, who happened to leave us on August 19, 1977, only three days after the death of Elvis Presley. Granted, Presley's death was both untimely and mysterious, whereas Groucho was an elderly man; still, the fact that the national hysteria over the King of Rock-and-Roll should have prevented the King of Comedy from getting his due is lamentable.

GO ON TO NEXT PAGE

55. The relationship of the first sentence to the rest of the passage is that of

(A) the general to the specific.

(B) superstition to fact.

(C) the rhetorical to the logical.

(D) data to interpretation.

(E) cause to effect.

The etymology of vulgar or profane words is a subject of both frustration and amusement for linguists. Because "dirty" words tend to be used in speech for a considerable length of time before they are ever used in print, their origins are often a subject of controversy. Often, urban legend will hold that a particular four-letter word originated as an acronym, but such after-the-fact explanations — jokingly dubbed "backronyms" — are inevitably spurious.

56. The passage suggests that the etymology of "dirty" words is often in doubt because

(A) linguists are reluctant to study them.

(B) deliberate disinformation is spread about them.

(C) they are absent from preserved records.

(D) their meanings change so rapidly.

(E) they frequently originate as acronyms.

DO NOT TURN THE PAGE UNTIL TOLD TO DO SO   STOP   DO NOT RETURN TO A PREVIOUS TEST

Part 2: Writing

TIME: 40 minutes for 40 selected-response questions

DIRECTIONS: Choose the best answer or answers to each question or statement. Mark the corresponding oval on the answer sheet.

DIRECTIONS: Each of the following questions consists of a sentence that contains four underlined portions. Read each sentence and decide whether any of the underlined parts contains a grammatical construction, a word use, an instance of incorrect or omitted punctuation, or capitalization that would be inappropriate in carefully written English. If so, select the underlined portion that must be revised to produce a correct sentence. If there are no errors in the sentence as written, select "No error." **No sentence has more than one error.**

1. Some people drink coffee for its taste, whereas
                    A   B
   many others simply use it as a delivery system
              C
   for the caffeine it contains. No error.
               D   E

2. Although many films inspired by books are
   well made and considered cinematic classics,
      A
   it's rare for a film to flesh out its characters as
           B
   fully as did the book by which it was based.
        C   D
   No error.
     E

3. Many people who believe the platypus to be a
           A
   marsupial because it's weird-looking and lives
     B
   in Australia, but it's actually a monotreme and
   more closely related to placental mammals like
         C
   humans than it is to the marsupials. No error.
          D   E

4. Turk Edwards was a star lineman for the
               A
   Washington Redskins in the 1930s whom was
                          B
   eventually inducted into the Football Hall of
   Fame, but, ironically, his career ended when
         C
   he injured his knee while walking away from a
                D
   pre-game coin toss. No error.
                E

5. While we don't know exactly how life arose
   on Earth, we can say that what distinguishes
     A   B
   a living organism from mere "chemical soup"
   is their ability to replicate in a manner that
     C
   passes on genes. No error.
     D   E

6. Should you have any questions about what the
        A
   data represent, please don't hesitate to ask
         B   C
   either Amy or myself. No error.
            D   E

7. The award-winning film *Braveheart* depicts
   its central characters as wearing kilts, but in
     A   B
   actuality the Scots did not wear kilts until four
           C
   centuries after the time of William Wallace.
            D
   No error.
     E

8. The children's museum is further away than
        A   B   C
   the waterpark, but it will presumably be both
   more educational and less crowded. No error.
               D   E

9. It didn't sell very many copies, but I thought
              A
   the album was one of the best-produced
                     B
   musical endeavors in which I have ever heard.
               C   D
   No error.
     E

GO ON TO NEXT PAGE

10. If you really want to effect change, then you
                      A   B
should make sure your arguments affect
                                  C
people's opinions, rather than merely shouting
                            D
them into silence. No error.
                    E

11. Olympus Mons, being a shield volcano on the
                  A
planet Mars with six calderas, dwarfs Mount
      B   C
Everest, as it's nearly three times taller.
            D
No error.
E

12. The treasurer of the society devoted to the
                       A
upkeep and preservation of historic disc-golf
courses were delighted by, but unsure of how
       B   C
best to allocate, the sudden influx of dona-
     D
tions. No error.
       E

13. I realize you've been searching frantically for
              A
him all evening, but if Danny had been here
                              B
earlier, I certainly didn't see him. No error.
C   D   E

14. Because we still had half a day's travel before
    A   B
us, we stopped for the night, but the weather
                             C
forecast failed to make us optimistic of the
                                       D
remainder of the trip. No error.
                       E

15. The principle reason most students give for
    A   B
opposing a tuition hike is suspicion that most
C   D
of the money will just be used on the sports
teams. No error.
      E

16. The theory that visual and auditory hallucinations caused by infrasound are actually the real
                            A
explanation behind most reports of hauntings
            B
is gaining credibly among scientists. No error.
C   D   E

17. Though his short lyric poems have often been
                                A
dismissed by critics as overly sentimental,
                        B
Lord Byron has more recently been given
                C
credit for the immense influence that his long
narrative poems have had for novelists.
                  D
No error.
E

18. The question of which British Kings
                 A
and Queens have been "great" since the power
    B
of the monarch was limited after the Glorious

Revolution of 1688 is a tricky one, as symbolic
C
moral leadership is obviously harder to evaluate than are executive decisions. No error.
    D   E

19. Though they are often depicted alongside
           A   B
dinosaurs in paintings or cartoon shows, the
Dimetrodon was actually not a dinosaur at all,
                                         C
but rather a mammalian ancestor called a
    D
synapsid. No error.
          E

20. Students may not enjoy learning grammar, but a teacher who doesn't teach grammar is not doing their job.

    (A) is not doing their job

    (B) is not doing their jobs

    (C) are not doing their jobs

    (D) is not doing his or her job

    (E) are not doing his or her job

21. There are actually six different species of giraffe, all with distinctive spot patterns.

    (A) all with

    (B) in which all have

    (C) all of whom having

    (D) they all have

    (E) each one has

22. Although he is widely considered the greatest novelist of the 20th century, but James Joyce never won the Nobel Prize for Literature.

    (A) century, but James Joyce

    (B) century, seeing that

    (C) century, James Joyce

    (D) century; James Joyce

    (E) century, however, James Joyce

23. The late Christopher Hitchens had the capacity both to delight with the force of his learning and wit, but was also shocking in his iconoclasm and bluntness.

    (A) wit, but was also shocking in

    (B) wit, while also being shocking by

    (C) wit, he also shocked with

    (D) wit but also to shock with

    (E) wit and to shock with

24. Having spotted the skyline in the distance, an attempt was made to reach town without making any more stops.

    (A) Having spotted the skyline in the distance, an attempt was made to

    (B) Having spotted the skyline in the distance, and we attempted to

    (C) Having spotted the skyline in the distance, we decided to try to

    (D) We spotted the skyline in the distance, therefore we attempted to

    (E) Spotting the skyline in the distance and trying to

25. Nineteenth-century Hungarian composer Franz Liszt was the first artist who female fans showed their appreciation for throwing their undergarments onto the stage.

    (A) who female fans showed their appreciation for throwing

    (B) who female fans were showing their appreciation for and throwing

    (C) to whom female fans to show their appreciation by throwing

    (D) for whom female fans showed their appreciation by throwing

    (E) to whom female fans showed their appreciation to throw

26. In about 6 billion years, the Sun will exhaust its supply of hydrogen and expand into a red giant, <u>and consume all the planets of our solar system, then collapse</u> into a white dwarf.

(A) and consume all the planets of our solar system, then collapse

(B) it will consume all the planets of our solar system and then collapse

(C) and it will consume all the planets of our solar system; then collapse

(D) consuming all the planets of our solar system and then it will collapse

(E) consuming all the planets of our solar system before collapsing

27. Madagascar, an island off the western coast of <u>Africa, a biodiversity hotspot, and over 90 percent of its wildlife is found</u> nowhere else on the planet.

(A) Africa, a biodiversity hotspot, and over 90 percent of its wildlife is found

(B) Africa, is a biodiversity hotspot, with over 90 percent of its wildlife being found

(C) Africa, being a biodiversity hotspot, over 90 percent of its wildlife found

(D) Africa and a biodiversity hotspot, with over 90 percent of its wildlife found

(E) Africa, it is a biodiversity hotspot, and over 90 percent of its wildlife is found

28. I have decided that I'm ready to take the test <u>now, however the rest of you may</u> delay for as long as you like.

(A) now, however the rest of you may

(B) now, however, the rest of you may

(C) now; the rest of you, however, may

(D) now; the rest of you however may

(E) now, the rest of you, however, may

29. Though he was unappreciated in his time, today the works of Vincent van Gogh are more celebrated <u>than are those of</u> any other Post-Impressionist painter.

(A) than are those of

(B) than

(C) compared to

(D) compared with

(E) compared than

30. It may look cool when people do it in the movies, but <u>the truth of it is firing</u> two guns at the same time is a very effective way of not hitting anything.

(A) the truth of it is firing

(B) the truth is that firing

(C) the truth is, if one is firing

(D) truly, if one is to fire

(E) truly to fire

1 The state of poetry in contemporary America really depends on whom you ask. 2 A certain type of person is likely to tell you that poetry is read by hardly anyone. 3 He will add that the few people who do read it comprise an insular cadre of specialists, which is ignored by the culture at large. 4 Another person may well say that we are living in a new golden age of American verse, one in which poetry events pack coffeehouses and even auditoriums with excited young people in numbers never seen before. 5 The explanation is that these two respondents are talking about two very different things when they say "poetry."

6 For centuries, the obvious definition of "poetry" has been that it is a genre of published literature, written by writers, submitted for publication in journals and anthologies, and read by poetry lovers in thoughtful solitude. 7 In recent decades, however, a populist subgenre of poetry called "slam" has been challenging that definition,

just as definitions are often challenged. 8 At slam events, poets take the stage in rapid succession for three to five minutes at a time, with the winners of each round being determined by applause and a single winner being crowned at the end of the night. 9 Unlike more traditional poets, many of whom have advanced degrees in poetry, slammers memorize their poems and act them out with gestures, impressions, and even sound effects, moving all about the stage in an effort to keep the crowd's attention. 10 This is a difficult task with any crowd.

11 Slam poets often argue that traditionalists — or, as they call them, "page" poets — are clinging to an outdated concept of poetry for the sake of elitism. 12 More traditional versifiers counter that slam poets — who are often ignorant of poetic history and cite popular songwriters or even stand-up comics as their primary influences — are simply crowd-pleasers who perform humorous, titillating, or shocking monologues and presume to call it poetry, with those who read more slowly or thoughtfully often getting booed off the stage for not putting on enough of a show. 13 Each camp sincerely believes that it is being "oppressed" by the other: Slammers think that page poets are privileged, closed-minded, and exclusionary, whereas page poets see slammers as the "cool kids" trying to turn poetry into a popularity contest.

GO ON TO NEXT PAGE

31. In context, what is the best way to combine Sentences 2 and 3 (reproduced here)?

A certain type of person is likely to tell you that poetry is read by hardly anyone. He will add that the few people who do read it comprise an insular cadre of specialists, which is ignored by the culture at large.

(A) A certain type of person is likely to tell you that poetry is read by hardly anyone except a few people who do read it and comprise an insular cadre of specialists, and that these people are ignored by the culture at large.

(B) A certain type of person is likely to tell you that poetry is read by hardly anyone, and that the few people who do read it comprise an insular cadre of specialists ignored by the culture at large.

(C) A certain type of person is likely to tell you that poetry is read by hardly anyone, only an insular cadre of specialists that is also ignored by the culture at large.

(D) A certain type of person is likely to tell you that poetry is read by hardly anyone who does not comprise an insular cadre of specialists ignored by the culture at large.

(E) A certain type of person is likely to tell you that poetry is read by hardly anyone, adding that the few people who do read it comprise an insular cadre of specialists, and specifying that they are ignored by the culture at large.

32. In context, what is best to do with Sentence 5 (reproduced here)?

The explanation is that these two respondents are talking about two very different things when they say "poetry."

(A) Leave it as it is.

(B) Take the word *poetry* out of quotation marks and put the word *very* in italics.

(C) Begin the sentence with "On the other hand."

(D) Make it the second sentence of the subsequent paragraph.

(E) Insert the word "however" between *respondents* and *are*.

33. In context, what is the best revision of the underlined portion of Sentence 7 (reproduced here)?

In recent decades, however, a populist sub-genre of poetry called "slam" has been challenging that definition, just as definitions are often challenged.

(A) just as definitions are often challenged.

(B) and you're about to find out how and why.

(C) with varying degrees of success.

(D) to the delight of some and the consternation of others.

(E) with methods as devious as they were unexpected.

34. In context, which is the best way to modify the underlined portion of Sentence 9 (reproduced here)?

Unlike more traditional poets, many of whom have advanced degrees in poetry, slammers memorize their poems and act them out with gestures, impressions, and even sound effects, moving all about the stage in an effort to keep the crowd's attention.

(A) many of whom have advanced degrees in poetry,

(B) who come from just as wide a range of backgrounds as do slammers

(C) who are not necessarily any older than the slammers are

(D) who are often more shy than slammers are, despite being more well-read

(E) who typically stand at lecterns and read from notes or a published book during recitals

35. Which version of Sentence 10 (reproduced here) would make the best conclusion to the second paragraph?

This is a difficult task with any crowd.

(A) This is a difficult task with any crowd.

(B) Some of them even burst into song, though usually not very skillfully.

(C) Their work is designed to be seen in performance rather than read.

(D) Can the use of props among slammers be far behind?

(E) The venues that host slams can't complain, because they always make money.

36. In context, which is the best transitional phrase to add at the beginning of Sentence 13 (reproduced here)?

Each camp sincerely believes that it is being "oppressed" by the other: Slammers think that page poets are privileged, closed-minded, and exclusionary, whereas page poets see slammers as the "cool kids" trying to turn poetry into a popularity contest.

(A) Ironically

(B) Therefore

(C) Undeniably

(D) On the other hand

(E) In conclusion

DIRECTIONS: The following selected-response questions are a test of your familiarity with basic research skills. For each question, choose the best answer. Remember, try to answer every question.

37. Downing, Thomas. (2012, April). "The Standardized-Test Conundrum." *Education*, 76, 93–99.

In the citation shown, which of the following is cited?

(A) a book

(B) a magazine article

(C) a newspaper article

(D) a blog entry

(E) a speech

38. In terms of research, the technical distinction between a primary source and a secondary source is that

(A) a secondary source yields less important information than a primary source.

(B) a primary source is quoted from directly, whereas a secondary source is not.

(C) a primary source represents original research, whereas a secondary source contains information already compiled by someone else.

(D) a primary source is a published work with an ISBN, whereas a secondary source might not have been published or even copyrighted.

(E) a primary source is the text or texts that the paper is about, and a secondary source is anything else.

39. When an author includes a quotation (from a poem, for example) below the title of the essay and above the text, the quotation is called an

(A) epigram.

(B) epigraph.

(C) epistle.

(D) epithelium.

(E) epitaxy.

40. The difference between a Works Cited page and a bibliography is that

(A) *Bibliography* is the term used in high school, and *Works Cited page* is the term used in college.

(B) a *Works Cited page* lists only cited sources, whereas a *bibliography* lists every source consulted.

(C) a *bibliography* lists only books, whereas a *Works Cited page* lists all types of sources.

(D) *Bibliography* is the term used in an unpublished paper, whereas *Works Cited page* is the term used in a published paper.

(E) *Works Cited page* is the preferred term in APA style, whereas *bibliography* is the preferred term in MLA style.

Argumentative Essay

Source-Based Essay

TIME: 30 minutes

DIRECTIONS: Both of the following sources address the philosophical paradox of the desire to see things as they are versus the need to appreciate them in a manner that makes emotional sense to us. Read the two passages carefully and then write an essay in which you identify the most important concerns regarding the issue and explain why they are important. Your essay must draw on information from *both* of the sources. In addition, you may draw upon your own experience, observations, or reading. Be sure to *cite* the sources, whether you are paraphrasing or directly quoting.

When paraphrasing or quoting from the sources, cite each source by referring to the author's last name, the title of the source, or any other clear identifier.

Source 1

Adapted from: Wisnewski, Jeremy J. "Mutant Phenomenology." *X-Men and Philosophy: Astonishing Insight and Uncanny Argument in the Mutant X-verse.* Hoboken, NJ: John Wiley & Sons, Inc. 2009. Print.

Phenomenology is a philosophical movement that has its roots in late-nineteenth- and early-twentieth-century thought, in thinkers such as Edmund Husserl (1859–1938) and Martin Heidegger (1889–1976). It is a systematic investigation into phenomena — that is, into the way things present themselves to us in experience. Both Husserl and Heidegger thought that things present themselves as they really are in our experiences, but that we often distort the truth that experience presents. We impose particular theories onto phenomena and insist that they conform to our preconceived notions about how the world is. To do phenomenology is to try and set aside our preconceptions and to uncover the actual *being* of things as they reveal themselves to us. In a way, it is to see past our preconceptions into the heart of things.

Source 2

Adapted from: Tschner, George. "High-Tech Mythology in X-Men." *X-Men and Philosophy: Astonishing Insight and Uncanny Argument in the Mutant X-verse.* Hoboken, NJ: John Wiley & Sons, Inc. 2009. Print.

Creating and believing in mythical heroes and heroic deeds are ways that human consciousness conceptualizes major forces and conflicts. The ancient Greeks satisfied the need to understand the how, the why, the origin of things, and the destiny of human beings beyond social and biological life through an elaborate polytheism that invested divinities with powers and personalities beyond the human. Mythology is a figurative and metaphorical way the human intellect grasps its world and answers and resolves some of the most fundamental questions. Unlike ancient Greece, today's society faces one of its most pressing issues in the relationship between humanity and technology. Contemporary technology has created the machine, which has dwarfed the natural abilities of the human body. The native capacities of the human mind are slow and meager compared to the speed and processing power of the computer. The major events of the nineteenth and twentieth centuries have been shaped by the use and development of the machine in manufacturing, war, transportation, and scientific research.

DO NOT TURN THE PAGE UNTIL TOLD TO DO SO **STOP** DO NOT RETURN TO A PREVIOUS TEST

Part 3: Mathematics

TIME: 90 minutes for 56 questions

DIRECTIONS: Choose the best answer to each question. Mark the corresponding oval on the answer sheet. Remember, try to answer every question.

1. A pair of u and w values is written on a card. The pair works as a solution to the equation $5u + 3w = 0$. Paul begins to write another pair of u and w values on a different card. He increases the value of w by 10 from the first card. What type of change must the value of u have from the first card in order for the new pair to also work as a solution to the equation?

(A) decrease of 6

(B) increase of 3

(C) decrease of 10

(D) increase of 6

(E) increase of 10

$8x + 3$

$2x$

© John Wiley & Sons, Inc.

2. If the preceding rectangle has a perimeter of 46 units, what is the area of the rectangle?

(A) 2

(B) 22

(C) 23

(D) 26

(E) 76

3. The following numbers are equal to each other, except for one. Which of the five numbers is NOT equal to the other four?

(A) 4.7

(B) $4\frac{7}{10}$

(C) $\frac{47}{10}$

(D) $\frac{470}{1,000}$

(E) 4.700

DAVID'S TEST SCORES

Test Number	Score
1	83
2	72
3	94
4	100
5	68
6	?

4. Based on the preceding chart, if David's test scores for the current term are 83, 72, 94, 100, and 68, what will he need to make on his next test to have an average test score of 85?

(A) 93

(B) 85

(C) 83.4

(D) 70

(E) 94

5. Brady is trying to solve the equation $5x + 7 = 42$. For his first step, he subtracted 7 from both sides of the equation. Which of the following should be his next step?

(A) Subtract 5 from both sides of the equation.

(B) Divide both sides of the equation by 5.

(C) Multiply both sides of the equation by 49.

(D) Add 5 to both sides of the equation.

(E) Divide both sides of the equation by 35.

6. A decimal number is multiplied by 0.1. That operation is the equivalent of which of the following? Select **all** that apply.

(A) multiplying by $\frac{1}{10}$

(B) moving the decimal point one place to the right

(C) multiplying by 10

(D) moving the decimal point one place to the left

(E) dividing by 10

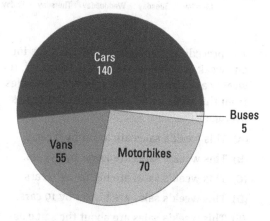

Cars
140

Buses
5

Vans
55

Motorbikes
70

7. In the preceding figure, cars are the preferred method of transportation. Approximately what percentage of the total people preferred vans?

(A) 20%

(B) 48%

(C) 55%

(D) 80%

(E) 149%

Sales

Marketing

Computer
Technology

Business Management

8. The preceding diagram represents areas of expertise of executives at a business. According to the diagram, which of the following statements is true?

(A) Not all of the marketing experts are business management experts.

(B) None of the sales experts are computer technology experts.

(C) None of the marketing experts are computer technology experts.

(D) None of the sales experts are marketing experts.

(E) All of the marketing experts are computer technology experts.

9. Which of the following is the simplified equivalent to $\dfrac{p^2 - 49}{p^2 - 2p - 35}$?

(A) $\dfrac{p-3}{p-7}$

(B) $p-5$

(C) $p+3$

(D) $\dfrac{p+7}{p+5}$

(E) $\dfrac{p-7}{p-5}$

> Any number that is 1 greater than the square of an integer is a prime number.

10. Which of the following numbers is a counter-example to the preceding statement?

(A) 5

(B) 17

(C) 37

(D) 65

(E) 101

11. What is the sum of $-2\frac{5}{7}$ and $12\frac{4}{5}$?

(A) $-34\frac{26}{75}$

(B) $-12\frac{1}{5}$

(C) $10\frac{3}{35}$

(D) $15\frac{18}{35}$

(E) $18\frac{1}{7}$

12. What is the greatest common factor (GCF) of the first 28 prime numbers?

(A) 0

(B) 1

(C) 2

(D) 4

(E) 28

13. Which of the following is the least common multiple of 8 and 14?

(A) 2

(B) 28

(C) 48

(D) 56

(E) 96

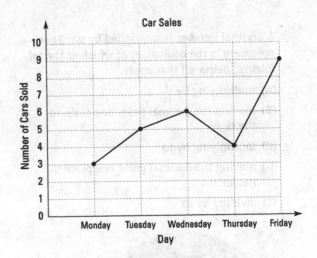

14. The preceding graph shows the car sales for one week at Bobby's dealership. Last year, the weekly average was 18 cars. How do the sales from this week so far compare to last year's average?

(A) This week's sales are lower by 9 cars.

(B) This week's sales are lower by 15 cars.

(C) This week's sales are higher by 9 cars.

(D) This week's sales are higher by 19 cars.

(E) This week's sales are about the same as last year's average.

23 41 78 83 41 54 85 92 76

15. Which statement about the preceding data set is false?

(A) The mean is greater than the median.

(B) The median is greater than the mean.

(C) The mean is greater than the mode.

(D) The mode is less than the median.

(E) The mean and the median are greater than the mode.

16. Martin wrote the first seven prime numbers on a piece of paper in order from least to greatest. What is the quotient of the last number he wrote divided by the first number?

(A) $\frac{2}{17}$

(B) 6.5

(C) 7

(D) 8.5

(E) 17

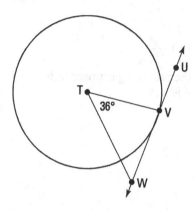

17. In the above diagram, line WU is a tangent to circle T. Point V is the point of tangency. The measure of ∠WTV is 36°. What is the measure of ∠TWV?

(A) 5°

(B) 17°

(C) 37°

(D) 48°

(E) 54°

18. Sharon drove from her home to the gym at a rate of 55 miles per hour. She returned home along the same route at the same speed. If she spent 45 minutes at the gym and was gone from home for a total of 1.5 hours, approximately how many total miles did Sharon travel?

(A) 10 miles

(B) 21 miles

(C) 41 miles

(D) 83 miles

(E) 100 miles

19. Which of the following is 245% in simplest improper fraction form?

(A) $\frac{21}{40}$

(B) $\frac{92}{45}$

(C) $\frac{43}{20}$

(D) $\frac{98}{40}$

(E) $\frac{49}{20}$

20. Al played 27 games of golf in a period of two weeks. The number of games he played in that period is 75 percent of the number he played in the previous two weeks. How many games of golf did Al play in the first two-week period?

(A) 1

(B) 2

(C) 20

(D) 36

(E) 277

GO ON TO NEXT PAGE

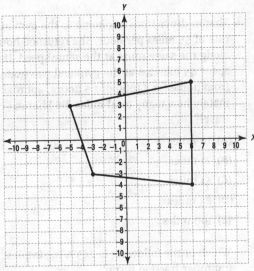

© John Wiley & Sons, Inc.

21. If the preceding quadrilateral is translated 7 units up and 4 units left, what will be the coordinates of the new vertices?

    (A) $(4, -3)$, $(5, 3)$, $(-6, -4)$, and $(-6, 5)$

    (B) $(-10, 1)$, $(-12, 7)$, $(-1, 0)$, and $(-1, 9)$

    (C) $(7, 4)$, $(9, 10)$, $(-2, 3)$, and $(-2, 12)$

    (D) $(-7, 4)$, $(-9, 10)$, $(2, 3)$, and $(2, 12)$

    (E) $(4, -7)$, $(10, -9)$, $(3, 2)$, and $(12, 2)$

22. If Adam's hourly wages increase from $16.50 to $19.60, what is his percent increase rounded to the nearest tenth?

    (A) 3.1%

    (B) 18.8%

    (C) 20.0%

    (D) 31.0%

    (E) 36.1%

23. The number of humans living on Earth is approximately 7.53 billion. What is that number in scientific notation?

    (A) 7.53×10^{-9}

    (B) 7.53×10^{-6}

    (C) 7.53×10^{9}

    (D) 7.53×10^{12}

    (E) 70.53×10^{12}

24. Erik, Kristi, and Brecken own a plot of land. Erik owns $\frac{2}{5}$ of the land, and Kristi owns $\frac{1}{3}$ of it. What fraction of the land does Brecken own?

    (A) $\frac{1}{5}$

    (B) $\frac{4}{15}$

    (C) $\frac{2}{7}$

    (D) $\frac{8}{15}$

    (E) $\frac{2}{3}$

25. $8v^2 - 7(u+v) + \frac{55}{w}$

    Evaluate the preceding expression for $u = 4$, $v = -2$, and $w = 11$.

    (A) 21

    (B) 23

    (C) 51

    (D) 68

    (E) 74

26. A polling company plans to poll workers of a large corporation on an issue not concerning the corporation. Which of the following methods would most likely involve polling an unbiased sample?

    (A) asking the president of the company questions and using his answers to represent the company

    (B) asking questions of every tenth worker who walks through the main entrance for work

    (C) polling every third cafeteria worker who enters the cafeteria for work

    (D) asking people questions as they stand in the lobby awaiting an executive meeting

    (E) conducting interviews of people who work in the mailroom

27. The distance from Mike's house to his office building is 4.72 km. The distance from Cindy's house to the same office building is 5,358 meters. How much greater is the distance from Cindy's house to the office building than the distance from Mike's house to the office building?

Select **all** such measurements.

(A) 4.886 kilometers

(B) 6,380 decimeters

(C) 4,886 meters

(D) 5,310.8 decameters

(E) 638 meters

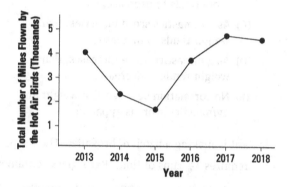

28. The preceding line graph shows the total numbers of miles flown by a hot-air balloon team in each of six years. In which of the six years did the team experience the second-biggest drop in number of miles flown from the previous year?

(A) 2014

(B) 2015

(C) 2016

(D) 2017

(E) 2018

29. Natasha is nine times Eric's age. In ten years, the sum of their ages will be 60. What is Natasha's age now?

(A) 4

(B) 14

(C) 36

(D) 46

(E) 60

30. Every square is all of the following types of figures EXCEPT

(A) parallelogram

(B) quadrilateral

(C) rectangle

(D) trapezoid

(E) rhombus

31. Peter has 20 coins in his coin collection. The total value of his coin collection is $3.65, and it consists of only quarters and dimes. If he has two more quarters than he has dimes, how many quarters does he have?

(A) 8

(B) 9

(C) 10

(D) 11

(E) 12

32. A triangle has a side with a measure of 3 m. It also has a side with a measure of 8 m. Which of the following could be a measure of a side of the triangle?

Indicate **all** such values.

(A) 5 m

(B) 7 m

(C) 9 m

(D) 11 m

(E) 13 m

GO ON TO NEXT PAGE

33. Linda flipped a quarter into the air four times, and it landed on heads all four times. If Linda flips the same quarter into the air again, what is the probability that it will land on tails? Write your answer in the space provided.

_____

34. Which of the following numbers is between $-\frac{19}{4}$ and -3.71?

(A) $-3\frac{3}{4}$

(B) $-3\frac{71}{100}$

(C) $-3\frac{3}{16}$

(D) -3.7

(E) -5

437 12 54 37 858 7 902 600 218 519

35. The set of data above represents the scores achieved by a group of students in a school video-game competition. What is the median of the set of scores?

(A) 37

(B) 218.5

(C) 219

(D) 327.5

(E) 364

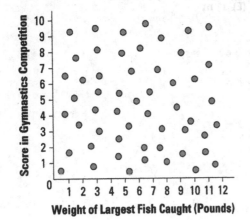

36. At the Jackson Gymnastics and Fishing Tournament, every participant competed in both a fishing contest and a gymnastics competition. Each ordered pair represented on the preceding scatter plot shows a participant's results. The goal in the fishing competition was to catch the biggest fish possible. None of the fish in the lake where the fishing contest was held weighed more than 12 pounds. Which of the following is indicated by the scatter plot?

Select all such statements.

(A) As fish weight increases, gymnastics score tends to increase.

(B) As fish weight increases, gymnastics score tends to decrease.

(C) As gymnastics score increases, fish weight tends to increase.

(D) As gymnastics score increases, fish weight tends to decrease.

(E) No correlation between fish weight and gymnastics score is apparent.

37. Kat is making a batch of brownies. The recipe requires $4\frac{2}{3}$ cups of flour. Kat's glass container can hold $\frac{3}{4}$ of a cup of flour. If she fills the container with flour multiple times and pours the flour into her cooking dish, how many times must she fill the glass container to pour the necessary amount of flour for the recipe?

(A) $6\frac{2}{9}$

(B) $6\frac{4}{9}$

(C) $7\frac{5}{8}$

(D) $8\frac{5}{12}$

(E) $8\frac{3}{4}$

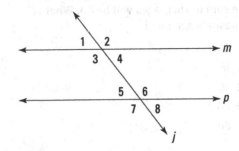

38. In the preceding diagram, line *m* is parallel to line *p*. Both lines are intersected by transversal line *j*. The measure of $\angle 1$ is 51°. What is the measure of $\angle 6$?

(A) 39°

(B) 41°

(C) 99°

(D) 129°

(E) 131°

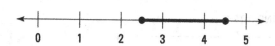

39. Which of the following are coordinates of points that are in the shaded interval on the preceding number line?

Indicate **all** such coordinates.

(A) 0^2

(B) 1^2

(C) 1.7^2

(D) 2^2

(E) 2.4^2

40. Triangle ABC and triangle PQR are similar triangles. Each side of triangle PQR is 3 times the length of its corresponding side in triangle ABC. How many times greater is the area of triangle PQR than the area of triangle ABC?

(A) 2

(B) 3

(C) 6

(D) 9

(E) 12

41. During the 2013–2014 baseball season, Mark hit the ball 48 out of 60 times he was up at bat. What percentage of the times Mark was up at bat did he NOT hit the ball?

(A) 20 percent

(B) 30 percent

(C) 50 percent

(D) 60 percent

(E) 80 percent

42. Tim is twice as old as Sarah. Rachel is $\frac{1}{3}$ Tim's age. If Rachel is 18, how old are Tim and Sarah?

(A) Tim is 36, and Sarah is 54.

(B) Tim is 27, and Sarah is 54.

(C) Tim is 81, and Sarah is 36.

(D) Tim is 54, and Sarah is 27.

(E) Tim is 72, and Sarah is 36.

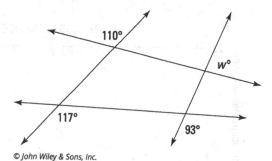

© John Wiley & Sons, Inc.

43. In the preceding diagram, what is the value of *w*?

(A) 40

(B) 46

(C) 84

(D) 94

(E) 100

Member	Number of Books Read
Nathan	12
Marcie	4
David	10
Richard	1
Carey	7
Sharon	3
Michael	2

44. The previous table shows the numbers of books read in one summer by the kids in a reading club. What is the range of the set of data?

(A) 2

(B) 4

(C) 5.57

(D) 11

(E) 12

GO ON TO NEXT PAGE

45. In the equation written out as "22 is p less than a third of r," which of the following equations indicates the relationship between p and r?

(A) $22 - p = \frac{r}{3}$

(B) $\frac{r}{3} - p = 22$

(C) $\frac{p}{3} - r = 22$

(D) $p - 22 = \frac{r}{3}$

(E) $\frac{r}{3} - 22 = -p$

TRENDS IN THE USE OF DATING SITES

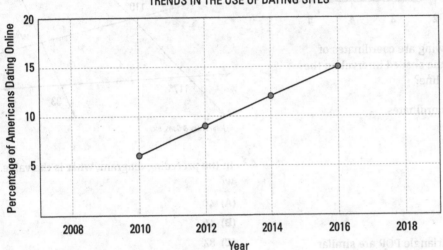

46. The preceding graph shows a trend in the use of dating sites. If this trend continues, how many people would be expected to date online in 2020?

(A) 15%

(B) 16%

(C) 18%

(D) 20%

(E) 21%

47. Twenty-four bees of a certain species formed a colony. Their population triples over a time period of exactly 1 week. If all bees remain in the colony, how many will be living in it precisely 8 weeks after the colony was formed?

(A) 5.2488×10^4

(B) 5.2488×10^5

(C) 1.57464×10^5

(D) 1.57464×10^6

(E) 4.72392×10^7

$$3x - 2y = -2$$
$$2x - 3y = -13$$

48. What is the solution to the preceding system of equations?

(A) (0, 0)

(B) (4, 7)

(C) (11, 15.5)

(D) (7, 4)

(E) (0, 11)

Stem	Leaf
1	0 3 6
2	1 6 7 8
3	5 5 6
4	1 1 5 6 9
5	0 3 6 8

Key: 3|5 = 35

49. The preceding stem-and-leaf plot reflects the ages of males who signed up for a volunteer golf tournament. How many males signed up?

(A) 5

(B) 10

(C) 19

(D) 50

(E) 53

50. Molly cut out $\frac{4}{5}$ of a full pizza and ate $\frac{2}{3}$ of that portion. Wes cut off and took $\frac{7}{8}$ of the rest of the portion and ate $\frac{2}{7}$ of what he took. What fraction of the full pizza did Wes eat?

(A) $\frac{1}{105}$

(B) $\frac{1}{15}$

(C) $\frac{2}{15}$

(D) $\frac{1}{5}$

(E) $\frac{3}{8}$

51. When a certain number wheel is spun, it has a $\frac{1}{4}$ probability of stopping on a red number. If it lands on a red number, the probability of that red number also being prime is $\frac{5}{11}$. If the wheel is spun, what is the probability that it will land on a red prime number?

(A) $\frac{5}{44}$

(B) $\frac{2}{5}$

(C) $\frac{11}{20}$

(D) $\frac{31}{44}$

(E) $\frac{3}{4}$

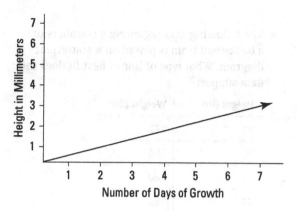

Number of Days of Growth

52. The preceding graph displays the height of an exotic plant after the presented numbers of days of growth of the plant. If the plant continues to grow at the same rate, which of the following will be the height of the plant, in millimeters, when it has reached 12 days of growth?

(A) 2

(B) 3

(C) 6

(D) 12

(E) 22

$$5451.38 \times 10^7$$

53. What can be done to the above expression to change it to scientific notation?

(A) Move the decimal three places to the left and make the exponent three higher.

(B) Move the decimal three places to the left and make the exponent three lower.

(C) Move the decimal two places to the left and make the exponent two higher.

(D) Move the decimal two places to the left and make the exponent two lower.

(E) Move the decimal four places to the left and make the exponent one higher.

GO ON TO NEXT PAGE

54. The following data regarding 5 members of a basketball team is placed on a scatterplot diagram. What type of line of best fit does this data support?

Height (in)	Weight (lb)
71	172
70	168
68	160
74	185
76	190

(A) a positive slope line

(B) a negative slope line

(C) a horizontal line

(D) a vertical line

(E) no line of best fit

55. Olivia wants to convert 65 feet per minute to a unit rate consisting of a number of inches per second. By which of the following can she multiply $\frac{65 \text{ feet}}{1 \text{ minute}}$ to make the conversion? Indicate **all** such factors.

(A) $\frac{1 \text{ minute}}{65 \text{ feet}}$

(B) $\frac{1 \text{ foot}}{12 \text{ inches}}$

(C) $\frac{1 \text{ minute}}{60 \text{ seconds}}$

(D) $\frac{60 \text{ seconds}}{1 \text{ minute}}$

(E) $\frac{12 \text{ inches}}{1 \text{ foot}}$

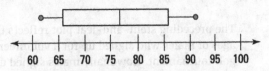

Biology Test Scores in Mrs. Cox's Fourth Period Class

56. Between what two numbers is the interquartile range of the set of data represented by the previous box-and-whisker plot?

(A) 5 and 10

(B) 15 and 25

(C) 30 and 50

(D) 65 and 90

(E) 75 and 80

Chapter **17**

Practice Exam 2: Answers and Explanations

I f this is the second practice exam you've taken, we hope that you've improved your scores and you're feeling more confident about taking the Praxis Core. Use the answers and explanations in this chapter to see how well you performed and to understand where you might have gone wrong on the answers you missed. Remember, the practice exam can help you determine where you need to focus your studies in preparation for the real Praxis Core. If you want to score your test quickly, flip to the end of the chapter, where the "Answer Key" gives only the letters of the correct answers.

TIP

If you want even more preparation for taking the Praxis, check out the instructions in the "Beyond the Book" section of the book's Introduction. Using those instructions, you can access the online test bank to take more practice tests, review the answers and explanations, and get a personalized summary of your performance.

Part 1: **Reading**

1. **E. change his legacy.** The passage explains that Nobel was dismayed by seeing himself referred to as "the merchant of death" in a newspaper. He didn't want to be remembered that way, so he endowed the Nobel Prizes so that he would be remembered for something else. In other words, he wanted to change his legacy.

    The right answer is not Choice (A) because the passage never indicates that Nobel made any money from the Nobel Prizes; on the contrary, he devoted the fortune he had made through other means to their establishment.

    The right answer is not Choice (B) because there's no indication that Nobel thought he would actually live longer as a result of endowing the Nobel Prizes. The idea was to be remembered differently, not to live longer.

    The right answer is not Choice (C) because, although Nobel did want the prizes to draw attention away from other things he had done, he wasn't specifically trying to cover those things up. People would still know that he had invented explosives; he would just be *more* famous for something else.

The right answer is not Choice (D) because the passage doesn't indicate that Nobel's motivation was to be famous forever as a result of endowing the prizes. He was already famous, but he wanted to be remembered for doing a good thing rather than causing destruction.

2. **C. report on new and exciting discoveries about killer whales.** The passage reports on recent discoveries about killer whales. As is often the case with such questions, the broadest answer is the correct one.

The right answer is not Choice (A) because, although the passage mentions that there are killer whale subspecies, it doesn't explain how they diverged or even focus entirely on the subspecies topic.

The right answer is not Choice (B) because the passage never implies any sort of disagreement between scientists and the general public.

The right answer is not Choice (D) because even though the passage closes by mentioning that most scientists now use the term *orca*, the passage as a whole is not an argument about proper terminology.

The right answer is not Choice (E) because the passage isn't particularly humorous and, although it's not written for an audience of experts, there's no indication that it's aimed specifically at children.

3. **C. evidence that nobody actually lived there.** The middle of the passage not only mentions the lack of evidence that Göbekli Tepe was residential but also establishes that the site dates from before humans established permanent residences at all. Therefore, its purpose must have been ceremonial.

The right answer is not Choice (A) because there's no reason to assume that an archaeological site was religious just because it's large. Religious structures are often large, but so are other types of structures.

The right answer is not Choice (B) because, although the passage explains that Göbekli Tepe had elaborate artwork, that fact in and of itself is not the primary evidence that it was a religious site.

The right answer is not Choice (D) because, although the passage does briefly compare Göbekli Tepe to Stonehenge, it doesn't imply a "close resemblance."

The right answer is not Choice (E) because the passage doesn't say that Göbekli Tepe played a role in the invention of agriculture; it mentions that people hadn't developed agriculture when Göbekli Tepe was built as support for the conclusion that the structure could not have been a permanent residence.

4. **D. inform readers about Hoffman and the controversy surrounding her work.** The best answer here is Choice (D) because the passage does inform readers about Hoffman and about the controversy surrounding her work. Other answers may be close, but Choice (D) is the most accurate description of the overall passage content.

The right answer is not Choice (A) because, although the passage does include details about Hoffman's life and work, it doesn't include enough personal detail to be called "a personal biography."

The right answer is not Choice (B) because the passage doesn't argue a specific viewpoint on the Field Museum's decision.

The right answer is not Choice (C) because the passage as a whole is about Hoffman and her work. It mentions that some people were offended by Hoffman's work and establishes what their reasoning was, but that doesn't serve as the basis of the passage.

The right answer is not Choice (E) because, although the passage establishes that there haven't been many famous female sculptors, that point isn't the main topic.

5. **A. trailblazing.** *Pioneering* is a synonym for *trailblazing* — breaking new ground in a certain area (in Hoffman's case, being among the first famous female sculptors).

None of the other choices is correct because they aren't what *pioneering* means in this context. Many of them may be words that accurately describe Hoffman or her work, but they don't fit what the question is asking for.

6. **B. multicultural sensitivity with celebration of the achievements of women.** The thorny paradox raised by the passage is that, although Hoffman's work was potentially offensive from a multiculturalist perspective, the same sensitivity that demands we address this also encourages us to celebrate the work of important women in the arts.

The right answer is not Choice (A) because how would we even know what the cultural values of the future are? The passage doesn't make any predictions.

The right answer is not Choice (C) because the passage doesn't set up any kind of paradox that pits science against art; rather, it pits the duty to honor women artists against the duty to respect the views of people who might object to her work.

The right answer is not Choice (D) because the passage doesn't pit *intentionalist criticism* (that is, approaching works of art from the perspective of the artist's original intentions) against *interpretive criticism* (prioritizing that art's effects on the audience). Even if you didn't recognize these terms, it should still be possible to eliminate this answer choice. It was there to try to trick people who automatically gravitate toward the most confusing answer choice.

The right answer is not Choice (E) because the passage doesn't really get into what the mission of a museum is. You can reasonably infer that the Field Museum decided to hide the sculptures because of public opinion, but the passage is about Hoffman's work itself, not the museum and its mission.

7. **A. It examines a familiar concept from an unorthodox viewpoint.** The familiar concept is the Renaissance, and the unorthodox viewpoint is the notion that it was caused by the preceding Black Plague.

The right answer is not Choice (B) because the passage doesn't address or imply any conspiracy theory.

The right answer is not Choice (C) because the passage never brings up a two-sided controversy.

The right answer is not Choice (D) because the passage discusses only one artistic period — the Renaissance — not two.

The right answer is not Choice (E) because, though the passage mentions how the Black Plague came to Europe, it doesn't scientifically analyze the origins of the epidemic.

8. **A. "artistic brilliance."** The preoccupation with the "human experience" mentioned in the second paragraph led to the "artistic brilliance" mentioned in the first. The Renaissance is primarily associated with the arts, and the other part of the sentence in the second paragraph clearly alludes to the "scientific advancement" previously mentioned, so the rest of the sentence is presumably about the arts.

The right answer is not Choice (B) because the first half of the sentence ("Desperation to stop the devastation had gotten people thinking . . ."), not the second, is what alludes to the "scientific advancement" mentioned in the first paragraph.

The right answer is not Choice (C) because the first paragraph mentions "violent political oppression" as a characteristic of the Dark Ages, not of the Renaissance.

The right answer is not Choice (D) because the "European golden age" indicates the Renaissance as a whole, not specifically the artistic side of it.

The right answer is not Choice (E) because "Europe's worst nightmare" refers to the Black Plague itself, not to the effect it had on people's relationship to art.

9. **E. coherent.** The feudal system collapsed after the Plague, so it was no longer *feasible* or *coherent* (it couldn't "cohere" or "hold together").

None of the other choices is correct because none gives a correct definition of *feasible*.

10. **C. Laborers became so scarce that they were in a better bargaining position.** The passage explains that the peasant population was so devastated by the Plague that laborers were suddenly in a better position simply because there were fewer of them.

The right answer is not Choice (A) because, although advances in ethical philosophy were made during the Renaissance, those advances aren't why feudalism ended. The collapse of feudalism was an immediate effect of the Plague, and the advancements of the Renaissance were an eventual effect.

The right answer is not Choice (B) because scientific discoveries aren't what gave the emergent middle class a wider range of job options in the early Renaissance. The opportunities occurred because so many commoners died during the Plague.

The right answer is not Choice (D) because trade between Asia and the Mediterranean is mentioned in the passage as contributing to the outbreak of the Plague in Europe, not as having led to "increased mechanization."

The right answer is not Choice (E) because the passage doesn't mention feudal lords fleeing their castles and abandoning their lands. They stayed in their castles, but there weren't enough peasants left to farm their lands anymore.

11. **B. The Renaissance was the inevitable result of the vastly reduced population.** The meaning of the given phrase, and the point of the passage as a whole, is that the Renaissance came about more or less because Europe's population was thinned out by the Plague.

The right answer is not Choice (A) because the passage never implies that the Renaissance didn't happen. The passage just makes an argument about what caused it.

The right answer is not Choice (C) because the passage says that the Black Plague, not the Renaissance, started in central Asia.

The right answer is not Choice (D) because the passage never implies that the Renaissance actually happened at a different time from when it reportedly did; it just makes an interesting argument about its causes.

The right answer is not Choice (E) because, although the passage does indeed offer a dark explanation for the causes of the Renaissance, it doesn't suggest that the term "Renaissance" itself is a *euphemistic* (whitewashed) expression signifying something else.

12. **B. correct a widespread misconception.** The author starts off by calling a term "misunderstood" and then goes on to explain what it means "in actuality." The goal is clearly to correct a widespread misconception.

The right answer is not Choice (A) because the passage isn't *espousing* (arguing for) a particular philosophy; it's correcting the erroneous usage of a particular term. Simply pointing out a correct definition is not the same as making an argument for a certain viewpoint.

The right answer is not Choice (C) because the author is not taking sides in a philosophical debate; no "debate" exists here. A popular misunderstanding is not a philosophical debate.

The right answer is not Choice (D) because the author isn't suggesting a new definition, just explaining what the original definition actually is.

The right answer is not Choice (E) because the correct usage of a term isn't an "unpopular viewpoint." Even if most people misunderstand the term, the simple correction of a definition isn't a debate.

13. **C. philosophers use to describe others' work rather than their own.** The author explains that actual philosophers always use the term *nihilism* pejoratively, as an insult for others' work, not as a description of their own.

The right answer is not Choice (A) because the author explains that philosophers do in fact use the term *nihilism*; they just do so as an insult.

The right answer is not Choice (B) because among actual philosophers, the term *nihilism* always means the same thing. Non-philosophers are the people who use it incorrectly.

The right answer is not Choice (D) because the passage never implies that philosophers used the term *nihilism* during one particular era of philosophy only.

The right answer is not Choice (E) because the passage establishes that young people accidentally misuse the term *nihilism*, which directly refutes the idea that they misuse it deliberately.

14. **D. dispassionate.** The author is simply explaining something in an unemotional fashion. The term for that sort of tone is *dispassionate.*

The right answer is not Choice (A) because the author isn't using irony or cracking jokes at anyone's expense, so calling the tone *sardonic* isn't accurate.

The right answer is not Choice (B) because the author isn't talking down to anyone, so the tone isn't *condescending.*

The right answer is not Choice (C) because the author doesn't seem to be particularly merry or gleeful, so the tone doesn't qualify as *jovial.*

The right answer is not Choice (E) because the author doesn't seem to be frightened, wary, or paranoid about anything, so the tone isn't *apprehensive.*

15. **E. jargon.** The word *jargon* refers to any language that would be used by the members of a certain group among themselves but not recognized by outsiders without an explanation, so to call these terms *jargon* is accurate.

The right answer is not Choice (A) because the terms aren't being used ironically; the definitions given are what they actually mean to people in the ASMR community.

The right answer is not Choice (B) because the words in italics aren't being emphasized more than others; they have special formatting because they're unfamiliar.

The right answer is not Choice (C) because even though some of the terms are in fact proper nouns, the italics don't identify that characteristic. The term YouTube is a proper noun, and it isn't italicized in the passage.

The right answer is not Choice (D) because the terms aren't being misused. They may be unfamiliar to most people, but they're being used to mean what they actually mean.

16. **C. use a specific animal as an example to explain a particular term.** The passage begins by talking about the dunnart, but it then becomes clear that it's using the dunnart just as a springboard to talk about the larger concept of convergent evolution. So this reading is one of those "specific example to general principle" passages that are such a common presence on tests like the Praxis.

The right answer is not Choice (A) because, even though the passage briefly compares a particular marsupial to a particular non-marsupial, the purpose of the passage as a whole isn't to distinguish between marsupials and non-marsupials. (If it were, the passage would have explained the difference.)

The right answer is not Choice (B) because, although the passage does specify that dunn-arts aren't mice, the passage as a whole is about convergent evolution, not specifically about mice.

The right answer is not Choice (D) because, although the passage does correct people, it would be a bit much to say it *excoriates* them. To *excoriate* is to severely and angrily criticize, so this would be a wild exaggeration of the passage's tone.

The right answer is not Choice (E) because the passage doesn't say or imply that the dunn-art itself is key to evolutionary theory; it's an example of convergent evolution, which is an important concept, but a lot of animals are examples of this process.

17. **C. It does not in fact provide a legal excuse for violence.** This answer choice is essentially a paraphrase of the final sentence of the passage, so it's definitely a point that the passage makes.

The right answer is not Choice (A) because the passage implies that a lot of people don't know what the *Chaplinsky* decision means, not that no one does.

The right answer is not Choice (B) because the passage never mentions anything about *Chaplinsky* being affected in any way by subsequent Supreme Court decisions.

The right answer is not Choice (D) because, although the defendant claimed the law was unconstitutional, the passage never takes a stance on this issue.

The right answer is not Choice (E) because one of the answer choices was in fact correct.

18. **C. explain that a very famous character was heavily based on a lesser-known one.** The passage does in fact explain that a famous fictional detective (Sherlock Holmes) was based on a lesser-known one (Auguste Dupin); that's all the passage does, so Choice (C) is the correct answer. In general, answer choices that use broad terms such as *explain* are more likely to be correct than answer choices that use more specific words such as *argue* or *accuse*.

The right answer is not Choice (A) because the passage specifies that Arthur Conan Doyle "admitted the obvious influence and gave Poe credit," so plagiarism isn't an issue.

The right answer is not Choice (B) because the passage doesn't get into whose stories were better from a critical perspective.

The right answer is not Choice (D) because the traditional explanation has always acknowledged, as did Conan Doyle himself, that Poe invented the detective story. Poe's stories aren't as broadly famous as Conan Doyle's, but critics have always known that Poe's came first.

The right answer is not Choice (E) because the passage doesn't address any confusion about Holmes and Dupin. It says that most people have heard of Holmes but not Dupin, not that people confuse the two.

19. **A. conjecture.** The fact that the sentence begins with "perhaps" is a clue that the final sentence of the passage is *conjecture* — a guess or hypothesis.

The right answer is not Choice (B) because the final sentence isn't a clue to what comes later, so it's not *foreshadowing*.

The right answer is not Choice (C) because *synecdoche* means "using a part to symbolize a whole," as in when you refer to your car as your "wheels." This figure of speech doesn't occur in the final sentence. (Don't be fooled into picking an answer just because it's a fancy word; these options are often tricks.)

The right answer is not Choice (D) because an *allusion* is a reference, and the final sentence doesn't contain a reference to anything.

The right answer is not Choice (E) because *poetic license* refers to an author describing something in an inaccurate or ungrammatical way for the sake of aesthetics, and the final sentence doesn't do this.

20. **B. gauche.** "Socially oblivious" in this context means "rude" or "unmannerly," and *gauche* is a fancy synonym for such terms.

None of the other choices is correct because none presents a close synonym of "socially oblivious."

21. **A. intellectual disdain.** The author spends the rest of the passage explaining why the "rule of thumb" alluded to at the outset is a stupid idea, so you can fairly say that the author has "intellectual disdain" for it. (*Disdain* means "contempt" or "revulsion.")

The right answer is not Choice (B) because the author may be cynical but doesn't appear to be *shocked* by anything.

The right answer is not Choice (C) because the author doesn't regret anything or seem to be melancholy.

The right answer is not Choice (D) because the author is discussing a problem that exists, not delusionally imagining one.

The right answer is not Choice (E) because, although the author is *dismissing* the idea that he criticizes, he is not being *dismissive*. He wants to combat the problem, not ignore it.

22. **E. self-contained.** *Discrete* means "separate," so the best answer is Choice (E), self-contained. (Remember, don't confuse *discrete* with *discreet*, meaning "secret.")

None of the other answers is correct because none is the definition of *discrete*.

23. **C. naïve administrators.** The second sentence of the passage lays the blame on administrators, and the passage in general explains why their policy is naïve.

None of the other choices is correct because the second sentence of the passage establishes that the author blames administrators. Nowhere does the passage indicate that the author blames teachers, students, scientists, or parents. It never mentions scientists or parents at all.

24. **B. draw the line at respecting opinions that are demonstrably untrue.** The last sentence of the first paragraph and the first two sentences of the second are the places where the passage most clearly states that the author's complaint is with professors being obliged to respect ideas that aren't true.

The right answer is not Choice (A) because the author never says or implies that professors should deliberately offend students. The point is that offense is sometimes unavoidable in education, not that it's desirable.

The right answer is not Choice (C) because the author's point is that facts need to be respected over opinions; the passage never suggests that professors should simply teach their own personal opinions.

The right answer is not Choice (D) because this statement is nearly the opposite of the author's point; the passage argues that professors *should* correct students' opinions and *not* merely their mechanics.

The right answer is not Choice (E) because the author never implies that professors should go out of their way to flunk students who appear unknowledgeable. The passage simply says that correcting students' general knowledge should be part of a professor's job.

25. **C. whether to retreat from the world or try to improve it.** Choice (C) is a clear paraphrase of the line from the passage that says "should a good person 'turn the other cheek' in the face of evil . . . or should he attempt to make the world a better place by actively combating the wicked?"

The right answer is not Choice (A) because, early on, the author flatly states that the famous soliloquy "is *not* about whether to commit suicide."

The right answer is not Choice (B) because, although the author explains that the paradox Hamlet confronts involves whether to take a certain piece of scriptural advice, the passage never indicates that the question is about God's existence itself.

The right answer is not Choice (D) because the author explains that the speech is about whether to fight evil at all or to passively ignore it, not about the methods one may use to fight it.

The right answer is not Choice (E) because the passage doesn't imply that "To be or not to be" is about something incomprehensible; the author explains one possible meaning.

26. **E. unacceptable.** The author states that "Hamlet already flatly ruled out suicide on ethical grounds" — that is, he decided suicide is unacceptable.

The right answer is not Choice (A) because the author states that Hamlet "flatly ruled out suicide on ethical grounds," which would indicate that suicide itself is unethical. And there's no indication Hamlet considers suicide the lesser of two evils.

The right answer is not Choice (B) because the "eternal paradox of morality" referred to in the passage is about whether to be active or passive in the face of evil, not about suicide.

The right answer is not Choice (C) because, although the idea that suicide is "attractive but frightening" is the common interpretation of the speech, the passage establishes early on that the author believes that interpretation to be wrong.

The right answer is not Choice (D) because nothing in the passage points to this answer.

27. **D. correct a misreading.** In the third sentence, the author states that "virtually everyone . . . is dead wrong about what [the speech] means," and then goes on to explain why. This establishes that the author's goal is to "correct a misreading."

The right answer is not Choice (A) because the author explains that Hamlet is wondering about whether to take an ethical stand; it's not the author's own goal in writing the passage.

The right answer is not Choice (B) because the author is trying to explain a complex piece of literature, not to simplify a complex issue. If anything, the author's reading of the speech is more complex than the common one.

The right answer is not Choice (C) because the author never warns about anything that might happen in the future.

The right answer is not Choice (E) because the author explains that other people often make a mistake in explaining the "to be or not to be" speech; the passage never indicates the author made a mistake or apologizes for having made one.

28. **A. Why should great apes have rights similar to human rights?** The final sentence — which begins with "The reasoning goes that . . ." — is where the passage does indeed answer the question of why great apes should have rights similar to human rights.

The right answer is not Choice (B) because the passage never fully explains the difference between a great ape and a monkey. Monkeys are never mentioned.

The right answer is not Choice (C) because, although the passage mentions that the founders of the Great Ape Project are Peter Singer and Paola Cavalieri, it never says that they're its most famous supporters. There may be more famous supporters whom the passage simply never mentions.

The right answer is not Choice (D) because the passage mentions that great apes are both exhibited in zoos and used in scientific research, but it never says which purpose more great apes are used for.

The right answer is not Choice (E) because, although the passage mentions that great apes are intelligent, it never explains how researchers know this or how apes' intelligence is measured.

29. **D. They do not make use of underground burrows.** The second sentence of the passage states that hares live in nests and that rabbits are the ones who live in burrows.

The right answer is not Choice (A) because that passage says that the hare is the only *mammal* with a jointed skull, not that it's the only *animal* with one.

The right answers are not Choice (B), (C), or (E) because all these statements are true of rabbits, not hares.

30. **C. Matter can be sent into the past, but not living beings.** The passage objects to the idea of time travel to the past by explaining that a human traveling to the past may cause a paradox. The idea that inanimate matter could be sent to the past, but not living beings, would get around the paradox, and thus resolve the objection.

The right answer is not Choice (A) because, though physicists do indeed believe exceeding the speed of light to be impossible, the passage doesn't raise any objection to a time travel theory based on this issue. So a discovery that surpassing the speed of light is somehow possible would not resolve an objection made in the passage.

The right answer is not Choice (B) because physicists already believe that exceeding the speed of light is impossible, so a confirmation of this fact wouldn't explain anything.

The right answer is not Choice (D) because the passage never mentions other dimensions, so the discovery would be irrelevant to the claims of the passage.

The right answer is not Choice (E) because the passage doesn't present any definitions of *time,* so the discovery would be irrelevant to the claims of the passage.

31. **B. exceptions and qualifications.** The expression *fine print* (like the words in small font at the bottom of a contract, where most of the catches are hidden) usually means something like "exceptions and qualifications," and that's what it means in this context, as well; time travel is possible, but not in the way you probably think.

None of the other choices is correct because none is the definition of *fine print* as it's used in the passage.

32. **D. It's a natural consequence of the relationship between speed and time.** The passage closes by saying that a time machine could be anything that goes fast enough — that is, that time travel is a natural consequence of the relationship between speed and time.

The right answer is not Choice (A) because the passage never says that humans have already achieved time travel.

The right answer is not Choice (B) because the passage never says that time travel to the future would resolve its own paradoxes, just that it wouldn't create any.

The right answer is not Choice (C) because, although the passage does explain that time travel to the future is to some extent a matter of perspective, that statement doesn't make time travel the same as an illusion. (It's actually happening, but only happening relative to something else.)

The right answer is not Choice (E) because, though the simple passage of time does technically constitute time travel to the future (in other words, you're traveling to the future right now because time is passing), that topic isn't addressed in the passage.

33. **D. Passage 1 explains the origin of a theory that Passage 2 then modifies.** Passage 1 explains where the asteroid theory came from, and Passage 2 then adds *to* the asteroid theory, rather than presenting a competing theory.

The right answer is not Choice (A) because the theories presented in the two passages aren't in fact *mutually exclusive* (a term meaning they can't be true at the same time). Passage 2 admits that the asteroid impact happened; it just argues that other things happened too.

The right answer is not Choice (B) because, although Passage 2 admits that the asteroid impact happened, that doesn't mean that the two passages are exploring the same theory from different angles. Passage 1 concerns the theory that the dinosaurs were killed by just an asteroid, and Passage 2 concerns the theory that they were killed by an asteroid, as well as other events.

The right answer is not Choice (C) because the theory in Passage 2 doesn't seek to replace the theory in Passage 1, just to modify it. Besides, to say that it has replaced the theory in Passage 1 would be incorrect because the readings establish that the theory from Passage 1 is still more popular.

The right answer is not Choice (E) because Passage 1 and Passage 2 present two (marginally) different theories, not the data and the conclusions for one single theory.

34. **A. ignoring.** When Passage 2 says that attributing the extinction solely to an asteroid would involve "writing off" the Deccan Traps, the best paraphrase is to say it would involve *ignoring* the Deccan Traps role in the extinction.

The right answer is not Choice (B) because the objection made by Passage 2 is that the asteroid theory involves believing that the Deccan Traps played no role in the extinction — that is, that the Deccan Traps are being ignored, not misrepresented.

The right answer is not Choice (C) because Passage 2 doesn't indicate that the theory from Passage 1 is *obscuring* (covering up or hiding) the role played by the Deccan Traps. It means that the theory from Passage 1 simply doesn't account for the Deccan Traps having played a role.

The right answer is not Choice (D) because the complaint of Passage 2 is that the Deccan Traps aren't being credited with enough of a role in the extinction, which is the opposite of saying that their role is being exaggerated.

The right answer is not Choice (E) because Passage 2 isn't accusing anyone of plagiarizing anything; it's saying that important data is being ignored, not stolen.

35. **C. One author believes it killed the dinosaurs, and the other believes it was one of multiple causes.** Passage 1 concerns the theory that the asteroid killed the dinosaurs, and Passage 2 concerns the theory that at least one other cause may have been involved. The place to confirm this answer is the final sentence of Passage 2 ("No one is denying . . .").

The right answer is not Choice (A) because saying that the author of Passage 2 doesn't believe an asteroid killed the dinosaurs is going too far.

The right answer is not Choice (B) because both authors agree about the timing of the asteroid impact.

The right answer is not Choice (D) because the author of Passage 1 characterizes the asteroid as being heavily composed of iridium, and the author of Passage 2 never challenges this description.

The right answer is not Choice (E) because the author of Passage 1 never appears to doubt that the asteroid theory is correct.

36. **E. Passage 1 explains the history of its theory, whereas Passage 2 does not.** Much of Passage 1 consists of an explanation of when and how the asteroid theory was developed and supported. Passage 2 never gets into the history of the idea that the Deccan Traps played a role.

The right answer is not Choice (A) because the two passages aren't each based on a different scientific discipline. They both involve both chemistry and physics. (Also, keep in mind that an answer choice that would require you to have outside knowledge of the topic is extremely unlikely to be correct; this is a reading test, not a science test.)

The right answer is not Choice (B) because, although the passages establish that the asteroid hit what is now North America and the Deccan Traps formed in what is now Asia, neither passage says that either of these locations is the only place dinosaurs lived.

The right answer is not Choice (C) because the two passages are very similar in tone and reading level, so there's no reason to assume that they were composed with different audiences in mind.

The right answer is not Choice (D) because there's no indication that the author of Passage 2 formulated the Deccan Traps theory, so it's not an original (to the author) theory.

37. **B. limited.** The theory from Passage 1 suggests one cause, and the theory from Passage 2 puts forth multiple causes that include the cause from Passage 1. Therefore, Passage 2 sees Passage 1 as limited — that is, true but incomplete.

The right answer is not Choice (A) because Passage 2 admits that the asteroid impact happened and played a role.

The right answer is not Choice (C) because Passage 2 never implies that the theory in Passage 1 is old and that its own idea is newer.

The right answer is not Choice (D) because Passage 2 never implies that the theory in Passage 1 is contradicting itself somehow.

The right answer is not Choice (E) because there's no indication that the author of Passage 2 sees the theory from Passage 1 as *elitist* (somehow snobbish or exclusionary).

38. **D. the causes of an agreed-upon event.** The "agreed-upon event" is the extinction of the dinosaurs, and both passages discuss its possible causes.

The right answer is not Choice (A) because the two authors agree about when dinosaurs lived, which you can tell by the fact that they're both discussing the extinction as having happened at the same time.

The right answer is not Choice (B) because neither author ever says anything about some dinosaurs disappearing at different times from other dinosaurs.

The right answer is not Choice (C) because the author of Passage 2 concedes that the asteroid struck Earth, and that it did so at the time that the theory in Passage 1 claims.

The right answer is not Choice (E) because neither author ever addresses the question of why one theory or another is popular, or even talks much about which theory is more popular.

39. **C. the Medieval Period and the Renaissance.** *The Middle Ages* and *the Medieval period* are two terms for the same time in history, and the Renaissance came after it. The correction the passage makes is that suits of armor are actually from the Renaissance, not from the Medieval period.

The right answer is not Choice (A) because, although the passage begins by mentioning that most children would be mistaken about when suits of armor were actually worn, it also says that most adults would, too.

The right answer is not Choice (B) because the passage doesn't distinguish between armor and regular clothing; it distinguishes between the armor of two time periods.

The right answer is not Choice (D) because, although the passage establishes that European warriors were the ones who wore suits of armor, the passage doesn't involve comparing them to warriors from other places.

The right answer is not Choice (E) because the passage actually compares wealthy and less-wealthy warriors, saying essentially that all Medieval warriors would have worn plate-and-mail suits.

40. **C. civilization hasn't existed long enough to substantially alter human instinct.** The point of the passage as a whole, as stated most clearly in the last two sentences, is that human instinct and genetics were formed for millions of years, and that civilization hasn't existed for nearly long enough to have substantially altered these things.

The right answer is not Choice (A) because the passage never suggests that common people are broadly wrong about how long civilization has been around; rather, the point is that most people don't know how long humans were evolving before that time.

The right answer is not Choice (B) because the point of the passage is that the development of civilization (government, agriculture, and so on) *didn't* substantially affect human genetics, simply because it happened too recently to have done so yet.

The right answer is not Choice (D) because the passage certainly doesn't say that human evolution stopped when civilization began, just that the previous evolutionary trajectory hasn't yet been significantly altered by civilization.

The right answer is not Choice (E) because the passage never implies that experts disagree about any of this information; it says that laypeople misunderstand it.

41. **B. apparently straightforward questions can be muddled by vague definitions.** Ultimately, the point of the passage is to call attention to the fact that the apparently straightforward question "What is the southernmost city in the world?" is not so easy to answer because it depends on what counts as a city.

The right answer is not Choice (A) because the point of the passage is not that geography is complex. The problem at hand is how many people a community needs in order to count as a city, which is not a geographic question.

The right answer is not Choice (C) because the passage never implies that the argument is silly. The author appears to think that the question is valid and interesting, though apparently unsolvable.

The right answers are not Choice (D) or Choice (E) because the passage never takes one country's side over the other's; it just explains the nature of the dispute.

42. **B. The first paragraph mainly presents details of William Tyndale's life, and the second deals more closely with his influence.** The first paragraph is mainly about Tyndale's life, and the second paragraph is mainly about his influence, so Choice (B) is clearly the best description.

The right answer is not Choice (A) because both paragraphs are mainly about Tyndale, not just the second one.

The right answer is not Choice (C) because the first paragraph is about Tyndale's life, not the influence of his Bible.

The right answer is not Choice (D) because the first paragraph is much more about Tyndale and only briefly mentions Shakespeare. Though the second paragraph does allude to Tyndale's influence on Shakespeare, that's not the main point of the paragraph.

The right answer is not Choice (E) because the first paragraph is mainly about Tyndale, not other Bible translations done before the invention of the printing press. (It only briefly alludes to Wycliffe's translation.) Furthermore, the second paragraph is specifically about Tyndale's Bible, not printed Bible translations in general.

43. **A. use him as the standard by which influence on the English language is measured.** Both allusions to Shakespeare invoke him as the greatest influence on the English language, in order to praise Tyndale by establishing his influence on both the language and on Shakespeare himself.

The right answer is not Choice (B) because only the second paragraph discusses Tyndale's influence on Shakespeare himself, and even then, it never says that Tyndale was the greatest influence on Shakespeare, just a major influence (don't pick a choice that goes further than you need it to).

The right answer is not Choice (C) because the passage never directly compares Tyndale's language to Shakespeare's.

The right answer is not Choice (D) because the passage never implies that people confuse figures of speech coined by Tyndale with those coined by Shakespeare.

The right answer is not Choice (E) because, although the passage certainly elaborates on the political constraints on Tyndale's work, it never mentions anything about political constraints on Shakespeare's.

44. **E. The character of modern literary English was largely established in the 16th century.** The passage cites Shakespeare and Tyndale as the two greatest influences on the form of literary English, and it establishes that they both did their work in the 16th century.

The right answer is not Choice (A) because the passage says that Shakespeare was influenced by Tyndale's use of language in his translation of religious texts, not necessarily by religion itself.

The right answer is not Choice (B) because the passage never addresses the question of political differences among various English translations of the Bible.

The right answer is not Choice (C) because nothing in the passage implies that Tyndale's Bible caused Henry VIII's break with Rome. The passage merely explains that the Roman Catholic Church was against English translations of the Bible, and that such translations (such as Tyndale's, even though he was already dead) became acceptable in England after the king broke with the Catholic Church.

The right answer is not Choice (D) because the passage never says that translations done by individuals are generally superior to those done by committees.

45. **C. who attempted a similar project to Tyndale's but was thwarted.** The lone mention of Wycliffe explains that, like Tyndale, he tried to translate the Bible into English, but was thwarted because his handwritten translations made it much easier for the state to seize and destroy most of the copies.

The right answer is not Choice (A) because the passage never says that Tyndale was directly inspired by Wycliffe, just that they both tried to do the same thing.

The right answer is not Choice (B) because the passage never says Wycliffe was as talented as Tyndale or mentions anything about Wycliffe's politics.

The right answer is not Choice (D) because the passage doesn't say that Wycliffe's influence on English is harder to measure than Tyndale's; on the contrary, you can safely assume that Wycliffe's influence was much smaller because his Bibles were destroyed.

The right answer is not Choice (E) because the passage never says Wycliffe was more religious than Tyndale.

46. **D. knack for.** To have an "ear for" something, in music or in writing, is to be finely attuned to its capacity for aesthetic beauty — that is, to have a knack for it.

None of the other choices is correct because, in this context, no other answer is an appropriate synonym for the phrase "ear for."

47. **2010.** All you need to do is look for the year above which the bottom and the middle lines are farthest apart. That's 2010, when there were apparently about 6 wolves in the Wenaha pack and 15 in the Imnaha pack.

48. **C, D. (C) 2011, (D) 2012.** In the years 2009 and 2010, the numbers indicated by the bottom and middle lines seem to add up to the number indicated by the top line — that is, the Wenaha and Imnaha wolf packs' populations added up to the total wolf population of the state. Thus, the right answer is not Choice (A) or Choice (B). For the years 2011 and 2012 (Choices [C] and [D]), however, the number indicated by the top line is greater than the sum of the numbers indicated by the bottom and middle lines, indicating that wolves that belonged to packs other than the Wenaha and Imnaha were in the state.

49. **B. 2010.** This question is a tricky one; you have to look at the closeness of the middle and top lines, but you also have to consider percentages. In 2009, there looked to be about 15 wolves total (top line) and 10 in the Imnaha pack, so that means that 2/3 of the wolves in

the state, or about 67 percent, were from the Imnaha pack. In 2010, the top and middle lines are also close together, but there look to be roughly 20 wolves total and 15 in the Imnaha pack, which means that 3/4 of the wolves in the state, or about 75 percent, were from the Imnaha pack. The answer is 2010, because 75 percent is more than 67 percent.

The right answer is not Choice (A), (C), or (D) because the percentage of total wolves that were from the Imnaha pack in those years is not the highest of the yearly percentages.

The right answer is not Choice (E) because the graph does in fact reveal the requested information.

50. **A. Both psychopathy and sociopathy are observable via brain autopsy.** The middle of the passage states that, concerning both psychopathy and sociopathy, "there is agreement that the conditions involve observable differences in brain structure."

The right answer is not Choice (B) because the passage states that only *some* professionals think that both psychopathy and sociopathy are synonymous with antisocial personality disorder.

The right answer is not Choice (C) because the passage states that only *some* professionals use the terms *psychopath* and *sociopath* interchangeably.

The right answer is not Choice (D) because the passage establishes (at the end) that, according to how an increasing number of professionals use the term, only psychopaths genuinely have no sense of right and wrong.

The right answer is not Choice (E) because the passage states that psychopathy and sociopathy are difficult, but not impossible, to detect via psychological examination.

51. **E. clear up confusion on the parts of general readers.** The passage aims merely to distinguish the ways that psychological professionals currently use the terms *psychopath* and *sociopath*.

The right answer is not Choice (A) because the passage is explanatory and informative, not critical — it never says that anyone is wrong.

The right answer is not Choice (B) because the passage never expresses a personal opinion; the author only explains what other people think.

The right answer is not Choice (C) because the passage never mentions any particular person; it's just about the terms *psychopath* and *sociopath*, in general.

The right answer is not Choice (D) because, although the passage mentions that psychopaths often try to evade detection, the goal isn't to warn professionals about this fact; the passage establishes that professionals already know it.

52. **C. logically expectable.** When the passage describes the average person's confusion as "forgivable," it does so as a way of introducing the idea that many professionals use the terms psychopath and sociopath in different ways. The idea is that the layperson's confusion is unavoidable and understandable, so the most correct answer is Choice (C).

The right answer is not Choice (A) because, although the term *forgivable* sometimes means "morally excusable," the passage doesn't regard the average person's confusion as a moral issue, so Choice (A) is not the best of the choices in context.

The right answer is not Choice (B) because the passage doesn't say that the average person's confusion is confusing itself. This choice is trying to fool you by repeating words.

The right answer is not Choice (D) because the passage never indicates that the author regards people's confusion as either disturbing or amusing.

The right answer is not Choice (E) because the passage never says or implies that the author considers the layperson's confusion annoying.

53. **B. idiosyncratic.** This is just a vocabulary question. The passage explains (at the end) that sociopaths have a sense of right and wrong that is massively out of line with most people's sense of these things. The fancy word for "different from other people" is Choice (B), *idiosyncratic*.

None of the other choices is correct because none of the other words means "different from other people." Choice (A), *ineffable*, means "inexpressible." Choice (C), *inextricable*, means "impossible to separate." Choice (D), *remunerative*, means "yielding money or reward." Choice (E), *eleemosynary*, means "related to or depending on charity."

54. **D. multifaceted.** The point of the passage is that Yeats's poetry went through many different phases and had many different sides to it. The fancy word for "having many dimensions or aspects" is *multifaceted*, Choice (D).

None of the other choices is correct because none represents the "having many dimensions or aspects" concept.

55. **A. the general to the specific.** The first sentence states a widespread principle or truism, and the rest of the passage talks about a specific example of it.

The right answer is not Choice (B) because, although the first sentence of the passage does make reference to a superstition, the point of the passage as a whole is not to distinguish superstition and fact.

The right answer is not Choice (C) because the passage is not divided between *rhetoric* (attempts at eloquence or persuasion) and logic.

The right answer is not Choice (D) because the first sentence of the passage doesn't provide data that the rest of the passage subsequently interprets.

The right answer is not Choice (E) because the first sentence of the passage doesn't state a cause with the rest of the passage and then delineate its effects.

56. **C. they are absent from preserved records.** The second sentence of the passage explains that "dirty" words are usually used in speech for a long time before they're written down in any way that survives to be studied. This gap is what makes pinning down their etymologies difficult.

The right answer is not Choice (A) because the passage never says that linguists are reluctant to study "dirty" words; on the contrary, it says that doing so is a source of "amusement" for them.

The right answer is not Choice (B) because, although the final sentence of the passage states that misinformation often circulates about the origins of "dirty" words, it explains that people do this mistakenly rather than deliberately.

The right answer is not Choice (D) because the passage never says or implies that the meanings of "dirty" words change more often than those of other words do.

The right answer is not Choice (E) because the passage explains that "dirty" words actually don't usually originate as acronyms, although urban legends often claim that they do.

Part 2: Writing

1. E. No error

The sentence does not contain an error.

The right answer is not Choice (A) because the *its* without the apostrophe is the possessive, so it's correct in this context.

The right answer is not Choice (B) because the conjunction *whereas* means something like "while on the other hand," so it's used correctly here.

The right answer is not Choice (C) because the sentence uses the adverb *simply* (meaning "merely") to clearly and correctly modify the verb *use*.

The right answer is not Choice (D) because this phrasing is grammatically correct as written. You may have picked this answer thinking it was missing the word *that*; although the phrase "that it contains" would also be correct, the omission of *that* doesn't create an error.

2. D. by which

A movie is based *on* a book, not *by* a book, so "on which" is the correct prepositional construction here.

The right answer is not Choice (A) because the movies in question are both "well made" and "considered cinematic classics." The construction is clear and correct, and no commas or other punctuation are necessary.

The right answer is not Choice (B) because *for* is the correct preposition in this context.

The right answer is not Choice (C) because saying that a movie didn't do something "as fully as did the book" (as opposed to "as fully as the book did") is perfectly correct, even though it's a bit more formal than everyday speech.

The right answer is not Choice (E) because there is, in fact, an error in the sentence.

3. A. people who believe

The word *who* should be omitted, because the first clause needs to be independent ("people believe" is an independent subject and verb, whereas "people *who* believe" subordinates the verb to a pronoun, resulting in an incomplete sentence).

The right answer is not Choice (B) because this phrase correctly uses the infinitive.

The right answer is not Choice (C) because this is a clear and correct usage of an adverb modifying an adverb that is modifying an adjective.

The right answer is not Choice (D) because *than* (not *then*) is the word used for comparisons.

The right answer is not Choice (E) because there is, in fact, an error in the sentence.

4. B. whom was

The pronoun is the subject of a subordinate clause, so *who* is correct.

The right answer is not Choice (A) because the regular past tense is fine here.

The right answer is not Choice (C) because using a comma after a conjunction is acceptable when the sentence is interrupted by a modifier (such as "ironically") at that point.

The right answer is not Choice (D) because the participial verb form is fine here.

The right answer is not Choice (E) because there is, in fact, an error in the sentence.

5. C. is their

The antecedent of the pronoun is singular ("organism"), so you need the singular possessive pronoun *its* rather than the plural *their* here.

The right answer is not Choice (A) because the past tense *arose* is perfectly correct here.

The right answer is not Choice (B) because the third-person singular *distinguishes* is correct here.

The right answer is not Choice (D) because the subject of the verb in question is *manner*, so the third-person singular *passes on* (meaning "transmits") is correct.

The right answer is not Choice (E) because there is, in fact, an error in the sentence.

6. D. myself

The speaker isn't performing a verb reflexively with themselves as the object, so *myself* is incorrect. They should simply have said *me*.

The right answer is not Choice (A) because *should you* is a correct construction here (to mean "If you should . . .").

The right answer is not Choice (B) because, although data is often used as a singular noun, it's actually plural, so *data represent* is correct.

The right answer is not Choice (C) because the infinitive is correct in this context.

The right answer is not Choice (E) because there is, in fact, an error in the sentence.

7. E. No error

This sentence doesn't contain any errors.

The right answer is not Choice (A) because the *its* without an apostrophe is the possessive, so it's correct in this context. (*It's* with an apostrophe is the contraction for *it is*.)

The right answer is not Choice (B) because although the *as* isn't necessary here, including it's not wrong. In fact, including it is more formal and correct.

The right answer is not Choice (C) because *Scots* (Scottish people) is a proper noun and should be capitalized.

The right answer is not Choice (D) because *after the time* (meaning after the time in which he lived) is perfectly clear and correct in this context.

8. B. further

Because the sentence is discussing physical distance, *farther* is the correct adjective.

The right answer is not Choice (A) because the word *children* should indeed be possessive here (even though the museum doesn't literally belong to actual children), and the apostrophe is in the right place.

The right answer is not Choice (C) because *than* (not *then*) is the word used for comparisons.

The right answer is not Choice (D) because *less* is correct here (as opposed to *fewer*, which would be used for countable quantities).

The right answer is not Choice (E) because there is, in fact, an error in the sentence.

9. C. in which

You don't hear *in* an album; you just *hear* an album, so the addition of *in* is unnecessary and incorrect. Plus, *which* is used incorrectly here; the phrase should read "*that* I have ever heard."

The right answer is not Choice (A) because *very many* is a perfectly clear and correct instance of an adverb modifying an adjective.

The right answer is not Choice (B) because *best-produced* forms a two-word adjective here (in which the first word isn't an adverb), so it should be hyphenated.

The right answer is not Choice (D) because the present-perfect *have ever heard* is correct in this context.

The right answer is not Choice (E) because there is, in fact, an error in the sentence.

10. E. No error

This sentence contains no error.

The right answer is not Choice (A) because the word *effect* can also be a verb meaning "to bring about."

The right answer is not Choice (B) because *then* (not *than*) is the word used for conditional statements ("if/then"), so it's correct here.

The right answer is not Choice (C) because *affect* is a verb meaning "to change," so it's correct here.

The right answer is not Choice (D) because *than* (not *then*) is the word used for comparisons, so it's correct here.

11. A. being

The word *being* is pointlessly inserted into the appositive phrase; the convention is for an appositive phrase to limit itself to the definition without the participle. When a verbal (*being*) is added, it creates a participial phrase.

The right answer is not Choice (B) because *planet* doesn't need to be capitalized.

The right answer is not Choice (C) because *dwarfs* is used correctly here as a verb meaning "to make something else seem small by comparison."

The right answer is not Choice (D) because *it's* (with an apostrophe) is the contraction for "it is," so it's correct in this context.

The right answer is not Choice (E) because there is, in fact, an error in the sentence.

12. B. were

The subject is *treasurer*, which is singular, so the verb should be *was*, not *were*.

The right answer is not Choice (A) because "devoted to the upkeep . . ." is an adjectival phrase modifying *society*, so this construction is correct.

The right answer is not Choice (C) because "unsure of how best to allocate" is perfectly correct, even though it may be a bit more formal than everyday speech.

The right answer is not Choice (D) because the infinitive is correct in this context.

The right answer is not Choice (E) because there is, in fact, an error in this sentence.

13. **B. had been**

The speaker is unsure of whether Danny ever actually arrived, so the hypothetical *was* ("if he *was* here") is correct, not the past-perfect *had been*.

The right answer is not Choice (A) because *you've been* — a contraction of the present-perfect *you have been* — is perfectly correct in this context.

The right answer is not Choice (C) because *earlier* (meaning "before now") is correct here.

The right answer is not Choice (D) because the regular past tense *didn't see* ("did not see") is correct here.

The right answer is not Choice (E) because there is, in fact, an error in the sentence.

14. **D. of**

Of is the wrong preposition here; correct options include *optimistic about* or possibly *optimistic for*, but not *optimistic of*.

The right answer is not Choice (A) because beginning a sentence with a subordinate *because* clause is fine as long as the clause is followed by a comma and an independent clause.

The right answer is not Choice (B) because the possessive *half a day's travel* (meaning "half a day's *worth of* travel") is a correct construction.

The right answer is not Choice (C) because the clause preceding it is independent, so the clause in Choice (C) must be preceded by a conjunction.

The right answer is not Choice (E) because there is, in fact, an error in the sentence.

15. **A. principle**

The words *principle* and *principal* are commonly confused. When the word means "primary or leading," as it does in this sentence, *principal* is correct.

The right answer is not Choice (B) because *students give* is correct subject/verb agreement.

The right answer is not Choice (C) because the verb form is correct here.

The right answer is not Choice (D) because the noun *suspicion* is used correctly in this context: The reason is suspicion.

The right answer is not Choice (E) because there is, in fact, an error in the sentence.

16. **D. credibly**

The proper word here is the noun *credibility*, not the adverb *credibly*.

The right answer is not Choice (A) because the noun performing the verb is *hallucinations*, which is plural, so the plural verb *are* is correct.

The right answer is not Choice (B) because *behind* is used correctly ("the explanation behind . . ."). You could also use *of* or *for*, but having other viable options doesn't automatically make the given wording wrong.

The right answer is not Choice (C) because the noun performing the verb is *theory*, which is singular, so the singular verb *is* is correct.

The right answer is not Choice (E) because there is, in fact, an error in the sentence.

17. D. have had for

The sentence uses the wrong preposition here. It should say that the poems had an influence *on* other writers, not an influence *for* them.

The right answer is not Choice (A) because the present perfect *have often been dismissed* is the correct tense in this context.

The right answer is not Choice (B) because *overly sentimental* is a correct instance of an adverb modifying an adjective.

The right answer is not Choice (C) because the present perfect *has more recently been given credit* is correct.

The right answer is not Choice (E) because there is, in fact, an error in the sentence.

18. B. Kings and Queens

The words *kings* and *queens* should not be capitalized here because they're used in the abstract, rather than as titles before the names of specific people.

The right answer is not Choice (A) because "the question of which" is the correct construction here.

The right answer is not Choice (C) because *Glorious Revolution* is a proper noun referring to a specific historical event, so it should be capitalized.

The right answer is not Choice (D) because *than* (not *then*) is the word used for comparisons, so it's correct here. As for the placement of the verb *are*, it's correct either before or after "executive decisions."

The right answer is not Choice (E) because there is, in fact, an error in the sentence.

19. A. they are

As the rest of the sentence shows, the *Dimetrodon* is being discussed in the singular, so you need the singular *it is* here rather than the plural *they are*.

The right answer is not Choice (B) because *alongside* is used correctly in this context.

The right answer is not Choice (C) because using *at all* for the sake of emphasis is perfectly fine (although not necessary).

The right answer is not Choice (D) because "rather a" is a correct construction in this context. You could also add *was* ("was rather a"), but omitting it is acceptable.

The right answer is not Choice (E) because there is, in fact, an error in the sentence.

20. D. is not doing his or her job

The teacher in the sentence is singular ("a teacher"), so you need a singular verb (*is*), pronoun (*his or her*), and direct object (*job*). The other choices are incorrect because they use plural versions of one or more of these items.

21. A. all with

The sentence is correct the way it is.

The right answer is not Choice (B) because the addition of the word *in* is incorrect; *which all have* would be acceptable, but not *in which all have*.

The right answer is not Choice (C) because you need *have* in this context, not the participial form *having*. (Also, *which* is preferable to *whom* in this case because the subject is an animal rather than a person.)

The right answer is not Choice (D) because it forms a comma splice.

The right answer is not Choice (E) because it forms a comma splice.

22. C. century, James Joyce

This choice is a correct example of an introductory subordinate clause (*although* is a subordinating conjunction) followed by a comma and an independent clause.

The right answer is not Choice (A) because the sentence doesn't need both the subordinating conjunction *although* before the first clause and the coordinating conjunction *but* before the second clause. Using one or the other would be correct, but not both.

The right answer is not Choice (B) because neither clause is independent.

The right answer is not Choice (D) because a semicolon here would not separate two independent clauses (an *although* clause is subordinate).

The right answer is not Choice (E) because *although* and *however* are doing the same job, so you don't need both of them (and if only *however* were there, you'd need to add a semicolon or to start a new independent clause).

23. E. wit and to shock with

This sentence presents a parallel-phrasing issue. The *both* is a clue that the sentence needs two of the same type of grammatical element, both being infinitives in this case, not separated by a comma: "the capacity both to delight . . . and to shock. . . ." The only answer that accomplishes that is Choice (E).

The right answer is not Choice (A) because the *both* is a clue that the two verbals (*to delight* and *to shock*) should be in the infinitive and not separated by a comma.

The right answer is not Choice (B) because the *both* is a clue that the two verbals (*to delight* and *to shock*) should be in the infinitive and not separated by a comma.

The right answer is not Choice (C) because this forms a comma splice (and a nonsensical one, at that, because the first independent clause says *both* but only includes one infinitive).

The right answer is not Choice (D) because the *both* is a clue that you need *and* rather than *but*.

24. C. Having spotted the skyline in the distance, we decided to try to

This sentence is a misplaced-modifier question. The modifier needs to attach to who or what spotted the skyline; as written, that subject is "attempt," and clearly an attempt can't spot something. The sentence is written in the first-person plural (we/us) point of view, so opening the independent clause with "we" makes sense.

The right answer is not Choice (A) because the "attempt" isn't who or what spotted the skyline, so the modifier is misplaced.

The right answer is not Choice (B) because the first clause would need to be independent for the second clause to begin with "and."

The right answer is not Choice (D) because this answer has a comma splice (because *therefore* isn't a conjunction).

The right answer is not Choice (E) because it's a long participial phrase, not a complete sentence.

25. D. for whom female fans showed their appreciation by throwing

Choice (D) is the only answer choice in which all the prepositions and verb forms agree: Liszt was the artist *for whom* female fans showed their appreciation *by throwing* their undergarments. Remember, all the verbs in a sentence don't always have to be in the same form.

The right answer is not Choice (A) because it's constructed to imply that the fans had an appreciation for the act of throwing undergarments itself rather than an appreciation for Liszt.

The right answer is not Choice (B) because the past-progressive form *were showing* rather than the regular past tense *showed* is both awkward and unnecessary.

The right answer is not Choice (C) because using the infinitive *to show* in place of the past-tense *showed* is nonsensical in context.

The right answer is not Choice (E) because the fans showed their appreciation *by throwing* their undergarments (it was the *means by which* they showed appreciation), so you need *by throwing* rather than *to throw*.

26. E. consuming all the planets of our solar system before collapsing

The participle *consuming* and the gerund *collapsing* are appropriate for the last part of the sentence. The participle is an adjective that modifies "Sun," and the gerund is a noun that functions as a an object of a preposition.

The right answer is not Choice (A) because the *and* should not have a comma before it (even if it didn't, the sentence as phrased would still be awkward).

The right answer is not Choice (B) because it forms a comma splice.

The right answer is not Choice (C) because a semicolon here wouldn't separate two independent clauses. (What follows the semicolon isn't an independent clause. In fact, it's not even a clause.)

The right answer is not Choice (D) because the sentence ends with an independent clause that's not preceded by a comma.

27. B. Africa, is a biodiversity hotspot, with over 90 percent of its wildlife being found

The subject of the sentence is *Madagascar*, and the verb is *is*; this choice sets it up so that the subject and verb are separated by an appositive phrase, and the sentence ends with a prepositional phrase.

The right answer is not Choice (A) because what precedes the independent clause isn't an independent clause. It's not even a clause (it has no verb). It would need to be an independent clause to be followed by a comma and "and."

The right answer is not Choice (C) because this isn't a complete sentence (*being* can't be the main verb).

The right answer is not Choice (D) because it's not a complete sentence (it has no main verb).

The right answer is not Choice (E) because the inclusion of *it* gives the sentence two subjects, so it doesn't grammatically agree.

28. C. now; the rest of you, however, may

This choice correctly joins two independent clauses with a semicolon (the second of which contains the adverb *however*, correctly set off with a pair of commas).

The right answer is not Choice (A) because it forms a comma splice (*however* is not a conjunction).

The right answer is not Choice (B) because it also forms a comma splice (*however* is not a conjunction).

The right answer is not Choice (D) because, although the semicolon is correct, the *however* in the second independent clause would need to be set off with two commas.

The right answer is not Choice (E) because it forms a comma splice (between *now* and *the*).

29. A. than are those of

The sentence is correct as it is. The construction may be a little more formal than you're used to hearing in speech, but it isn't wrong.

The right answer is not Choice (B) because you're comparing *the works of* van Gogh to *the works of* other painters, not to the painters themselves, so you need to say *than are those of* (meaning the works of) any other, rather than simply *than* any other.

The right answer is not Choice (C) or Choice (D) because the *more* is a clue that you need *than*, rather than *compared* (the preposition you use after it — *to* or *with* — doesn't matter, because *compared* itself is wrong).

The right answer is not Choice (E) because you need *than* rather than *compared*, not both words.

30. B. the truth is that firing

This is the only choice that forms a coherent, correct sentence.

The right answer is not Choice (A) because the construction "the truth of it is" would require a comma afterwards, in place of the omitted "that."

The right answer is not Choice (C) or Choice (D) because the presence of the word *is* later in the sentence causes those phrasings to become nonsensical. (Always read the whole sentence to determine whether a choice makes sense in context.)

The right answer is not Choice (E) because it needs a comma after *truly* (and even then, it's extremely awkward).

31. B. A certain type of person is likely to tell you that poetry is read by hardly anyone, and that the few people who do read it comprise an insular cadre of specialists ignored by the culture at large.

None of the choices is incorrect from a technical standpoint, but Choice (B) is the most concise and efficient of the answer choices.

The right answer is not Choice (A) because this sentence is unnecessarily repetitive and could be more concise by eliminating "and that these people are."

The right answer is not Choice (C) because it's unnecessarily repetitive and could be more concise in the "only an . . ." and "that is also . . ." portions.

The right answer is not Choice (D) because it's terribly awkward, particularly the phrase "hardly anyone who does not comprise."

The right answer is not Choice (E) because it's unnecessarily repetitive and could be more concise in the "adding that . . ." and "specifying that . . ." portions.

32. A. Leave it as it is.

The sentence makes perfect sense exactly where it is and as it's written.

The right answer is not Choice (B) because the word "poetry" belongs in quotation marks; the sentence refers to the act of saying it. Plus, there's no particular reason to italicize the word *very*.

The right answer is not Choice (C) because beginning the sentence with "on the other hand" would make no sense; Sentence 5 doesn't present a counterpoint to the previous sentence.

The right answer is not Choice (D) because this sentence would be out of place as the second sentence of the next paragraph; the explanation it alludes to would have already begun.

The right answer is not Choice (E) because the sentence doesn't present a counterpoint to the previous sentence, so you don't need to insert the word *however*.

33. **D. to the delight of some and the consternation of others**

The point of the paragraph is that slam poetry has both its supporters and its detractors, so the phrase "to the delight of some and the consternation of others" makes the most sense in context.

The right answer is not Choice (A) because although definitions are often challenged, that isn't the most relevant statement to be made about the specific topic under discussion here.

The right answer is not Choice (B) because simply announcing that something is about to be explained is usually an unnecessary rhetorical move; another answer choice is clearly more necessary.

The right answer is not Choice (C) because the paragraph as a whole doesn't address any "varying degrees of success" on the part of slam poets. Another choice makes more sense in context.

The right answer is not Choice (E) because the passage doesn't refer to slam poets employing any "devious" or "unexpected" methods. The reference makes no sense in context.

34. **E. who typically stand at lecterns and read from notes or a published book during recitals**

Because the rest of the sentence describes the performance style of slam poets, the best choice for the underlined portion is the phrase that contrasts this style with the style of traditional poets.

None of the other answer choices is correct because none addresses the true subject of the sentence as a whole, which seeks to contrast the *styles* of traditional and slam poets.

35. **C. Their work is designed to be seen in performance rather than read.**

The concluding sentence aims at a characterization of the slammers' work as a whole, and to say that it "is designed to be seen in performance rather than read" sums it up nicely.

The right answer is not Choice (A) because this vague and obvious statement adds very little to the paragraph. It is true, but it could just as well not be there, which isn't what you want from a conclusion.

The right answer is not Choice (B) because, although true, it's a minor, unnecessary detail. Another answer choice performs a much more logical function in this context.

The right answer is not Choice (D) because speculation about slammers using props in the future is an odd tangent and not the most effective way to end the paragraph and transition into the next.

The right answer is not Choice (E) because changing the subject to slammers making money for their venues is a tangent that is never addressed elsewhere.

36. A. Ironically

The fact that each group thinks it's being oppressed by the other is ironic, so "Ironically" is a perfectly logical way to begin the sentence.

The right answer is not Choice (B) because the sentence isn't a result of what was being discussed immediately prior, so "Therefore" doesn't make sense as a transition word.

The right answer is not Choice (C) because the emphatic "Undeniably" adds little in this context. This portion of the passage isn't weighing evidence and/or attempting to persuade the reader.

The right answer is not Choice (D) because the sentence isn't a counterpoint to the previous one, so "on the other hand" doesn't make sense as a transition.

The right answer is not Choice (E) because you don't need to say "In conclusion" just because it's the last sentence. It would seem out of place here.

37. B. a magazine article

You can tell this citation is for a magazine article because it includes a month in the publication date, it lists two titles (the article in quotation marks, followed by the title of the publication itself in italics), and it notes an issue number and the page numbers of the article.

The right answer is not Choice (A) because the inclusion of a month in the publication date, as well as the two titles, is a clue that the cited work isn't a book.

The right answer is not Choice (C) because newspapers come out daily, not monthly, so a magazine is more likely.

The right answer is not Choice (D) because blogs don't have page numbers.

The right answer is not Choice (E) because the lack of a specific date (day instead of just month), the presence of two titles, and the inclusion of page numbers are all clues that the cited work isn't a speech.

38. C. a primary source represents original research, whereas a secondary source contains information already compiled by someone else.

These are the correct definitions of "primary source" and "secondary source."

None of the other choices gives the correct definitions of *primary source* and *secondary source*.

39. B. epigraph.

A quotation below the title and above the main body of the text is called an *epigraph*.

The right answer is not Choice (A) because an *epigram* is any saying or proverb.

The right answer is not Choice (C) because *epistle* is a fancy word for a letter (the kind you mail).

The right answer is not Choice (D) because *epithelium* is a type of animal tissue in biology.

The right answer is not Choice (E) because *epitaxy* refers to the deposition of crystal in geology.

40. B. a *Works Cited* page lists only cited sources, whereas a *bibliography* lists every source consulted.

These are the correct definitions of *bibliography* and *Works Cited page.* None of the other answers give the correct definitions.

Argumentative Essay

Take a look at the following essay written in response to the opinion that's presented in Chapter 16. To score your own essay, flip back to Chapter 11, where you can find a checklist to help you evaluate your own writing.

The idea that "high-school and college creative-writing classes should seek to foster an emotionally nurturing environment above emphasizing the development of technical skill" is the kind of recommendation that almost anyone would want to support when he or she first hears it. It pits kindness and sensitivity against elitism, and who would want to appear to be on the side of the elitists? The problem with it, however, is the same as the problem with many statements: It oversimplifies a complex issue into a simple either/or problem, and it fails to consider that not everyone who works with young people has the same job to do.

Would most young people who sign up for creative-writing classes prefer to vent about personal problems than to be nitpicked about whether their work is good enough for publication? Of course they would. But young people would probably rather vent about personal problems in math class instead of doing math too — that's just what young people are like. Yes, creative work certainly has more to do with personal expression than math does, but a class in school is still a class in school, and the students are in the class because there's something they're supposed to be learning. It may make a teacher feel like a great guy to tell everybody that his or her poem or story is fantastic just the way it is and then let the class use discussion time simply to share their feelings, but nobody learns anything that way.

A lot of young people struggle with issues in their lives, and it would help them to talk about those issues in a supportive environment. But that's what a therapist is for. Therapy is great, and many kids could benefit from it, but that doesn't mean it's the teacher's job. The writing teacher isn't obligated to be everyone's therapist instead of teaching writing, any more than it's the job of the math teacher or the science teacher to be a therapist instead of teaching math or science. If the writing teacher would rather help kids work out their problems than teach them how to write, then she should get a degree in psychology and become a therapist. And more importantly, a kid with a serious problem should be seeking help from someone who is specifically trained to address it instead of assuming that the English teacher is qualified to do so.

Perhaps most troubling is the fact that the question lumps together "high-school and college creative-writing classes" as though they are the same thing. A ninth-grader and a college student aren't taught the same things in the same way in any other subject, so why should they be taught writing in the same way? There's a world of difference between a 15-year-old and a 20-year-old, and what seems sensitive and encouraging to the former might seem patronizing and pointless to the latter. High-school freshmen may sign up for a creative-writing elective because it seems like an easy class, but a young adult who registers for a college course in the same subject may be considering a career as a writer and looking for tough and honest feedback. If the teacher just smiles and praises this student instead of helping him hone his skills as much as possible, then the college is essentially stealing his money because he isn't learning what he paid to learn.

This isn't to say that writing teachers should be insensitive. Nobody is a brilliant writer right off the bat, and it often takes years of encouragement about work that isn't truly very good before a young person manages to pen anything worthwhile. But it's still the students' work that should be discussed in the classroom, rather than their personal lives.

Source-Based Essay

Take a look at the following essay written about the paradox of wanting to see things as they are versus appreciating them in a way that makes emotional sense. To score your own essay, flip back to Chapter 11 and use the checklist to help you evaluate your own writing.

To a great extent, the history of human civilization has been a battle between those who seek to comprehend the natural world as it really is and those who are more concerned with the feelings, experiences, and behavior of the human beings who live in it. This conflict could be said to have reached its apex in the 20th century, during which science and technology advanced by breathtaking leaps and bounds even as human suffering and existential despair were exasperated by countless wars of unprecedented scale. Now, in the early years of the 21st century, we understand the world more clearly than ever before from a scientific and philosophical perspective, but we also feel more lost in that world than we ever have.

According to Jeremy Wisnewski, the philosophical discipline of phenomenology, as developed by such thinkers as Edmund Husserl and Martin Heidegger, is an attempt to "set aside our preconceptions and to uncover the actual *being* of things as they reveal themselves to us" and "to see past our preconceptions into the heart of things" (Wisnewski, 2009). No thinking person could argue that this is not, in theory, an admirable goal. Many of the people we love would not be here today had science not succeeded in doing this to a significant extent. No one with a friend or relative whose life was saved by modern medical science could wish for a return to the days when human beings interpreted even everyday events like illness in personalized terms of spells and demons instead of in a coldly objective — and therefore effective — manner.

On the other hand, however, people want to enjoy their lives, not merely to stay alive for the sake of doing so. We evolved our capacities for reason and intellect so we could bond and live in harmony with one another, not because we had some pressing need to figure out what is going on in the middle of a black hole. There is a wide range of subjective human experiences of existence, and what is fascinating to a philosopher or a physicist might well be frightening to the average person. As George Tschner pointed out, "mythology is a figurative and metaphorical way the human intellect grasps its world and answers and resolves some of the most fundamental questions" (Tschner, 2009). The tales of Odysseus's decade-long attempt to return home or of Orpheus's descent into the underworld in search of his lost bride will never help us cure a disease or colonize an alien planet, but they were never intended to do so. A viewpoint that constitutes a wrong answer to one question may be the right answer to another.

To return to Wisnewski's words, yes, we humans do "impose particular theories onto phenomena and insist that they conform to our preconceived notions about how the world is" (Wisnewski, 2009). But this is not a moral or an intellectual failing so much as it is something we evolved to do for a reason — and that reason is that it keeps our awareness of the cold, vast, unfeeling "reality" of existence from driving us to despair and madness. The scientific and philosophical methods are not a model for how everyone should live, and science and philosophy admit as much by reminding us that their disciplines are concerned with reality and results rather than with ethics and emotions. Objectivity and reason are not wrong, of course, and more spiritually inclined people would do well to stop fearing and demonizing them, but just because they are not wrong, that doesn't mean that they are how everyone should think all the time. The scientific method is a means to certain ends, and the mythological method is a means to certain other ends. Both missions are admirable and necessary, and both ways of seeing the world are therefore respectable.

Part 3: Mathematics

1. A. decrease of 6

Because the value of w in the equation $5u + 3w = 0$ is increased by 10, the value of the left side of the equation is increased by 30. That is because the coefficient of w is 3. For every 1 the value of w is increased, the value of $3w$ is increased by 3 since $3w$ is 3 times greater than w. In order for the left side to maintain its value, the increase of 30 must be accompanied by a decrease of 30. That means the value of $5u$ must decrease by 30. If u is decreased by 6, $5u$ is decreased by 30, and the value of $5u + 3w$ does not change, so the new pair also makes the equation true.

2. E. 76

$$8x + 3 + 2x + 8x + 3 + 2x = 20x + 6$$
$$20x + 6 = 46$$
$$20x = 40$$
$$x = 2$$
$$length = 8(2) + 3 = 19$$
$$width = 2(2) = 4$$
$$A = lw$$
$$A = (19)(4)$$
$$A = 76$$

By adding the four side measures in terms of x, you get the expression $20x + 6$ for the perimeter. If you set that equal to 46 and solve the equation, you can determine that $x = 2$. Then, you can put 2 in for x in the length and width expressions to find that the length is 19 and the width is 4. Because the area of a rectangle is length times width, the area of this rectangle is $A = (19)(4)$, which is 76.

3. D. $\frac{470}{1,000}$

All of the choices except (D) are equal to 4.7, which is the form of Choice (A). The 7 in that decimal number is in the tenths place, so it represents 7 tenths, or $\frac{7}{10}$. Therefore, 4.7 is equal to $4\frac{7}{10}$, Choice (B). In improper fraction form, $4\frac{7}{10}$ is $\frac{47}{10}$, Choice (C).

$$4\frac{7}{10} = \frac{10(4) + 7}{10}$$
$$= \frac{40 + 7}{10}$$
$$= \frac{47}{10}$$

You can also put a fraction into decimal form by dividing the numerator by the denominator. Your calculator can show you that $47 \div 10$ is equal to 4.7. If 0 is the only digit that follows a non-zero digit after a decimal point, putting more 0's on the end does not change the value of the number, so 4.700, Choice (E), is equal to 4.7. You can put $\frac{470}{1,000}$ into mixed number form or decimal form and see that it is equal to $\frac{47}{100}$, or 0.47, not 4.7.

4. A. 93

Because a mean is the sum of all items of data divided by the number of items of data, you can add all the test scores and a variable representing the missing test score and then divide that sum by the number of test scores, which is 6. If you set that ratio equal to 85 and solve for the variable, you can determine that the missing test score is 93.

$$\frac{(83+72+94+100+68+x)}{6} = 85$$

$$\frac{417+x}{6} = 85$$

$$417+x = 510$$

$$417+x-417 = 510-417$$

$$x = 93$$

5. **B. Divide both sides of the equation by 5.**

Brady subtracted 7 from both sides of the original equation, so the resulting equation is $5x = 35$. The goal in solving an equation is to get the variable by itself on one side so that the other side can represent the value of the variable. That can be achieved here by dividing both sides by 5. The resulting equation would be $x = 7$, which is a statement of the solution to the original equation.

6. **A, D, E. (A) multiplying by $\frac{1}{10}$, (D) moving the decimal point one place to the left, (E) dividing by 10.**

In 0.1, the 1 is in the tenths place, so the number represents 0 and one-tenth, or one-tenth. Multiplying by it is the same as multiplying by $\frac{1}{10}$. That's what results from moving a decimal point one place to the left because doing so pushes each digit one place to the right. A digit's place value is always 10 times what it would be if it were one place to the right and $\frac{1}{10}$ what it would be if it were one place to the left. Multiplying by a number is the same as dividing by its reciprocal, so multiplying by $\frac{1}{10}$ is the same as dividing by 10.

7. **A. 20%**

To calculate percentages, first get the total number of people surveyed.

$$140+70+55+5 = 270$$

You also know that $\% = \frac{\text{part}}{\text{whole}} \times 100\%$. Therefore, $\frac{55}{270} \times 100\% \approx 20.3\% \approx 20\%$.

8. **C. None of the marketing experts are computer technology experts.**

In the Venn diagram, the figures representing marketing and computer technology don't overlap. That means none of the marketing experts are also computer experts. None of the other statements expresses a correct situation concerning overlapping areas of expertise.

9. **D. $\frac{p-3}{p-7}$**

You can factor the top and the bottom of the original expression, and then cancel their common factor. The top of the expression is a difference of perfect squares, so you can factor it by getting the square root of the first term and subtracting the square root of the subtracted term, and then multiplying the resulting binomial by its conjugate (same binomial, except with the opposite operation).

$$\frac{p^2-49}{p^2-2p-35} = \frac{(p-7)(p+7)}{(p-7)(p+5)}$$

$$= \frac{p+7}{p+5}$$

10. **D. 65**

65 is 1 greater than 64, which is the square of the integer 8. 65 is not a prime number. All of the other choices are 1 greater than the square of an integer, but they are prime numbers.

11. C. $10\frac{3}{35}$

Convert the mixed numbers to improper fractions and then add them.

$$-2\frac{5}{7}+12\frac{4}{5}=-\frac{7(2)+5}{7}+\frac{5(12)+4}{5}$$

$$=-\frac{14+5}{7}+\frac{60+4}{5}$$

$$=-\frac{19}{7}+\frac{64}{5}$$

$$=-\frac{19(5)}{7(5)}+\frac{64(7)}{5(7)}$$

$$=-\frac{95}{35}+\frac{448}{35}$$

$$=\frac{-95}{35}+\frac{448}{35}$$

$$=\frac{-95+448}{35}$$

$$=\frac{353}{35}$$

Next, divide the numerator by the denominator. Write the integer part of the quotient next to a fraction with the remainder over the denominator, 35.

$$\frac{353}{35}=10\text{ R }3$$

$$=10\frac{3}{35}$$

12. B. 1

A prime number is a whole number that has exactly two factors — itself and 1. It's therefore impossible for any two different prime numbers to have a common factor other than 1. The greatest common factor of the first 28 prime numbers is 1, and the greatest common factor of the entire infinite set of prime numbers is 1.

13. D. 56

Write the first few multiples of each number. Look for the first multiple they have in common. That is their least common multiple (LCM). You can stop writing the multiples of 14 when you see the first one it has in common with 8.

Multiples of 8: 8, 16, 24, 32, 40, 48, 56, 64, 72 . . .

Multiples of 14: 14, 28, 42, 56 . . .

The least common multiple of 8 and 14 is 56.

14. C. This week's sales are higher by 9 cars.

Based on the graph, the following numbers of cars were sold: Monday — 3; Tuesday — 5; Wednesday — 6; Thursday — 4; Friday — 9. That brings the total for the week to 27 cars sold. If the weekly average for last year was 18, then you can subtract to compare. $27-18=9$.

15. A. The mean is greater than the median.

The mean can be determined by adding all the data figures and then dividing by the number of data figures. The mean is 63.666 . . .

The median is found by putting the data in order from least to greatest and then determining the middle number or the average of two middle numbers. In this case, it is a single middle number, 76.

The mode is the number that appears the highest number of times in the set. That number is 41.

Using the exact numbers for mean, median, and mode, you can compare them and determine that the only false statement is Choice (A). The mean is 63.666 . . ., which isn't greater than the median, 76. All of the other statements are true.

16. D. 8.5

A prime number is a whole number that has exactly two factors — itself and 1. The first seven prime numbers are 2, 3, 5, 7, 11, 13, and 17. The first number in that set is 2, and the last is 17. The last number divided by the first number is $17 \div 2$, or $\frac{17}{2}$, which is equal to 8.5.

17. E. 54°

A radius that has an endpoint that's a point of tangency is perpendicular to the tangent. That means TV is perpendicular to $\overline{WU}$, so $\angle TVW$ is a right angle and therefore has a measure of 90°, making $\triangle TVW$ a right triangle. Another angle in $\triangle TVW$ is 36°. The sum of the interior angles of a triangle is 180°, so the measure of $\angle TWV$ is 54°.

$$180 - (90 + 36) = 180 - 126$$
$$= 54$$

18. C. 41 miles

Identify what the question is asking for first: the total number of miles driven. What else did she do on her 1.5-hour or 90-minute trip? She was at the gym for 45 minutes. That leaves 45 minutes of drive time or 0.75 hours.

$$\text{distance} = \text{speed} \times \text{time}$$
$$\text{distance} = 55 \, \frac{\text{miles}}{\text{hour}} \times .75 \, \text{hour}$$
$$\text{distance} = 41.25 \approx 41 \, \text{miles}$$

19. E. $\frac{49}{20}$

To convert a percent to a fraction, drop the percent sign (%) and write the number over 100.

$$245\% = \frac{245}{100}$$

Now you can simplify by dividing the numerator and denominator by their greatest common factor (GCF). Really, you can divide them both by any common factor, but if it is not the GCF, further reducing will be necessary.

$$\frac{245}{100} = \frac{245 \div 5}{100 \div 5}$$
$$= \frac{49}{20}$$

20. D. 36

The question is essentially asking this: 27 is 75 percent of what number? To find the answer to the question, you can translate it into mathematical language and then solve for the unknown. You can use the equation 27 = 0.75x, where x represents the unknown. Solving the equation reveals that x is 36. The other choices can result from incorrect translations of the question.

21. D. (−7, 4), (−9, 10), (2, 3), and (2, 12)

The vertices of the quadrilateral before the translation are (−3, −3), (−5, 3), (6, −4), and (6, 5). To translate the quadrilateral 7 units up and 4 units left, add 7 to each y-coordinate and subtract 4 from each x-coordinate. The resulting coordinates are (−7, 4), (−9, 10), (2, 3), and (2, 12). The other choices can result from performing the wrong operations on the original coordinates, or placing them in incorrect orders, or both.

22. B. 18.8%

To find percent increase, do the following:

$$\frac{\text{new value} - \text{old value}}{\text{old value}} \times 100\%$$

$$\frac{19.60 - 16.50}{16.50} \times 100\% \approx 18.8\%$$

23. C. 7.53×10^9

7.53 billion is $7.53 \times 1{,}000{,}000{,}000$, which is 7.53 times a 1 with nine zeros. A 1 followed by nine zeros is 10^9, so 7.53 billion is 7.53×10^9. That expression is in scientific notation because the first factor has one digit (it isn't and can't be 0) before the decimal point, and that factor is multiplied by 10 with an exponent.

24. B. $\frac{4}{15}$

The land owned by Erik, Kristi, and Brecken is 1 whole. The fractions they own are fractions of 1. To find the fraction of land Brecken owns, add the fractions owned by Erik and Kristi, and then subtract the sum from 1.

$$\frac{2}{5} + \frac{1}{3} = \frac{2(3)}{5(3)} + \frac{1(5)}{3(5)}$$
$$= \frac{6}{15} + \frac{5}{15}$$
$$= \frac{11}{15}$$

Together, Erik and Kristi own $\frac{11}{15}$ of the land. Brecken owns the rest. You can determine his fraction by subtracting $\frac{11}{15}$ from 1.

$$1 - \frac{11}{15} = \frac{1}{1} - \frac{11}{15}$$
$$= \frac{1(15)}{1(15)} - \frac{11}{15}$$
$$= \frac{15}{15} - \frac{11}{15}$$
$$= \frac{4}{15}$$

Brecken owns $\frac{4}{15}$ of the land.

25. B. 23

Put the given variable values in for their respective variables, and then simplify. Follow the order of operations by using GEMDAS.

$$8v^2 - 7(u+v) + \frac{55}{w} = 8(-2)^2 - 7(4 + (-2)) + \frac{55}{11}$$
$$= 8(4) - 7(2) + 5$$
$$= 32 - 14 + 5$$
$$= 18 + 5$$
$$= 23$$

26. B. asking questions of every tenth worker who walks through the main entrance for work

Asking questions of every tenth person who walks through the main entrance would most likely result in answers from people of varying departments and other categories that may affect poll results. The other choices involve samples that lack diversity and could therefore cause biased results.

27. B, E. (B) 6,380 decimeters, (E) 638 meters

To do operations with measurements, express measurements (of the same measurement category) with the same unit. In this case, one option is to convert 5,358 meters to a number of kilometers. Since main units and kilometers are three spaces apart on the metric prefixes chart, you need to move the decimal three spaces. There are fewer kilometers than meters in any distance, so the resulting number will be smaller. That means you need to move the decimal to the left. Thus, you need to move the decimal three spaces to the left.

5,358 meters = 5.358 kilometers

Now you can calculate the difference between the distances.

5.358 − 4.72 = 0.638

The distance from Cindy's house to the office building is 0.638 kilometers greater than the distance from Mike's house to the office building. However, that representation of the measurement isn't one of the choices, so you need to do more converting. There are 1,000 times as many meters as there are kilometers in a distance, and that's why the kilo level is three spaces up from main units on the metric prefixes chart. So, you can multiply 0.638 by 1,000 by moving the decimal three spaces to the right to determine the number of meters.

0.638 kilometers = 638 meters

That measurement is also equal to 6,380 decimeters. The deci– level on the metric prefix chart is one space below main units, so you need to move the decimal one space to the right when converting from meters to decimeters. There are 10 times more decimeters than meters in a distance. Multiplying by 10 is the same as moving a decimal point one space to the right.

638 meters = 6,380 decimeters

28. B. 2015.

The line graph shows three decreases from one year to the next. They are from 2013 to 2014, 2014 to 2015, and 2017 to 2018. That's shown by the fact that the line goes down from left to right for all of those intervals. The other two changes, from 2015 to 2016 and 2016 to 2017, are increases. The line goes up from left to right in those intervals. You can see that the decreases greatly vary by looking at how far the line goes down in each case. The biggest drop is from 2013 to 2014. It's a decrease of approximately 1,800 miles (the numbers in the vertical column represent thousands of miles). The decrease from 2017 to 2018 is the third largest of the three. It's a drop of approximately 200 miles. The second-biggest drop is from 2014 to 2015. It shows a decrease of about 650 miles.

29. C. 36

You can use a variable to represent Eric's age and 9 times that variable to represent Natasha's age. You can call Eric's age x and Natasha's age $9x$. In 10 years, their ages will be $x+10$ and $9x+10$. Then you can write an equation based on the situation described. The sum of their ages in 10 years can be represented by $x+10+9x+10$, which is equal to 60. By solving the equation $x+10+9x+10=60$, you can determine that x is 4, so Natasha's age is $9(4)$, or 36.

30. D. Trapezoid

A square is a type of polygon that has four sides, so it's a quadrilateral. Both pairs of opposite sides are parallel, and that makes it a parallelogram. Because a square is a quadrilateral in which all four interior angles are right angles, a square is a rectangle. The four sides of any square are congruent, so every square is a rhombus. There are no exceptions to these rules. Because a trapezoid, by definition, has a pair of opposite sides that aren't parallel, a trapezoid can't be a parallelogram and therefore can't be a square.

31. D. 11

First, you must set up an equation, using variables to represent the currencies. If q represents the number of quarters and d represents the number of dimes, you can set up the following equation:

$$.10d + .25q = \$3.65$$

Then, to get only one variable in an equation, determine the relationship between d and q. The question tells you that Peter has two more quarters than dimes. Therefore:

$$q = d + 2$$

Now substitute this new expression in for q:

$$.10d + .25(d + 2) = 3.65$$
$$.10d + .25d + .50 = 3.65$$
$$.35d + .50 = 3.65$$
$$.35d + .50 - .50 = 3.65 - .50$$
$$.35d = 3.15$$
$$\frac{.35d}{.35} = \frac{3.15}{.35}$$
$$d = 9$$

So there are 9 dimes. Because there are two more quarters than dimes, there are 11 quarters.

32. B, C. (B) 7 m, (C) 9 m

When two segment measures are given, there's a range of possibilities for what the measure of a third segment can be to make forming a triangle possible. That range is between, and not including, the positive difference of the two segment measures and the sum of the two given measures. That's because no two segments can join at their endpoints and form an angle and still join their other endpoints to the endpoints of a segment that is longer than both of them combined. Any combination of two segments must cover more distance than the other segment. In this case, the two given segment measures are 8 m and 3 m.

Their sum is 11 m, and their positive difference is 5 m. Therefore, any third segment that could join endpoints with the 8 m and 3 m segment must be between 5 m and 11 m. They can't have those measures, only values greater than 5 m and less than 11 m. The choices that are between those measures are Choices (B) and (C).

33. $\frac{1}{2}$

The probability of an event is the ratio of the number of qualifying outcomes to the number of possible outcomes. For a single quarter toss, landing on tails is 1 qualifying outcome out of 2 possible outcomes. Thus, the probability that a quarter toss will result in landing on tails is $\frac{1}{2}$. That's the case no matter how many times the quarter has already landed on heads or tails. The probability remains the same.

34. A. $-3\frac{3}{4}$

$-\frac{19}{4}$, -3.71, and all the answer choices can be written as improper fractions, mixed numbers, or decimals. When they're all in the same form, you can see which numbers are greater than others. For example, $-3\frac{3}{4}$ is the only choice that is between $-\frac{19}{4}$ and -3.71, which can be written as $-4\frac{3}{4}$ and $-3\frac{71}{100}$ by converting to mixed numbers.

35. D. 327.5

The set of data doesn't have just one middle number; it has two middle numbers. When the numbers are in order from least to greatest, the two middle numbers are 218 and 437. The mean of those two numbers is the median of the set of data, and that mean is 327.5, so 327.5 is the median of the set of data.

36. E. No correlation between fish weight and gymnastics score is apparent.

The scatter plot does not show a pattern in which one variable tends to increase or decrease as the other one increases or decreases. The plotted points are placed very randomly, and no line of best fit can be determined. In the lowest and highest levels of fish weight, and throughout the intervals between them, very high, very low, and mediocre gymnastics scores are represented. No apparent correlation is implied by the scatter plot.

37. A. $6\frac{2}{9}$

The number of times the glass container must be filled is the number of times $\frac{3}{4}$ goes into $4\frac{2}{3}$. That is the quotient of $4\frac{2}{3}$ divided by $\frac{3}{4}$.

$$4\frac{2}{3} \div \frac{3}{4} = \frac{3(4)+2}{3} \div \frac{3}{4}$$
$$= \frac{12+2}{3} \div \frac{3}{4}$$
$$= \frac{14}{3} \div \frac{3}{4}$$
$$= \frac{14}{3} \times \frac{4}{3}$$
$$= \frac{56}{9}$$
$$= 6 \text{ R } 2$$
$$= 6\frac{2}{9}$$

38. D. 129°

The measure of ∠1 is 51°. Since ∠1 and ∠4 are vertical angles and are therefore congruent, the measure of ∠4 is also 51°. ∠4 and ∠6 make a pair of same-side interior angles formed by a transversal that intersects two parallel lines, so ∠4 and ∠6 are supplementary. That means their measures have a sum of 180°. You can use a variable to represent the measure of ∠6.

$$51 + x = 180$$
$$51 + x - 51 = 180 - 51$$
$$x = 129$$

39. C, D. (C) 1.7^2, (D) 2^2

The shaded part of the number line covers approximately the interval from 2.5 to 4.5. The only two choices with values in that interval are Choices (C) and (D). To square a number, you can use your calculator to multiply the number by itself. The value of 1.7^2 is equal to 1.7×1.7, or 2.89. The value of 2^2 is 2×2, or 4. None of the other choices have values within the interval of 2.5 to 4.5. The value of Choice (A) is 0, the value of Choice (B) is 1, and Choice (E) is equal to 5.76.

40. D. 9

The scale factor of triangle PQR to triangle ABC is 3 because each side measure of triangle PQR is 3 times that of its corresponding side measure in triangle ABC. Side measure is a one-dimensional measure, but area is a two-dimensional measure. When an issue of measure ratio is taken from the first dimension to the second dimension, the ratio is squared. In other words, if a scale factor of side measures is a number, the ratio of the figures' areas is that number squared. In this case, the ratio of the side measures of triangle PQR to the side measures of triangle ABC is $\frac{3}{1}$, which is equal to 3, so the ratio of the area of triangle PQR to the area of triangle ABC is equal to 3^2, or 9.

41. A. 20 percent

Mark hit the ball 48 out of 60 times he was up at bat, which converts to 80 percent. If Mark hit the ball 80 percent of the time, then he didn't hit the ball 20 percent of the time he was up at bat.

42. D. Tim is 54, and Sarah is 27.

To set this up in mathematical language, start with what you know first. Tim is twice Sarah's age, so: $T = 2S$.

Next, Rachel is one-third Tim's age, so: $R = \frac{1}{3}T$.

Then substitute one term for the other:

$$R = \frac{1}{3}(2S)$$
$$R = \frac{2}{3}S$$
$$18 = \frac{2}{3}S$$
$$3 \times 18 = \frac{2}{3}S \times 3$$
$$54 = 2S$$
$$\frac{54}{2} = \frac{2}{2}S$$
$$27 = S$$

If Sarah is 27, then Tim is 54 because he is twice Sarah's age. Choice (D) is the correct answer.

43. D. 94

The angle that's *w* degrees is a vertical angle to an angle in the quadrilateral, as is the 110-degree angle. All vertical angles are congruent, so those are the measures of two of the angles of the quadrilateral. The 117-degree angle is supplementary to another angle in the quadrilateral, and the 93-degree angle is vertical to the remaining one. The interior angles of a quadrilateral have a sum of 360 degrees. By adding the angle measures of the quadrilateral and setting the sum equal to 360 degrees, you can solve for *w*. The result is 94 degrees. The other choices result from combinations of mixing the rules of supplementary angles with those of vertical angles.

44. D. 11

The range of a set of data is the positive difference of its highest number and lowest number. It's the *numerical span*, the amount that's covered by the set. You can find the range by subtracting the lowest number from the highest number. In the set of data here, the highest number is 12, and the lowest number is 1.

$$12 - 1 = 11$$

The range of the set of data is 11. Choice (B) is the median of the data set, and Choice (C) is the mean, rounded to the nearest hundredth.

45. B. $\frac{r}{3} - p = 22$

A third of *r* can be written as $\frac{r}{3}$ and *p* less than that as $\frac{r}{3} - p$. All of the other choices involve false representations of those expressions.

46. E. 21%

This question involves the reading of a graph. You can note significant points on the graph such as the following: In 2010, the percentage was about 6; in 2012, about 9; in 2014, about 12; and in 2016, about 15. That shows an increase of 3% every two years. From 2016 to 2020 is four years, so there should be an increase of 6% from the last data point. $15 + 6 = 21$. Therefore, if this trend continues, in 2020, about 21% of Americans should be using online dating sites.

47. C. 1.57464×10^5

The colony starts with 24 bees, and it gets 3 times greater every week. In 8 weeks, the number of bees in the colony will be 24×3^8. That is $24 \times 3 \times 3 \times 3 \times 3 \times 3 \times 3 \times 3 \times 3$, which is 157,464.

You need to convert that number to scientific notation because the answer choices are in scientific notation. That requires putting the decimal point in front of the first non-zero digit, 1, and compensating for the change by multiplying the result by 10 with an exponent equal in magnitude to the number of places you move the decimal. That number is 5. Because the value is positive, moving the decimal point to the left makes the value less, so you need to multiply by 10 with an exponent that makes the value greater to compensate. You need to move the decimal 5 places to the left and multiply the result by 10 with an exponent of 5.

$$157,464 = 1.57464 \times 10^5$$

48. B. (4, 7)

x is 4, and y is 7. One method you can use to find the solution is elimination. By multiplying both sides of the top equation by 2 and both sides of the bottom equation by −3, you get two equations in which the coefficients of x are opposites.

$$3x - 2y = -2$$
$$2(3x - 2y) = 2(-2)$$
$$6x - 4y = -4$$

$$2x - 3y = -13$$
$$-3(2x - 3y) = -3(-13)$$
$$-6x + 9y = 39$$

You can add the resulting bottom equations to get rid of x.

$$6x - 4y = -4$$
$$-6x + 9y = 39$$
$$5y = 35$$

Then solve for y, which is 7.

$$\frac{5y}{5} = \frac{35}{5}$$
$$y = 7$$

You can then put 7 in for y to determine that x is 4.

$$3x - 2(7) = -2$$
$$3x - 14 = -2$$
$$3x = -2 + 14$$
$$3x = 12$$
$$x = 4$$

You can put the solution into both equations to see that it works for them.

49. C. 19

To find the number of participants in the tournament based on this stem-and-leaf plot, simply count the number of leaves. There are 19 numbers under the "leaf" side. So there are 19 males who signed up for the tournament. The stem side can be used to indicate their full ages: 10, 13, 16, 21, and so on, but it is not enough for determining the number of participants.

50. B. $\frac{1}{15}$

Molly ate $\frac{2}{3}$ of $\frac{4}{5}$ of the pizza, and Wes took $\frac{7}{8}$ of what remained of Molly's portion. What remains from $\frac{2}{3}$ is $\frac{1}{3}$ because those two fractions add up to 1. That means Wes took $\frac{7}{8}$ of $\frac{1}{3}$ of $\frac{4}{5}$ of the pizza

$$\frac{7}{8} \cdot \frac{1}{3} \cdot \frac{4}{5} = \frac{28}{120}$$
$$= \frac{7}{30}$$

West took $\frac{7}{30}$ of the pizza. He ate $\frac{2}{7}$ of that portion.

$$\frac{2}{7} \cdot \frac{7}{30} = \frac{14}{210}$$
$$= \frac{1}{15}$$

A more concise perspective is that Wes ate $\frac{2}{7}$ of $\frac{7}{8}$ of $\frac{1}{3}$ of $\frac{4}{5}$ of the pizza.

$$\frac{2}{7} \cdot \frac{7}{8} \cdot \frac{1}{3} \cdot \frac{4}{5} = \frac{56}{840}$$
$$= \frac{1}{15}$$

Wes ate $\frac{1}{15}$ of the pizza.

51. **A.** $\frac{5}{44}$

To find a probability within a probability, multiply the probabilities. In other words, the probability of two outcomes, of separate categories, both happening is the product of their individual probabilities. The probability that the wheel will land on red is $\frac{1}{4}$. Within that $\frac{1}{4}$ chance, there is a $\frac{5}{11}$ chance of the number being prime. The probability that the wheel will land on a red prime number is the product of $\frac{1}{4}$ and $\frac{5}{11}$.

$$\frac{1}{4} \times \frac{5}{11} = \frac{5}{44}$$

The probability that the spinning wheel will stop on a red prime number is $\frac{5}{44}$.

52. **C. 6**

The line graph increases at a constant rate, and it indicates that the number of millimeters the plant is tall is very close to half the number of days the plant has been growing. Therefore, at 12 days of growth, the plant will be approximately 6 mm tall. It will be much closer to that measure than any of the other choices.

53. **A. Move the decimal three places to the left and make the exponent three higher.**

Scientific notation consists of a number in which a single digit is followed by a decimal point (except in some cases of single-digit whole numbers, for which decimal points are not required) and the number is multiplied by 10 with an exponent. The number in the question has four digits before the decimal, so the decimal must be moved three places to the left. To keep the original value, the exponent of 10 has to increase by three to make up for moving the decimal three places to the left.

$$5451.38 \cdot 10^7 = 5.45138 \cdot 10^{10}$$

54. **A. a positive slope line**

A line of best fit is a single line that represents the nature of the points in a scatterplot. If the points in the chart were plotted on a coordinate plane, they would give a line similar to the one that follows:

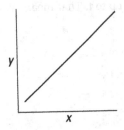

This line indicates a positive slope; while one entity is increasing, so is the other. Based on this particular scenario, as the heights of the players increase, so do their weights. Be careful that you don't read too much into the data. Base conclusions on what's presented. Even if you know of a case where the heights and weights don't necessarily correlate, you can't bring that information to this problem.

55. **C, E.** (C) $\dfrac{1 \text{ minute}}{60 \text{ seconds}}$, (E) $\dfrac{12 \text{ inches}}{1 \text{ foot}}$

A way to multiply unit rates in order to get a unit rate with the desired units is to multiply unit rates that are equal to 1 because the numerator and denominator are equal but expressed with different units, such as $\dfrac{12 \text{ inches}}{1 \text{ foot}}$. A desired unit should be in just a numerator if you want it in the numerator of the product and in just a denominator if you want it in the denominator of the product. Any unit you want to cancel needs to be in a numerator and a denominator, once for each, or at least an equal number of times for each. Any value that's a factor of a numerator and a denominator, an equal number of times for each in a product of fractions, can be canceled. For this problem, $\dfrac{65 \text{ feet}}{1 \text{ minute}}$ needs to be multiplied by a unit rate that has a number of inches in the numerator and a number of feet in the denominator. The unit rate that fits that standard and is equal to 1, and therefore does not cause a change of value when a value is multiplied by it, is $\dfrac{12 \text{ inches}}{1 \text{ foot}}$. Multiplying by that unit rate will result in a product that has inches in the numerator. Seconds can already be in the denominator as a result of cancellation.

$$\frac{65 \text{ feet}}{1 \text{ minute}} \times \frac{1 \text{ minute}}{60 \text{ seconds}} \times \frac{12 \text{ inches}}{1 \text{ foot}} = \frac{780 \text{ inches}}{60 \text{ seconds}}$$

$$= \frac{13 \text{ inches}}{1 \text{ second}}$$

$$= 13 \text{ inches/second}$$

56. **B. 15 and 25**

The interquartile range is the distance from the first quartile (Q_1) to the third quartile (Q_3). You can find it by subtracting the first quartile from the third quartile. The first quartile is the number that's represented by the left side of the box, and it's approximately 67. The third quartile is the number that's represented by the right side of the box. It's about 87. The interquartile range is therefore approximately 67 less than 87.

$$87 - 67 = 20$$

The interquartile range is about 20, so it's between 15 and 25. Choice (D) represents an interval of numbers that the first quartile and third quartile are within, but the interquartile range is the value of $Q_3 - Q_1$, not an interval of numbers.

Answer Key

Part 1: Reading

1.	E	15.	E	29.	D	43.	A
2.	C	16.	C	30.	C	44.	E
3.	C	17.	C	31.	B	45.	C
4.	D	18.	C	32.	C	46.	D
5.	A	19.	A	33.	D	47.	2010
6.	C	20.	E	34.	A	48.	C, D
7.	A	21.	A	35.	C	49.	B
8.	A	22.	E	36.	A	50.	A
9.	E	23.	C	37.	B	51.	E
10.	C	24.	B	38.	D	52.	C
11.	B	25.	C	39.	C	53.	B
12.	A	26.	C	40.	C	54.	D
13.	C	27.	D	41.	B	55.	A
14.	D	28.	A	42.	A	56.	C

Part 2: Writing

1.	E	11.	A	21.	A	31.	B
2.	D	12.	B	22.	C	32.	A
3.	A	13.	B	23.	E	33.	D
4.	B	14.	B	24.	D	34.	E
5.	C	15.	A	25.	D	35.	C
6.	D	16.	A	26.	E	36.	A
7.	E	17.	D	27.	B	37.	B
8.	B	18.	B	28.	C	38.	C
9.	C	19.	A	29.	A	39.	B
10.	E	20.	D	30.	B	40.	B

Part 3: Mathematics

1.	A	15.	A	29.	C	43.	D
2.	E	16.	D	30.	D	44.	D
3.	D	17.	E	31.	D	45.	B
4.	A	18.	C	32.	B, C	46.	E
5.	B	19.	E	33.	$\frac{1}{2}$	47.	C
6.	A, D, E	20.	D	34.	A	48.	B
7.	A	21.	D	35.	D	49.	C
8.	C	22.	B	36.	E	50.	B
9.	D	23.	C	37.	A	51.	A
10.	D	24.	B	38.	D	52.	C
11.	C	25.	B	39.	C, D	53.	A
12.	B	26.	B	40.	D	54.	A
13.	D	27.	B, E	41.	A	55.	C, E
14.	C	28.	B	42.	D	56.	B

6

The Part of Tens

Check out ten common math errors to avoid.

Know what to be on the lookout for in the reading and writing questions, and discover how your own instincts may trip you up.

Chapter **18**

Ten Common Math Errors to Avoid

nowing how to perform certain types of math operations is a big part of solving problems correctly, but knowledge isn't everything: Caution is also important. Avoiding common math errors involves both. Think back to times when you saw what you missed on math tests and thought, "Oh yeah, I had this mixed up with that!" This chapter helps you avoid that exact situation. Errors are always a threat. Don't let them get you.

Misusing Negative Signs

In our observations, math mistakes occur most frequently when negatives are involved. Negatives are to math problems what land mines are to war zones (except they're only dangerous to math scores). That's the good news. When you see a negative sign, you should turn your level of caution up a notch or two. Such a small symbol has so much power to transform a quantity. Imagine being told that you have $1 million in a bank account and then being told, "Oh, I'm sorry. I didn't see the negative sign. You have –$1 million. You are that much in debt." It's a completely different picture. One misuse of a negative sign can usually wreck an entire answer. See Chapter 4 for the lowdown on negative numbers.

REMEMBER

Multiplying by an odd number of negative factors results in a negative product, and multiplying by an even number of negative factors results in a positive product. Also keep in mind that the sum of two negatives is a negative and the sum of a negative and a positive has the sign of the number with the greater absolute value.

TIP

You'll have a calculator to use on the Praxis Core exam. When you work with negative numbers, you should always use the calculator, even when you feel like you don't need it. Safety is a big issue in math.

Confusing Perimeter and Area

Many people mix up the formulas for perimeter and area. Remember that *perimeter* is the distance around something. If it's expressed in units, it's expressed in one-dimensional units, such as meters (m), centimeters (cm), feet (ft.), and inches (in.). Area is two-dimensional. It's the amount of a plane a two-dimensional figure covers. In other words, area is the size of a piece of a plane. When area is expressed in units, the units are two-dimensional and have an exponent of 2. Such units include m², cm², ft², and in². For more details on calculating perimeter and area, turn to Chapter 6.

REMEMBER

The perimeter of a circle is also called the *circumference*. A lot of people mix up the formula for circumference with the formula for the area of a circle. Both formulas involve only π, r, and 2 on the right side, but in different arrangements. The formula for the circumference of a circle is $C = 2\pi r$. The formula for the area of a circle is $A = \pi r^2$. So you see how they're especially easy to confuse — it happens all the time. Be very careful with the formulas for area and perimeter. If you can remember that perimeter (specifically circumference, in this case) is a one-dimensional measure and area is a two-dimensional measure, it will help you distinguish the formulas. $C = 2\pi r$ has r with an understood exponent of 1 (one dimension), whereas $A = \pi r^2$ has r with an exponent of 2 (two dimensions).

Incorrectly Combining Like Terms

Only like terms can be combined, and terms have to meet certain conditions to be like terms. They have to either have no variables or have exactly the same variables with the same exponent per corresponding variable. Remember that when a variable is shown without an exponent, its understood exponent is 1. $5xyz$ and $4xyz$ can be added to get $9xyz$. And $4x^2y^3z^4$ can be subtracted from $5x^2y^3z^4$ to get $x^2y^3z^4$. However, $5x^2y^3z^4 + 4x^2y^3z^5$ can't be simplified because the two terms are not like terms. z doesn't have the same exponent in both terms. Take a look at Chapter 4 for a review of exponents and Chapter 5 to see how they work in algebraic terms and equations.

Messing Up When Moving Decimals

Some really common math errors involve calculations and rewritings that require moving a decimal to the right or left. The two major areas of math that entail decimal movement are converting to and from scientific notation and converting between decimals and percents. Both involve doing something and then making up for it by undoing it. You can do this smoothly if you keep in mind that multiplying by a multiple of 10 can be done by moving a decimal to the right and dividing by a multiple of 10 can be accomplished by moving a decimal to the left. Decimals and percents are reviewed in Chapter 4.

Not Solving for the Actual Variable

Solving an equation or inequality involves stating what a variable equals or could equal. A mistake people commonly make is saying what something that almost looks like a variable could equal. For example, you may think an equation is solved by the conclusion $-x = 15$. That's not a solution. It shows a value for the opposite of the variable. To solve for x, you need a statement about x at the end, not $-x$. Solving for x (or any other variable) is all about the value of x (or whatever the variable is). Your final statement must be about what x equals, not about what $3x$, or $1/x$, equals, for example. Chapter 5 tells you everything you need to know about solving for variables.

Misrepresenting "Less Than" in Word Problems

When an operation is described with English words rather than mathematical symbols, part of your challenge is to represent the operation correctly. The most common mistake made in doing that is incorrectly representing a certain amount less than a number. The quantities are often falsely reversed. For example, "6 less than a number" can be represented by $x - 6$, but it cannot be represented by $6 - x$. The latter represents a certain amount less than 6, not 6 less than a certain amount. Check out Chapter 5 for a more detailed review of this concept.

WARNING

The confusion that commonly exists here results from the fact that the subtracted quantity is mentioned in the description before the quantity from which it is subtracted. Be careful with that. 4 less than 7 is $7 - 4$, not $4 - 7$.

Mixing Up Supplementary and Complementary Angles

The words *supplementary* and *complementary* are often confused. Preparing ahead of time to avoid that confusion can help keep your work safer. Complementary angles have measures that add up to 90°, and supplementary angles have measures that add up to 180°. Here's a silly but effective mnemonic statement to help you remember the difference: *If you live to be 90, you deserve a complement. If you live to be 180, you are super.* You can find out all about angles in Chapter 6.

Finding a False Median

The most common mistake that happens in finding a median of a set of data is failing to put the data in order. The median is the middle number, or the mean of the two middle numbers, of a set of data *when the data is in order*. Getting that for a set of data that isn't in order is not very likely to result in the actual median. If you want to find the correct median, write the values from least to greatest or greatest to least first. Get the lowdown on determining the median, mean, and mode in Chapter 7.

Fearing Fractions

So "fearing fractions" isn't a specific mistake, but fraction problems create all sorts of opportunities for errors, and that scares people.

REMEMBER

Common denominators are necessary for adding and subtracting fractions, not for multiplying or dividing them. The distinction is extremely important.

Multiplying fractions involves multiplying the numerators and multiplying the denominators, and dividing by a fraction is the same as multiplying by its reciprocal. Adding and subtracting fractions involve getting a common denominator and then operating with only the numerators. The denominator doesn't change unless the sum or difference has to be simplified. You can review computing with fractions in Chapter 4.

Forgetting about Fractions in Formulas

Some of the formulas you need to know have 1/2 in them, and the 1/2 is often neglected. That can wreck your answer. For example, the formula for the area of a triangle is $A = (1/2)bh$. That is half of bh, so calculating just bh won't give you the area of a triangle. The area of a parallelogram is bh because a parallelogram can be split into two congruent triangles. Knowing that can help you remember that the formula for the area of a triangle has 1/2 in it. Also, don't be afraid to replace 1/2 with 0.5. They mean the same thing and result in the same answers. The topic of area is covered in Chapter 6.

Chapter 19

Ten Mistakes to Avoid on the Praxis Reading and Writing Exams

We have instincts for a reason, but they don't always serve us well in every context. If you've ever played baseball or softball, you've probably learned that "an outfielder's first step is always back" — this is an example of a rule that players have to internalize in order to help them *unlearn* their natural instinct to run forward when the ball is hit. Running toward the ball is what your mind *wants* you to do, but by doing so, you run the risk of misjudging the ball and watching it sail over your head.

Just like sports, test-taking is an arena where your mind sometimes encourages you to do the wrong thing, and in those situations, you have to learn *not* to follow your instincts. This chapter helps you steer clear of common errors that test-takers make on the writing and reading portions of the Praxis Core.

Avoiding Mistakes Common to the Writing and Reading Tests

Before we turn to specific pieces of advice about the writing and reading tests, the following section gives you a couple of tips to keep in mind on both of them.

Don't look for patterns in the answers

The human brain has evolved to see patterns in everything. This capability is helpful when a pattern really is at work, but it can trip you up when you're confronting something truly random. For example, the fact that the ball of a roulette wheel has landed on an even number three times in a row doesn't mean that an odd number is due to come up next. Perhaps the biggest mistake that a test-taker can make on the Praxis is to look for a pattern in the answers. It's a waste of time and energy, and it won't help you get any more of the answers correct — in fact, it will probably cause you to select *wrong* answers that you wouldn't otherwise have picked.

Say you've eliminated three of the answer choices on a particular question, and now you're down to a 50/50 split between Choices (B) and (D). There are many logical ways to proceed, depending on what sort of question it is, but one thing you should never do is base your answer on how many (B)s or (D)s you've selected so far or which answer letter you selected most recently. The fact that you chose (B) for two of the previous three questions doesn't mean that the right answer to this question is any less likely to be (B) than (D) — and even if it did, you may have been wrong on one of the previous questions.

Where this instinct *really* has a tendency to trip up even very good test-takers is on those questions in the writing test that offer the choice "No Error." It's easy to feel paranoid about whether you've selected "No Error" too many or too few times. But the best thing to do with that nagging little voice is ignore it. Even though it seems like a "special" answer, "No Error" is statistically no more or less likely to be right than any other answer. Every test is different, and the Praxis writing test you take may have a lot of correct "No Error" responses, or it may have only a couple. The best method is always to mark the answer you think is correct for each individual question on a case-by-case basis, paying absolutely no attention to how many or how few times you've selected the same answer choice previously.

Remember, this goes for "in-a-row" logic too: The fact that it seems unlikely that the correct answer would be Choice (C) three times in a row is no reason *not* to choose (C) if you genuinely think it's the right answer. There are few guarantees in life, but one thing you can take to the bank is the fact that looking for patterns on the Praxis Core is *always* a bad idea.

Don't change answers merely for the sake of changing them

The computer-delivered Praxis test allows you to skip and return to questions or even to look back over questions you've already answered. But just because you're allowed to do it doesn't necessarily mean it's a good idea!

The trickiest question to answer as test-prep tutors is when students ask us, "Should I go back and check over my answers if I have time left over?" There's no one right answer to that question because every student is different. Some test-takers tend to actually catch their careless mistakes when they look back, and others tend to get nervous and change answers that were right the first time.

TIP

To see which type of test-taker you are, go back over one of the practice tests in this book after you finish (but before you check your answers) and see whether you tend to catch real mistakes and improve your score when you go back and change answers, or whether you tend to outsmart yourself and change answers that were right the first time.

If you *do* end up deciding to go back and change an answer, you should be thinking more about whether the first answer you put is wrong than about whether the other answer you're considering seems right. It's common for more than one answer choice to seem right, and the way to avoid the problems this can cause is *never* to change an answer unless you can articulate to yourself *a reason why it's wrong*. "If it ain't broke, don't fix it" is an expression for a reason!

Sidestepping Mistakes on the Writing Test

The section "Avoiding Mistakes Common to the Writing and Reading Tests," earlier in this chapter, gives you some general pointers about multiple-choice tests as a whole. The following subsections turn your attention specifically to the Praxis writing test. The tips in the first two subsections are about the multiple-choice questions, and the next two subsections pertain to the essays.

Don't equate different with wrong

Quick! Which is correct: to say, "I walked *down* the street" or "I walked *along* the street?" Well, based on the title of this section, you probably correctly guessed that either one is perfectly acceptable. Keep that in mind when you're taking the Praxis writing test: Just because you can think of a way to phrase something other than the way the question phrases it doesn't necessarily mean that the phrasing in the question is grammatically incorrect. There's often more than one correct way to say something.

This is a problem for a lot of test-takers on questions with the "No Error" answer choice. The fact that you can think of another word or phrase that could be substituted for underlined portion (B) doesn't mean that underlined portion (B) is an error. The sentence may have no errors, or portion (B) may be distracting you from another underlined portion that really *does* contain an error.

REMEMBER

Those questions aren't asking whether anything about the sentence *could be different* — they're asking whether anything about the sentence is *wrong*. You're supposed to be on the lookout for broken rules, not arbitrary stylistic matters.

Don't assume something must be correct just because it sounds fancier or more complex

Are you familiar with the term *overcorrection?* It's a mistake that occurs as a result of trying extra-hard to be right, and it's a common pitfall in grammar. An example is saying, "Just between you and *I*," even though "Just between you and *me*" is actually correct. Most people are insecure about their grammar, and grammatically stressful situations — such as taking a test or having a conversation with an English professor — can exacerbate that insecurity and cause people to say things in a way they wouldn't normally say them, even if the way they'd normally say them is fine.

Perhaps no single word in the English language pops up unnecessarily more often as a result of overcorrection than *whom*. Nervous students writing essays may slap unneeded m's onto the end of the interrogative pronoun right and left. They're so nervous about saying *who* when they should say *whom* that they end up saying *whom* when they should say *who*. (See Chapter 12 for a review of when to use "who" and when to use "whom.")

Verb tenses are another area where you'll want to watch out for overcorrection. If "I *drove* to the store yesterday" sounds perfectly fine in context, resist the urge to select "I *had driven* to the store yesterday" just because the past-perfect tense sounds more complex than the regular past tense.

REMEMBER

Fancy words, such as *whom*, or fancy tenses, such as the perfect tenses, aren't right *all* the time or even *most* of the time — they're right when they're right. So, trust your ear and select the answer choices that sound correct in context, rather than always going for the fancy ones.

Don't turn the essay into a thesaurus explosion

Deploying ostentatious diction due merely to the fact that your extemporaneous prosody is slated for appraisal is egregiously unadvisable.

Does the preceding sentence sound good to you? Or would "Using big words just because you're taking an essay test isn't a good idea" be something you would rather read? That's what we thought.

The idea that you get extra points for big words is probably the most persistent urban legend about standardized tests. Nevertheless, you should ignore the urge to use a 50-cent synonym for each everyday word that pops into your head.

WARNING

Stopping to think of big words you wouldn't normally use eats up precious time, and it won't make your score go up anyway because — contrary to popular belief — the graders don't "count big words." If anything, adopting an unnatural style will probably make your score go *down* because it sounds robotic and obnoxious (and if you don't normally use those words, chances are pretty good that you're using the big words incorrectly anyway).

The graders of the essay look for a sense of ease with written communication. You want to sound thoughtful, personable, persuasive, and, above all, as if you think writing is fun. If it seems like your main concern is trying to work in as many big words as you can, you'll end up looking like you're trying to disguise the fact that you're uncomfortable with the writing process.

Don't paint yourself into a corner with a rigid thesis

The first of the two essays on the Praxis writing test is thesis-driven; it asks you to adopt a stance on an issue or defend a viewpoint. You want to carve out a clear position and sound like you believe in what you're saying, of course, but it's not a good idea to start off by asserting your thesis so stringently that you can't acknowledge an exception or gray area that occurs to you, for fear of appearing to contradict yourself.

REMEMBER

When it comes to theses, you don't get extra points for extremism. If you think each side of the issue has some valid points, it's entirely okay to say so. You're graded on how well you write, not on your opinion. You want to steer clear of the dreaded essay-test dead end where you think of something bright and interesting to say halfway through your writing process but feel as if you can't say it because it doesn't fit in with your uncompromising thesis statement.

This doesn't mean you have to hem and haw. You can state your opinion clearly up-front and add an "on the other hand, I can understand why someone might think . . ." later. That way, if an exception to your thesis pops into your head, you can say so. This strategy not only helps you out when it comes to length, but it also gets you points for what essay graders call *anticipating objections* — demonstrating that you're able to see the issue from the other side's point of view, even though you don't agree with it. That's a sign of philosophical maturity (and it earns you points).

Evading Mistakes on the Reading Test

Reading comprehension is not as rule-based as grammar, but there are still a few definite traps you want to avoid falling into on the Praxis reading exam.

Don't rule out the "too obvious"

No one's saying the Praxis is easy, but there's no point in making things tougher on yourself by expecting it to be harder than it is. We can't tell you how many times we see students about to circle the correct answer, only to change it at the last second. When asked why, they often say that the first (and correct) answer was "too obvious."

So, we can't stress this enough: There is no such thing as "too obvious." There's only *right* or *wrong*.

The "too obvious" mistake is really a confidence problem: You expect the test to be hard, so when a question seems easy, you assume you must have missed something and question your (good) instincts. Some students even say they whittle the answer choices down to 50/50 and then pick the one they think is *wrong* because they're so sure that there must be some trick that they're missing!

REMEMBER

One of the answer choices will be right, and the other four will be wrong. There's no such thing as a question with an easy right answer or a hard right one. When a right answer seems obvious to you, give yourself some credit and assume that you're getting pretty good at this, rather than being tricked.

Don't word-match

Do you know what students who don't speak English very well do when they have to take a multiple-choice test in English? They look for the answer choice that has the greatest number of words from the passage in it and pick that one. The people who write multiple-choice standardized tests like the Praxis reading test know this, and they use it to try to trick you. Inserting a string of matching words from the passage into one of the wrong answer choices as bait for people whose reading comprehension is weak is a common method that test-writers use to compose the wrong answer choices.

We're not saying that you should *always* pick the answer choice that has the *fewest* words in common with the passage, of course. We're just saying that you shouldn't base your answer on anything to do with how many words or phrases from the passage appear in a particular choice.

Don't ignore your outside knowledge

Unlike the writing exam, for which you need to know as many grammar rules as you can cram into your head, the Praxis reading exam doesn't test you on outside knowledge. A passage presents you with some information, and then you answer the question you're asked based solely on the information in the passage. For example, if a passage is about economics, you don't have to know anything about economics in order to get the question right — the passage is designed to tell you everything you need to know.

But just because you don't *need* to know anything other than what the passages tell you in order to correctly answer the questions, you shouldn't ignore or forget about things that you *happen* to know from real life. Now, we're *not* saying you should try to select *right* answers based on what you think is true in real life — when the question says, "according to the author" or "according to the passage," it means that you need to identify what the text says, not give your personal opinion. However, outside knowledge is frequently useful when it comes to eliminating *wrong* answers.

Many of the passages may involve unsettled matters of opinion, but none of the authors is ever out-and-out *wrong* about anything. You may see a passage by a scientist who thinks life exists on the moon of Jupiter known as Europa, or you may see a passage by a scientist who thinks such life doesn't exist. According to current scientific thought, either opinion is plausible. But you'll never see a passage by a scientist who thinks there are panda bears on Mars because that's just crazy! So, although you're not supposed to select right answers based on your own knowledge or opinions, if you see an answer choice that you happen to know is *definitely, factually false,* you can cross it off immediately.

Don't try to answer more than the question asks you to

"Answer the questions" probably seems like unnecessarily obvious advice. Of course, you're supposed to answer the questions — you're taking a test! But you'd be surprised how many test-takers forget to follow that advice. The question following a passage may ask something like "Which of the following claims is explicitly made in the passage?" You may see an answer choice that does indeed paraphrase a claim that was explicitly made in the passage, but then avoid picking it because the claim wasn't the author's main point. Huh?! The question didn't ask you what the author's main point was — it *just* asked you which of the claims was explicitly made in the passage. So, answer *that* specific question and that specific question *alone.*

The same confusion can even occur with a simple vocabulary question. When the question says "The author is using this word most nearly to mean . . .," it isn't asking you what that word means most of the time or for the fanciest thing it could possibly mean in another context. It's just asking you what the author used it to mean in one specific place, so *just answer that question.*

Index

infinitive verbals, 200
informative/explanatory essay, 233–234
  citing sources, 190
  making outline for, 189
  mastering, 233–234
  prompts for, 187, 193–194
  sticking to facts in, 188
initial subject-related chapters, 15
inscribed angle, 104
integers. *See* whole numbers
interior angles, 99
interquartile range (IQR), 131
interrogative pronouns, 206
intersecting graphs, 116
intersection, origin of, 112
intransitive forms, 199
introduction, writing, 195, 196
isosceles triangle, 100

J
jargon, 191

K
key ideas, 8
Kirkland Group, 13
knowledge, integrating, 8

L
language skills, 8, 9
least common multiple, 46
"less than," in word problems, 413
like terms, in algebra, 68–69
likelihood of an event, 140
line graph, 169
linear equations, 113–115
linear function, 139
linear models, in data analysis, 139
linear pair, 97
lines, 94. *See also* number lines
  parallel, 95
  perpendicular, 98
  slope of, 113
  transversal, 98

long-passages, 163–168, 181
  argumentation/support questions, 164
  "if" questions, 164–165
  purpose of, 163–164
  sample questions, 166–168
lower quartile, 130, 131

M
magnitude, orders of, 58
main idea, of short-passages, 159–160
mathematics, 145–149. *See also* geometry; numbers
  approximation, 147
  budgeting time for test, 13
  calculating in head, 148
  common errors to avoid, 411–414
    confusing perimeter and area, 412
    confusing supplementary and complementary angles, 413
    finding false median, 413
    incorrectly combining like terms, 412
    involving fractions, 413–414
    misrepresenting "less than" in word problems, 413
    misusing negative signs, 411
    not solving for actual variable, 412–413
    when moving decimals, 412
  common wrong answers, 150–151
  constructed responses, 151–153
  eliminating obviously wrong answers, 149–150
  estimation, 147
  guessing, 148–149
  practice exams
    answers, 305–326, 393–407
    questions, 27–29, 267–276, 354–364
  question categories, 10
  using calculator, 147
  working backward, 149
mean, 135–137
measure of central tendency, 135
measurement, systems of, 61
median, 130, 135–137, 413
me/I, 206
metric system prefixes, 61
middle paragraph, 189, 195
middle quartile, 130, 131
midpoint point, 115
misplaced modifiers, 215–216

P

visual- and quantitative-information questions, 168–171, 183

visual literacy, 183

volume, 61, 110

W

weather/whether, 218

weight, 61

we/us, 206

"What's the point of this part?" question, 163

whether/weather, 218

"Which of these statements can be true by itself?" method, 184

whiskers, 131

whole numbers, 41–48

  basic operations with, 42–43

  divisibility rules, 44–45

  exponents, 47

  factors of, 43–44

  greatest common factor, 46–47

  least common multiple, 46–47

  multiples of, 45

  square roots, 47–48

who/whom, 206

word choice, 228

word pictures, in essays, 191

word problems

  in algebra, 85–86

  misrepresenting "less than" in, 413

words

  big, 191, 418

  conditional, 232

  original, 163

  red-flag words, 184

  "squirrel words", 208

work cited, 189

writing. *See also* essays; grammar

  budgeting time for test, 14

  common errors to avoid, 417–418

  practice exams

    answers, 25–26, 291–301, 381–392

    questions, 33–34, 257–266, 345–353

  selected-response questions on test, 227–232

  identifying and correcting errors in, 232–233

  types of, 227–232

X

x- and *y*-axis number lines, 112